FREE MINDS
&
FREE MARKETS

TWENTY-FIVE YEARS OF REASON

FREE MINDS

&

FREE MARKETS

TWENTY-FIVE YEARS OF REASON

edited by

Robert W. Poole, Jr.
and
Virginia I. Postrel

Pacific Research Institute for Public Policy
San Francisco, California

The Pacific Research Institute is a nonprofit organization that advocates individual liberty through the fundamental principles of free markets, private property, and limited government. PRI focuses on current public policy issues and promotes a better understanding of those issues among opinion leaders in government, the media, academia, and the business community. For further information on the Pacific Research Institute's programs and publications, please contact:

Pacific Research Institute for Public Policy
177 Post Street, San Francisco, CA 94108
(415) 989-0833 FAX (415) 989-2411

ISBN 0-936488-72-7

Printed in the United States of America
1   2   3   4   5   6   7   8   9   10

Library of Congress Cataloging-in-Publication Data

Free minds & free markets : twenty-five years of Reason / edited by
    Robert W. Poole, Jr. and Virginia I. Postrel

p.   cm.

ISBN 0-936488-72-7

1. Libertarianism. 2. Libertarianism—United States. 3. Free
    enterprise. 4. Free enterprise—United States. 5. Social
    history—20th century. 6. United States—Social policy.
    I. Poole, Robert W., Jr. [date]. II. Postrel, Virginia I. [date].
    III. Reason. IV. Title: Free minds and free markets.

JC571.F644   1993   93-20435

320.5′12—dc20   CIP

Research and Editorial Director: *Steven Hayward*
Director of Publications: *Kay Mikel*
Cover Design: *Arrowgraphics*
Interior Design: *Kay Mikel*
Printing and Binding: *Data Reproductions Corporation*

Contents

Foreword

This anthology celebrating the 25th anniversary of *Reason* will find different uses among different people. It makes an excellent gift for the unconverted, for example. There's nothing like a few *Reason* articles to prove to your friends that some very smart people depart radically from the accepted wisdom of Republicans and Democrats without being weird. Or it can serve the purposes of nostalgia, evoking for us middle-aged readers memories of battles from bygone days. Or it can remind younger readers that many of their exciting new ideas have a history.

But for me, this book is like a refuge, a sort of literary Galt's Gulch. I spend my days writing books of a particular kind. They are about social policy, they draw on complex (often opaque) social science research, and they are written for people who do not agree with me. So all day, every day, I am engaged in a mental dialogue with this imaginary reader, an intelligent and fairminded fellow who nonetheless is temporarily inclined to dismiss me given the slightest opportunity. This keeps me on my toes (I can't skirt his best arguments), and it encourages civility (if I ridicule his position, he's going to stop reading). It is an attempt at intellectual seduction of a sort, but benign. If more people on the other side wrote that way, I could get through a lot more of their books.

But what a strain civility can be, when so often it means being respectful of ideas that are palpably, on the face of them, WRONG. How much simpler life would be if I could just write knowing that everyone agreed on the obvious truth that human beings should be free to live their lives as they see fit, up to the point beyond which doing so interferes with the same right enjoyed by every other human being, and that this truth necessarily puts strict limits on the proper powers of government.

What could be more self-evident? And yet we live in a world where people who think that way are seen as oddballs. Probably most of the readers of this foreword live and work in places where we are the only persons who hold such views.

When we try to explain the simple truths, we find that few can come to grips with what they really mean. People say that they agree with us, that of course human beings should be free to live their lives as they see fit—which is why, also "of course," the government should pass laws that forbid landlords to choose freely among prospective tenants and laws that force businesses to provide access to the handicapped. How else can human beings live their lives as they see fit, if the government does not pass such laws? And when we argue, when we try to explain the nature of voluntary agreements, when we try to say that there are certain things the government may not legitimately do, no matter how good the intention, we meet a blank stare. As of the end of the 20th century, most Americans find it impossible to hold in their heads these two thoughts at the same time: (1) situation

X is deplorable or behavior Z is deplorable and yet (2) the government should not do anything to try to remedy situation X or behavior Z.

It can be very frustrating. Why don't more people understand? Is there anybody else out there who *does* understand? And that is why this book is a refuge. It is all very well to spend one's life trying to appear like a sensible fellow, but there are occasions when one wants company, when one wants to be able to talk to someone who understands. This anthology is full of excellent company. The views within it are diverse—in some respects, the differences that divide thinkers in this book are as great as the things that divide most *Reason* readers from mainstream politics. But the underlying kinship of assumptions about liberty and the dignity of the individual and the principles on which human beings can live in harmony transcend those differences. In reading this anthology, as in reading *Reason*, we are for once among friends.

There is another quality to these writings that is not just comforting but inspiring, for hardly any of these writings calls to the brand of icily pure libertarianism that, frankly, puts me off. Instead, they are mostly commentaries on how this nation, in this era, can make progress toward a society that is closer to the ideal. If the arguments in these writings have not yet gotten the hearing they deserve, they are getting more of a hearing than they used to, for this excellent reason: It is no longer wishful thinking, but hard-headed realism, to conclude that advancing technology and burgeoning wealth are making possible huge gains in liberty. Government control of industry is dying because government-controlled industries cannot compete, even in the rigged market that a government tries to fashion for itself. Government control over the economy is undermined because government does not have it in its power to control the wisps of electrons that now constitute international finance. Government control over knowledge is vanishing, as individuals gain access to computing power and data bases that even governments did not possess only a few decades ago.

The wonderful lesson of recent decades is that advances in wealth and technology are not neutral in the cause of liberty. They tend to play into the hands of individuals, and they make obvious the parasitic nature of government as it exists. Meanwhile, the failure of the American government to perform its core function of protecting individuals against coercion (by other individuals and by the government itself) may serve to revitalize an awareness of what that core function really is. Against this backdrop, the energetic and pragmatic arguments of the articles in this anthology must get a hearing, for their message is too reasonable to ignore.

I trust that these writings will also draw attention to the idealism that is embedded in the classical liberal tradition. In the last 15 years, most people have come to accept that free markets are more efficient at producing economic growth than planned economies. But this misses the main point and will doom reform to the margin as long as governments grudgingly allow people just enough freedom to keep the golden goose alive. The crucial next step is to bring the idealism back to center stage, letting the next generation understand limited government as the Founders understood it, not just as a way of encouraging economic growth but as the system that enables men and women everywhere, of all talents and temperaments, to realize the best that is in them. Do that, and everything becomes possible. Hoping for a little luck of several kinds, I aspire to write a foreword for the Golden Anniversary anthology in which I may celebrate the reconstituted Jeffersonian republic.

Charles Murray

Acknowledgments

This volume would not have been possible without the very hard work of the *Reason* staff: Charles Oliver, who proofed articles and trimmed the lengthy Reagan interview; Jacob Sullum, who scanned in and proofed many, many articles; and Elizabeth Larson, who did that and much, much more.

We also thank Petr Beckmann, Roger Bissell, David Brudnoy, Edith Efron, Milton Friedman, Phil Gramm, Thomas Szasz, Jack Wheeler, and Karl Zinsmeister for granting permission to reprint their articles.

The Pacific Research Institute staff, especially Pam Riley and Kay Mikel, deserve great thanks for their patience with amateur book editors, as does our PRI editor Steve Hayward, who was both careful and ruthless enough to hack our tremendous manuscript down by 30 percent. Steve has also paid me back, in full, for all the times I've bugged him about missed story deadlines.

Finally, I'd like to add personal thanks to Steven Postrel, who discovered *Reason* in 1981, and to Bob Poole, who created the *Reason* we discovered and has kept it going, growing, and improving for 25 years.

Virginia I. Postrel

Introduction

The surprising thing about think magazines, to paraphrase Samuel Johnson, is not that they are done well, but that they exist at all. Something like nine out of ten magazine startups fail to last as many as two years, so for a small magazine begun by amateurs to celebrate its 25th anniversary is something of an occasion.

Reason was founded in 1968 and was published for its first two and a half years by a journalism student at Boston University named Lanny Friedlander. Inspired by the ideas of Ayn Rand, he started *Reason* as a voice of protest against the nihilism and collectivism of the New Left, which was routinely using force to shut down campuses to protest not merely the Vietnam War but the whole capitalist system of "Amerika."

The fledgling magazine acquired several hundred readers from among the burgeoning libertarian movement. But by the end of its second year, it had run out of money. At that point, two of its early contributors, Tibor Machan and I, decided to mount a rescue effort. Convinced that there should be a market for a magazine of ideas that was neither liberal nor conservative, we drafted a business plan and tried to raise funds from others who shared our libertarian views. Though we raised only a few thousand dollars, with Manuel Klausner and several others as partners, we plunged ahead anyway.

From January 1971 through June 1978 *Reason* was published by our hand-to-mouth partnership, growing from under 1,000 subscribers to well over 12,000. It was truly a labor of love. The only paid staff was a secretary/office manager, and for most of those years the office was a spare room in my house or apartment, the warehouse was half of my garage, and the actual paste-up took place on my kitchen table.

In the early partnership years, the editorship rotated among the partners. But by the time the partnership had shrunk to just Tibor, Manny, and me, my career situation gave me the most time to put into the magazine. While struggling to make a living as a privatization consultant, I became *Reason*'s editor-in-chief.

During those years, the magazine was aimed primarily at people whose views were already libertarian; while addressing some current issues, it included fairly theoretical pieces and articles about the libertarian movement, its controversies, and personalities. By 1978, however, *Reason* seemed to have reached a plateau in circulation among the hard core. Both its inward-looking editorial approach and its shaky finances prevented it from growing into the serious national magazine we had envisioned in our business plan.

In the meantime, my work on privatization led to creating a think tank to do free market policy research. For the cash-poor magazine, the new nonprofit, tax-exempt Reason Foundation seemed a natural home. In mid-1978 we opened the foundation's doors in Santa Barbara, with three full-time, paid staff members:

our secretary/office manager, me, (now on salary!), and our formerly unpaid book review and copy editor, Marty Zupan.

The ability to raise funds from foundation grants and individual donors gave the magazine something of a financial base, enabling it not only to pay our salaries but to begin paying more than token amounts to authors and to conduct larger scale subscription mailings. The results were dramatic.

With its relaunch as a general interest think magazine, *Reason* began attracting better writers and its articles began to be noticed. Our first foray into investigative reporting (a piece about a union's illicit use of federal grant funds) made the wire services and was picked up by NBC's weekly newsmagazine program. Other newsworthy (and sometimes award-winning) investigations followed, several of which are included in this volume. Circulation grew fairly steadily, passing 20,000, then 25,000 by the early 1980s.

By *Reason*'s 15th anniversary in 1983, the growing demands of running the Reason Foundation took me more and more away from editing the magazine. Increasingly, Marty was becoming the editor in fact. So in late 1983, we recognized that reality and promoted her to the editorship. Under Marty's guiding hand, the magazine began building a real staff and developed a much larger network of writers. Circulation continued upward, reaching the 30,000 range by the late 1980s.

When we moved from Santa Barbara to Los Angeles in 1986, Marty hired as an assistant editor Virginia Postrel. Coming to *Reason* from *Inc.* (and before that, *The Wall Street Journal*), Virginia was our first professional journalist. By mid-1989, when Marty decided to move to the Institute for Humane Studies, Virginia was tapped to take over as editor.

The past three years have been *Reason*'s best by far. The magazine has reached a new level of sophistication and journalistic quality under Virginia's guiding hand. Circulation has climbed to more than 45,000. And *Reason* is increasingly reviewed and quoted from in national media.

One of the most satisfying aspects of publishing *Reason* has been working with its wonderful roster of authors. Even in the early poverty years, *Reason* attracted occasional pieces by such notables as Milton Friedman and Edith Efron. In addition, *Reason* in the 1970s was among the first to publish articles by people who would subsequently become much better known—including Doug Bandow, Phil Gramm, Alan Reynolds, and Paul Craig Roberts.

Deciding what to include in this 25th anniversary volume was an agonizing task. In so many areas, *Reason* was far ahead of its time. Our September 1971 issue foresaw the breakup of the Bell monopoly, and we made the case for airline deregulation and energy price decontrol long before these actions were taken. *Reason* was the first national magazine to write about privatization of public services. It has been a champion of entrepreneurs in areas ranging from space launch vehicles to urban jitneys.

Finding examples of private solutions to difficult problems (such as Houston's use of deed restrictions rather than zoning) has also been a *Reason* speciality. Many fascinating articles had to be omitted, simply to make the book a publishable length. We've also been able to include only a few of the nearly 100 *Reason* interviews with provocative thinkers that have graced our pages and just a sampling of the many pieces of investigative journalism.

It was especially interesting to go back over more than two decades of editorializing to relive the issues that had stirred our passions over the years. Some (the UN's proposed Moon Treaty, Nixon's wage and price controls, the draft) are long since dead issues, where liberty ultimately triumphed. Many others, of course, including our odious drug laws and the ever-growing welfare state, are still with us. Still, the net gains for freedom in the world over the 25 years of *Reason*'s existence are little short of astounding. The collapse of communism, the loss of credibility for socialism and central planning, the growth of worldwide markets, and the stunning advances in liberating technology all point to a future that should be much freer than any of us could have imagined in the dark days of 1968.

Nonetheless, the threats of a burgeoning "father knows best" state still loom large here at home in the 1990s. Today's market liberals—believers in free minds and free markets—still have our work cut out for us. Since eternal vigilance is the price of liberty, *Reason* still has much to do as we move into our second 25 years.

Robert W. Poole, Jr.

PART ONE

PLOTTING THE COURSE

Which Way for Capitalism?

By Milton Friedman

May 1978

W hat is the future of capitalism?—by which I mean the future of competitive capitalism, free enterprise capitalism. In a certain sense, every major society is capitalist. Russia has a great deal of capital, but it is under the control of governmental officials who are supposedly acting as agents of the state. That turns capitalism (state capitalism) into a wholly different system from a system under which capital is controlled by individuals in their private capacity as owners and operators of industry. What I want to take up here is the future of private enterprise—of competitive capitalism.

The future of private enterprise capitalism is also the future of a free society. There is no possibility of having a politically free society unless the major part of its economic resources are operated under a capitalistic private enterprise system.

The real question, therefore, is the future of human freedom. The question that I want to consider is whether or not we are going to complete the movement that has been going on for the past 40 or 50 years, away from a free society and toward a collectivist society. Are we going to continue down that path until we have followed Chile by losing our political freedom and coming under the thumb of an all-powerful government? Or are we going to be able to halt that trend, perhaps even reverse it, and establish a greater degree of freedom?

One thing is clear—we cannot continue along the lines that we have been moving. In 1928, less than 50 years ago, government at all levels—federal, state, and local—spent less than 10 percent of the national income. Two-thirds of that was at the state and local level. Federal spending amounted to less than 3 percent of the national income. Today, total government spending at all levels amounts to 40 percent of the national income, and two-thirds of that is at the federal level. So federal government spending has moved in less than 50 years from 3 percent to over 25 percent, total government spending from 10 percent to 40 percent. Now, I guarantee you one thing. In the next 50 years government spending cannot move from 40 percent of the national income to 160 percent. Legislatures cannot repeal the laws of arithmetic.

In judging whether we will keep trying to continue on this path until we have lost our freedom, it's worth considering where we are and how we got there. Let me say at the outset that, with all the problems I am going to talk about, this still remains a predominantly free society. There is no great country in the world (there are some small enclaves, but no great country) that offers as much freedom to the individual as the United States does. But having said that, we ought also to recognize how far we have gone away from the ideal of freedom and the extent to which our lives are restricted by governmental enactments.

In talking about freedom, it is important to distinguish two different meanings, on the economic level, of the concept of free enterprise, for there is no term which is more misused or misunderstood. The one meaning that is often attached to free enterprise is that enterprises shall be free to do what they want. That is not the meaning that has historically been attached to free enterprise. What we really mean is the freedom of individuals to set up enterprises. It is the freedom of an individual to engage in an activity so long as he uses only voluntary methods of getting other individuals to cooperate with him.

If you want to see how far we have moved from the basic concept of free enterprise, you can consider how free anyone is to set up an enterprise. You are not free to establish a bank or to go into the taxicab business unless you can get a certificate of convenience and necessity from the local, state, or federal authorities. You cannot become a lawyer or a physician or a plumber or a mortician (and you can name many other cases) unless you can get a license from the government to engage in that activity. You cannot go into the business of delivering the mail or providing electricity or providing telephone service unless you get a permit from the government to do so. You cannot raise funds on the capital market and get other people to lend you money unless you go through the SEC and fill out the 400 pages of forms that they require. To take the latest restriction on freedom, you cannot any longer engage in voluntary deals with others or make bets with other people on an organized exchange about the future prices of commodities unless you get the approval of the government.

Another example of the extent to which we have moved away from a free society is the 40 percent of our earnings, on the average, which is co-opted by the government. Each and every one of us works from the first of January to late in April or May, in order to pay governmental expenses, before we can start to work for our own expenses.

If you want to look at it still another way, the government owns 48 percent of every corporation in the United States. We talk about ourselves as a free enterprise society. Yet in terms of the fundamental question of who owns the means of production in the corporate sector, we are 48 percent socialistic because the corporate tax is 48 percent. Once when I was in Yugoslavia some years ago I calculated that the difference in the degree of socialism in the United States and in Communist Yugoslavia was exactly 18 percentage points, because the U.S. government took 48 percent and the Yugoslav government took 66 percent of the profits of every corporation. And of course, those numbers grossly understate the role of the government because of its effect in regulating business in areas other than taxation.

Let me give you another example of the extent to which we have lost freedom. About a year or so ago, I had a debate in Washington with that great saint of the U.S. consumer, Ralph Nader. I posed the question of state laws requiring people who ride motorcycles to wear helmets. Now I believe that in many ways that law is the best litmus paper to distinguish true believers in individualism from people who do not believe in individualism, because the person riding the motorcycle is risking only his own life. He may be a fool to drive that motorcycle without a helmet, but part of freedom and liberty is the freedom to be a fool!

So I expressed the view that the state laws which make it compulsory for people who are riding motorcycles to wear helmets are against individual freedom and against the principles of a free society. I asked Ralph Nader for his opinion, and he gave the answer I expected. He said, "Well, that's all very well for a different society. But you must realize that today, if a motorcyclist driving down the road without a helmet splashes himself on the cement, a government-subsidized ambulance will come to pick him up, they will take him to a government-subsidized hospital, he will be buried in a government-subsidized cemetery, and his wife and children will be supported by government-subsidized welfare. Therefore we can't let him!" What he was saying was that every single one of us bears on our back a stamp that says, "Property of the U.S. government. Do not fold, bend, or mutilate."

That is essentially the fundamental principle that animates the Ralph Naders of our time—the people who want the power to be in government. You see it everywhere. You see it in a law passed a few years ago which requires the Treasury Department to report to the Congress a category called Tax Expenditures—taxes which are not collected from you because of various deductions permitted by the law (such as interest or excess depreciation). The principle is that you are, after all, the property of the U.S. government. You work for the government, and the government lets you keep a little of what you earn in order to be sure that you'll keep working hard for them. But the rest is the property of the U.S. government. And if the government allows you to deduct something from your taxes, it's a government expenditure. You have no right to keep it. It's theirs!

We have gone very far indeed along the road to losing freedom. But you may say that I am talking only about economic matters, about whether you can enter a profession or an occupation. What about political freedom? What about the freedom of speech? How many businessmen have you heard in the past 10 years who have been willing to stand up on some public rostrum and take issue with governmental policies? Many a businessman gets up and expresses general sentiments in favor of free enterprise and of competition, but very few get up and criticize particular measures taken by government. I don't blame them. They would be fools to do it! Because any businessman who has the nerve to do that has to look over one shoulder and see what the IRS is going to do to his books the next day. And he has to look over the other shoulder to see whether the Justice Department is going to launch an antitrust suit. And then he has to find two or three more shoulders to see what the FTC is going to do. You can take any other three letters of the alphabet and you have to ask what they are going to do to you. In fact, a businessman today does not have effective freedom of speech.

But you may say that businessmen don't matter. What about the intellectuals? Suppose I take a professor from a medical school whose research and training is largely being financed by the National Institutes of Health. Do you suppose he wouldn't think three times before he gives a speech against socialized medicine? Suppose I take one of my colleagues in economics who has been supported by a grant from the National Science Foundation. I personally happen to think there is no justification for the National Science Foundation. (As it happens, I have never received a grant from them, though I might have. It isn't that they have turned me down; I haven't asked them!) But nevertheless, do you suppose my colleagues would not be inhibited in speaking out? In fact, I have often said that about the only people who have any real freedom of speech left are people who are in the fortunate position of myself—tenured professors at major private universities on the verge of retirement!

An even more chilling story about freedom of the press comes from Britain. The *London Times* was prevented from publishing for one day by the pressmen's unions because the issue would have carried a story that was critical of the policies of the unions.

So there is no way of separating economic freedom from political freedom. The only way you can have the one is to have the other.

So much for the present. What about the past? The closest approach to free enterprise we have ever had in the United States was in the 19th century. Yet your children will hear over and over again in their schools and in their classes the myth that that was a terrible period when the robber barons were grinding the poor, miserable people under their heels. That's a myth constructed out of whole cloth. The plain fact is that at no other time in human history has the ordinary man improved his condition and benefited his life as much as he did during that period of the 19th century when we were the closest to free enterprise.

Many of us, I venture to say, are beneficiaries of that period. I speak of myself. My parents came to this country in the 1890s. Like millions of others, they came with empty hands. They were able to find a place in this country, to build a life for themselves, and to provide a basis on which their children and their children's children could have a better life. There is no saga in history remotely comparable to the saga of the United States during that era, welcoming millions of people from all over the world and enabling them to find a place for themselves and to improve their lives. And it was possible only because there was an essentially free society.

If the laws and regulations that today hamstring industry and commerce had been in effect in the 19th century, our standard of living today would be below that of the 19th century. It would have been impossible to have absorbed the millions of people who came to this country.

What produced the shift? Why did we move from a situation in which we had an essentially free society to a situation of increasing regimentation by government? In my opinion, the fundamental cause of most government intervention is an unholy coalition between, on the one hand, well-meaning people seeking to do good and, on the other, special interests (meaning you and me) seeking advantage from government.

The great movement toward government has not come about as a result of people with evil intentions trying to do evil. No, it has come about because of good people trying to do good. But they have tried to do good with other people's money, and doing good with other people's money has two basic flaws. In the first place, you never spend anybody else's money as carefully as you spend your own. So a large fraction of that money is inevitably wasted. In the second place, and equally important, you cannot do good with other people's money unless you first get the money away from them, so that force—sending a policeman to take the money from somebody's pocket—is fundamental to the philosophy of the welfare state. That is why the attempt by good people to do good has led to disastrous results.

It was this movement toward welfare statism that produced the phenomenon in Chile which ended with the Allende regime. It is this tendency to try to do good with other people's money that has brought Great Britain—once the greatest nation of the earth, the nation which is the source of our traditions and our values and our beliefs in a free society—to the edge of catastrophe.

When you start on the road to do good with other people's money, it is easy at first. You've got a lot of people to pay taxes and a small number of people for whom you are trying to do good. But the later stages become harder and harder. As the number of people on the receiving end grows, you end up taxing 50 percent of the people to help 50 percent of the people—or really, 100 percent of the people to distribute benefits to 100 percent!

Where do we go from here? People may say, "You can't turn the clock back. How can you go back?" But the thing that always amuses me about that argument is that the people who make it, and who accuse me or my colleagues of trying to turn the clock back to the 19th century, are themselves busily at work trying to turn it back to the 18th century.

Adam Smith, in 1776, wrote *The Wealth of Nations*. It was an attack on the government controls of his time—on mercantilism, on tariffs, on restrictions, on governmental monopoly. But those are exactly the results which the present-day reformers are seeking to achieve.

In any event, that's a foolish question. The real question is not whether you are turning the clock back or forward but whether you are doing the right thing.

Some people argue that technological changes require big government and you can no longer talk in the terms of the 19th century when the federal government only absorbed 3 percent of the national income.

That's nonsense from beginning to end. Some technological changes no doubt require the government to engage in activities different from those in which it engaged before. But other technological changes *reduce* the need for government. The improvements in communication and transportation have greatly reduced the possibility of local monopoly which requires government intervention to protect the consumers. Moreover, if you look at the record, the great growth of government has not been in the areas dictated by technological change. The great growth of government has been to take money from some people and to give it to others. The only way technology has entered into that is by providing the computers which make it possible to do so.

Other people will say, "How can you talk about stopping this trend? What about big business? Does it really make any difference whether automobiles are made by General Motors, which is an enormous bureaucratic enterprise employing thousands of people, or by an agency of the United States Government, which is another bureaucratic enterprise?"

The answer to that is very simple. It does make all the difference in the world, because there is a fundamental difference between the two. There is no way in which General Motors can get a dollar from you unless you agree to give it to them. They can only get money from you by providing you with something you value

7

more than the money you give them. If they try to force something on you that you don't want—ask Mr. Henry Ford what happened when they tried to introduce the Edsel.

On the other hand, the government can get money from you without your consent. They can send policemen to take it out of your pocket. General Motors doesn't have that power. And that is all the difference in the world. It is the difference between a society in which exchange is voluntary and a society in which exchange is not voluntary. It's the reason why the government, when it is in the saddle, produces poor quality at high cost, while industry, when it's in the saddle, produces high quality at low cost. The one has to satisfy its customers and the other does not.

Where shall we go from here? There are two possible scenarios. The one is that we shall continue in the direction in which we have been going, with gradual increases in the scope of government and government control. If we do continue in that direction, two results are inevitable. One is financial crisis and the other is loss of freedom. Great Britain is a frightening example to contemplate. It moved in this direction earlier than we and has gone much farther. The effects are patent and clear. But at least when Britain moved in this direction and thus lost its power politically and internationally, the United States was there to take over the defense of the free world. But I ask you, if the United States follows the same course, who is going to take over from us? That's one scenario, and I very much fear it's the more likely one.

The other scenario is that we shall, in fact, halt this trend—that we shall call a halt to the apparently increasing growth of government, set a limit, and hold it back. There are many favorable signs from this point of view.

I may say that the greatest reason for hope, in my opinion, is the inefficiency of government. Many people complain about government waste, but I welcome it. I welcome it for two reasons. In the first place, efficiency is not a desirable thing if somebody is doing a bad thing. A great teacher of mine, Harold Hotelling, a mathematical economist, once wrote an article on the teaching of statistics. He said, "Pedagogical ability is a vice rather than a virtue if it is devoted to teaching error." That's a fundamental principle. Government is doing things that we don't want it to do; so the more money it wastes, the better.

In the second place, waste brings home to the public at large the fact that government is not an efficient and effective instrument for achieving its objectives. One of the great causes for hope is a growing disillusionment around the country with the idea that government is the all-wise, all-powerful big brother who can solve every problem that comes along, that if only you throw enough money at a problem it will be resolved.

Several years ago John Kenneth Galbraith wrote an article in which he said that New York City had no problem that could not be solved by an increase in government spending in New York. Well, since that time, the budget in the city of New York has more than doubled and so have the problems of New York. The one is the cause and the other effect. The government has spent more, but that meant that the people have less to spend. Since the government spends money less efficiently than individuals spend their own money, as government spending has gone up, the problems have gotten worse. My main point is that this inefficiency, this waste, brings home to the public at large the undesirability of governmental intervention.

There are also many unfavorable signs. It's far easier to enact laws than to repeal them. Every special interest, including you and me, has great resistance to giving up its special privileges. I remember when Gerald Ford became president and called a summit conference to do something about the problems of inflation. I sat at that summit conference and heard representatives of one group after another go to the podium—a representative of business, a representative of the farmers, a representative of labor, you name the group—they all went to the podium and they all said the same things: "Of course, we recognize that in order to stop inflation we must cut down government spending. And I tell you, the way to cut down government spending is to spend more on me." That was the universal refrain.

Many people say that one of the causes for hope is the rising recognition by the business community that the growth of government is a threat to the free enterprise system. I wish I could believe that, but I do not. You must recognize the facts. Business corporations in general are not defenders of free enterprise. On the contrary, they are one of the chief sources of danger.

The two greatest enemies of free enterprise in the United States, in my opinion, have been, on the one hand, my fellow intellectuals and, on the other hand, the business corporations of this country. They are enemies for opposite reasons.

Every one of my fellow intellectuals believes in freedom for himself. He wants free speech. He wants free research. I ask him, "Isn't it a terrible waste that a dozen people are studying the same problem? Oughtn't we to have a central planning committee to decide what research products various individuals undertake?" He'll look at me as if I'm crazy, and he'll say, "What do you mean? Don't you understand about the value of academic freedom and freedom of research?" But when it comes to business he says, "Oh, that's wasteful competition. That's duplication over there! We must have a central planning board to make those things intelligent, sensible!"

So every intellectual is in favor of freedom for himself and against freedom for everybody else. The businessman and the business enterprises are very different. Every businessman and every business enterprise is in favor of freedom for everybody else, but when it comes to himself, that's a different question. We have to have that tariff to protect us against competition from abroad. We have to have that special provision in the tax code. We have to have that subsidy. Businessmen are in favor of freedom for everybody else but not for themselves.

There are many notable exceptions. There are many business leaders who have been extremely farsighted in their understanding of the problem and will come to the defense of a free enterprise system. But for the business community in general, the tendency is typified by U.S. Steel Company, which takes ads to extol the virtues of free enterprise but then pleads before Congress for an import quota on steel from Japan. The only result of that is for everybody who is fair-minded to say, "What a bunch of hypocrites!" And they're right.

Now don't misunderstand me; I don't blame business enterprise. I don't blame U.S. Steel for seeking to get those special privileges. The heads of U.S. Steel have an obligation to their stockholders, and they would be false to that obligation if they did not try to take advantage of the opportunities to get assistance. I don't blame them. I blame the rest of us for letting them get away with it.

Where are we going to end up? I do not know. I think that depends upon a great many things.

I am reminded of a story which will illustrate what we may need. It has to do with a young and attractive nun who was out driving a car down a superhighway and ran out of gas. She remembered that a mile back there had been a gas station. She got out of her car, hiked up her habit, and walked back. When she got to the station she found that there was only one young man in attendance there. He said he'd love to help her but he couldn't leave the gas station because he was the only one there. He said he would try to find a container in which he could give her some gas. He hunted around the gas station and couldn't find a decent container. The only thing he could find was a little baby's potty that had been left there. So he filled the baby potty with gasoline and gave it to the nun. She took the baby potty and walked the mile down the road to her car. She got to her car and opened the gas tank and started to pour it in. Just at that moment, a great big Cadillac came barreling down the road at 80 miles an hour. The driver was looking out and couldn't believe what he was seeing. So he jammed on his brakes, stopped, backed up, opened the window, and looked out and said, "Sister, I only wish I had your faith!"

Secular Fundamentalism

By Edith Efron

November 1977

Recently, in *National Review*, a libertarian named Jerome Tuccille published an attack on the libertarian movement. It was a short description of a small group of libertarian cultists, and of their characteristically futile patterns of thought. The description, in many ways, was accurate, and Tuccille may have performed a service by bringing the problem out into the open. The need to discuss it does not lie in some medieval quest for self-mortification, but rather in the fact that one cannot cure a malady that one does not acknowledge.

The most important perspective one can acquire on the problem of the cultist mentality is to see its universality. It is not unique to libertarians. The problem, in fact, is epidemic in every cultural and political group in the land. The country is literally overrun by liberal robots, emitting their latest trendy responses; by conservative robots emitting the entrenched prejudices of their grandfathers; and by socialist robots, consumerist robots, Black Panther robots, health food robots, gay robots, Moonie robots, feminist robots, etc., etc.—all reciting their sacred texts. To the degree that there is sense or sensibility in any of these movements, they are almost obliterated by the ritualistic incantations.

The reasons for this phenomenon are hard to grasp when the robot is an ally, but they are glaringly obvious when he is not. The knee-jerk liberal, who exists in the greatest numbers, is quite transparent. His reflexive concepts clearly serve as a substitute for knowledge, for thought, for judgment, for independent moral vision. His automated repertoire gives him the illusion that he understands a complicated world, and, above all, that he is a vessel of rectitude. But that is also an explanation of every other kind of "movement" robot. The same mental process is occurring in all—and in all cases it hurls the individual out of contact with reality.

If the libertarian cultist is similar, in principle, to all other cultists, he differs strikingly in details. Characteristically, he is young and inexperienced. He gulps down a few books by libertarian writers and rushes to change this society before he has understood either this society or the books. He tends to restrict himself to a shrunken conceptual repertoire. It generally consists of a one-note opposition to the evil of government intervention, and frequently this is the only aspect of social reality of which he seems to be aware. Monumentally important political, social, cultural, and intellectual problems leave the cultist indifferent. He is only concerned with government misdeeds. His "thinking," consequently, is eternally out of context, and his value system flattened and hostile. His disconnection from what he often refers to as "the real world" leaves him ignorant of the workings of this society. Fixated on a handful of concepts lifted from Ayn Rand or Murray Rothbard

11

or both, he reduces all experience to those concepts and shelters his reductionism with severe moral rigidity. He is, to cite the illuminating phrase of Michael Novak, a "secular fundamentalist." And it is of interest to note that Novak was speaking of morally rigid liberals when he identified the phenomenon.

Now, is there a solution for this problem? There is, indeed—and that is why it's so useful to think about cultism-in-general, and not just about the libertarian form thereof. All cultists are gripped by the desire for a simple world which can be explained by a few all-purpose formulas. Thus, the first solution is simply to face the fact that it isn't that kind of world at all. How does one go about such "facing"? By reading. The prescribed regimen is six months of steady reading of specialized journals and books in a half-dozen fields. The cultist will emerge from that regimen staggering in salutary confusion and equipped with a new kind of certainty. He will know that the world is a very complicated place and that a pocketful of formulas will not explain it. At one fell swoop, he will lose the worst form of his ignorance— his ignorance of being ignorant. And his sense of moral superiority falsely hitched to three and a half ideas will die a swift death. He will, we must suppose, still remain attached to the idea of political liberty—but he will realize that just saying his beads ferociously will get him no place.

The second solution emerges from the other major trait of all cultists— namely their disconnectedness from social reality. And again, the solution is tailor-made to the symptom: To cure disconnectedness, one must connect. Connect with what? In the case of a libertarian, he must connect with those individuals or groups who are moving in the direction of liberty. In other words, he must look for fellow travelers. If he does, he will discover from his reading that the country is now full of them. There are the philosophers who now know that by defining "rights" as arbitrary grants from the state, they have destroyed the concept of "rights." There are the economists who now know that their Keynesian-interventionist formulas are bankrupt. There are the neoconservatives who now know that the powers of the state must be curbed. There are the businessmen, labor leaders, and workers who now know that the "public interest" regulators are destroying industries and jobs. There are the black leaders who now know that turning blacks into wards of the state is destroying their humanity. All are moving in the right direction. And people who are walking in the direction of liberty should be joined. One should not repudiate such fellow travelers because of philosophical differences; one should connect with them in the area of philosophical similarities. That connectedness will destroy cultism forever, as the libertarian learns what a fight for real liberty, among real people, in a real society, really means. He will learn that he cannot leap, by fantasy, into an ideal world—he must fight for it step by step, with the aid of others.

Jerry Tuccille did not mention it, for reasons best known to himself, but there are many libertarians, today, who are already functioning effectively in this society, who are already struggling to solve specific problems, who are already connected to real people in a real world who share some, if not all, of their goals. Many such libertarians arrived at this sensible state by the simple act of growing up; usually they are older than the cultists. But there's no point in hanging around until one ripens like a cheese. There's work to be done. The most important message I would give to young libertarians is this: Libertarianism isn't an imaginary world; it isn't a bible; it isn't a spiritual state; it isn't a chastity belt. It is a *compass*.

Libertarian Realpolitik

By Robert W. Poole, Jr.

August 1976

The Libertarian Party is currently running candidates for president, vice president, the Senate and House, and various state offices. Party members, friends, and sympathizers are being asked to contribute large sums of money, volunteer to circulate petitions, and devote time in other ways to working for these candidates. Although the L.P. has grown rapidly in the four years since its founding, its candidates to date have achieved only miniscule vote totals, generally in the vicinity of 1 percent (and at a cost of several dollars per vote). This lack of electoral support has occurred despite attractive candidates and the obvious openings created by the Watergate and CIA/FBI revelations, the failure of Great Society programs, a growing tax revolt, the emergence of decriminalization and deregulation as live issues, etc.—and despite media attention considerably greater than the L.P.'s actual size would warrant.

Obviously, something has prevented Libertarian candidates from getting votes (even where they appear on the ballot), despite a climate of opinion that appears inherently favorable. It would appear that Libertarian candidates simply are not being taken seriously by the electorate. What we have, in other words, is a failure of communications—of marketing libertarian ideas. To understand this failure, we must examine the nature of most Libertarian campaigns to date.

Ostensibly, the purpose of a political campaign is to elect the candidate to office. Yet most Libertarian political campaigns have been run principally to "educate the voters " in libertarian political philosophy. Thus, much time is spent on detailed expositions of the party's theoretical position on every conceivable issue, showing how this seemingly diverse collection of views is really a consistent philosophical whole. Some candidates have taken pride in their ability to shock the voters with their consistent radicalism and are pleased when a presentation to 500 people results in five or six potential new converts (apparently ignoring the possibility that of the other 495, 295 may be bored and 200 permanently alienated). The net effect of such activity is indeed to increase awareness of the libertarian philosophy—and to guarantee the hostility or indifference of the vast majority of voters.

To a certain extent this pernicious effect has been masked by the interest shown in L.P. candidates by media people. Many candidates report spending long hours with reporters, explicating the libertarian classics. Reporters are fascinated with such ideas as private roads, competing private defense agencies, individual secession, completely voluntary financing of government, etc. As a result, press conferences tend to focus on questions of the "How would the blind be cared for in a libertarian society?" variety. The candidate glibly answers that private charity will solve all such problems once the state is abolished. The reporter is pleased for having obtained sensational copy ("Candidate favors welfare cutoff"), but the audience, though "educated," is largely frightened and turned off by what appears to be a naive, utopian, and irresponsible position.

Libertarian politicians are thus faced with a basic choice. They must decide whether their first purpose is to educate people in political philosophy (in which case they can forget about electing candidates and accept the likelihood of alienating a majority of the populace) or to elect candidates who can get on with the task of rolling back the state (leaving to nonparty vehicles the task of teaching political philosophy). If the latter alternative is selected, as we would urge, then a fundamental change in marketing policy is required.

If a campaign's purpose is to elect candidates, then the focus of its marketing must be on what the specific candidate can and will do during the term of office for which he/she is elected. What is required, in other words, is a specific program which can be seen as potentially realizable during the time period in question. Such a program would be evolutionary in nature, taking into account today's political realities (e.g., the existence of foreign threats, of millions of people dependent on welfare and Social Security, etc.). It would purposely begin with proposals by which a large majority would benefit while only a small vested interest would lose. Each element of such a program would be a step in the direction of less government control and greater personal freedom, and each could be justified in terms of appropriate libertarian principles. But any prolonged discussion of the ultimate libertarian utopia would be scrupulously avoided, as irrelevant to a specific campaign for a specific office.

Such a program for candidates to national office in 1976 might include such elements as abolishing the most vulnerable regulatory agencies (CAB, ICC, OSHA), deregulating energy pricing, repealing the postal monopoly, repealing *federal* laws against marijuana and pornography, enactment of a constitutional amendment prohibiting deficit spending, and setting up a 10-year plan to convert from Social Security to private retirement programs. Each of these proposals is potentially saleable to a majority of Americans, if presented in an appropriate context and using nonthreatening rhetoric. Notice that the list does not include abolishing income taxes or welfare or the FDA—ideas whose time has not yet come, since people today cannot see how to do without these institutions. Until viable replacements can be researched, developed, and popularized, people's needs and fears must be taken seriously if a candidate is serious about being elected.

Those who will attack this approach as compromising or unprincipled should keep several points in mind: (1) The purpose of a political party is to elect people to office. Those libertarians who find this unpalatable should leave politics to the politicians and start or support educational libertarian groups. (2) It is not compromise to face the necessity for evolutionary change and, therefore, to implement a long-term plan a step at a time. (3) Libertarians are under no obligation to advertise their ultimate goals every time they make a public statement, so long as they don't misrepresent or conceal their principles. In short, we must learn the

15

art of strategy and tactics and develop marketing approaches at least as sophisticated as those used to introduce a new breakfast cereal.

The stakes are very high. What we are talking about is the survival of liberty in America, and perhaps the world. If libertarian politics is to play a part in this struggle, those involved must develop programs that can actually get candidates elected. It will be a tragedy if the impressive talent now commanded by the Libertarian Party alienates voters who could accept the first steps of a libertarian program to free the country.

To Ourselves and Our Posterity

By Charles Murray

May 1988

A false premise prevails in the latter half of this century, one that will seem as naive to our grandchildren as the Victorians' confidence in the permanency of empire now seems to us: that democracy is a stable form of government. It is as if we need worry only about how well we are making democracy serve whatever policies are in vogue, not whether democracy itself will continue to survive. Thus, when I recently suggested before an audience that I thought my children would probably live to see the end of American democracy, the reaction was not so much "Why do you think that?" as "Don't be silly."

The Framers knew better. They examined history as carefully as they studied political theory, and the signal lesson they drew from history is that Democracies Don't Last. They don't because of faction—citizens "who are united and actuated by some common impulse of passion, or of interest, adverse to the rights of other citizens," in Madison's words. It was not theory, the Framers observed, but a statement of fact: If factions are permitted to work their will on the polity, they destroy first liberty and then democracy itself—invariably.

So the Framers prepared a Constitution that arrayed all the structures of government against the effects of factions, by substituting representative democracy for direct democracy, by dividing power within the government, and above all by radically restricting the things that the central government was permitted to do. And thereby they hoped to secure the blessings of liberty to themselves and their posterity.

People engaged in the business of policy analysis have largely forgotten that the design of the Constitution was driven by fear for democracy's survival, not hope for its achievements. There are a few exceptions to the forgetfulness, thankfully, especially in the scholars of the "public choice" school. But in all the effusion of talk about the Constitution during the bicentennial year just past, in all the self-congratulatory talk about the success of "checks and balances" and "the living document," I cannot recall hearing this ultimately simple message: If the Framers were right in their reading of history and human nature, we cannot go about democracy the way that the United States (and every other Western democracy) has been doing it recently—not just should not but can not, if we want democracy to last much longer.

Most of contemporary policy is based on the assumption that the Framers were wrong. It is believed, apparently by a very large majority of people in every modern democracy, that humans can act collectively with far more latitude than the Framers believed: If humans seek a more even distribution of resources, they

17

may achieve it by using government to take money from one set of people and giving it to another. If humans want an end to racial inequality or sexual inequality, it is within their grasp to have it; all they have to do is pass the right laws. The world can be made constantly fairer if human beings use the instruments of government to reduce unfairnesses.

If the Framers were wrong, we may continue to be optimistic in the face of failures and the ubiquitous "unintended outcomes" that have followed such policies; we may assume that the proper response is to try again with another and better political solution. Most importantly, if the Framers were wrong, then we may assume that this expansive use of a centralized government can continue over the long run, because men have it in them after all to use the power of the state to do good.

If, on the other hand, the Framers were right, then we are already in big trouble. Democracies, they told us, begin to degrade when a faction is able to use the state to impose its vision of the good on the rest of society. And a relentless use of the state in just that fashion—to determine what is the majority faction, then permit that faction to impose its vision of the good on everyone—is the essence of contemporary policy.

That the contending factions are intent on using the state is not new. What is new is that so many now think that democracy can survive the success of a majority faction, that a majority faction is not dangerous as long as its causes are good. The left and the right struggle over whose vision of the good the government will enact. The only way to preserve democracy is to ensure that visions of the good cannot be enacted.

Here is where I ought to offer my solution, but I am deeply pessimistic and have none in which I place confidence. I do not see how to put the genie back in the bottle, how to restore old limits and say, "This time, let's not fool with them." But we have to try.

In that spirit, let me suggest that we resurrect another of the Framers' neglected insights: To preserve liberty, it is much more important that the *central* government be strictly limited than that *all* government be strictly limited. If the citizens of Bridgeport pass a bad law, that's too bad, but it is fairly easy to move out of Bridgeport, and a marketplace of governments that must compete for taxpayers restrains government's worst features. When Washington, D.C., passes a bad law, there's no recourse and no competition. I raise this point partly because of my own attraction to the virtues of community as well as to the freedom of individuals, but also as a practical matter. I sympathize with those who argue that governments at all levels ought to be limited for reasons of principle. But they will never convince a popular majority to go along with them. It seems increasingly clear that in ordinary situations most people prefer to live in extensive states.

Assuming that to be true (I will not try to prove the point here), then the only hope for sustaining democracy and the considerable level of freedom that citizens of the United States still enjoy is to make the case for tolerating diversity. For while most people prefer extensive states for themselves, I think most people—or at least most Americans—can still be persuaded that national uniformity is not necessary. It just might be possible to put together a majority of voters who believe that people should be free to live according to their beliefs, which means that people should be free to form communities as they see fit within a few overarching constraints—a majority who will agree, as it were, to take seriously once more the Ninth and Tenth amendments.

In seeking to restore that pragmatic outlook that underlay the original Constitution—restricting the national government above all and leaving considerable latitude to the lower levels of government—lies the best chance for mobilizing a majority and in the process securing the blessings of liberty to our own posterity.

Things Are a Lot Groovier Now

By Robert W. Poole, Jr.

May 1988

It was 20 years ago today
Sgt. Pepper taught his band to play.

The year of *Reason*'s founding was a year of violence. It was the height of the Vietnam War, the war that defeated Lyndon Johnson. That summer Soviet tanks rolled into Czechoslovakia, stamping out the *glasnost* and *perestroika* of Alexander Dubcek. Both Robert Kennedy and Martin Luther King were cut down by assassins' bullets. Across the country, students protested the war and were often attacked by the police, most notably during demonstrations outside the Democratic Party convention in Mayor Daley's Chicago. On some campuses, student radicals called strikes and occupied campus administration buildings, protesting not just the war but the "system"—the university, government, capitalism, whatever.

It was the campus violence, in particular, that motivated a Boston University journalism student named Lanny Friedlander to create a mimeographed little magazine. Inspired by the writings of novelist-philosopher Ayn Rand and seeking to uphold the standards of learning and rationality proper to a university—and the freedom of thought and action on which they are based—he called the publication *Reason*. Rather than simply criticizing the actions of SDS and its allies, he took aim at their *principles*. While opposing the war and the draft and the corporate state, *Reason* raised the banner of individualism in opposition to SDS collectivism, of free markets in opposition to SDS socialism. Neither left-wing nor right-wing, *Reason* was, presciently, libertarian.

What a difference 20 years makes, even in the everyday accoutrements of life. In 1968 you could still get in trouble for hooking up a "foreign attachment"—like an answering machine or a designer extension—to your phone line. There was, of course, only one long-distance telephone company, and if you didn't like what Ma Bell provided, tough. Believe it or not, cable TV was banned in the largest 200 cities (to "protect" broadcast TV, of course). And if you had a package that had to be somewhere by the next day, uh, forget it.

Self-service gas stations were illegal in most places (fire hazard, you know). The typical car got about 12 miles per gallon and was made in Detroit. It had sloppy steering, soft suspension, and bias-ply tires that wore out after 12,000 miles. Sure, there were a lot of little VW beetles around, and a few of those funny-looking little Toyotas and Datsuns—but mostly in weirdo California. Hondas were motorbikes

("You meet the nicest people on a Honda"), not yuppie sedans. And BMWs were nowhere to be found.

If you wanted cash, you had to go to a branch of your bank (between 10:00 AM and 3:00 PM on weekdays) and stand in line for a teller; no 24-hour ATMs on the street corner. (And if you were in another state, forget about getting cash, Charlie.) Unless you had $10,000 to purchase T-bills, the most you could earn on your savings was 5 percent or so in a savings account; money-market funds hadn't been invented yet, and banks were forbidden to offer higher rates on CDs.

To travel long distance, you could choose between two (or sometimes three) airlines. You asked your travel agent what the price was—not what discount fares were available but simply the price, the one set by the government. The round-trip coach fare from New York to Los Angeles was $948 in today's dollars.

Numerous personal freedoms that we take for granted were very tenuous in 1968. Unmarried couples staying in hotels had to pretend they were married—sex between consenting adults was still illegal in numerous states. In many states, including Massachusetts, you could get arrested for displaying contraceptives or advocating their use. Condoms were kept beneath the counter in drugstores, not advertised on billboards.

Erotic films were just beginning to be tolerated in polite society, helped along by the introduction of the movie rating system. But there was nothing like today's videocassette smorgasbord. Homosexuals were known to exist but were not discussed in public. Most of them lived in fear of exposure, harassment, and loss of their jobs.

The revolution in women's roles was only just beginning in 1968. Women still constituted only a few percent of the students majoring in engineering, law, business, and medicine. The sexual double standard prevailed, though the Pill would soon put women on a more equal footing with men.

Hanging over the life of every young man was the specter of the draft. It's difficult to convey the extent to which one's local draft board was feared for its life-and-death power.

The maximum rate of income tax was 70 percent, compared with 28 percent now; and the IRS was no less fearsome than it is today. It was illegal to own gold—that's right, illegal.

If you were a doctor or a lawyer in 1968, it was illegal for you to advertise. There were no such things as legal clinics or prepaid legal services or doc-in-a-box storefront clinics or HMOs. Competing on price was not only "unethical" in these professions; it was grounds for legal action.

Internationally, pundits told us that the real threat was no longer the Soviet Union. No, the real danger was the Red Chinese; the movie version of Ian Fleming's *Goldfinger* was altered from the book to make the ultimate villain a Chicom, and subsequent Bond films dropped all mention of SMERSH, the Soviet terror organization that had been a key player in many of the books. Whether Soviet or Chinese, the march of communism seemed to many to be inevitable. The idea of *mujaheddin* going up against the Soviet army or of anti-Soviet freedom fighters in Angola was unthinkable.

Defense Secretary Robert McNamara by 1968 had won the battle to make

"mutual assured destruction" the basis of U.S. strategic policy, purposely disman-
tling this country's air defenses and forswearing defenses against ballistic missiles.
Thus began 20 years with no defense but the threat of Armageddon.

In Europe, socialism was the dominant philosophy of government. Britain's
Labour and Conservative parties alternated in power, with the Tories presiding over
each new plateau of nationalized industries and the welfare state. The idea of
"privatizing" state enterprises, especially utilities such as airports and telecoms,
was unimaginable.

The idea of the Third World as an undifferentiated mass of underdeveloped
countries made poor by colonial exploitation was the received wisdom, not just at
the United Nations (which was still respected) but among most educated people.
Taiwan, South Korea, and the other tigers of South Asia were still poor; to have
forecast that Hyundai would by 1988 be the best-selling import car would have marked
one as loony.

To be sure, some things have gotten worse in the past 20 years. The federal
government now consumes 25 percent of GNP instead of 21 percent. Social
Security taxes have doubled. New regulatory agencies (OSHA, CPSC, EPA,
EEOC) and new bureaucracies (both DOEs) have grown up among us. Rent control
has made a comeback in some cities, and land-use controls have assumed dangerous proportions.

But the past 20 years have witnessed some profound gains for human
freedom, thanks to the power of ideas and the liberating influence of new technologies. The next time a doom-and-gloom friend starts telling you how the world is
going to hell in a handbasket, ask him if he'd really prefer the violent, constrained
world of 1968. If so, he deserves it.

Dynamic Tension

By Virginia I. Postrel

November 1992

Bovine growth hormone. Japanese cars. Gay marriages. Corporate restructuring. Food irradiation. Breast implants. Mobile phones. Temporary workers. Plastic grocery bags. Rock videos. Surrogate motherhood. Aseptic juice boxes. Salvadoran nannies. Indian surgeons. Ethiopian cab drivers.

From the cows to the cabbies, they all create controversy. They're new. They're different. And they're deeply politicized.

Today, our political culture stands divided between dynamic and static visions of the good society. On one side are those who see civilization as an ever-evolving process of discovery and who seek to preserve the liberal institutions that make that process possible. On the other side are those who envision a single best order for society and who seek to alter the current culture—often radically—to achieve and conserve an unchanging end state.

Most people, and certainly most politicians, don't yet recognize the divisions, which are still masked by Cold War alliances. That's one reason this election season seems so odd, so frustrating, and so empty. Neither George Bush nor Bill Clinton speaks to the issues. Both seek to straddle the divide. Both lead fractious coalitions that encompass representatives of both camps.

Those rare politicians who do elicit strong public reactions—positive and negative—tend to be people whose visions and attitudes are clearly defined, even if their policies are inconsistent. Pat Buchanan, for instance, supports cultural stasis. Jack Kemp supports economic dynamism. Searching for political allies and intellectual soulmates, each has gradually expanded his vision beyond its original arena. Buchanan now supports economic protectionism, a static policy. Kemp advocates social tolerance.

The collision of static and dynamic visions is most obvious in the struggle to protect technical innovation from antitechnology greens. The ideology of "sustainability" requires a "steady-state" economy in which self-sufficiency replaces specialization and geographic isolation supplants trade. The goal is to slow down change and, ultimately, to end it.

So if genetic engineering cures diseases, if irradiation keeps food fresh, if the juice box replaces the Thermos, stasis supporters seek to stop the change, preferably by law. Since every change, indeed every choice, entails risk, anyone can easily find fault with any innovation, often fault enough to block regulatory permissions. The result is a legal bias against the new, a squelching of the experimental.

One man's stagnation is another man's utopia. Some California air regulators are delighted with the state's economic slump. It's a lot easier to meet traffic-reduction targets when people are leaving the state. Bureaucrats are pleased. So are the environmentalists who spent the '80s campaigning against growth.

The conflict of visions extends beyond environmental disputes, however, to every sphere of human endeavor. Each vision encompasses not merely some policy prescription but an entire world view.

Stasis is utopia—whether the environmentalists' Eden or Ozzie and Harriet's America. It is planning—the old time Progressives' rational order. It is control—the protectionist paradise of big business and big labor, of growth without change.

Dynamism, by contrast, is continuous improvement, discovery, adaptation. It is "muddling through" environmental problems with cleaner fuels or better materials. It is "experiments in living," through which family life adjusts to a world in which women have education and contraception. It is market competition and diversity of enterprise.

Dynamism doesn't promise perfection. Experiments, by their nature, often fail. Dynamism is deeply historical; it understands that the past was different from the present and that the future will be different still. Dynamism seeks to learn, while stasis claims to know. Stasis divides and conquers. Dynamism lets a thousand flowers bloom.

Stasis is an end. Dynamism is a means. And that means is the heart of our culture. It is both liberty's product and its rationale.

Proponents of stasis are cultural revolutionaries. They seek change, radical change, to achieve their picture of the good. But once captured, that picture becomes a still photograph. It does not move.

Consider this year's leading culture warriors. Pat Buchanan says we're in the midst of a "religious war" requiring "force, rooted in justice, and backed by courage," to "take back our cities, and take back our culture, and take back our country."

Meanwhile, Al Gore says we need a new "central organizing principle" to subordinate every aspect of life to his environmental vision. He calls for "struggle, sacrifice, and a wrenching transformation of society." He equates American materialism with Nazi totalitarianism. He, too, declares a culture war.

Buchanan and Gore are political enemies. But they stand on the same side of the great divide. Both crave a static utopia, to be achieved by drastic action. Both see adaptation as appeasement, tolerance as treason.

Both Buchanan and Gore want stasis, but neither wants to live in the other's utopia. And the political weakness of stasis is just this: Its adherents seek mutually exclusive static worlds.

Dynamism, by contrast, can accommodate competing ideas of the good life. It provides a framework within which many people can test different hypotheses about everything from which fashions will sell to what religion best provides spiritual meaning.

A dynamic society also encourages people to discover new ways of sheltering themselves from its very turmoil. Commodities traders develop hedging strategies; insurance spreads risk; families, churches, and ethnic communities create anchors of stability. (Hence, for instance, the great strength of religious havens in immigrant communities, where individuals have uprooted themselves from their home-lands.)

Dynamism does not, however, accommodate everything. It does not, cannot, enforce uniformity. It permits the imposition of mores but also allows for their evolution. It is the product of liberalism.

"The liberal position," wrote F.A. Hayek in *The Constitution of Liberty*, "is based on courage and confidence, on a preparedness to let change run its course even if we cannot predict where it will lead . . . .[C]onservatives are inclined to use the powers of government to prevent change or to limit its rate to whatever appeals to the more timid mind. In looking forward, they lack the faith of the spontaneous forces of adjustment which makes the liberal accept changes without apprehension, even though he does not know how the necessary adaptations will be brought about."

But just as "change" supporters may in fact be utopian reactionaries seeking to impose stasis, dynamism's proponents may seem quite conservative. A dynamic system requires four freedoms: freedom of conscience, freedom of speech, freedom of contract, and property rights. To conceive and communicate ideas, to carve out spheres of experimentation, to make commitments and plans, these freedoms are essential. And their existence, by unleashing individual choice, creates a dynamic society.

For civilization to evolve, for adaptation to take place, these freedoms must be conserved. The process, not a particular result, is the point. Liberty and dynamism are not identical, but they are interdependent.

In the real world of politics, of course, most people lack "the vision thing." Few advocate anything definitely recognizable as either stasis or dynamism.

Given our current political culture, that means a sort of stasis wins—not the rarified stasis of Jeremy Rifkin or Russell Kirk, a coherent ideological vision, but the mundane stasis of regulatory gridlock. This is what Milton and Rose Friedman call "the tyranny of the status quo," or what *National Journal*'s Jonathan Rauch, drawing on the work of economist Mancur Olson, recently dubbed "demo-sclerosis." Established interest groups block both governmental reform and economic innovation. Often they block both simultaneously.

Writes Rauch: "No one starting anew today would think to subsidize wool farmers, banish banks from the mutual fund business, forbid United Parcel Service to deliver letters, grant massive tax breaks for borrowing. Countless policies are on the books not because they make sense in 1992, but merely because they cannot be gotten rid of. They are dinosaurs that will not die. In a Darwinian sense, the universe of federal policies is ceasing to evolve."

Nowhere is bureaucratic stasis more obvious than in the regulation of telecommunications. There are too many interest groups—phone companies, cable monopolists, broadcasters, cable networks, movie studios, equipment manufactur-ers, mobile phone companies, newspaper publishers, even electric utilities—and too much political intervention. Insiders block outsiders and everyone squeezes consumers.

The result is "anti-industrial policy," as Robert Samuelson described it in a recent column focusing on a tiny corner of the mess, a dispute over mobile-phone frequencies. In one of the most technically innovative industries in the world, stasis predominates.

This trend, which is by no means confined to telecommunications, threatens the experimental nature of capitalism itself. Notes economist Nathan Rosenberg, "Historically, one of the most distinctive features of capitalistic economies has been the practice of decentralizing authority over investments to substantial numbers of individuals who stand to make large personal gains if their decisions are right, and who stand to lose heavily if their decisions are wrong, and *who lack the economic or political power to prevent at least some others from proving them wrong.*" (Italics in the original.)

In today's politics, self-interested protectionists and static ideologues feed off each other. So, for instance, Rifkin opposes bovine growth hormone because it is unnatural, the product of genetic engineering. But regulatory approvals are on hold not because Rifkin hates technology but because dairy farmers, fearing greater milk supplies and lower prices, raised a ruckus.

Despite the pull of stasis, there is still a strong constituency for what Hayek called "the party of life, the party that favors free growth and spontaneous evolution." The American spirit favors dynamism. The human spirit does as well.

Most people like freedom. They like to order their lives by their own lights. They like to create new businesses, new products, new social arrangements. They don't want to enlist in culture wars.

People know what they like. But they don't understand how to protect it. We don't see immigrants forming coalitions with biotech companies or mobile-phone entrepreneurs allying with surrogate mothers. Until those coalitions begin to form, until the party of life, the party of dynamism, articulates its interests and defends free institutions, American politics will continue to seem irrelevant.

PART TWO

ENTERPRISE

Future Shock in the Grocery

By Robert W. Poole, Jr.

August 1975

Technology, by its nature, is dynamic, forward-looking. Every development, every invention, every improvement upsets the status quo, changes the people and society, threatens the Establishment.

Ben Bova, editor of *Analog*

Future shock is as old as the Industrial Revolution. In 1815 fearful English workers, led by half-wit Ned Lud, set upon and destroyed labor-saving textile machines. Although the Luddites failed to prevent the introduction of the new machinery, their spiritual descendants have never given up attacking technological advances that threaten their contentment with the status quo. But today's opposition to new developments goes beyond simple fear of the new and unknown. The man in the street may react with this type of generalized fear, but all too often his fears are encouraged by relatively small vested interests which stand to lose from new developments. These amplified fears then become the excuse for new laws prohibiting or restricting the use of new technology which is designed to benefit consumers.

Two examples of this process are occurring today in America's supermarkets. One concerns the introduction of the Universal Product Code (UPC), the pattern of lines and numbers now appearing on most grocery items. The UPC, a key element in computerized check-out systems, is a symbol that encodes the manufacturer's name, product type, and package size. It is designed to be read by a scanning device at the checkout counter, hooked into a computerized cash register terminal. The terminal automatically looks up the product's current price and sales tax to compute the bill and prints both the price *and* the product's name on the customer's receipt tape. The Grocery Manufacturers' Association spent millions of dollars developing the UPC system because of the substantial economies it can bring to supermarket operations. In addition to such benefits as faster checkout, instant inventory, and automatic reordering (which are made possible by the computerized cash register), the UPC's big payoff comes from eliminating the costly, labor-intensive step of stamping the price on every one of the 170 billion cans and boxes sold by grocers each year. (The price would still be marked on the shelf, of course.) The GMA estimates that full implementation of the UPC will save several hundred million dollars each year and permit the average supermarket to reduce its number of retail clerks from 22 to 18.

Predictably, the Retail Clerks International Association is up in arms over the UPC plan. According to the GMA, the union is funneling money to consumer groups to agitate against UPC and, regrettably, many consumer groups are falling into line. The Consumer Federation of America, representing 208 member organizations, is waging a propaganda war against "packages without prices," arguing that buyers will be unable to comparison-shop, *despite* the presence of prices on both the shelf and on the register tape, and the advantage of having an itemized register tape containing the name as well as the price of each item. (The consumerists also point out that the new system could make it easier for supermarkets to commit fraud—which may be true, but is relatively easy for either officials or consumer groups to check up on.) The CFA and the Retail Clerks union are backing a Federal "Price Disclosure Act," which would force stores to continue stamping prices on every item, regardless of their investment in UPC. Already 59 members of Congress have endorsed the bill, and similar measures have been introduced in more than a dozen states, including California, Arkansas, and Maryland.

The other new development also concerns computerized systems and supermarkets (among other locations). This time the issue is the computerized remote banking terminal, an innovation that permits bank-teller service (deposits, withdrawals, check-cashing) at such convenient locations as supermarkets, airports, and department stores. Part of the problem here is that banking is highly regulated, with different categories of banks prohibited from competing with one another. Thus, since the different regulators have moved at different speeds to permit use of Customer-Bank Communications Terminals (CBCTs), problems have arisen. The process began with a ruling by the Federal Home Loan Bank Board in January 1974 allowing federally chartered savings and loans to install CBCTs, followed in December of that year by the Comptroller of Currency's ruling that national banks could do the same thing; the latter ruling established that CBCTs were not legally bank branches, and thereby were not to be restricted by state bank branching laws.

Innovative institutions quickly took advantage of these rulings—and soon ran into Luddite reactions from their conservative competitors, in league with the state. First Federal Savings and Loan of Lincoln, Nebraska, installed CBCTs in two Hinky Dinky supermarkets. Five commercial banks, rather than mount an aggressive attack on the laws preventing them from doing likewise, promptly obtained an injunction against First Federal, charging unfair competition. After much harassment by the Nebraska attorney general, leading to a six-month shutdown of the system, the Nebraska Supreme Court ruled in May that the CBCTs were not acting as S&L branches. There are now terminals in 21 Hinky Dinky supermarkets, and two other S&Ls have teamed up with First Federal to offer the service. Elsewhere, the City National Bank and Trust of Columbus, Ohio, is installing 125 CBCTs in 60 major stores and supermarkets, and Atlanta's Citizens and Southern National Bank is franchising its "Instant Bank Key" CBCT system to smaller banks in seven southern states. Both Bankamericard and Master Charge are planning similar systems.

Nonetheless, many smaller banks are afraid of the challenge posed by CBCTs and are backing legislation to prohibit their use. The Ohio state banking superintendent is suing banks in Cincinnati and Dayton that are trying to set up CBCT systems, a similar suit is under way in Colorado, and the 7,800-member Independent Bankers Association of America is suing the Comptroller of Currency, seeking to overturn his ruling that CBCTs are not branches. Comptroller Smith retreated a step in May by announcing a new rule that prohibits CBCTs from being located more than 50 miles from a bank branch. And Sen. William Proxmire has introduced legislation to prohibit all CBCT operations until a federal study commission has decided how they should be regulated, around the end of 1976.

These examples demonstrate once again the dynamic, ever-changing nature of capitalism. And sadly, they also demonstrate that Luddism is still with us. Only today, instead of destroying isolated machines, the Luddites have access to the machinery of total, nationwide coercion: the state. Defenders of economic freedom must fight not only the specific laws restricting innovation but also the underlying conservative, anticonsumer attitudes that revere the status quo. It is these attitudes that sanction the special pleadings of those who cannot or will not face the challenges of a dynamic, competitive economy.

Two Utilities Are Better Than One

By Jan Bellamy

October 1981

DATELINE: LUBBOCK, TEXAS. "This bill is simply too high," Alma Jones told the customer service representative on the phone. "Last year's July electric bill was half this amount despite the hotter weather."

"I'm sorry, Mrs. Jones," the representative responded, "but our bill simply reflects the meter reading for July."

"Well, your meter reading is wrong," Mrs. Jones replied, "and I want to speak to the customer service manager."

"Mr. Wilson is away from his desk," cooed the cool voice on the phone.

"Well, then, I want a meter reader to come out and check his figures. Something has to be done!" Mrs. Jones was on the verge of tears.

"That isn't possible at this time, Mrs. Jones," the impersonal voice continued, "but our field service representative will be making his regular rounds in two weeks."

"I can't wait two weeks!" Alma Jones cried desperately into the phone. "If you won't resolve this mess today, I'm changing companies!"

"As you wish, Mrs. Jones," the faceless voice retorted.

A woman of her word, Alma Jones slammed the receiver into place just long enough to disconnect that sweet voice. Picking it up again, she dialed the other electric company. "I've paid my last bill to the competition," she informed the service representative who answered. "I want my electric service changed immediately." Three days later, Mrs. Jones was the happy customer of another electric utility, which she believes responds more positively to her requests for assistance.

Though the details of this little scenario are fictitious, such calls take place routinely in Lubbock, Texas. In this west Texas city, consumers enjoy the benefits of competition between Lubbock Power and Light (LP&L) and Southwestern Public Service (SPS) Company. The two companies compete for business despite the preachments of economists who swear by Lord Keynes that competition cannot work in the electric utility industry.

And Lubbock is not an isolated case. Competition between a municipally owned and an investor-owned utility—what economists call a "duopoly" situation—exists in other cities and towns across the country.

How It Works in Lubbock

The competition in this city of some 200,000 residents is active and fierce. LP&L and SPS enthusiastically push and pull for customers in an open market. Yet the rivalry is basically a friendly, cooperative one, I found out on a visit to Lubbock last spring. At least, that's how the two men running the respective operations described it to me over lunch at the country club.

Carroll McDonald is director of sales and service for city-owned LP&L, while Jake Webb serves as district manager for investor-owned SPS (which operates in three states besides Texas). Interestingly, McDonald spent 26 years with SPS before moving over to LP&L two years ago.

"Conceivably, a customer could change service every three days," McDonald told me, though frequent switching is quite uncommon. But the procedure for switching is quite simple. A company sales representative fills out a form for the customer who wishes to change service, and a copy goes to the competition. Every morning at 7:00, an LP&L and an SPS employee stops by the competing firm's offices, a block apart, and picks up an envelope containing the notices of orders for service change. Each company then has 24 hours to convince its customers not to change service.

If the order form is confirmed, the new company goes out and changes the meter. The meters are stored at the main service facilities operated by each company. Each firm sets aside a special wall on which the meters of the competition hang, awaiting the call of a serviceman sent to retrieve them.

To make such switching possible, of course, the entire city must be covered by two sets of electric lines. Doesn't that make for "visual pollution"? I asked Webb and McDonald. They quickly pointed out that many cities have two sets of poles and lines already—one for the electric company and another for the phone company.

In Lubbock, the most common arrangement is for SPS and the telephone company to share one set of poles, while LP&L shares poles with the local cable-TV system. (Although, as I was later to learn, pole sharing *between* competing electric utilities exists in some of the other duopoly cities, the LP&L/SPS cooperative competition has never extended to joint use of the same poles.) In newer Lubbock neighborhoods, all utility lines are underground, removing the aesthetics issue altogether. Interestingly, both LP&L and SPS began "undergrounding" in the mid-1950s, well before most monopoly utilities did.

What about "wasteful duplication," that traditional objection to competition between utilities? Apart from the very minor cost of the dual set of lines, about the only real duplication in Lubbock is the salaries of the two companies' sales reps, who solicit new customers and changes of service. As far as the really large costs—those of power generation—are concerned, each firm has geared its generating capacity to the size of its market share (split about 48/52 between LP&L and SPS, respectively, and relatively stable over time). Thus, neither suffers from wasteful overcapacity.

Service with a Smile

Despite the fact that each company serves the entire city and tries to win customers away from the other, it cannot offer the lure of a lower price: electricity rates in Lubbock are set by the city council—and kept the same for both firms. Consequently, the competitors must fight it out in the service offered to customers.

This nonprice competition definitely affects the attitudes of the employees.

"If we don't treat you right, you have a place to go," mused McDonald over lunch. "People come in and say, 'Wish we had two phone companies in town.'"

Awareness of the importance of courtesy and service doesn't stop with the top managers at either company. Both firms' offices, I noticed when I visited, sport displays in the forms of rugs on the floors or posters on the walls, reminding employees that the customer is *always* right in Lubbock, Texas.

SPS takes great pride in its Consumer Services Department, which serves Lubbock among seven cities in Webb's district on the southern plains of Texas. The nine-member department offers a home demonstration service and provides advisory assistance in the design of facilities for commercial and residential builders, upgrading of lines and fixtures, and engineering of commercial cooking facilities. Webb stresses the company's involvement in promoting Lubbock as the site for new industries.

Not to be outdone, in or out of the office, McDonald argues that city-owned LP&L offers every service outlined by SPS—with the exception of those three home advisers, who, McDonald snipes, spend more time in cooking schools than in homes and actually compete with every home appliance store in town. Webb just grins; the verbal barbs are part of the game.

Both companies schedule specific appointments for placing their meters so that the customer does not have to sit at home all day waiting. Webb points out that SPS follows that procedure in all of its service areas. Could it be an indirect influence of the competition in Lubbock?

Neither company cuts off a customer unless a bill goes unpaid for up to 60 days. And if, as sometimes happens, a resident gets confused and calls the wrong company about an outage, standard procedure for each firm is to notify the other.

Sitting across the table from these two men, I could understand why, as long-time friends and business associates, they could accept such a truce: the cooperation simply makes good business sense. Neither Webb nor McDonald hesitates to say that he would *prefer* to run the only electric company in town, but neither will aspire to put the other out of business: The citizens of Lubbock, Texas, like things as they are, they assured me.

Bottom-Line Benefits

It sounded almost too good to be true. So I decided to check out consumer reaction myself, spending an afternoon walking through a Lubbock subdivision with camera and cassette recorder, knocking on doors. More than one door was opened wide to me with an invitation to "sit a spell" and hear the praise homeowners heaped upon either one or both companies.

"Competition helps hold down prices and results in better service," one homeowner offered. A petite brunette lost no time in informing me, "I like free enterprise."

"I like having the opportunity to change service. We changed because the first electric company wasn't cooperative when a check bounced," explained another while holding back an overly affectionate Doberman.

The majority agreed with one gentleman who stated, "Competition keeps rates down!" And he appears to be correct. The basic rate for residential service in

Lubbock is 2.62¢/kilowatt-hour (kwh). Outside Lubbock, areas served by SPS pay 3.13¢/kwh—nearly 20 percent more. (Total electric bills in Lubbock are sometimes slightly higher because of a fuel pass-through charge—based on LP&L's more expensive fuel—added by the city onto *both* companies' bills. Absent this government intervention, SPS's rates could undercut LP&L's.)

In answer to my query, one homeowner slid his hands into his pockets, grinned at me, and replied, "Competition is the best thing in the world."

Kenneth May, associate editor of the *Lubbock Avalanche-Journal,* agrees. "I think Lubbock residents have voted their approval of the competition each time they voted to pass a bond issue so that LP&L can expand."

LP&L's McDonald agrees, "As long as SPS is competitive [with us] it is a plus for residents. We don't wait a day or two to get out there and service a customer; we do it right away, or that customer may change his service."

Looking Back

Local residents, the media, and the heads of the two electric companies are so convinced that competition benefits the community because competition has proven itself again and again in the last 60-plus years in Lubbock, Texas.

It all began in March 1916, when then-monopoly Texas Utilities refused a rate cut demanded by the Lubbock city council. The city fathers emerged from a closed-door meeting to announce that Lubbock would build a city-owned electric utility company to compete with Texas Utilities. The city refused Texas Utilities' offer to sell its facilities, presumably because the price was too high. The city of Lubbock began operation of its utility in 1917, and the competition was on. (Southwestern Public Service Company bought out Texas Utilities in the 1940s.)

That competition continues to this day. You might even say that this west Texas city is a monument to the competition that once thrived in the electric utility industry throughout the country. That's right. Competition was once the rule in the provision of electricity. At one time, the majority of cities in America saw competition between two, three, or even more electric utility companies.

Several years ago, preparing to begin his Ph.D. thesis, Gregg Jarrell of the University of Rochester wondered why electric utility competition began dying out in the 20th century. Poring over old records, Jarrell found that in 1887, in New York City alone, six competing electric light companies were organized. By 1905, some 45 electric utilities had been granted franchises to operate in Chicago (only one of them an exclusive franchise granting the sole right to serve a territory). Prior to 1895, five electric lighting companies served Duluth, Minnesota, and four operated in Scranton, Pennsylvania, in 1906—to name but a few. Competition was not only common but persistent.

What happened to this frenetic pace of competitive activity? The conventional explanation is that it proved unworkable.

By 1907, New York and Chicago had seen a wave of mergers, and most of the firms had been consolidated into single entities with de facto monopolies. It was argued that city governments, lacking technical and economic expertise, had allowed too many firms to go into the electricity business and thus were in large part responsible for the overcapacity and undercapitalization that ended up in bankruptcies, mergers, and the emergence of powerful monopolies. Once entrenched, these monopolies could cut back output and force up prices, with the poor consumers at their mercy. So the idea of state regulation of electric utilities by well-trained professionals became a common political battle cry.

New York and Wisconsin were the first to create statewide public utility commissions, in 1907. In the next seven years, 27 more states followed suit. At first, utility firms fought the trend, but by 1912, Jarrell found, they had become "the main champions of the movement" for state regulation.

It was that shift that intrigued Jarrell and suggested the substance of his Ph.D. research. Why did the utilities switch sides? Could it be they expected to be better off under regulation than under competitive conditions? In short, he asked, "Was state regulation of the electric utility industry primarily motivated by a concern for the public interest, or was it a policy designed to benefit the private interests of the utilities?"

To answer this question Jarrell looked at where the demand for regulation first appeared. If the conventional view—that regulation was promoted in the interests of consumers—was correct, he reasoned, regulation would have been demanded the loudest and occurred first in states where the excesses of monopoly were the worst—that is, states whose utilities enjoyed fat profits thanks to restricted output and high prices.

In fact, Jarrell discovered, the first states to come around to regulation were those whose utility rates had been much lower (by an amazing 46 percent) than those of late-regulating states. Profits, too, were lower (by 38 percent) and output was higher (by 23 percent). In short, it appeared that regulation was sought most avidly precisely in those states with the least monopolistic utilities, those least able to manipulate output and prices. This finding bore out the suspicion that it was the utilities themselves that wanted regulation, to protect themselves from competition.

Further confirmation came from Jarrell's second finding. After five years of state regulation, he discovered, the utilities' prices and profits had both *increased,* while electricity output *fell.* Regulation was creating the very monopolistic results the public was told it would counteract!

Academic Apologists

How were the utilities able to pull it off? Although populist arguments about the greed of monopoly corporations held some sway with the public, a key factor in selling the idea of state regulation was the rationale provided by economists. As long ago as 1848, John Stuart Mill advanced the idea that utility companies are "natural monopolies."

The core of the economists' argument ran as follows: A utility is a business characterized by substantial *economics of scale*—as its size increases, the costs of its expensive plant and equipment can be spread over more customers, so that the cost per unit of output decreases with increasing size. Thus, to serve a city of 200,000 people, one firm sized for an output of 200,000 can produce at lower average cost than two firms geared to serve 100,000 each.

If government stands aside, the theory went, the workings of the marketplace will inevitably lead to the most efficient result of a single firm winning out, because of its ability to offer lower prices thanks to lower average costs. But then, having secured its monopoly position (buying out rivals, etc.) the monopolist will be free to jack up the rates, earning "monopoly profits" at the expense of hapless consumers whose alternative suppliers have all gone out of business. (And because of the large investment required, potential competitors are supposed to be unlikely to risk taking on the monopolist.)

The economists' solution was to have government offer the utilities a Faustian bargain. Since the business is a natural monopoly anyway, they reasoned, let's grant an exclusive franchise, thus protecting the utility against competitive threats. In exchange, government would control the rates charged consumers. That way, the rates could be kept at "reasonable" (nonmonopoly) levels, and customers would still reap the benefits of the natural monopoly's economies of scale.

The basis for rate setting would be a specified rate of return on the company's investment. The experts on the regulatory commission would keep tabs on the utility's total investment (called its "rate base") and allow it to set rates so as to earn up to a maximum percentage return (for example, 10 percent) on that rate base each year.

That, at least, was the theory. And after being discussed by economists for decades, it took the country by storm in the teens and twenties, becoming the basis for legal monopolization of the nation's telephone system as well as nearly all gas and electric utilities. Hardly an economics text in the country omits a discussion of the natural monopoly theory of public utilities, dutifully assuring the students that exclusive franchises, public utility commissions, and rate-of-return regulation are the best ways to protect consumers from the evils of utility monopolies.

Economic Revisionist

Although a few economists have questioned the efficacy of regulation via public utility commissions, it was not until the 1970s that a serious challenge to the natural-monopoly theory arose. It came from Walter J. Primeaux, today a professor of economics at the University of Illinois at Urbana. Primeaux has spent the past 13 years single-mindedly researching electric utility competition.

It all started back in 1968, in a classroom at Louisiana State University. "I was lecturing the students on the subject of 'natural monopoly,'" Primeaux recalls. "I was discussing the theory as applied to electric utilities when a young gentleman raised his hand. 'That's not the way it is in Lubbock, Texas,' he said. I assured him he perhaps misunderstood, but he contended he had lived in Lubbock where there was successful competition between two electric companies.

"I couldn't shake the thought—that years, even decades of economic theory, could be disproven in one Texas town; and I wondered, 'Could there be other cities in which competition survives, even grows?' And that's when I began my studies."

After combing through records compiled by the old Federal Power Commission, Primeaux traveled to some of these cities and spent time learning the history of the competition, assessing public attitudes, checking on the nature and extent of competition (which sometimes included price competition but more often was restricted to service competition, as in Lubbock).

Among Primeaux's discoveries was the fact that electric utility competition seemed to be dying out. By 1972 the number of cities with competition had dropped from 49 to 35. And today Primeaux's tally reveals only 23 competitive cities.

Turning his research to the cause of this demise, he found that the opponents of competition were not consumers in the area but regulatory officials committed to its elimination on theoretical grounds. Like their predecessors, public utility regulators remain convinced that electric utilities constitute a natural monopoly and should therefore be subject to rate-of-return regulation.

In Oregon, for example, when Pacific Power & Light met the competitive price of the Northern Wasco County People's Utility District, there were cries of protest—not from the public at large, but "from sources whose interests are the result of social and government theories." Surveying public utility commissions in all 50 states, Primeaux found that competition is outlawed in all but a handful of states.

Yet, despite the pressure of legislatures and state regulatory commissions, where residents have a choice they always vote in favor of competition. In Sikeston, Missouri, voters were asked in 1967 to approve a bond issue to allow the local Board of Municipal Utilities to buy up the facilities of Missouri Utilities, thereby ending competition between the two. The bond issue failed, and Primeaux found that among the reasons voters cited was a desire to retain competition between the two firms. Residents told Primeaux that they believed the competition guaranteed better service and helped maintain lower rates.

In Hagerstown, Maryland, voters also rejected an attempt in 1965 to buy out the local investor-owned facilities. Again, Primeaux found that voters believed competition forced the competing companies to supply better service. (Unfortunately, this competition was subsequently ended by the state regulatory commission.)

In Lubbock, by contrast, the city fathers wrote into the city charter that any change in the competition between Lubbock Power & Light and Southwestern Public Service Company must be approved by three-fourths of the registered voters. Nowhere in the country do three-fourths of the registered voters even vote, much less agree!

The Theory Challenged

Primeaux did more than simply amass case studies, however. He also collected data on how costs and prices compare under conditions of competition and monopoly. After all, the natural monopoly theory maintains that costs—and hence the rates allowed by the regulatory agency—will be less under regulated monopoly conditions than under competitive conditions.

So Primeaux set about collecting data to compare the prices charged to electricity consumers in cities with and without competition. Using standard statistical techniques, he eliminated whatever price differences could be explained by a number of possible factors (income effects, climatic conditions, extent of residential versus commercial and industrial sales, population density, etc.), so that in the end he would have a measure of the extent of price variations attributable to the existence or nonexistence of competition.

Even Primeaux was surprised by the magnitude of the results. In competitive cities the marginal price (the price for an additional unit) was 16 to 19 percent *lower* than in monopoly cities, while the average price was a whopping 33 percent lower. And the statistical adjustments for other factors revealed that it was the competitive market that largely accounted for these differences.

But what about the economies-of-scale argument? How *could* smaller, competing utilities actually be able to charge less than larger monopoly ones? Primeaux discovered what he thinks is the answer in the work of another economist, Harvey Leibenstein. In a landmark 1966 article in the *American Economic Review,* Leibenstein developed his concept of "X-efficiency."

Simply put, the idea is that in general neither people nor organizations work at maximum efficiency or effectiveness all the time. Competition plays an important role in the intensity with which people work. Where there is little competitive pressure to perform, many people opt for less work effort and better interpersonal relations in the workplace. Leibenstein's X-efficiency theory postulates that because of such effects, a firm's costs will be lower when it faces competition than when it does not, because its employees will be given greater incentives to think, plan, and work efficiently.

Once again Primeaux used data from competitive and noncompetitive utilities, this time focusing on costs rather than prices. What he found was that competition lowers the average cost of production, exactly as the X-efficiency theory predicts.

His analysis also revealed that the X-efficiency effect was more significant for smaller firms than for larger ones. In fact, Primeaux's rough estimate, based on data from the 1960s, was that the cost-reducing effects of X-efficiency outweigh economies-of-scale effects for small firms and for medium-sized ones, up to an annual power output of 222 million kilowatt-hours (kwh). Above that size, he concluded, economies of scale become so important that a single firm *would* be more efficient than competing firms.

Yet there is reason to think that Primeaux was too cautious in his assessment of the reach of X-efficiency. Consider once again the example of Lubbock. Electricity rates there are 20 percent lower than in nearby Texas areas. Yet LP&L and SPS together produce over 1.5 billion kwh per year—far higher than Primeaux's cutoff point.

Lubbock was not one of the cities in Primeaux's data base, and when I told him that figure he was quite pleased. "I have every reason to believe that if Lubbock had been in the sample years of data the earlier results would have been even more impressive," he told me. In fact, he pointed out, only 3 of the 23 competitive cities he analyzed had power outputs exceeding 200,000 kwh, so the 222,000-kwh cutoff had been based on very limited data. If more large cities had competition, we might have a lot more evidence in support of X-efficiency.

Not being a whiz at math, I couldn't really assess Primeaux's statistical results. But a chart I picked up at SPS in Lubbock brought home to me what X-efficiency is all about. It showed SPS's cost of building a new coal-fired power plant in the late 1970s versus that for comparable plants in Wisconsin, Oregon, and Pennsylvania (based on calculations by the Electric Power Research Institute). The other three plants averaged $739 per installed kilowatt—fairly typical for modern 500-1,000 megawatt plants. But here was SPS able to build the same thing for only $296 per kilowatt!

If that's what X-efficiency means in practice, then I'm a believer. Those people really *have* figured out how to produce electricity cheaper! (In fact, SPS's installed cost per kilowatt is the lowest in the nation.)

There's one final nail in the coffin of the old economies-of-scale argument for regarding utilities as natural monopolies. It is that for large firms—the ones Primeaux tentatively excluded from eligibility for competition—economies of scale no longer exist. It turns out that the economics of producing electricity underwent a fundamental shift in the latter half of the 1960s.

What happened, notes utility analyst Ernst R. Habich, Jr., was that rising costs of production began overtaking the pace of technological change. The result? Utilities shifted from being a declining-cost to an increasing-cost industry. Each new increment of generating capacity cost so much more to build that the net effect was to *raise* average costs instead of lowering them. In short—no more economies of scale.

Rate-of-Return Ruin

Conventional utility regulation is a bad deal for consumers. By forcing a monopoly structure on electricity production, it has raised utility costs by promoting X-inefficiency, has led to higher utility rates, and has restricted consumer choice and the availability of good service. (In Sikeston, Missouri, the competing utilities provide the following customer services at no charge: cutting down trees, providing poles for TV antennas, providing free electrician services, and installing the wiring from the power pole to the building.) Ironically, though utilities fought for and benefited handsomely from regulation, today they are being strangled by it.

As noted earlier, the basic approach to pricing employed by public utility commissions is rate-of-return regulation. Because the system is designed to allow up to a specified return on the company's installed capital infrastructure—the rate base—it is in the company's interest to load everything possible into that rate base. The more it costs to build a power plant—and most coal-fired plants cost $700-$1,000 per installed kilowatt—the more the utility can make at its allowed 10-percent return on the rate base. The utilities have every incentive to build plants as inefficiently as possible—they're rewarded by the regulators for doing so. Without competition as a counteracting force, they've historically done just that, and the consumer takes it in the pocketbook.

This part of the rate-of-return gravy train is still in motion. Another part of it, though, has turned around and now threatens to ruin the utilities. That other part is regulatory lag.

During the 40-odd years when electric utilities were declining-cost firms, the purpose of regulatory rate hearings was to decide on the size of rate *decreases*. All during that period, technological improvements and economies of scale in going to larger power plants led to continuing declines in the cost and price of electricity. The average price dropped from 7.45¢/kwh in 1920 to 6.03¢ in 1930, 3.84¢ in 1940, and 2.88¢ in 1950 (measured in constant 1967 dollars).

Because of this downward cost trend, it was clearly in the utilities' interest to have rate-hearing procedures that were thorough, complex, and time-consuming—the more time-consuming the better. The length of time between the initiation of a regulatory agency proceeding and its final resolution is referred to as regulatory lag. And for 10 years, regulatory lag worked in favor of the utilities, putting off the advent of rate decreases.

Then came the 1960s, and when utility economics changed, so did the significance of regulatory lag. Now the purpose of a regulatory proceeding was to obtain a rate *increase*. But the well-oiled gears of the regulatory machinery ground on at their accustomed snail's pace, aided and abetted by consumer and environmental groups who arose to challenge the wisdom of virtually every rate-increase request.

Regulatory lag began cutting off the utilities' access to capital, right when they needed it the most. Faced with skyrocketing prices of oil and natural gas, rising coal prices, and huge increases in construction costs, utilities desperately need the ability to make their own investment decisions in a timely fashion. But regulatory lag means they must spend two years arguing over what was needed two years ago instead of getting on with today's job.

This is no trivial problem. The financial markets have reflected the dramatic decline in the utilities' financial health. Over the past decade, utility bond ratings have dropped from AAA and AA to the A and BBB category, indicating higher risk. By 1981 the value of utility stocks had dropped to 75 percent of book value—that is, to less than the firms' facilities are worth.

According to Harvard energy researcher Peter Navarro, "the root of the problem is electric utility regulation." Because of regulatory lag, Navarro says, rates set by regulators based on outdated cost figures prevented any major regulated utility from realizing its allowed rate of return in 1980. And in nearly every case, the rate of return it did earn was below its cost of obtaining capital—a sure route to bankruptcy. It's not surprising, then, to learn that more than half of the new electric generating capacity scheduled for 1979 through 1988 has been delayed or deferred—the utilities simply can't raise the money.

The solution increasingly being proposed is...deregulation. No less an authority than the director of the Harvard Energy Security Project raised the idea on the op-ed page of the *Washington Post* in April. Reviewing the utilities' sad plight, Alvin Alm concluded that there are really only two ways out: an enormously costly federal bailout, or deregulation. By removing at least new plants from regulation, he suggested, new firms or deregulated subsidiaries of existing utilities would be able to raise capital more easily because the plant's construction and operation would be free of regulatory control.

Alm is not alone in this idea. In his article he pointed out that at a recent conference sponsored by the California Public Utilities Commission, the heads of both the California and New York PUCs, John Bryson and Chuck Zielinski, "both advocated decontrol as the best solution to the utility crisis." And Zielinski, going further than Alm, urged that *all* generating plants—not just new ones—be freed from regulation. "In the long run," notes Bryson, "a deregulated market would force rigorous decisions on the most cost-effective means of supplying electricity needs." Even regulators are advocating deregulation!

But it's not just electric utility experts who are coming to favor deregulation. So are authorities on the regulated telephone utility—and for similar reasons. Nina Cornell was chief of the Office of Plans and Policy of the Federal Communications Commission until early this year. In her years at the FCC she saw first-hand how rate-of-return regulation works in the telephone industry. In an article in *Regulation* in November 1980, she analyzed the assumptions behind such regulation and found them wanting.

Utility regulators operate as if both consumer demand and technology (supply) remained essentially static, she noted, rather than being dynamic and hard to predict. As a result, regulation tends to lock regulated firms into obsolete technologies and to stifle innovation. One explicit way it does this is by encouraging long depreciation periods, matched to the physical life of the equipment rather than to its economic life. Thus, telephone companies are still utilizing huge quantities of obsolete electromechanical relays in their switching systems. Likewise, electric utilities have resisted replacing economically obsolete oil-fired plants and seem unable to cope with the variety of new small-size energy sources. As Cornell sums it up:

> *Rate-of-return regulation with price and entry controls has the effect of slowing product innovation and technological change by regulated firms; by firms that might want to enter the market, using a better idea to make the very same output; and by firms that might develop new products to serve the same basic functions.*

It seems quite likely that it is because of rate-of-return regulation that the fraction of its revenues that the electric utility industry invests in research and development (0.6 percent) is among the lowest in all of American industry.

In fact, explains Cornell, what we have is a vicious cycle. Due to the possibility of monopoly and its potential for harm to consumers, regulation was created to guarantee and (supposedly) control the monopoly. But the regulation itself serves to perpetuate the conditions that make for monopoly in the first place—by forbidding the challenges that come from innovation, which in turn spring from competition. Thus, concludes Cornell, "rate-of-return regulation does not work, creates distinctly bad side-effects, and takes on the status of a self-fulfilling prophecy."

Opening Doors

Primeaux, Leibenstein, Cornell—the lesson is that the production and sale of electricity is not a natural monopoly and probably never was. Power plants operate more efficiently when they face competition than when they are monopolies. While regulation has not protected consumers from monopoly, it has managed to protect monopolies from competition at the expense of consumers.

Moreover, there have always been substitutes for power-plant electricity. There are other sources of heat than electricity (oil, coal, gas, wood, solar), other sources of cooking fuel (gas, wood), and decentralized sources of electricity as well (cogeneration, small hydro, windmills, etc.).

In addition, as economist Harold Demsetz pointed out in 1968, even if a single utility firm had significant economies of scale in an area, there is good reason to think that the potential for competition from rival firms moving into the area would serve to keep prices below monopoly levels. And if individuals or consumer groups owned the local distribution lines, Demsetz noted, they could seek competitive bids from electricity generating companies rather than being stuck with a monopoly supplier.

Movers and shakers are starting to take electricity deregulation seriously. Justice Department antitrust chief William Baxter told *The Wall Street Journal* in June that he thinks the idea is worth exploring. A congressional subcommittee headed by Rep. Richart Ottinger (D-N.Y.) is advocating local experiments in electricity deregulation. Even the Edison Electric Institute, the industry's rather staid trade group, has launched a study. "Deregulation is going to be a major item of the next decade," predicts Edison Vice-President Terry Farrar.

But what most of these people mean by deregulation is exemption of electricity *generation* from controls. Distribution systems are still viewed as natural monopolies. Yet as we have seen in Lubbock and 22 other cities, actual head-to-head competition in production *and* distribution not only is possible but is actually more economical, thanks to the discipline forced on companies by competition (that good old X-efficiency).

Today, more than ever, with the rebirth of cogeneration, the rush into small-scale hydropower turbines, the revival of wind energy systems, and future prospects for fuel cells and solar panels, the dead hand of monopoly and rate-of-return regulation is the last thing we need. There's a dynamic, competitive industry lurking in the shadows of the smokestacks and cooling towers, waiting to step forth into the sunshine—if only the politicians and bureaucrats will let it.

"When should an industry be subject to classical public utility regulation?" asks Nina Cornell. "The answer is 'never.' This form of regulation, widely viewed as protecting the public from abuse of monopoly power, in fact has never done so, never could, and never will....It is both a snare and a delusion—and an unacceptable fraud on the public." With electric utilities fighting for survival and with energy entrepreneurs waiting in the wings, the time to end that fraud is now.

Space Entrepreneurs

By Patrick Cox

January 1985

G ary Hudson needs $100 million, maybe $200 million. He needs the money to fulfill a dream: He wants to build a spaceship. If he succeeds, he is certain that he will make a fortune—and that anyone who backs him will, too. But first, he needs $100 million, maybe $200 million.

Hudson is one among a number of entrepreneurs who have been trying to develop "launch vehicles" for transporting things into space—satellites, people, manufacturing facilities, whatever. These entrepreneurs and their efforts to develop low-cost alternatives to government-funded and government-controlled space-transportation systems have caught the imagination of documentary filmmakers and the mainstream media, from *Esquire* to *The Wall Street Journal.*

They are a colorful lot, and they've had their small successes. But the story of the conquest of space by private enterprise can't be written yet. And upon investigation, it appears unlikely that that story will be written for some years to come.

The roaring, enthusiastic energy that was associated only several years ago with the beginnings of the free-enterprise launch business has taken on a bitter edge. The groups of mostly young entrepreneurs and engineers are running up against a major obstacle to their dreams of space exploration and financial success. That obstacle is not a lack of energy or talent or ideas. Ironically, it is the National Aeronautics and Space Administration, the very organization that has fueled so many Americans' fascination with space.

The problem is that NASA is a taxpayer-funded monopolist of space trans-portation—a bureaucratic empire, with a budget of billions, that presents its Space Shuttle as *the* best, *the* most economical—*the only*—way to get into space. Its current, on-the-record, official line is one of encouraging "the commercialization of space." But behind the scenes there are NASA policies, actions, and attitudes reflecting a dogged determination to keep space transportation a government monopoly.

Yet for people like Gary Hudson and others who are trying to develop low-cost space transportation, NASA's monopolistic stance amounts to a war against those efforts. This investigation has turned up evidence that at a high level NASA has even resorted to "hardball" pressure tactics in an attempt to deliberately stifle the development of a private space transportation industry. But for the most part NASA's war against space entrepreneurs is a subtle war; the obstacle it poses can be traced to its very existence.

There are at least two ways to think about space. From one perspective, space is a commercial frontier, a place where generations of entrepreneurs will build businesses and fortunes, in communications, manufacturing, mining—even tourism.

Already, there is a successful and rapidly growing communications-satellite business, providing telecommunications at the speed of light all over the world. Gold prices, telephone calls, and reruns of *I Love Lucy* are bouncing around the geosynchronous orbit, 22,300 miles overhead, at this very instant.

Navigational radio services are available to anybody with the right receivers. Satellite imaging services relay pictures of the Earth and its atmosphere to geologists, shipping lines, and others, although the best stuff is reserved for the military. Weather satellites are providing three-dimensional images of myriad meteorological phenomena from pole to pole.

In the not-too-distant future, there are even more spectacular developments. The processing of materials in space, where there is little gravitational force, promises cheaper, purer, and more-exotic pharmaceuticals. The first astronaut sent into space aboard the Space Shuttle by a private firm (McDonnell Douglas) monitored the manufacture of a secret substance for Johnson & Johnson—a substance that reportedly can be produced 500 times faster in the microgravity of space than on Earth. And John Deere, the farm-equipment maker, has performed metallurgical research in space that may lead to the manufacture of better and cheaper alloys on Earth.

Space, too, provides the ideal waste-disposal site—intensely hot suns, giant incinerators in the heavens above. Our own sun provides a source of energy, bounced to Earth from orbiting solar plants, that could someday make fossil and nuclear fuels obsolete. Conditions in space could also provide help for people with medical problems that cannot be treated effectively on Earth. Even asteroid mining is foreseen. And only time will reveal wonders that are as yet unimagined.

There is another way to look at space, a romantic one. A generation ago, children played at cowboys and Indians. Television and film were filled with the Old West, reflecting a longing affection for the frontier that almost seems programmed into Americans' chromosomes. But now there is the *Star Trek* generation. Cowboys are out, Han Solo, Luke Skywalker, and E.T. are in.

Space has become a symbol of freedom and adventure for the generation that broke all TV-viewing records one summer day in 1969, when the space vessel *Eagle* landed on the moon. I remember that day much better than the usual "Do you remember what you were doing when?" day, the day that President John F. Kennedy was shot. Indeed, Kennedy may one day be remembered mainly as the president who rose to the Soviets' Sputnik challenge, sent Americans into space, and thus inaugurated a new era of exploration.

When Neil Armstrong set foot on the moon on July 20, 1969, and flubbed his line, we the American people were not so much excited by the advances of nation or science—we were excited by the potential for us, each one of us. The implications were personal. We saw ourselves taking that giant step—not for mankind, but for ourselves, individually.

But whatever the cause that sets pioneers in search of promised lands, they cannot accomplish anything without transportation. From the Phoenicians to the

Vikings to Christopher Columbus, shipping was a vital ingredient of their varied successes. Hannibal attacked Rome with elephants. The Arabs beat all comers with camels. The Spanish took the Americas with ships and horses. In the United States, the railroad joined the East to the West. The automobile followed, reshaping the continent; then the airplane, reshaping the globe.

I belabor the obvious for a reason: Transportation is the key to space. Nothing of historical importance ever happens until people get there. And nothing really important happens until people can transport more than national flags. Transportation links the practical side of space exploration with the romantic dreams.

The history of space transportation is not a long one. The first U.S. rockets were launched into space by the Defense Department in the 1950s, using technology derived from military missiles. The military's immediate objective was to launch "spy" satellites: Essentially, a satellite equipped with a camera and transmitter was put atop a big, unarmed missile and fired into space. The satellite, high enough to escape Earth's gravity, coasted into orbit. The missile itself, the "launch vehicle," fell away during the spaceward flight (in "stages," or segments) and disintegrated during its descent or dropped into the ocean, broke up, and sank. Because such a rocket can be used only once, it is called an "expendable launch vehicle," or ELV.

NASA was created by Congress in 1958 to research and develop space technology for peaceful purposes. It joined the military in producing ELVs of several different designs. These vehicles differ among one another primarily in size and power—that is, in how heavy a payload the rocket can boost how far into space. Observational satellites, which relay pictures of the planet and its atmosphere back to Earth, are launched to low earth orbit (LEO), roughly 100 to 200 miles above Earth. Communications satellites—the "birds" that relay phone calls, TV signals, and a variety of other electronic stuff—are deposited in geostationary, or geosynchronous, orbit (GEO), 22,300 miles above Earth. In that orbit, satellites move synchronously with Earth, so that they appear from the ground to be fixed in the sky.

By the mid-1960s, the government's rockets had proven themselves reliable, paving the way for commercial uses of the ELVs, and the first commercial communications satellites were spun into orbit—aboard NASA rockets. Space entrepreneurs were a phenomenon of the future. Even had dreamers perceived the potential for a launch business, though, they would have run into a massive wall of "national security" concerns. During this early period of space-flight development and the Cold War environment in which it occurred, much of the launch technology now commonly available was highly restricted.

When NASA had completed its first major mission in 1969—beating the Russians in sending a human to the moon—it turned to its next challenge: the development of a manned "space truck," a fully reusable spaceship that could ferry people and cargo between Earth and space. Like the cost of an airplane, the shuttle's cost could be spread over a great number of users, making the journey to outer space economically feasible. The expensive, disposable ELVs—the original workhorse rockets—would be replaced with an economical alternative, and the high frontier would at last be opened to development. So the vision went.

The reality was that NASA's Space Shuttle, finally operational in 1981, turned out to cost three times more to develop than originally projected. Likewise, its cost of operation keeps escalating. Yet NASA determinedly promotes the Shuttle as a low-cost space vehicle, setting a low price for commercial users and making up the difference out of the taxpayers' kitty.

Meanwhile, in 1983 the Reagan administration directed NASA and the military to turn over their expendable launch vehicles—primarily NASA's Delta and Atlas launchers and the Air Force's Titan rocket—to private operators. So major aerospace corporations are now poised to compete with the Shuttle in getting satellites and such into space. It's a situation that makes NASA very testy.

Joining NASA and the private ELV operators on the space-transportation scene is a third element: the entrepreneurs. They see a growing market for launch services and, typically, think they can do it for less than either NASA's Shuttle or the privatized ELVs.

It was just two years ago that the barrier to a free-enterprise launch industry appeared to have finally been breached. On September 9, 1982, Space Services Inc. (SSI), a Houston-based firm headed by Texas real-estate millionaire David Hannah and former astronaut Donald Slayton, launched its $2.5-million *Conestoga I* rocket from Matagorda Island, off the Texas coast, 196 miles into the sky. Only little more than a year before, Hannah's group (Slayton was not yet part of it) had seen $1.5 million and months of development work go up in smoke when their *Percheron* rocket blew up on the Matagorda pad during a launch attempt.

The *Conestoga I* was actually a surplus NASA "sounding," or research, rocket incapable of delivering a commercial payload into orbit. But its successful launch was funded and carried out from start to finish by a private company. Among entrepreneurs, enthusiasm ran high: The big money would now come their way, because at last investors had seen that a private company could do what till then only government had done. But investors didn't reach for their checkbooks.

Even for SSI, the launch firm that some observers consider the most likely to succeed, disappointment was in store. Following its *Conestoga I* launch in 1982, the firm started developing what would be its operational rocket, the *Conestoga II,* and hoped to sign up customers. Space Vector, a small California aerospace firm that executed the first launch under contract to SSI, was hired to work on development of *Conestoga II.*

By the beginning of 1984, SSI decided to no longer fund work on the project, and Space Vector struck out to develop its own commercial rocket, the LEO 3. Two years after the *Conestoga I* launch, Hannah and company are still seeking their first customer, and they've hired another firm, Space Data, to develop the *Conestoga II.* They're also interested in acquiring rights to market NASA's Scout, a sounding rocket that can deliver small payloads to low earth orbit.

Another high point for entrepreneurs came in August 1984, when Starstruck Inc., launched its sounding rocket, the *Dolphin*, from the Pacific Ocean, off the Southern California coast. It was the young firm's fourth try—and first success—at launching the *Dolphin.*

But that up was immediately followed by a down. Just a few weeks after the August 3 *Dolphin* launch, Starstruck president Michael Scott—who in 1982 had left his position as chairman and chief executive officer at Apple Computer to head Starstruck—laid off nearly all of Starstruck's 50 employees. The apparent austerity move touched off a reorganization of Starstruck's management; the firm's board of directors was reconstituted, and Starstruck cofounder Tucker Thompson replaced Scott as president. Thompson put together a skeletal staff to keep operations going, and the firm plans to continue developing its operational rocket, the *Constellation*.

Gary Hudson's career, too, resembles something of a roller-coaster ride. Hudson got his chance to realize a long-time dream when, with David Hannah's backing, he designed the *Percheron* rocket. After the *Percheron* met its explosive fate in July 1981, Hudson and Hannah's partnership ended. But Hudson formed Pacific American Launch Systems, which is now developing his new dream vehicle, the *Phoenix*.

Other private launch initiatives include Len Cormier's Third Millenium. Cormier envisions a "Space Van," a Shuttle-like manned spacecraft launched in midair from atop a jumbo jet. He is reportedly trying to set up a public stock offering to get funding for the project, but as yet no stock has been put on the block.

Robert Truax's Truax Engineering, meanwhile, has plans to develop two very large and powerful launch vehicles, the *Excalibur* and *Sea Dragon* rockets. But to publicize his company's efforts in order to attract investors, Truax is pursuing his Project Private Enterprise—a plan to launch a person into a brief suborbital flight aboard a small rocket. He has constructed most of the rocket and conducted several engine test firings for the press. According to Tom Brosz, the editor of *Commercial Space Report*, Truax needs about another $1 million "to polish off the project."

And there's OTRAG, a West German firm that for several years appeared to be gathering momentum in developing a rocket, from a base of operations in Libya. OTRAG has ended the Libyan connection but is reportedly continuing with its plans to develop a commercial rocket.

One of the revealing features of these private launch initiatives is that they do not share a single approach to space transportation. Some, like Space Services with its *Conestoga*, or Space Vector with its LEO 3, aim to develop a more or less conventional expendable rocket. Others—Starstruck, for example—are adding unconventional twists to otherwise conventional rocket designs.

Starstruck's *Dolphin* uses a hybrid engine that incorporates a liquid oxydizer and a solid fuel, a revival of technology that the Air Force developed and then abandoned. The hybrid engine is said to offer certain performance advantages over an all-solid engine (like that of SSI's *Conestoga II*, for example) and greater safety than a liquid-fuel system such as the Titan's. The *Dolphin*, appropriate to its name, is launched from *in* the sea, rather than from a launch pad on land. Starstruck not only is spared the expense of building launch pads but also will have great flexibility in choosing a launch site. In addition, Starstruck's idea is to develop modular rocket units that can be put together in various numbers to create more-powerful launchers.

Hudson's *Phoenix*, too, is a quite different approach to designing a launch vehicle. The way to radically bring down launch costs, says Hudson, is to create a reusable vehicle. If a rocket is used only once, the price charged—by a private firm, anyway—must cover the vehicle's full production costs as well as development and operating costs. But if a single vehicle gets used over and over again, each user pays only a portion of its production cost. The more users, the lower the cost to each user, all other things being equal. Hudson is placing his bet on a reusable rocket.

Unlike Len Cormier's Space Van (and NASA's Shuttle), Hudson's *Phoenix* is not a winged vehicle—it is a ballistic, or missile-like, vehicle. This design, says Hudson, results in much less stress and heat build-up, especially during reentry into Earth's atmosphere. Hudson's explanation of his design criteria is lucid, and his logic seems quite solid. Yet major investors don't want any part of it. Why they don't requires a lot of digging into the way NASA goes about its business.

Mention "Shuttle pricing" to a space entrepreneur, and he's likely to turn purple. It's one of the subtle ways NASA sits athwart the private road to space, and it's probably the most important.

Ever since the Space Shuttle's much-applauded maiden flight in the spring of 1981, it's been ferrying things into orbit for private firms (and, dramatically, fixing or fetching some). NASA charges users of the Shuttle, of course, just as users have been paying for launches via government-operated ELVs. But NASA *undercharges* commercial users, according to outsiders—pricing launches at half their actual cost and perhaps even at a quarter of their cost.

Phillip Salin, a cofounder of the firm Starstruck, is an outsider who has looked closely at NASA's Shuttle pricing. In February 1984, he was invited by Rep. Harold Volkmer (D-Mo.), head of the House Subcommittee on Space Science and Applications, to testify on the economics of Shuttle pricing.

Salin, who has a background in economics, spent two weeks tracking down financial information about the Shuttle. His job was not easy: There are no balance sheets for the Shuttle, it being a commercial venture of an agency that is manned by scientists instead of business people. And to judge from what Salin discovered, it is possible that had standard accounting practices been applied to Shuttle pricing policies, space development might have taken a quite different course in the last few years.

In February 28, 1984, Salin walked into the Rayburn Office Building of the U.S. House. Four congressmen and 100-odd interested parties in the audience were there to hear his testimony. Subcommittee chair Harold Volkmer ran the show. Salin was nervous, because even he was surprised at the numbers he had uncovered in his marathon "audit" of NASA.

According to the space agency's own projections of costs, budgets, and an expected 53 launches from October 1985 to October 1988, Salin declared, the average cost per Shuttle launch during those three years will be approximately $250 million. That figure, he noted, includes apportioned ongoing costs for maintaining, operating, and improving the Shuttle.

The $250-million-per-launch estimate does *not* include some *$20 billion* in "sunk costs" for the Shuttle: $10 billion on R&D, $3 billion to construct orbiters, $2 billion to construct facilities, and $5 billion to conduct the first eight launches. A private company would somehow have to cover these costs, but Salin didn't add them in, he says, because of the difficulty in comparing government R&D man-dated by "national interest" considerations and a private enterprise's R&D.

Even excluding that $20 billion, Salin noted in his testimony, NASA's proposed pricing policy is not based on full-cost recovery, on average annual cost recovery, on average per-launch cost recovery, or on any other methodology comparable to the way a business firm would have to set charges. Instead, NASA's pricing policy for the Shuttle is based on a cost concept of its own devising, which it calls "out-of-pocket costs." Significantly, Salin charged, the taxpayers end up paying at least half of the actual costs of sending satellites into orbit for profitable corporations such as RCA and AT&T and for various foreign governments.

Salin's testimony put NASA in a tizzy. Within days the agency had circulated a memo to every remotely interested party in Washington, attempting to rebut his analysis. The memo, dated March 7, 1984, charged that "Mr. Salin had a basic misunderstanding of both the Shuttle cost structure and the principles underlying the pricing policies for commercial and foreign customers." The six-page attack on Salin's analysis ended with the assertion that "it is the commercial and foreign customer who is subsidizing the cost of Government launches and not the oppo-site."

That the document's author did not sign the memo has probably spared the unknown bureaucrat much embarrassment. Only five months later, NASA chief James Beggs testified before a congressional subcommittee that each Shuttle launch actually costs $150 million to $200 million. NASA was apparently not so misunderstood by Salin as the agency had charged.

Yet three months after Beggs testified on Shuttle costs, when the head of NASA's Office for Commercial Programs, Isaac T. Gillam, was interviewed for this article, he called Salin's cost estimates "preposterous." Gillam admits that Salin took pains to get all available cost data from NASA, but he contends that Salin's analysis was seriously flawed—essentially because Salin included Shuttle ex-penses that shouldn't, by NASA's lights, be counted as costs of a commercial launch.

What is at stake is evident from a quick review of Shuttle pricing (all in 1982 dollars). NASA currently charges only $35 million to take a full cargo bay load into low earth orbit (cargo that doesn't take up the whole bay is prorated). In late 1985 the charge is to go up to $71 million. But from October 1988 on, President Reagan has told NASA, it must charge commercial Shuttle users a full-cost-recov-ery price.

So NASA has analyzed its costs and projected business and submitted to the White House a post-1988 pricing proposal. NASA's "full cost recovery" price: $87 million! It's no wonder that the agency has been so eager to dismiss Salin's cost figures.

For his part, Salin concedes that some of NASA's criticisms may be valid. But he doesn't see how the average cost could be gotten below $200 million per launch. And that leaves a huge tab for taxpayers—and gives NASA a tremendous leg up on the potential competition in the space-transportation business.

Against the highly subsidized Shuttle, then, private ELV operators cannot compete on price. Without its huge subsidies, the Shuttle would be a hands-down loser. But since taxpayers pick up somewhere between half and three-quarters of the actual *cost* of a commercial Shuttle launch, the Shuttle beats ELVs in *price* by a significant margin.

And, figures the astute venture capitalist, yet-to-be-proven alternatives couldn't compete either. And so investment funds for alternative vehicles remain scarce. That is precisely the problem that smacks entrepreneurs like Gary Hudson in the face. The Shuttle's artificially low price is freezing out the competition.

Of course, NASA has a benign view of its pricing policy. As Chris Kraft, former director of NASA's Johnson Space Center in Houston, told an *Esquire* reporter recently, "Until you capture the market, you've got to subsidize it." Eventually, with lots of users over which to spread its fixed costs, taxpayers won't have to subsidize Shuttle users. The nation's space agency will thus have made good on its promise to provide low-cost space transportation.

At best, that thinking is desperate. In the mid-1970s, NASA projected nearly 600 launches in the first 12 years of Shuttle operation. That figure was later lowered to less than 500, and in 1982 the projection was again lowered, to *less than 250.* In 1984, the Shuttle's fourth year of operation, it made only 5 of 10 planned launches, and observers say that NASA's goal of a launch a month in 1985 looks doubtful.

Moreover, suppose the present average cost per launch is, as Phil Salin found out and NASA now concedes, something between $150 million and $250 million. Even the most elastic imagination is tested by NASA's supposition that it can increase its volume, price, and operational efficiency enough to recover its costs, especially if the agency's record on cost overruns holds into the future. In 1982, the General Accounting Office, the federal government's internal auditor, found that NASA's projected average Shuttle launch cost increased 73 percent between 1976 and 1980.

Consider, too, that for a single launch the fuel, external tank, and engines that are expended cost $25 million or so. And NASA employs 12,000 to 14,000 people to carry out a Shuttle launch from start to finish. How much personnel cost to attribute to the cost of a single Shuttle launch is not easy to calculate, but the magnitude at issue is clear.

Officials at NASA say that as they learn more with each Shuttle mission, they will rapidly achieve efficiencies. But NASA's descent on the "learning curve" would have to be precipitous—especially for a government bureaucracy that has little incentive to reduce costs—in order to achieve the kind of reduction it suggests.

For NASA officials, then, getting all the customers they can is their only hope for keeping up the Shuttle's facade as an inexpensive vehicle. And that means keeping competitors at bay—whether with subsidized pricing or by other means.

NASA's machinations to scuttle a private launch industry extend at least as far back as 1975. In January of that year, NASA employee Tenney Johnson sent a memo to his colleague Jerome Patterson about a Boeing proposal to develop the Minuteman 3 missile, a military rocket, as a commercial launch vehicle. Boeing was nearing the end of a production run on the missile and was looking for a way to keep up manufacture.

"Private rocket launchings, unregulated, would interfere with NASA's program, as the agency responsible for the space activities of the United States,"

Johnson wrote in his memo. But he speculated that the agency "would have the authority to regulate private launchings, not only to insure safety *but to further the goals of the National Aeronautics and Space Administration*" (emphasis added).

Johnson acknowledged that "since NASA is not a regulatory agency, it could not promulgate rules prohibiting private launchings." Other means came to mind. "NASA could oppose an application for a radio license for such a rocket before the FCC [Federal Communications Commission] or, in cooperation with the Administrator of the FAA [Federal Aviation Administration], formulate a policy which could be effected through the regulatory authority of the FAA." The memo pointedly noted that "no one would wish to project a rocket into outer space if he could not communicate with it through the use of radio. In order to do this, he must have a license....Thus, the withholding of a license would effectively prevent the private launching of rockets."

In any event, NASA did not have to employ such tactics. Boeing's proposal involved a foreign launching site, but that was nixed by the State Department on the grounds that Boeing would be "exporting sensitive technology." The issue of government authority over private launches, meanwhile, remained in limbo until the Reagan administration settled on the Department of Transportation.

Despite its abundant subsidies, however, NASA is still worried about competition from the private sector. That concern was well in the forefront of NASA chief James Beggs's mind when he pegged the Shuttle's per-launch cost at $150-$200 million in congressional testimony last July. Beggs had a sticky dilemma for Congress to puzzle over: Through cost reductions and price increases, Shuttle operations could be made self-sustaining by 1990, he claimed—if the Department of Defense doesn't go elsewhere for its substantial launch services.

In fact, NASA worries a lot about the military's loyalty as a Shuttle patron. The Defense Department isn't as crazy about the Shuttle as it once was—it complains about the frequent delays and long preparation time, questions aspects of the Shuttle's reliability, and has other, strategic reservations about using the Shuttle for all military missions. Consequently, the Pentagon now urges the importance of an expendable launch vehicle capability, and the Air Force even plans to purchase 10 ELVs over the next several years. "This kind of thing," confides a close observer of the NASA-Pentagon feud over ELVs, "makes NASA go absolutely berserk."

"If it had cost $2 million to send a man across the Atlantic," Phil Salin suggests, "imagine how long it would have taken to explore, settle, and develop America." Salin, a cofounder of Starstruck, uses this thought experiment to drive home a main point: A dramatic reduction in the cost of getting there is the key to developing space for human use. And people at NASA would agree with this axiom as readily as would, say, Gary Hudson. NASA, after all, bet its future on the Space Shuttle, and for more than a decade poured all its resources and energy into the Shuttle, as a low-cost alternative to expendable launch vehicles.

As a government bureaucracy, however, NASA in fact has little if *any* reason to develop cheap space transportation. Though this claim might sound paradoxical at first—isn't it in the agency's interest to get the most out of its budget?—it becomes evident once one understands the specific incentives that NASA officials face.

Consider, first, the fundamental difference between how entrepreneurs are rewarded in the marketplace and how government bureaucrats are rewarded in the public sector. The potential for entrepreneurs' personal gain—for profit—increases as they decrease the costs of their operations. So *minimizing costs* is their fundamental incentive.

Public-sector managers, by contrast, are generally rewarded in accordance with the size and scope of their programs—they stand to gain no profits by cutting costs. So their incentive is to expand existing programs and create new programs—to increase their budget, that is.

At NASA, that incentive historically has led the agency to go all out for manned, rather than unmanned, systems. There is high publicity value in the glamour of astronauts, and this is an important element in an agency's bid for funds from Congress. And manned systems, requiring a far higher degree of reliability than unmanned systems, are more costly, too.

Phil Salin and many others argue that at this stage in our technological development, a *manned* reusable vehicle is a seriously mistaken approach to achieving economical space transportation. The Shuttle may be useful for certain types of advanced research, concedes Salin, but for the business of launching satellites, unmanned rockets—"big dumb boosters," as they are sometimes affectionately called—make the most economic sense right now.

Other entrepreneurs would not agree with Salin on this. Len Cormier of Third Millenium, for instance, is trying to develop a manned, Shuttle-like "Space Van." Salin's response to this: "Let each entrepreneur test his idea in the marketplace—without taxpayer subsidies."

Reinforcing NASA's incentive to inflate costs are the contractors who do the actual manufacturing on NASA projects. Because their fortunes rise and fall as NASA's programs expand and contract, it is in their interest, too, to promote high-cost approaches to space projects and to continually push new, more-advanced technology.

NASA's costs are also driven up by its need to satisfy politically influential constituencies. This often means making decisions based on criteria other than what is most economically rational. A prime example is the way in which the Shuttle's design had to be modified and remodified to satisfy demands from powerful quarters.

When the Nixon administration wouldn't fund NASA's plans for a manned space station, interests backing the station forced NASA to incorporate aspects of a space station, such as extended habitation in the vehicle, into the Shuttle. This significantly raised the Shuttle's cost beyond that of building a simple space truck. The truck became a *mobile home*.

Then, in order to win the Air Force's support, NASA again modified the design to accommodate larger military payloads and greater maneuverability. These changes led to a redesigned, complex wing and required the use of the infamous, troublesome heat-shield tiles, causing long delays and major cost increases. The Shuttle had become a *paramilitary* mobile home.

Finally, due to cuts in NASA's development funds, the original concept of total reusability had to be abandoned, thereby leading to higher operating costs. Some observers say the idea of a fully reusable vehicle was a questionable one, anyway, based on the premise that somewhat higher development costs would be offset by lower operating costs. But by changing horses midstream, the Shuttle ended up costing much more both to develop and to operate than purely expendable vehicles.

Risk, too, is handled by government bureaucrats in a way that inflates costs. Public-sector managers have Congress looking over their shoulders. They have little to gain if they take a risk and succeed—a cost-cutting breakthrough will not bring them profits. But if they fail, Congress may cancel their program. Understandably, NASA managers have a risk-avoidance mindset.

Ronald Cordes, a former NASA engineer on the Apollo program, has spoken at length on the subject. Faced with a choice between a $50-million system that is 60 percent reliable and $300-million system that is 90 percent reliable, says Cordes, NASA will choose the latter. A private firm, on the other hand, would probably go with the first option—it's simply good business.

Assume that a private firm fails in its first and second launches but succeeds on the third try. In three tries, each with a 60 percent chance of succeeding, the overall probability of success is 93.6 percent—at a total cost of $150 million. NASA's risk-averse strategy, however, has only a 90 percent chance of succeeding, and at twice the cost. But that's the approach NASA will choose, because failure on the first two 60 percent launches would be politically too risky.

So NASA's first concern is not to maximize its overall cost-effectiveness but to avoid politically risky errors that could lead Congress to cut its budget. And for NASA's contractors, too, the reflex to avoid political risks is second nature.

"This is caused not simply by individual decisions to reduce risks, regardless of cost," points out Eric Drexler of the Massachusetts Institute of Technology. "This pattern is ingrained into the structure of government-funded development organizations, into the way they operate." And Drexler drives home the point: "There need be no money-wasting devils to result in a devilish waste of money."

The upshot is that NASA's approach to space transportation is fundamentally inappropriate to the goal of getting into space cheaply. In contrast to the multiple, trial-and-error approaches of profit-seeking entrepreneurs, the government's space program is run as a centralized monopoly. After exhaustively studying the options, and after taking into account all the political aspects of the program, a committee of bureaucrats—scientists and technicians, yes; but bureaucrats nonetheless—selects what it sees as the single best approach to a problem, then massively funds it until it is made to work. Obviously, this brute-force method is likely to produce a higher-cost design. But in addition, it is exactly contrary to how innovative breakthroughs come about.

A comparison of the U.S. computer and telephone industries provides an illuminating case in point. The entrepreneurial, decentralized computer industry had seen a tremendous rate of innovation resulting in dramatic cost decreases, while for decades the phone industry lay in a technological coma. It was not until the phone industry was deregulated—opening the way for a multitude of entrepreneurs to test their ideas—that real innovation returned to this area. The lesson is clear: It is open competition, not centralized monopolization, that fosters cost-reducing innovation.

It is not NASA that will prove or disprove the feasibility of Starstruck's hybrid-engine, sea-launched *Constellation* rockets; or Gary Hudson's reusable *Phoenix*; or Len Cormier's manned Space Van; or Space Vector's and Space Services's quick and simple rockets. Each of these approaches is based on different notions of what will work best and of what users will need.

Each approach must be tested in the market—first in the market for investment capital, then, perhaps, in the market for customers. So the entrepreneurs behind these efforts must, at each step, ask themselves, How can I get the best results in the cheapest way? NASA officials, on the other hand, don't ask that question—they don't have to.

Money. When you talk with these entrepreneurs, you soon discover that they're not getting it—at least not enough to carry their ideas to a marketable point.

At first, the situation looks familiar enough—part of what one investment expert who follows the space industry calls "the continuing dialectic between entrepreneur and investor." The entrepreneur, brimming with enthusiasm, tries to convince the investor of some profitable new idea. And the investor clings to his skepticism, looking hard for ways he might get burned. But in the field of space transportation, the entrepreneur–investor struggle is complicated by the looming presence of NASA—a huge, monopolistic government bureaucracy that provides the only model of space transportation that investors can look to.

Gary Hudson, 34 years old and with a life-long passion for space transport, has tried to tap many investors' pockets to fund his *Phoenix* rocket. It's still only an idea on paper. But Hudson is convinced that the *Phoenix* will dramatically reduce launching costs—to about $66 per pound of payload delivered into low earth orbit, assuming that the vehicle sees 100 launches. *$66!* The highly subsidized price of a Shuttle launch still costs a user about $1,300 per pound delivered into low earth orbit and about $4,600 a pound aboard a Delta rocket.

"Fantastic," remarked James Connor when the $66 figure was reported to him. Connor, of the investment firm First Boston Corp. in Dallas, is considered an astute analyst of the private space industry and its investment opportunities. He does not dismiss out of hand the remarkable claims of space-transportation entrepreneurs like Hudson, but he wonders where such huge cost reductions are to come. The entrepreneurs' plans, notes Connor, do not involve the application of some radically new technology that in one fell swoop will bring down the costs of space transportation several times over, as the silicon chip did for the price of computers.

Hudson has answers. Because the vehicle is reusable, with nothing but the fuel expended on a mission, the vehicle's $25-million production cost could be spread among many users, just as airlines spread the multimillion-dollar cost of a jetliner over many users, not just a single planeful.

And the operation of a launch vehicle, says Hudson, doesn't require *nearly* the number of people that NASA uses—some 1,200 for a single Delta launch. As evidence that fewer people are needed, he cites the military, which uses a crew about one-tenth the size of NASA's for a similar launch. Hudson expects *Phoenix* launches to be handled by five-person crews. Moreover, he says, operational overhead can be cut even further by simplifying launch sites and control procedures (NASA's are extremely elaborate).

Developing his *Phoenix* to a commercial stage, Hudson estimates, will cost between $100 million and $200 million. But he can't get that kind of backing.

Gregg Fawkes, who heads the Space Enterprise Project of the U.S. Chamber of Commerce's National Chamber Foundation, has polled investors about going in on start-up space-transportation ventures. What he's found is universal reluctance. "The assumption among investors," says Fawkes, "is that the development costs would be *at least* $200 million and probably more like $500 million."

Why can't Hudson and others convince investors that development costs need not be so high? Here the specter of NASA looms large.

Say an entrepreneur has worked out a concept on paper in great detail—technical, financing, and marketing aspects—and meets with a prospective investor. The investor may be impressed by the idea but has no expertise about the subject, so he gets advice from a "technical evaluator." Wanting someone who is knowledgeable about rockets and such, the investor goes to a retired aerospace industry or NASA engineer—someone, that is, who has always operated within the environment of government bureaucracy in which cost is of little or no concern.

"There *are* no experts on this issue," says Starstruck cofounder Phil Salin, "because no one can answer the question the marketplace is asking: How much does it cost to develop a commercial launch vehicle? No one has ever done it, so no one really knows." Indeed, the entrepreneurs could be underestimating the development costs that face them: To achieve a quasi-successful test launch of just its prototype rocket, the *Dolphin,* Starstruck entrepreneurs spent four times as much money and three times as long as they had calculated.

Even if the technical evaluator judges the concept technically sound, he is almost certain to give the idea low marks on the feasibility of developing it within the cost limits the entrepreneur is suggesting. Tom Brosz, editor and publisher of *Commercial Space Report,* explains that the evaluator's attitude is, "if this could be done, NASA would have done it already." Adds Gary Hudson: "If the idea was obvious, the entrepreneurial opportunity wouldn't be there—Boeing or somebody would already be doing it."

And to top it off, observes banker James Connor, there is "an unspoken concern about what the government intends to do—in contrast to what official policy might be." The worry, he explains, is "whether the government will take the market for launches by underbidding" private operators, as NASA is doing with subsidized Shuttle pricing.

"The real money will flow to the entrepreneurs," Connor predicts, "when they can show that users will sign contracts for their services. But users are saying, Why should we sign up with these guys when we've already got a pretty good deal from the government?"

If there were a firm policy resolution to end subsidized government launch services, Connor predicts that investors would move into the business "reasonably quickly—there wouldn't be much reason to hesitate any longer." But as long as

NASA is in the launch business, there is the impression, as Connor puts it, that "the elephants are dancing and some mice will be crushed."

Yet it's still too early for the mammoth space agency to do a dance of victory. Ultimately, there may be too many mice to trample—especially on foreign shores.

When the Shuttle was nearing operation—it first flew in the spring of 1981—NASA's announced intention was to keep ELVs only as back-ups to the Shuttle and to phase them out altogether by 1986. All looked pretty rosy for NASA, but in 1983 came President Reagan's order to privatize the ELVs. Firms bid on the commercial rights to NASA's Atlas and Delta rockets and to the Air Force's Titan. General Dynamics, maker of the Atlas for NASA, won commercial rights to it, and Martin Marietta got the rights to the Titan, which it had developed for the Air Force. McDonnell Douglas, maker of the Delta for NASA, did not bid on commercializing the rocket, and the marketing rights to it went to Transpace Carriers, Inc.

NASA wanted very much to direct the government office that would oversee the private ELV industry. But Reagan assigned that duty to the Transportation Department, which then created for the purpose an Office of Commercial Space Transportation (OCST). Observers of the politics affecting the ELV industry say that Transportation Secretary Elizabeth Dole wants to help the private launch operators get off the ground and that she is likely to urge Reagan to take a firm stance on full-cost-recovery pricing for the Shuttle when the president makes a decision early in 1985. That may be all that's needed to get the private ELV industry going—and to loosen up investment funds for launch entrepreneurs.

How President Reagan decides the Shuttle-pricing question will be crucially important to the future of the American launch industry. NASA, of course, will be pushing hard to get Reagan's approval of its own proposal for a full-cost-recovery price: $87 million (in 1982 dollars). However, the agency may not have many allies this time around.

Also studying the pricing issue are the Department of Transportation's OCST, the Office of Management and Budget (OMB), and the Congressional Budget Office (CBO). Their studies, according to informed sources in Washington, are likely to contend that commercial use of the Shuttle costs more than NASA's analysis indicates.

Moreover, Transportation Secretary Dole, in urging true cost-based pricing for the Shuttle, may well present the issue to Reagan from the subsidization angle: Why, she might ask, should taxpayers subsidize users such as RCA or AT&T, especially when taxpayers face a massive federal deficit? She may explain that her office doesn't want *subsidies* for private launchers—just a fair shake from government by forcing NASA to charge a true cost-based price. That argument may well appeal to the administration's fiscal conservatives, especially OMB director David Stockman.

Another twist in the situation may also put some heat on NASA. On June 1, 1984, Transpace Carriers, the firm that acquired the marketing rights to NASA's Delta rocket, filed a petition with the U.S. Trade Representative's office to investigate "dumping" by Arianespace, the European government-backed consortium: Arianespace charges American users of its Ariane rocket a lower price than European users, thus undercutting Transpace's own prices. Arianespace responded to the charge by accusing NASA of being the most unfair price cutter of all. That squabble is bound to initiate further investigation of Shuttle pricing.

Still, NASA is a powerful force in Washington politics, with many strong supporters both in Congress and in high places within the Reagan administration itself. In addition, commercial Shuttle users do not, of course, like the prospect of having to pay a full-cost price, and they will likely lobby hard for continued subsidies. So there is a good chance that the NASA position will prevail.

But if a myopic U.S. policy thus continues to block efforts in private space transportation, there are other sources of advance. The Europeans' Arianespace probably will not go very far, because, subsidized by Common Market governments, it has many of the same problems as NASA's Shuttle.

It is the Japanese who could eventually dominate space transportation. They are not known for new technologies, but they don't need them to get into space. The tools are already available, and the Japanese have already begun to develop a launch capability. NASA may be able to throw its weight around in the U.S. space industry, squeezing out private operators and entrepreneurs. It will not similarly be able to lean on the Japanese.

Without question, space will be developed. Also without question, Americans will be involved in some way—whether or not their efforts originate from American soil. In the really long run, space represents more than something American or Japanese—it is the domain of individualists, people with political, cultural, and economic claustrophobia. The bureaucratic barriers are therefore destined to fall. The question now is how soon. A lot of us can't quite give up hope that it will happen in time for us to help shape those vast promised lands above.

Plowing Under Subsidies

By Karl Zinsmeister

October 1989

C harles West is six-and-a-half feet tall, and broad. His speech is clipped, his energy level is high, and he walks with a pronounced limp—but fast. Vegetable farming is a quick-paced business, where up to three crops are harvested from a field in a single season, where you have only a few hours to get the job done when it comes time to pick, where tens of thousands of dollars worth of perishable goods can disappear in a blink, due to wilt, hail, or insect hatching. You've got to move to keep up with Charles West.

Luckily I've got him trapped in a pickup. The CB radio crackles with messages between combine cabs, mobile managers, and farm offices. The cellular phone chirps irregularly. As we bang along the field roads, we come upon an evening harvest. Eight migrant laborers and a fleet of machines stuff four mesh-sided tractor trailers with fresh spinach—sloe green and smelling like money. Within an hour the still-bleeding leaves will be swept away to West's 10-minute tunnel freezer. By early the next morning the entire great mound will be locked in crystalline suspension.

The farm lies on the Delmarva peninsula, a dangling tonsil of land rimmed with saltwater—the Chesapeake Bay to the west, the Atlantic Ocean just five miles east. The coastal land is as flat as a calm sea, which is critical for vegetable culture, since field moisture must soak in evenly and mechanical pickers need absolutely level terrain to jostle their quarry out of ground-hugging vegetation.

We circle to a nearby field where three massive, matching eight-wheel-drive tractors drag 10-point plows, shoulder to shoulder. As we watch, this 1,000-horse-power flying wedge turns a hundred acres of sandy earth into a dusty cocoa-colored powder. "Vegetables are terribly hard on the land," West booms above the telecom cackle. To put humus back into the soil and break pest cycles, he alternates vegetables with more traditional field crops. "After growing spinach—hey—barley or wheat or soybeans are like an antiseptic on a sore. We plant them for that reason, though we don't expect to make money on them."

West and his son, Stanley, farm 8,700 acres, nearly two-thirds of that in multiple crops of peas, lima beans, sweet corn, cucumbers, carrots, and spinach. Their Milford, Delaware, operation is the second-largest vegetable farm in the 23-state northern region, according to *American Vegetable Grower* magazine.

Vegetable growing is big business—accounting for 15 percent of total U.S. crop receipts these days and growing fast. It is also far and away the most demanding segment of farming. Eighty-five percent of West's land is irrigated by massive spray booms. That investment has proved a godsend in the heat and dryness of recent years, but it is expensive. Vegetable farming costs from $500 to $1,000 per acre, compared to $400 to $500 for the next most intensive crop (rice), and approximately $200 to $300 per acre for wheat or corn. Growing vegetables also makes heavy demands on management skills, and it requires hired labor. Charles West Farms employs 26 full-time workers and 22 seasonal hands.

But there is a lot of money to be made in return for these efforts. West started from nowhere, leaving a furniture store job in 1953 with nothing but a $24,000 loan he somehow talked a local banker into staking on a lima bean visionary. Today, his farm grosses $4.2 million a year; his packing operation brings in another $10 million. So where are the local imitators of this one-man farming tornado?

In the main, they're farming something a lot less risky: government row-crop subsidies. Though vegetable growing has greater profit potential than any other type of agriculture, its rigors scare away lots of farmers. As a result, two-thirds of our broccoli and cauliflower are now grown abroad, as well as much of our green beans, peas, strawberries, and other produce crops. West evinces little sympathy for his more-timid brethren.

"It's simple: They're lazy," he barks. "It's *easy* to grow corn; any half-wit can do it. Most of those guys on the programs only actually farm for 9 to 12 weeks of the year. They don't want to have to think about anything during the winter. They don't want to mess with hiring labor. They'd rather get a boat and go to Florida."

What frustrates West most is the way government programs encourage warped farming. Since he built his freezing plant he has had an opportunity to deal with many of his neighbors from the vantage point of a processor as well as a fellow farmer. "Look," he says, "there are *no* vegetables in the country right now available to packers. There isn't any sweet corn, no limas, no peas. None to speak of. If I want to make up some mixed vegetable bags at my freezer plant I've got to look for supplies outside the country.

"Right now, I got a load of peas in from Poland—full of snails! Junk. But you can't tell until they come in. If I had my choice I'd never deal with those particular suppliers again. But we will, because we can't get enough American farmers to grow this stuff!"

He continues, "I've also got some frozen Polish green beans a grocery store chain brought me for packaging. They were supposed to be snapped in 1 1/2-inch lengths. Well, they arrived in 4-inch lengths. *We can't fit them in the boxes!* We have to put up with this kind of quality crap all the time, because American farmers are all too busy growing wheat and corn and other subsidized stuff so much in surplus we don't know where to put it, instead of growing unsubsidized vegetables.

"I used to have 8 or 10 growers in this area who ran their stuff through my freezing plant. This year they all dropped out because they can make more growing crops with government payments. So I had to go out and lease some land and get another harvester to keep up with my customers' demands for frozen vegetables. I'm currently packing 22 million pounds of product in my plant. I've got capacity to pack 28 million pounds. And I could sell 55 million! If I could get it."

Asked for his opinion on the best solution, West is even blunter. "These guys all want to do things like they always have, instead of getting with the times, specializing, taking some risks, hooking up in co-ops. The only thing to do now is starve them out. Put 'em on the street. It's this simple: There should be no subsidies in farming."

One of this nation's deepest and broadest collective attachments is to what one observer has called "agricultural fundamentalism." American romantic devotion to the image of the "family farm" is nearly universal. The power of that attachment is illustrated by the fact that every five years or so, in this country's only extended dalliance with economic central planning, we formulate a top-down national policy influencing even the most minute details of farm existence, then put billions of dollars behind it.

The 1990 version is being cobbled and quibbled over even now. And if the past is any guide, it will be founded in many places on some breathtakingly faulty assumptions about who farmers are and what they need. As we will see in this and subsequent articles, present farm subsidies and controls are inflicting heavy penalties on U.S. agriculture. We've long known the financial costs of farm programs to taxpayers and consumers. They are measured in the tens of billions of dollars annually. More recently, farmers themselves have learned that there is a price tag: in increased costs, distorted production, lost markets, lagging technology, unsound conservation and environmental practices, decreased long-term income, and diminished independence and self-worth.

When the executive director of the Australian National Farmers' Federation visited Capitol Hill in the spring of 1989, he told dozens of members of Congress that he is a farmer and he is against subsidies. "They refused to believe me," Rick Farley told me. "They insisted it was a contradiction to both be a farmer and be against government subsidies. An economist, OK, but not a farmer."

Anyone who actually goes out and talks to American farmers today, however, will quickly discover the members of Congress are badly mistaken. Though their views may not be reflected in the Washington offices of the farm lobbies, a large and growing number of farmers now believe that an intrusive, expensive farm policy is the last thing agricultural America needs.

Most of the public and many politicians don't realize that *most* of American agriculture already operates free of government entanglement. Only about 30 percent of U.S. farms participate in direct payment programs. The unsubsidized two-thirds of American agriculture includes more than 200 commodities, and not coincidentally this segment is the healthiest, the most profitable for farmers, and the most efficient for consumers.

Nothing fundamental requires one part of agriculture to be protected while the rest is not. Dairy producers say their product is too perishable to be traded on a free market. That may once have been true, but it isn't any longer in an age of refrigeration, reconstitution, and fast roads. Besides, eggs are also perishable, and unprotected by farm programs, yet that hasn't prevented any Americans from having access to fresh eggs.

California and Arizona orange growers claim they couldn't possibly get their crop to buyers in an orderly way and at a reasonable price without government marketing orders, which artificially restrict supply. Yet Florida orange orchardists do just fine without any help, as do livestock and poultry growers, most vegetable and fruit producers, and others in market-based sectors. The competitive successes of America's unsubsidized farmers confound the claim that agriculturalists cannot survive in a free economy.

Moreover, measures enacted for the benefit of one group of farmers often penalize another. Farm policy is a vast, tangled, often internally contradictory web. Iowa Rep. Fred Grandy (R) likes to say that "farm policy subdivides more times than a chromosome." Very often the constituent parts end up pitted one against another.

When the federal government paid for the slaughter of a million cows to support milk prices for the benefit of dairy farmers, beef prices tumbled. Cattle ranchers—independent and free of handouts—suffered for more than a year. When Charles West goes out to lease more land for his operation, he must bid against row-crop farmers whose margins are fattened by a yearly government check. When pumping water out of his wells to slake his cucumber fields, he must compete with counterparts in California who have the benefit of water subsidies. Those same subsidies allow California rice growers to discomfit Gulf Coast farmers, who must flood their own paddies.

One clear example of the differential effects of farm programs concerns feed-grain farmers and animal raisers. About half of U.S. farm income comes from animal production. Poultry, beef cattle, and hogs primarily eat corn, as well as milo, barley, and other program crops. Feed costs account for about two-thirds of the expense of pork production. The figure is even higher for beef, slightly lower for poultry.

Obviously, then, changes in government price supports on corn and other feed grains can make or break unsubsidized livestock farmers. "Whenever low grain prices give poultry farmers a chance to make big profits," Virginia poultry producer R.H. Strickler told *The Wall Street Journal,* "there's this inclination to do something for the grain farmers." Yet "the government never does anything to reduce the cost of grain to those of us who have to buy it."

Texans are notably open-minded about speed limits, and as you flash south out of Dallas it doesn't take long until you begin to get to some hilly, tree-covered land. Approaching Richland (Pop. 260) the spaces are wide open and the very air vibrates with agricultural rhythms. The ditches and roadsides along Farm to Market Route 3194 are thick with great splashes of Texas wildflowers: buttercups, primroses, fiery spikes of Indian paintbrush, and yellow tumbleweed blooms. And of course bluebonnets, the lupinelike natives that stain entire pastures an unnatural azure and drench the air with a sour, cloying perfume.

As I pull up the gravel road leading to Bobby Wilson's small split-level, the visual music unexpectedly glissades even higher. The house perches on the edge of a great faultline, and down below a valley stretches forever, dotted with tree clumps and watering holes and cattle. Bobby Wilson's cattle.

Wilson is a thin sandy-haired man, quick to make a point, with the cautious and skeptical temperament you might expect from a father of four daughters. He runs 150 cows with some bulls and every year they produce a crop of offspring that he either sells for fattening or grazes himself to yearlings. At any one time he has up to 600 head of stock on hand.

Wilson is a small-scale but respected rancher in the nation's leading ranching state, where 12 million cattle are sold every year. He is active in the Farm Bureau and the Cattlemen's Association and is up on the latest developments in breeding, marketing, and exporting. And he knows exactly what he wants Washington to do for him in the next farm bill: "The best thing the government could do is stay out of the way," he says quietly.

The constantly changing rules, the subsidies for competing products, the elevated costs of inputs, the distorted markets—these are his experience of farm programs. And Wilson worries that thanks to the increasing politicization of American agriculture, the next farm bill will become a target of the burgeoning swarm of Washington-based environmentalists. Then he will be saddled with a heavy load of new controls and regulations, despite never having received a government check in his life.

The feeling of political vulnerability is growing among all farmers. They realize that in an era of long-term fiscal pressure their subsidies—which grew at a faster rate than any other part of government during the early 1980s—are being eyed hungrily by all manner of budget wolves. They know that although farm income is now near an all-time high, it is a highly artificial accomplishment. Seventy-two percent of Iowa's net farm income last year came in the form of government checks. In Illinois it was 94 percent. Nationwide, Uncle Sam provided 36 cents of every dollar of agriculture profit.

"These programs are simply costing too much and not doing us a damn bit of good," worries Illinois farmer Ray Cheline. "Judgment Day is coming."

One of the first things one notices when studying the U.S. farm programs is how very little they have evolved in the more than 50 years since they were born, in the same Depression spasm that gave us the National Youth Administration, the Civilian Conservation Corp, the Works Progress Administration, and other perishables. "Agricultural stabilization" (described by New Dealers as "the greatest single experiment in economic planning under capitalist conditions ever attempted") may be the only portion of the vast New Deal legacy, other than Social Security, that continues to operate in more or less unaltered form.

Having walled off a significant number of farmers from the rest of the economy for a half century, insulating them from both negative pressures and positive innovations, the programs have led many to avoid hard choices and new thinking. "Farmers don't cut back as much as you might expect—as much as they ought to—when prices are bad," one Kansas farmer told me. An Indiana grower reported, "I tend to think in terms of a five-year average before I start considering changing something." Even given the environmental fluctuations that complicate farming, that is a very slow uptake, one that would lead to ruin in nearly any other economic sector.

Some farmers aren't even sure when they are making money and when they aren't. Specialists who consult with farmers on financial matters estimate that only 10 to 25 percent know their true costs of production. As Iowa extension agent Mike Duffy points out, "Corn farmers around here don't really *need* to know their costs today. Government support levels are set so high even the poorest performers can cover their expenses."

Nor are some farmers inclined to adopt business practices. "Most farmers chose their occupation thinking that it didn't require office work," notes farm consultant Eldon Hans. "They think: This is a job where you can work in the open air and run machinery. They don't want to be students of business management. They don't want to sit at a desk."

Part of the problem is generational. Literally since the nation's founding, as an intrinsic part of industrialization, the number of farmers has been shrinking. As a result, agriculture is always top-heavy with older practitioners. The 1980 census found that 23 percent of the nation's farmers were age 65 or older, and 41 percent were between 45 and 64. Only 36 percent of all farmers were under 45. By contrast, more than 70 percent of all other U.S. workers are under 45.

Older farmers understandably tend to favor traditional ways. Many grew up with the deeply embedded notion that industrial America aims to exploit rural America and that farmers cannot compete on free terms. They often distrust processors, commodities traders, bankers, consultants, and brokers, and sometimes fear antifarmer conspiracies.

Many are skeptical about market-based solutions to agricultural problems. They tend not to be as export-oriented as their younger fellows. They are usually not attuned to the idea that farmers must increasingly create markets as well as grow crops. They are nervous about attempting new production and conservation techniques. They are not information-oriented. Some of them feel they were led to believe that the government would take care of all these things, and they are frankly bewildered.

Leo Zilik is a hearty, unkempt, friendly man. Though strongly opinionated and possessed of a colorfully filthy vocabulary, he is naturally good humored and verbose. From his Slavic ancestors he inherited a love for the polka and the waltz, and many Saturday evenings find him on the dance floor in one of the rural halls that sustain Texas swing music. Handing me a plastic cup of iced tea across his kitchen table, he begins to wind up.

Zilik (not his real name) grew up in another era and feels betrayed by modern times. A series of ill-advised and careless blunders have kept his farm in trouble for years. Broken down in his yard is an advanced tractor too complicated for him to maintain and too costly for him to have serviced. He borrows a neighbor's equipment much of the time. A hasty decision a few years ago to try growing rice, a high-paying but difficult-to-husband crop, ended in disaster. Stumbling toward the retirement he has craved for years, he keeps hanging on to pay one more set of bills. A few years ago the bile he nurses for a world rushing by him perforated his ulcer, so he now indulges his grudges in short fits only.

Zilik's golden age came during the fatly subsidized 1950s and '60s. Since then, things have become too complicated and too costly, and he doesn't understand why someone doesn't *do something about it.* Any farmer who works hard, as he clearly does, *deserves* a good living, Zilik believes. It's only that the goddamn city people and the politicians and the rich are trying to starve the farmers out with a "cheap food" policy.

"The guy that wants to work needs what? A lunch bucket and a car!"

screeches his wife from under her rollers. "The farmer—look at what he gotta invest! It ain't fair."

A member of the Texas Farmers' Union, a follower of controversial Agriculture Commissioner Jim Hightower, and a self-described "populist," Zilik prescribes an aggressive, even violent, politics. He believes that all prices are set in offices somewhere and that only by "fighting the sonsabitches" will farmers get a "fair deal." In this he represents the same strain of sentiment that led the American Agricultural Movement, the one-time "tractor-cade" organizers and current enthusiasts for "supply control" as a route to agricultural salvation, to demand in 1978 that Congress simply pass a law decreeing that wheat could not be traded for less than $5.00 a bushel (market prices were about $2.50 at the time).

This idea, after all, is not radically different from the way farm programs already operate, and that is where the sadness comes in. Zilik has obviously suffered genuine humiliation from his farming travails. Mostly, he feels abused and manipulated by the failure of the government to deliver to him the automatic prosperity he feels the farm programs promise.

Once he tried to give up farming and make a go of it as a welder, a trade at which he is quite skilled and from which he no doubt could have supported his family with pride. But he was lured back by the delusions of a guaranteed income and false hopes inspired by a brief uptick—the ephemeral prosperity that periodically surges through rural America, thanks to government policies that presume to suspend the laws of economics and human nature. Eventually discovering he remained susceptible to economic gravity after all, he hardened into a bitter, tragic figure.

Today the chatty dancer has abandoned even life's most sacred loyalties. He openly resents the money he must pay on his ailing wife's health insurance. He vents his reluctance to pass the farm on to his son—who has labored beside him for years—threatening instead to sell it for cash proceeds. He vituperates against his nation, his Texas, his neighbors.

Happily, for every Leo Zilik there are several Loy Snearys. Son of an asphalt contractor in Dallas, Sneary grew up assuming he'd end up in his father's business. He went to college at Texas A&M, majoring in sociology and psychology, and chuckles to think that at one point he thought about going to work in urban planning. But he got himself a wife and her daddy was a rice farmer, one of the pioneers who farmed with mules in the early years after the industry took root south of Houston during the 1920s. The father-in-law offered the newcomer a chance to become a rice grower.

Weighing their options carefully, Sneary and his wife decided to split their furniture and get two apartments—one in Dallas, where Loy coated parking lots during the winter, and one in Bay City near the Gulf Coast, where he flooded fields and grew rice plants all summer. Eventually, he made rice his life.

Sneary is now one of the leading growers in Texas, in many ways the nation's most important agricultural state. In the afternoon of the day we met, he was scheduled to head off to Austin to participate in a Texas Farm Bureau project on the role of government in farming. The group is charged with making recommendations to the state's farmers on what their priorities ought to be in the 1990 farm bill and beyond.

Sneary has a 350-acre rice base, but the plant can be grown economically on a particular field only once every three years, so he rotates his plots over a much larger spread and pastures 500 head of cattle on the fallow land. Rice farming is a tricky, scientific undertaking. To achieve a uniform flood on the paddies, the earth must be precision-leveled using laser-guided land planes. A lot of seeding and chemical application is done aerially, at high cost and considerable danger, and water expenses are high. In this area, the sources are deep wells, 1,100 feet down, which cost more than $100,000 to sink.

As I follow Sneary on his morning rounds, he carefully lubricates, then starts the large new diesel engine he has installed to power his pump more economically than an electric motor. Soon an 8-inch pillar of icy groundwater is pounding out and coursing through the intricate network of routing canals.

A handsome, athletic man with salt-and-pepper hair, Sneary seems to be able to work without rumpling his spotless khaki shirt and crisp jeans. He is a precise person who states repeatedly, "We need to get educated on this...," or "I tried to educate myself on that...." Water flow rates, fuel costs, chemical usage levels and suchlike are on the tip of his tongue. He is an advanced, forward-looking young producer, one of the impressive number of farmers I met during my 12-state wanderings who could have made successes of themselves in any occupation.

But his is not a typical industry. At the moment, rice is one of the most heavily subsidized of all American crops. Farmers are getting $10.80 per 100 pounds of rice they produce. Of that amount less than two-thirds comes from their market sales. The rest arrives in the mailbox from Uncle Sam. As market prices fluctuate, the reliance on federal payments varies. But the current situation clearly leaves Sneary uneasy. "To be honest, if I was a construction worker in Dallas instead of a rice farmer, and I paid income tax and saw what farmers got, I would have lots of problems with that," he says.

"There's no way I can say that most farmers haven't lost some self-respect, whether they admit it or not," he sighs. "Don't get me wrong—I'm critical of the programs, but I participate in them. So long as they exist, I've got to." His position is similar to that of the person who continues to claim an objectionable tax deduction while campaigning against it. So long as it is on the books, available to competitors and distorting underlying economic relationships, most business owners have no choice. That is why it is so important to think clearly about the incentives we set up in federal farm programs—because as soon as they are in place, they dictate the required behavior.

"No question, I think government ought to be a lot less involved in agriculture than it is," says Sneary. "When I first started farming more than a dozen years ago, the talk among farmers was positive—yields, new products, growth. Now everything is defensive: What are the new government programs going to do? What will the target price be?

"I'll tell you," he concludes, "the efficiency of American agriculture has been reduced so much in the last 10 years thanks to paper shuffling it isn't funny."

Sneary knows whereof he speaks. He is one of three farmers elected to serve on the citizen review committee of the local Agricultural Stabilization and Conservation Service (ASCS) board. There is an ASCS office in each of the nearly 3,000 agricultural counties in the nation. They are the local government entities that police and implement this nation's farm policy, and they have staggering authority over the nittiest gritty of farm production—what will be planted, where, when, and so forth. Doing a term on the ASCS panel is a kind of obligation of good citizenship for leading local farmers. For several of the growers I spoke with, their service led to a turning point in their thinking.

"In the last three years, the number of hours required of our [ASCS] committee probably tripled," says Sneary. "Between the federal, state, local, and county requirements, it's mind boggling how much interference there is with our production decisions. It's definitely getting worse."

Some of this growing intrusion stems from calculated bureaucratic expansionism. The rest is just an unavoidable complication of the spiraling of a planned economy. Take tractors, explains Sneary. When the Congress pushed crop support prices way above market prices beginning in the early 1980s, some individual farmers got very gaudy payments from the taxpayers. The killer from a public relations standpoint came when a distressed family farmer named the Prince of Lichtenstein got a check for a million bucks to help his East Texas spread scrape by. In the aftermath, Congress established a cap of $50,000 as the most any one farmer can receive in direct payments.

That doesn't sound so bad. But rice, as we've seen, is a capital-intensive crop. There is a lot of cash flow when a rice farmer sells his harvest, but there is also a lot going out every week in expenses. A $50,000 federal payment cap means that the largest operation that is economical is only around a couple hundred acres. Which gets us back to Sneary's tractor story.

"There were lots of guys who were geared up to grow 1,200 acres of rice. They'd sunk the wells, they'd bought a bunch of big tractors and combines, and so on. Suddenly they had five or six times as much equipment as they could effectively use." Why didn't they just drop out of the federal program and farm as much as they wanted without any government payments? Because the federal programs by their very nature depressed market prices to the point where they didn't adequately cover the costs of production. As a result, a lot of family farmers who'd stretched themselves to get modern had to take several steps back down the efficiency ladder. Back toward Sneary's father-in-law and his mules.

Even without perverse farm program incentives, it can be hard for farmers to adapt to the high-tech, fast-moving demands of modern agriculture. For every instinctive progressive like Loy Sneary, there is another farmer who needs a jolt to help him break old ways and try something new. A little less than two years ago, Randy Justiss lost an 18-year-old daughter. "I spent a lot of time just sitting here, thinking about that, and about a lot of other things." His grief and period of withdrawal seem to have led eventually to a fresh willingness to approach old problems in new ways.

That winter he finally sat down and learned to be comfortable with the IBM PC jr. he had bought four years earlier and never used. Today he follows real-time quotes of commodities futures and options prices in Chicago and Kansas City. He can punch up a weather advisory or a crop report at his office terminal. Recently, he and a brother-in-law became partners in a grain elevator. They bought local farmers' output on forward contracts and immediately sold the promised goods back to brokers in the commodities centers.

With his son and one Mexican-American helper, Justiss farms 2,700 acres of wheat and milo. He is one of only about a dozen farmers left in fast-growing Dallas County, but he has found a way to prosper in spite of the high land prices development has brought on. Except for the site of the barn where he stores his three tractors, two combines, and other vehicles and rigs, all of his land is now leased. He is gradually going to lose access to his fields, he knows, as subdivisions and industrial parks creep outward from Big D. Meanwhile, though, he is able to do quite well—because speculators keep rents low so they can take advantage of agricultural-use property tax reductions.

Market prices for wheat are rising toward the high government-guarantee levels—thanks to tight supplies brought on by last season's drought—and Justiss has dropped out of the federal wheat program. He is planning to lease as much land as he can lay his hands on next year and put it all in wheat. He is also considering buying put options in the futures market to hedge much of the crop. In short, Randy Justiss is bursting out all over. He is running his farm like the capital-intensive, speculative, highly modern business it is.

A barrel-chested, deep-voiced man in a plaid shirt and a cap, Justiss is a model of the new American farmer—hard-working and rugged as ever, but also fastidious and attentive to mental detail. As I sit watching in his tidy office he tickles a price quote for July wheat out of his computer. "It's easy when you're a farmer to just keep on doing things the way you've been doing them," he admits. But habitual ways are beginning to change all across agricultural America, in some places fast.

Ignorance is no longer an excuse. American agriculture has always had a superb technical dissemination wing for new production techniques. For years, land-grant colleges, the USDA's Agricultural Research Service and field agents, and various private groups have empowered common farmers with the latest research in an astonishingly successful way. When it came to the financial and business end of farming, however, the resources were thinner.

But farming is now jumping into the entrepreneurial age. Justiss is hooked up to an on-line service offered since 1981 by the American Farm Bureau Federation to any of its 3.7 million member families. For $20 to $40 a month, any farmer can have toll-free access to all the national financial exchanges, a national news wire from Washington, D.C., a local and state news service, a 5-day, 10-day, and long-term weather forecast, a database of government reports with all current releases, a Farm Bureau advisory service, and more. With a satellite dish the farmer can get it all even more cheaply. The Farm Bureau will also sell any farmer a computer, at a reduced rate, and supply three days of training right at the farm.

State extension services continue to be tremendous grassroots resources in rural America. Fourteen states also have chapters of the Farm Business Association, a nonprofit private group that offers a wide range of specialized consulting for a nominal fee (about $500). Among other services, its consultants will visit a farm to advise on tax planning, diagnose animal diseases, suggest crop rotations, or aid with bookkeeping and sales decisions. The bottom line: Probably no other small business sector in the American economy has as much competent and low-cost technical advice available to it as family farming.

And farmers are picking up on it. They are computerizing. They are beginning to form marketing clubs with pooled money and information as a way of initiating themselves into private commodities trading. They are setting up accounts with brokers. They are diversifying into new ventures. They are adopting new technologies. They are self-insuring against weather hazards and price downturns. "As people get started," says Justiss, "word of mouth spreads. And when folks get so they understand it and realize what's now possible, I guarantee they will be interested."

After years of relying on others to guard their economic security, farmers are taking measures to increase their competence and flexibility, to protect the birthright of their farm equity, to increase their economic independence and cut their reliance upon the federal sugar teat. A privatized structure of agricultural income support is at last beginning to rise.

Justice Goes Private

By Paul Gordon

September 1985

Virgilio Razzo, a retired painter, and his wife, Matilda, were kept awake by a barking dog in their neighborhood.

Walter Kocher is the vice president and general counsel of a corporation that had a multimillion-dollar lawsuit on its hands.

Don and Karyn Souther, a couple with two daughters, were getting a divorce.

A barking dog, a corporate lawsuit, a marriage ending—each of these problems is conventional enough. And if they had come up a few years ago, everyone involved would have assumed that the only place they could go with these problems was to court.

Yet in all three cases, they made a quite different choice: They opted for "alternative dispute resolution," doing in the private sector what most people consider solely within the province of the official, government-operated courts.

Opting out of the system to obtain protection of rights is not an outlandish proposition. Policing was once done almost completely by police, but today there are more private security personnel than there are police officers on government payrolls. Meanwhile, volunteer organizations such as the Guardian Angels and community groups such as Philadelphia's House of Umoja, which was set up to reduce gang warfare and provide guidance for juveniles, are a most welcome part of quite a few urban neighborhoods. In this context, it's no surprise to hear that the Salvation Army is handling probation privately in several Florida counties for some misdemeanants.

What's happening elsewhere in the legal system—opting out—is also happening to the courts themselves. Without fanfare, more and more people are taking their conflicts to private mediation, arbitration, and other alternative methods of dispute resolution. The phenomenon by now even has earned an acronym—ADR.

On a small scale, Americans have been resolving disputes privately for centuries. In *Justice Without Law,* published in 1983 by Oxford University Press, legal historian Jerold Auerbach traced the pedigree of private ADR all the way back to the Puritans in the 1600s. Throughout the 1800s, an astonishing number of Christian utopian communities were set up around the country, and many shunned established legal institutions. And in the late 1800s and early 1900s, Jewish emigrants from Europe brought along their own tradition of resolving conflicts outside the law. The Dutch in colonial New Amsterdam, the Scandinavians in the Midwest, and the Chinese on the West Coast also employed private ADR as a vehicle of ethnic solidarity. And Auerbach discovered that businessmen without a religious or non-English bone in their bodies had as early as the 1600s established arbitration as a firm fixture along the New York-Philadelphia commercial axis. In 1768, the New York Chamber of Commerce set up the first private tribunal in America for settling business disputes.

Americans today are returning to their ADR roots in ever-greater numbers. After decades of fairly steady but unremarkable growth, the 59-year-old American Arbitration Association saw its annual caseload almost double between 1970 and 1984. Innovations that didn't exist 10 years ago, such as volunteer neighborhood "community boards" and corporate mini-trials, are spreading. Even the American Bar Association, where the pace of reform is often glacial, is getting into the act; the organization is busily conducting workshops and seminars in several areas of the law for attorneys who want to learn about ADR, and its Special Committee on Dispute Resolution now maintains an office in Washington, D.C.

One of the reasons explaining why private ADR looks so good is that traditional litigation these days looks so bad. Going to court has never been a barrel of laughs. "I must say that, as a litigant, I should dread a lawsuit beyond almost anything else short of sickness and death," the respected jurist Learned Hand declared and that was in 1926. Since then, the judicial system has only gotten worse.

There is little agreement on the cause for it but widespread agreement that the system is overburdened. Civil case filings in the federal courts have grown sixfold since 1940, while the nation's population hasn't even quadrupled in the same period. Business cases that last for years and produce truckloads of documents have become commonplace, and people are no longer shocked to hear of strange cases such as a child suing his parents for "malparenting."

Yet the often-voiced perception that America has become a litigious society, with everyone suing everyone at the drop of a hat, isn't borne out by the facts. An estimated one percent of the American population receives 95 percent of the legal services provided. And there is some evidence that, because the system is so slow and inefficient, people are often reluctant to pursue their grievances or claim their rights via legal action.

Anyone who does take the plunge into the legal system certainly needs a full reservoir of patience. Economist Bruce Benson argues that court congestion serves to "ration" justice: Those who are willing and can afford to wait and wait some more might get a trial—if the judge doesn't throw out the case somewhere down the line.

Even the pillars of the system admit that something is wrong. Chief Justice Warren Burger warns: "We have reached the point where our systems of justice—both state and federal—may literally break down before the end of this century." And Derek Bok, the president of Harvard University and former dean of the law school there, writes that the system is "strewn with the disappointed hopes of those who find [it] too complicated to understand, too quixotic to command respect, and too expensive to be of much practical use."

The speeches are bracing and the editorials rousing, but little changes for the better. The crisis seems almost impervious to resolution. But investigation of the scene from Los Angeles to New York reveals that in a growing number of places and an increasing range of circumstances, the private sector is providing a way out through alternative dispute resolution.

Lots of digging for information doesn't turn up any good count of how many individuals and groups across the country are offering ADR. They're springing up so quickly, it's not surprising.

Last year, though, the Washington-based National Institute for Dispute Resolution, an information clearinghouse that opened its own doors only in 1983, published a Dispute Resolution Resource Directory of 100 organizations handling problems that would very likely have headed for the courts—or nowhere at all—a few years ago. The organizations range from Call for Action, a group of radio and television stations offering help with consumer complaints, to Western Network, a private organization in New Mexico that mediates water-management and land-use disputes, and the Children's Hearings Project in Cambridge, Massachusetts, which handles conflicts between adolescents and their parents.

Few of the listed organizations are more than five years old, but there is one very important exception to the rule—the grande dame of private dispute resolution, the American Arbitration Association.

But in its maturity the AAA, funded mainly by fees for services and by dues and contributions from more than 5,000 members, has greatly expanded upon its original purpose. Commercial disputes weren't even a fourth of the nearly 40,000 cases the organization took last year. Today, the AAA also handles interpersonal disputes, labor-management problems, and uninsured-motorist claims. It also puts out eight periodicals, maintains a research institute, trains arbitrators, and tallies upwards of a million votes every year in elections conducted for private organizations. And it's even taking on a few mediation cases lately.

But arbitration—a procedure in which a neutral third party hears both sides, then independently comes up with a binding solution—is still how the AAA usually does things, and it is one of the most common ADR mechanisms. An indication of arbitration's wide acceptance is that 47 states, the District of Columbia, and the federal government all have arbitration statutes, most of which recognize arbitrated resolutions as enforceable contracts that can almost never be appealed in court.

But arbitration and the AAA are by no means the only ADR show in town. Not all disputants want or need a third party with the power of an arbitrator. Larry Ray of the American Bar Association's Special Committee on Dispute Resolution notes that other ADR methods include: direct negotiation, which dispenses with a neutral third party altogether; conciliation, whereby the third party is merely a conveyor of information between disputants; and mediation, in which the mediator's role is essentially to guide the flow of information and make suggestions, while the disputants themselves arrive at a solution (and unlike arbitration, the outcome is usually not considered legally binding).

These distinctions among types of ADR are logical enough. In real life, though, there are now many creative combinations and mutations of them.

Perhaps the least court-like alternative to the courts is to be found in San Francisco. There, in 25 neighborhoods, Community Boards provide an informal apparatus for San Franciscans to solve conflicts with the help of their neighbors. They're a "deceptively simple" operation, as syndicated columnist Neal Peirce has observed. And there is no convenient label with which they can be tagged.

In a recent interview, Community Boards founder Ray Shonholtz listed the sort of differences handled by the Boards: "landlord-tenant disputes, merchant-consumer disputes, neighborhood harassment problems, gay versus Hispanic conflicts, arguments between roommates, neighbors opposed to a high school's off-campus policy." A law professor and still the president of the organization, Shonholtz explained that the Boards act as "third parties who intervene in a conflict before the legal system gets involved."

Since Community Boards got off the ground in 1977, hundreds of volunteers—some doctors and lawyers, others without high-school degrees—have been trained by the Boards organization in basic communication and problem-solving skills. This pool of volunteers, currently numbering about 380, is drawn on for panels that help disputants work out their conflicts. Volunteering for Community Boards isn't a casual commitment: In addition to 26 hours of training, a typical panelist devotes about 125 hours annually to the organization. Community members can avail themselves of the service for free.

Putting a panel together (there are usually three to five members) is something of an art. The members usually come from the same neighborhood as the disputants. Moreover, in a dispute between, say, a Chinese and a Hispanic, the Boards would try hard to recruit at least one Chinese panelist and one Hispanic panelist.

It was to Community Boards that Virgilio and Matilda Razzo, who live in the Visitacion Valley area of San Francisco, took the problem of the barking dog this spring. "We have a hill in back of our house," Mrs. Razzo recently explained, "and we'd heard the dog barking night and day. We couldn't see exactly where it was coming from because of trees blocking the view, but for five years we'd heard the barking."

Finally, after finding out the address where the dog was located, Mrs. Razzo recounted, she sent a letter of complaint to the owner. She received no response. She called the Society for the Prevention of Cruelty to Animals and the police, both also to no avail.

It was then that she called Community Boards. "I'd heard about them," she said. "They'd distributed flyers around the neighborhood saying they were available."

The first step the Boards organization takes after receiving a complaint, according to Shonholtz, is to have a "case developer" visit both sides at home to determine whether a meeting would help. "That's enough by itself," he noted, "to solve about a third of the complaints we handle."

In this instance, the owners of the dog were a couple named John and Maria Arnott. The case developer happened to be Mr. Arnott's sister, and it was she who first told Ms. Arnott about the complaint.

"My sister-in-law said, 'Look, someone's complaining about your dog,'" she later recalled. "We didn't know that our dog was causing a problem, and our attitude was, 'Sure, we'll be happy to talk to them.'"

From time to time, the meeting with a Community Boards panel becomes quite heated. This did not. "They were very good about working it out," said Mrs. Razzo. And Ms. Arnott recalled, "I didn't feel any animosity or tension at the meeting. The panel was trying to figure out how to solve the problem. They asked if there are any other dogs around the neighborhood, and they asked what our schedules are—when we get back from work and when Mr. Razzo is at home—and they suggested some things we should try."

In the end, they put together an agreement signed by Virgilio Razzo and John Arnott. The Arnotts would move the dog house to a lower level and keep the dog where it wouldn't bother the Razzos. Mr. Razzo agreed that he or his wife would call right away if the dog's barking bothered them again. And the Arnotts would check with the Razzos later to make sure that the barking problem was ended.

"The day after the meeting," Mrs. Razzo recounted a few weeks later, "we didn't hear any barking. We haven't needed to call, because the dog barks only once in a great while, and it's just for a few minutes. It's like a miracle."

One of the three panel members was Ben Goodman, a retired utility official and a veteran of Community Boards panels. "We panelists try to set the stage so that both sides will think of each other as humans, not opponents," he explained. "We try to see what they have in common—maybe they both have kids going to the same school, or whatever."

Goodman figures it's important for the panelists "to be at ease and not think of it as 'downtown law.'" And ground rules are spelled out. "The first is that both sides should treat each other with respect. The second is, don't interrupt anyone when they're speaking, because you'll have an opportunity to tell your side. Then, in this case, we said to Mr. Razzo, 'Please tell Mr. Arnott how you felt at night when the dog kept you up.' That kind of thing can help."

Not incidentally, Mrs. Razzo is now an ardent Community Boards booster. "About 80 percent of the cases I've seen end this way," said panelist Goodman with obvious satisfaction. "It can be very wrenching with some of the disputes, but it can be very gratifying. That's why I'm in it."

There was a time when many, if not most, lawyers were repulsed by the idea of private dispute resolution. During an American Bar Association debate in 1919, an overoxygenated Massachusetts lawyer even implied ominous parallels between contractual arbitration and the Bolshevik revolution in the Soviet Union—"where they have taken the lawyers and put them out to work in the fields and factories, where they have closed down the courts."

Some of his successors in the law feel a bit less threatened. They have noticed that there's a growing demand for efficient, inexpensive dispute resolution—and they've also noticed that there are more than a few disputants who are willing and able to pay well for it. Streamlined private dispute resolution is not the kind of thing that attorneys are usually trained for, but many have been learning quickly.

In California, for example, lawyer-entrepreneurs and retired judges are offering "rent-a-judge" services, in which they render legally binding but appealable decisions. The state has a law dating back to 1872 that allows for such services ("general references," as the law calls them), but it's only in the last few years that the practice has flourished, as typical court delays have grown.

Among the more famous California rent-a-judge cases is the divorce of est founder Werner Erhard, which began last year and was still continuing as of June. The law permits general references in any civil (noncriminal) case, and the hired judge doesn't even have to be a lawyer.

California isn't alone: At least 10 other states have some rent-a-judge provisions in their laws. But this is hardly the ceiling on opportunity for entrepreneurial lawyers. Several are setting up full-fledged dispute-resolution businesses, rent-a-judge laws or no. Jonathan Marks of Washington, D.C., is one of those lawyers.

Marks comes to his current endeavor by way of the *Harvard Law Review*, of which he was president while in law school; the District of Columbia, where he served as a federal prosecutor; and then the high-powered Los Angeles law firm of Munger, Tolles & Rickerhauser. He and a Munger, Tolles colleague, Eric Green, were working eight years ago on a complicated patent case for TRW, a technology conglomerate that was embroiled in a conflict with another company, Telecredit. The case promised to be protracted and expensive.

Exasperated executives on both sides concluded that there must be a better way of handling the problem, so they improvised. They set up a private two-day hearing, with a neutral adviser present, at which lawyers for both sides presented summaries of their cases to executives of both companies. Marks recalls that it wasn't even an hour after all the arguments were ended before the executives from TRW and Telecredit had worked out an agreement. In the process, they jointly saved an estimated million dollars in legal costs.

The concoction was dubbed a "mini-trial." Was it an entirely new idea? Maybe so, maybe not. "It's conceivable that there were mini-trials in the past but they were never identified as such," says James Henry of the New York-based Center for Public Resources, which promotes and conducts mini-trials.

Marks and his friend Green (today a Boston University law professor) knew a good thing when they saw it. They soon formed a small company called EnDispute to arrange and conduct mini-trials not only in corporate disputes but also in simpler situations such as uninsured-motorist cases. Today, EnDispute has offices in Washington, Los Angeles, Chicago, and Boston, and the mini-trial is only one of its services.

For fees that are calculated at $150 to $250 an hour and usually come to a minimum of about $800, EnDispute will set up and conduct a mini-trial, provide neutral analysis, arrange a voluntary-settlement conference or arbitration, or work out another mode of dispute resolution suitable for the occasion. If need be, they'll conduct a management audit of a company to see how it can reduce the cost of its disputes. Or they'll provide any number of other consultant services.

Others are running the trail blazed by EnDispute, including Dispute Resolution in Hartford, Judicate in Philadelphia, Civicourt in Phoenix, and a handful of small firms, often with a single retired judge, in California. Since the TRW-Telecredit resolution in 1977, mini-trials facilitated by various enterprises have led to the settlement of a multimillion-dollar contract case between Wisconsin Electric and American Can Company; a $10-million liability claim against the Insurance Company of North America; a case brought by Gillette involving theft of trade secrets; and others.

Some of the biggest of the corporate mini-trials have been conducted by the Center for Public Resources, a nonprofit organization with a dues-paying membership. CPR's Judicial Panel—a roster of attorneys and legal scholars who can be hired to preside at mini-trials—includes former attorneys general Elliot Richardson and Griffin Bell, former Yale Law School dean Harry Wellington, and others of their stature. In addition to spreading the idea that the mini-trial is a sensible and useful mechanism, the Center acts, in president James Henry's words, as "a non-profit R&D effort to build the state of the art."

Walter Kocher, vice president and general counsel of the Borden Corporation, knows from first-hand experience how a CPR mini-trial works. His company settled a $200-million antitrust dispute with Texaco because of one.

Borden had filed a complaint in federal court in May 1980. "The case started out according to normal procedure," Kocher recalled recently in an interview. "Hundreds of thousands of pages were turned over by both sides. After we'd been in the case for more than two years, we were preparing for trial when, in a discussion between attorneys for both sides, it was suggested that we both try to resolve the case with a mini-trial. Both attorneys were members of CPR at the time, so they were familiar with it."

CPR's Henry later wrote that the rules at the Borden-Texaco mini-trial were simple: Attorneys for both sides would make presentations to executive vice presidents of both companies; the presentations would be on neutral ground (a private club in New York); and the attorney for each side would have an hour to make his presentation, plus time for rebuttal.

It worked. The meeting took less than four hours altogether. After "sometimes difficult" discussions between Borden and Texaco executives over the next two months, a solution was hammered out: No money changed hands, but they did negotiate a new gas-supply contract that hadn't even been an issue in the case. It was greeted by both parties "as a win-win settlement," observed Henry.

If private dispute resolution has any emblem of success, it is the win-win settlement. In divorce cases, where the emotional stakes are usually more substantial than in an antitrust dispute or a problem with a barking dog, the possibility of both sides winning can be especially appealing.

That's essentially why Karyn and Don Souther, a Los Angeles-area couple, went to a mediator when they decided to get divorced. "To have two lawyers would have been distasteful to us," Karyn Souther explained. "If you don't have a lot of difficulties already, a lot are created for you with the adversarial relationship in the divorce courts."

The Southers' family therapist recommended that they use the services of mediator Joel Edelman, an attorney and adjunct law professor at the University of Southern California and Loyola University. After Edelman had spoken to both of them on the phone, their first meeting was set up.

"In the first meeting," Mr. Souther recalls, "Joel explained his role. He told us he wasn't there to represent one side or another—he was there to help us decide the things we needed to decide. And he asked us why we wanted to divorce."

The second session was far more difficult. "It was long and drawn out," according to Ms. Souther. "During part of the session, I felt that Joel was favoring my husband, and I brought that up. It was a tough session. In the third session, though, the two of us came to an agreement. Don and I actually worked out part of it while Joel was taking a phone call." The third session was their last.

The agreement that the Southers and Edelman worked out is somewhat unconventional—not the kind of settlement that normally comes out of divorce court. "There were so many trade-offs they made that only they knew the reasons for, and no judge ever would," Edelman said. One of their two daughters is to live with her grandmother in Sacramento, while the other will live part-time with each parent. Ms. Souther is paying Mr. Souther child support, and although he is not providing any money for her to continue her education—as many courts might well have ordered—he is buying out her share of a jointly owned house.

It's not at all clear how many couples are like the Southers in that mediation can make their divorces easier and less painful. Edelman believes the Southers' divorce went as smoothly as it did because they "were a couple who had a great ability to understand each other and communicate with each other." In his experience, "Mediation works best when the people are basically sane and no one's off the wall—and neither one wants to get the other, emotionally or financially."

Edelman's experience with mediation goes back to 1969 during the Columbia University student strikes. He was on loan from the Rand Corporation (a California think tank) to the New York Police Department when a police executive learned that Edelman was a graduate of Columbia. "Next thing I knew," Edelman recounted recently, "I was mediating the Columbia student strike and getting hooked on it—as if mediation was one of those rare novels you just can't put down once you've started reading it."

Eight years later, the Los Angeles County Bar Association "drafted" him to set up a Neighborhood Justice Center. The first mediation center in Southern California, it started with "not many standards to speak of except common decency, common sense, and uncommon organizational curiosity," he wrote.

"For me," observed Edelman, "mediation has been life-affirming, all-encompassing, fulfilling, and rewarding. On all levels." These days, he is teaching mediation to law students in Southern California, running small divorce-mediation workshops, and working as a mediator in Santa Monica, frequently with couples like the Southers.

While observers agree that divorce mediation is no cure-all, nor will it work for everyone, it is a growing alternative to often bitter and unsatisfactory court battles over custody and property. No one seems to have tallied how many people are turning to divorce mediation, but there are already several organizations serving the growing market.

An obvious question is whether private dispute resolution is better than the judicial system. Turning up an answer to that is not so easy, though, for several reasons.

First, ADR comes in so many sizes and shapes as to be virtually uncountable. Besides arbitration, mini-trials, for-hire judges, and mediation, there are media-sponsored consumer hot lines, Better Business Bureau complaint resolution, industry-sponsored groups handling complaints for a single industry (such as autos), and numerous others.

Second, private ADR and litigation don't compare on many qualities. As Richard Abel, a law professor at the University of California at Los Angeles, has pointed out, informal ways of processing disputes aren't bureaucratic in the way that the legal system is, and they're not set apart from the larger society like the courts are. He describes ADR as "vague, unwritten, commonsensical, flexible, ad hoc, and particularistic." Those features sound just fine to a lot of people, while others are satisfied and secure with bureaucracy, the rule of law, precedent, and due process.

And while anecdotes about ADR are a dime a dozen—and many of them do ring true—there's very little good hard data about it. That's partly because many of the ADR methods are themselves so new and informal. But it's also because even established and fairly formal institutions like the American Arbitration Association carefully protect the confidentiality of their cases.

This is not to the liking of some observers. A search through the ADR literature turned up, for example, the worries of Berkeley anthropologist Laura Nader. At a conference several years ago, she recounted how AAA officials "weren't about to let us come in" for an external review of the organization's track record. "The reason they gave had to do with confidentiality," Nader relayed dubiously. "They said they had to protect the consumer." Earlier, in a *Yale Law Journal* article, Nader had suggested that it would be advantageous if public and private mediation and arbitration agencies were required to open their case files for public inspection.

The fact is, of course, that confidentiality can be a real blessing for disputants (no doubt many litigants have yearned for more privacy than the courts usually allow) and something they have a right to preserve. But the same confidentiality means that it can be difficult for consumers—and reporters—to check out the record of an ADR service or compare ADR to the traditional court system.

And yet, some comparisons are possible. For example, there's good reason to think that much of the time, private ADR is cheaper than litigation.

Take arbitration, which is quite similar in structure to what the courts do—so much so that it qualifies for being dubbed a "private court" if anything does. After all, arbitration usually entails an adversarial presentation before a neutral third party; the arbitrator renders a binding (and very judge-like) decision that's enforceable in the "real" courts; and in most arbitrated cases (at least the ones that the AAA handles) both parties have their lawyers with them. Yet, even though arbitration replicates the courts in so many ways, savings can often be realized by going to arbitration.

Herbert Kritzer is a political scientist at the University of Wisconsin, where the prestigious Disputes Processing Research Program has been examining the court system and ADR for eight years. He and Jill Anderson Dean, formerly at the University of Wisconsin and now an attorney in Alaska, compared 755 tort (wrongful act) and contract cases that went through the federal or state courts with 147 similar cases handled by the AAA. Their study is considered the best independent comparison available. They found that, on average, legal expenses were higher in AAA cases when the stakes in the case were over $5,000; but when the stakes were less, the AAA was the more economical way to go.

But that's arbitration. Discussion with various people involved suggests that the farther a private ADR moves from the traditional court model, the greater the chance of saving money. The typical mini-trial, for example, is enormously simpler and more informal than the complex litigation that it is intended to replace. While independent data on mini-trials is virtually nonexistent, James Henry of the CPR cites an estimate that a successful mini-trial can result in savings of as much as 90 percent on legal costs.

In recalling the Borden-Texaco mini-trial, Borden counsel Walter Kocher figures that if it hadn't taken place, "you could have expected four to six years of additional litigation. There was so much at stake that neither side would have accepted a negative decision until all the avenues for appeal had been exhausted." And the cost? "Millions of dollars. Let's face it—when you get lawyers and very competent technical people, you pay by the hour, and the hours add up."

It's possible that mini-trials haven't yet reached their full potential. Former Attorney General Griffin Bell, who now practices law in Atlanta and is available for hire through the Center for Public Resources to conduct mini-trials, believes that the day may come when mini-trials or similar ADR mechanisms will be a way to save even more in legal costs, not to mention time and energy. "Where there are thousands of cases against one company, such as in the asbestos litigation and the Dalkon Shield cases, there's got to be some way to marshal all these cases in one place," he observed when interviewed. "It would work well if there were 5,000 cases around the country that could be brought together, but we're not there yet."

For an entirely different kind of dispute, the kind that the Community Boards handle in San Francisco, one can't even begin to compare disputants' costs with what they'd have to invest in litigation. When they go to Community Boards, it doesn't cost them anything. The Board's organization itself doesn't charge them; there's no reason to pay for attorneys, because Boards' rules are that an attorney can't participate in a case unless he or she is a disputant; and all the panel members are unpaid volunteers. Virtually the only expenses in the whole Community Boards system—which, so far, has been funded entirely by private contributions—are for a small staff and rent for an administrative office and three storefronts around San Francisco.

Overall, observes Bowdoin College sociologist Craig McEwen, who's sympathetic to ADR, its purported cost advantage isn't proven. But the reliable evidence that's available does suggest that much of the time, ADR is a lot cheaper than litigation.

When it comes to speed in processing disputes, however, the advantage of ADR is much less ambiguous. By and large, the innovative private alternatives are considerably faster than the courts.

When Herbert Kritzer and Jill Anderson Dean compared court cases with AAA cases in five parts of the country, they found that in one area, the AAA was "appreciably faster" for contract cases but not torts; in a second area, the AAA and the court "had similar patterns"; but in three areas, the AAA is "clearly faster." Moreover, Kritzer and Dean noted that the AAA's speed advantage overall might have been even larger if they'd been able to carry out their technical analysis further.

Speed seems to be a hallmark of nearly every private dispute resolution proceeding. Mini-trials, when they're successful, reportedly take days or at most weeks to resolve cases that have sometimes been festering for years and typically would take years more in the courts. The four-hour meeting and two months of negotiations that led to a resolution of the Borden-Texaco conflict was, according to Center for Public Resources spokesperson Anne Glauber, somewhat longer than with the usual mini-trial.

In a divorce like the Southers', there's no way of knowing how long it would have taken if they had gone through the courts, even in a "no-fault divorce" state like California. But in the event, it took only three sessions with Edelman, each lasting only a few hours. He then drew up the divorce papers and sent them to Karyn and Don Souther for their approval. The only delay now is in the court system itself: The Southers are in the middle of a mandatory waiting period before the divorce is made final.

It's not so surprising that a mode of dispute resolution vastly different from the legal system—the Community Boards—is also one of the quickest. Usually, when the organization takes a dispute, both sides and the panel of neighbors gather on a free evening in a Boards' storefront or a church basement, set up some folding chairs, talk, and put an agreement in writing before the evening is done. Precious few courts, including those handling the simplest of cases, could boast of doing nearly as well.

There's no question about the fact that alternative dispute resolution offers an appealing way out of a creaky legal system. But it would be a mistake to think that they exist in some vacuum completely independent of the system. They don't.

Almost everywhere, arbitration decisions are legally enforceable—and enforced when necessary—in the courts. The results of mediation, such as in the Southers' divorce, often need the imprimatur of the state to carry any weight. For mini-trials, it's often the same story.

Even the Community Boards group has a close working relationship with local government officials, including the San Francisco police. They "have a good reputation here," Lt. Tim Thorsen, the head of the San Francisco Police Department's Community Service Division, said in an interview. "I've had them to staff meetings, and the Police Department has referred cases to them."

So alternative dispute resolution mechanisms don't function in a stateless society, and the ones that thrive reflect that fact in various ways. But at the same time, they're quietly making news so obvious that it's easy to overlook. It is this: Some shrewd, occasionally visionary, usually creative people are coming up with ways to opt out of a tottering legal system that's not doing its job well at all. They're not doing it because they want to erode the government's old monopoly on dispute resolution. They just want to meet people's need to work out conflicts, and several are doing just fine at it. As the Razzos and the Arnotts, the Southers, Walter Kocher, and anyone who's had the misfortune of spending even a week in court would probably attest, that is an impressive accomplishment.

Is the Kibbutz Kaput?

By Tom Bethell

October 1990

The Israeli kibbutz has long been hailed as proof that the principle "from each according to his ability, to each according to his needs" is compatible with both wealth and freedom. The kibbutz is considered, in philosopher Martin Buber's words, "an experiment that did not fail," the shining exception to the general failure of socialist economics—voluntary, productive, prosperous.

Kibbutz members, or kibbutzniks, own their property collectively; on the first kibbutz, Degania (founded in 1909), they even shared clothing. Over the years, the kibbutzim have loosened their restrictions on private property, allowing members to own not only clothing, but also furnishings, books, and tools; individuals now live in private flats rather than share living quarters. And, in sharp contrast to their original vision of Jews working the land, some kibbutzim employ Arab workers, and most have added factories.

True to their egalitarian ideals, however, the kibbutzim continue to separate output from income, the individual's contribution from his reward. Both economic theory and the history of communal experiments, from the Plymouth Colony to today, predict that this arrangement would give rise to the "free-rider problem," a situation in which the incentives encourage slackers, or consumers, to take advantage of hard workers, or producers.

But, say the kibbutz's supporters, this hasn't happened: "The problem on some kibbutzim is not getting members to work, but restraining them from overwork," wrote Lawrence Meyer in *Israel Now*, published in 1982. "On one kibbutz I visited, members show up at the factory on Saturday, the Sabbath, even though the factory is not officially functioning." As an economic enterprise, Meyer concluded, "the kibbutz undoubtedly is a success."

But is it really? Beginning last year, reports that the kibbutzim had wracked up tremendous debts began to cast doubt on their supposed economic success. "Debts Make Israelis Rethink an Ideal: the Kibbutz," ran the *New York Times* headline. Approximately 127,000 Israelis, or only 3 percent of the Jewish population, live on the kibbutzim, but among them they had accumulated a debt of $4 billion—about 13 percent of GNP. As *The Wall Street Journal* reported, this was "about 30 times that of Mexico on a per capita basis."

The kibbutzim raise many interesting questions. First and foremost, is it really true that they were able to achieve economic success despite incentives that have proved crippling everywhere else in the world? If so, how was this achieved?

How then did these vast debts arise, and what is the likely future of the kibbutz movement? To piece together some answers, I went to the kibbutzim themselves.

Kibbutz Tsuba is 10 miles southwest of Jerusalem, more than 2,000 feet above sea level, and set on a hill referred to in the biblical second Book of Samuel. A community of 550, Tsuba has 220 kibbutz members, 10 percent of whom are Holocaust survivors. The 330-odd nonmembers are visitors, volunteers, and children of the kibbutzniks. Founded shortly after Israel's war of independence in 1948, Tsuba is one of 180 kibbutzim affiliated with the United Kibbutz Movement, whose political orientation is "center-left" by Israeli standards (more to the left by ours). Another 80 kibbutzim are affiliated with a definitely left-wing organization, Artzi. Altogether there are 277 kibbutzim in Israel, and the remaining 17 belong to two religious groupings.

I was met in the parking lot by Joel Dorkam, a cheerful man of 61 who told me that he had grown up in Germany, immigrated to Israel after World War II, and spent nearly all of his adult life on Kibbutz Tsuba. Optimistic and friendly by nature, Dorkam was also candid. He had been thinking that day about the possibility that Tsuba, with its biblical associations, might one day become an "interfaith biblical theme park." Old Testament...New Testament...In short, he was worrying about the financial future of the kibbutz—of Tsuba in particular, and the kibbutz movement in general.

For years the movement had shown a slow but steady population growth— sometimes 3 percent yearly. "But in the last two years we have had about 1 percent negative growth," he said. Initially, he admitted, "we thought the kibbutz movement would grow much more. But we are aware now that the kibbutz can never encompass the whole population."

There was barely a trace of wistfulness when he said it. Once, the kibbutzim were thought of as laboratories for the transformation of human nature. "The purpose of the kibbutz," Murray Weingarten wrote in 1955, "is not only to set up a new economic framework for society [but] to create a new man." Long before New Soviet Man was heard of in the West, there emerged in Palestine, at about the same time as the Russian Revolution, this quiet confidence that a New Jewish Man would soon appear.

"But it turned out that this way of life is difficult and it is inherently selective," Dorkam told me. "Many cannot take the demands that the kibbutz makes on the individual. It is an intensive, 24-hour way of life. The society is in a position to evaluate your whole personality...." Here he paused to restate the point with greater emphasis. "Your whole personality is constantly on view to the whole community," he said. "It makes for a great strain for many people."

He explained the implied contract of the community. "You get all that you need from the kibbutz," he said: food, clothing, lodging, health care, education for the children, "cultural formation" for the adults. Your retirement worries are taken care of; higher education, vacations, and travel abroad all are subsidized by the kibbutz.

In return, individuals donate their labor. They work on the farm or in the factories, at Tsuba making laminated windshields for automobiles or self-assembly furniture. All families at Tsuba receive the same monthly stipend (about $330), whether the work they do is easy or difficult, managerial or subordinate.

I asked Dorkam how the kibbutz manages to circumvent the free-rider problem, and he admitted that it is very difficult. "We have no court, no laws, no police," he said. But there are ways of "creating an antagonism" against the stubborn egotist. And as a rule, such individuals either reform or leave. In Tsuba's 41-year history, only three people have been expelled.

Dorkam took me outside, and we walked down pleasant paths, through well-kept gardens. Tsuba itself was very quiet. It had the sunny, midmorning tranquility of a campus when everyone is still in class. Dorkam said that child psychologist Bruno Bettelheim had stayed at the kibbutz in the mid-1960s while researching his 1969 book *Children of the Dream*. For decades, kibbutz children were reared in special "children's houses," apart from their parents. This in turn produced a vast serial pilgrimage from the sociology departments of American universities, to test theories of child rearing.

The children at Tsuba no longer live in children's houses—five years ago there was an 80-percent vote to make this important change. Almost all other kibbutzim have likewise changed, or soon will. And, yes, when they grow up the children have been moving away, to the high-rise suburbs north of Tel Aviv.

"One-third stay, two-thirds leave," Dorkam told me. Of all the people in Israel I talked to about the kibbutz, he was the only one who gave so unpromising a statistic. Others said that half left, or were noncommittal. Formerly, Dorkam's ratio was reversed. Two-thirds stayed. "More and more are leaving, and that's a big problem we have, and the ideological strength of youth declines," Dorkam said—a personal psalm of sorrow, I thought. I admired him for uttering it unflinchingly.

Bettelheim saw it quite differently 20 years ago: "The founding generation has slowly acquired some private property, usually just a handful of things, some of them presents from relatives outside the kibbutz. But owning them makes quite a difference. And though they try to restrict and regulate such gifts, the wish for possessions seems so strong that there are many infractions of the principle of common property....Things are very different for the second generation....For them, communal property is not an idea defensively or consciously embraced, but the only normal way to live."

Among the majority of children who stayed on the kibbutz, then, Bettelheim saw more or less successful indoctrination; communal property was "the normal way to live." For Dorkam, however, the "ideological strength of the youth" had declined. No doubt what we really see here is a fairly long period (lasting perhaps until Menachem Begin's election in 1977) when collectivist ideals were by and large accepted by those born on the kibbutz (of whom there have been two or three generations, depending on the kibbutz). Only recently has this given way to a real, and worldwide, decline of the collectivist faith.

In the afternoon Dorkam took me to see the windshield factory, which was started 10 years ago—at the request of the children, he said. Agriculture was becoming less and less profitable. The assembly line was in operation, and no one even looked up when we entered. Tsuba produces 100,000 windshields a year and sells them on the world market, two-thirds to the United States and Europe, one-third for domestic use.

Making laminated safety windshields, with a thin layer of PVP plastic inserted between a sandwich of tempered glass, is a complex operation, requiring skill, precision, and care. This is real work, not just idle kibbutzniks playing at "Factory." The factory employs 50 workers, 35 of them kibbutz members, 10 volunteers, 5 from other kibbutzim. It is on its third manager, the first two having been rotated back into other jobs.

It is "not so popular" to work in the factory, Dorkam admitted. People work in teams of six to eight "on a strict schedule," and many look forward to being rotated back into farm or administrative work. Dorkam himself had worked in the quality-control unit, where they test the new windshields against the standards of British and German institutes.

Dorkam mentioned the "disconnection between contribution and retribution," as he put it. (But, unlike many in Israel, he spoke excellent English.) With the financial crisis now afflicting the kibbutzim, I mentioned the suggestion I had heard that the linkage of pay to performance should be restored.

"That would be in my opinion the end of the kibbutz," he said. Surely he is right. Its most distinctive feature would have been discarded, and there would be no remaining reason for the communes not to convert completely into corporations.

Before I left he said that the "hidden assumption of the kibbutz" is that "talented people, or people who are above average, have to make a personal sacrifice." This is true, and it is not normally pointed out. He also told me that the kibbutzim are all interlinked economically; profitable kibbutzim must subsidize the loss makers. And this "causes resentment," he said. "Some kibbutzim built themselves dining rooms and cultural facilities three times as costly as ours." Nonetheless, Dorkam was discomforted by the suggestion that the kibbutzim should be separated from one another. The political clout of the kibbutzim (and their ability to extract subsidies from the Ministry of Finance) depends on their remaining unified.

I was impressed by Kibbutz Tsuba. Yes, it is subsidized, but people are working despite poor incentives, and an arid hill of stones has been turned into a functioning community with two factories and a farm, their output sold in world markets. And it has survived for over 40 years.

The kibbutz, of course, has all along enjoyed the great advantage, as Dorkam reminded me, that its values are voluntarily embraced. Those who do not like it are free to leave at any time; new applicants are carefully screened for good work habits and "socially compatible" attitudes and must receive a two-thirds vote to be admitted. In addition, the external military threat to the country has imparted a sense of mission to the kibbutzim, a mission often made explicit by assigning them a specific defense role; most of the country's military leaders, as well as many elite units, have come from the kibbutzim. These factors in combination may have enabled the kibbutzim to overcome, at least to some extent, the free-rider problem that has been the ruin of communes everywhere else.

Still, as I drove back to Jerusalem, I realized that despite Dorkam's helpfulness (I had only given him half an hour's notice of my arrival), I really didn't know whether Kibbutz Tsuba was economically self-sustaining or not. With the embedded nature of the subsidies, some of them applying across the board in Israeli society (e.g., price supports for much agricultural produce), it is possible that many kibbutz members themselves do not really know. I would encounter vagueness about financial matters throughout my visits to the kibbutzim.

This vagueness was most striking at Shefayim, a kibbutz on the Mediterranean coast, 12 miles north of Tel Aviv. It began as I checked into the kibbutz-owned hotel: The clerk quoted me three different prices for the same room. I had the feeling that if only I knew the password, the room could be had for free.

The next day, I met Beny Kaz Nelson, a gaunt, white-haired Marlboro smoker who had been born on this kibbutz in 1933, "a very bad year in the history of mankind," he said. His father came from Poland, his mother from Riga—"pioneers of the Zionist Youth Movement," and his mother-in-law, now 92, still lives on Degania, the first kibbutz. The kibbutz way of life, Nelson said, "is not natural, it belongs to the realm of ideas, of mind." But he thinks it is "part of the essence of the Zionist movement."

Currently, he said, there is a great crisis for those who espouse socialism, "both in the communistic and the social-democratic world." For the "capitalistic way," he said, in his good but idiosyncratic English, "it is a moment of flourishing." In the 1920s, he said, "every good fellow was a socialist. In our times, it will not be so. So I am sure that this change will have an influence on the kibbutz."

"A negative influence?"

"Yes."

Nelson has held a number of government and kibbutz jobs, including three stints as general secretary of Kibbutz Shefayim. I asked him if he could tell me how much the annual family stipend was at Shefayim. "Something near to 2,000 shekels [about $1,000] per family," he said. "But I don't want to give you figures that are not exact. I will telephone to the treasurer."

He picked up the phone by his side and asked for someone, who was out but apparently would call back.

He told me that Shefayim is a successful kibbutz, "one of the 20 richest." So much so that a part of its income goes to other kibbutzim—nearly 2 million shekels, he thought. They have a "very successful" plastics factory and the tourist trade is also successful, if uneven.

When I asked him how people are motivated to work, he said that only the day before a guest from Hungary had asked the same question. "I think the answer lies in identification with others," he said. "When you are at home you clean the family's dishes without asking yourself why, because that is your home. Only in a moment of crisis do you ask."

He took out another Marlboro and a son, in his 20s, came through the room and glanced across at us without much sign of interest. One-half of the children who grow up in kibbutzim stay on, Nelson estimated. "Thirty years ago, it was 60 to 70 percent. So I am not so sure about the future. If we stay as we are, we will not have a future. But if we change..."

The telephone rang, and it was the treasurer of the kibbutz, returning his call. Nelson was happy to share the information with me. The stipend for a family of four is 7,000 shekels. The income of the kibbutz is 30 million shekels. And they give 500,000 shekels to other kibbutzim, not 2 million as Nelson had guessed. Forty percent of revenue comes from industry, 30 percent from tourism. "And our expenses are lower than our income," he said, repeating these last words into the receiver, before saying thank you and hanging up. "I speak with the treasurer because I want to give you correct figures," he told me.

It was puzzling, that his earlier estimate of the stipend should have been off by 350 percent. I could only assume that he never looked at the checks—in short, that money wasn't something that he worried about. It wasn't that he was trying to hide anything from me—on the contrary. The truth was that he really didn't know very much about the finances of the kibbutz, even if he lived on it, and didn't mind if it showed. Probably (it was later suggested to me) he receives a government salary and regards the kibbutz stipend as a minor detail.

Like Nelson, the kibbutzim themselves rarely have had to worry about finances. Until the 1930s, they couldn't balance their budgets, Eliyahu Kanovsky reported in a rare study of kibbutz finances published in 1966. But aid from the World Zionist Organization and other philanthropic sources allowed them to survive, and the Depression made it possible to buy agricultural equipment cheaply. The 1940s constituted a "golden age" for the kibbutz movement: The world war cut off supplies from abroad, and the Allied armies in the Middle East provided a ready market for agricultural and industrial products at favorable prices.

The first few years following independence were likewise financially "successful," at least on paper. The new government provided both direct subsidies and protection from competition, while mass immigration created a ready market. Even so, in the late '50s and early '60s, the Jewish Agency had to "adopt" about 100 newer kibbutzim to save them from insolvency. A joint fund established by the government, the Jewish Agency, and the Workers' Bank of the Histadrut union bailed out those kibbutzim that couldn't repay their debts to private commercial banks and suppliers.

According to Gershon Kaddar, then the agricultural adviser of Israel's largest bank, all but the oldest kibbutzim lost money even in the supposedly profitable years 1954-57, once the depreciation of their assets is properly accounted for. "He concluded that, in effect, the kibbutzim were consuming their assets, which had been provided them by the government, the Jewish Agency, and the other public bodies in Israel," Kanovsky wrote.

Lavish agricultural subsidies from the government and Jewish Agency accounted for the "profits" of the older kibbutzim. Kanovsky concluded that the kibbutzim were, in aggregate, in deficit from 1954 to 1960 but may have shown a small profit in the next two years. Since then, the kibbutzim have become increasingly dependent on the government for land grants, protection from competition, government salaries for some kibbutz members, and direct subsidies.

More important than direct aid, however, has been inflation. The government seems to have followed, whether consciously or not, a strategy of bailing out debtors by inflating the currency. Since 1948, the Israeli currency has been devalued by a factor of 80,000. This de facto debt forgiveness enabled the kibbutzim to maintain an appearance of solvency and to claim the success of the kibbutz experiment. And for much of this time, a steady infusion of cash from abroad—some of it from the U.S. Treasury and some of it voluntary Jewish philanthropy collected worldwide and funneled into the Jewish Agency (now amounting to about half a billion dollars a year)—preserved a semblance of financial stability.

But with the massive inflation of the 1980s, reaching 450 percent in 1984, this strategy became no longer feasible. Since bank loans as well as savings were thereafter indexed to inflation, debt could no longer be inflated away. Israelis began to bank abroad, and the task of bailing out debtors by devaluing everyone's savings became more and more difficult. The insolvency of the kibbutzim was exposed to view.

"The economic problems associated with the kibbutzim have been endemic since the day they were started," says Steve Hanke, a professor of applied economics at Johns Hopkins University and a senior fellow at the Institute for Advanced Strategic and Political Studies in Israel. "They only recently became visible to the untrained eye because the hemorrhaging grew so large that it was impossible to cover up. The subsidies required for their bailout are too massive to disguise."

So the kibbutzim are being bailed out again, but this time publicly. Jacob Gadish, an economist and member of Kibbutz Yavne, a religious community of 850 (400 kibbutz members, one-third of whom are over 65) helped to negotiate the bailout. "For each kibbutz we found out what is its ability to repay the money it owes," he told me, "and then to create a repayment schedule so that they can repay over 25 years." Some of the debt (about half) is being forgiven outright.

For two years in the 1980s, Gadish worked for the government, heading the budget division of the treasury. Today he runs a consulting business in Tel Aviv, commuting from Yavne, the largest religious kibbutz. Yavne's main business is poultry farming, producing one-seventh of all the poultry marketed in Israel; its annual income is $23 million. After expenses and taxes, Gadish said, "we have about $7 million net profit."

Gadish told a *Jerusalem Post* reporter: "I was conversing with a comrade from a kibbutz whose debts equal the combined debt of the whole Kibbutz Dati [the federation of all 17 religious kibbutzim]. The man told me he had spent a month overseas the year before and a fortnight again in the current year. I informed him that in our kibbutz nobody may go abroad more than once in eight years. He could not believe me." He added that about 20 kibbutzim are incorrigible. "If their debts are totally written off, they will pile up new ones tomorrow."

A strong believer in the kibbutz ideal, Gadish worries that the present system of interlinked kibbutzim may "destroy the entire movement." The bailouts are imposing continuing costs on the whole of Israel, and the political will to keep propping them up cannot last forever. The danger is that dead-weight kibbutzim will drag down those that are making a sincere effort.

"The kibbutzim do continue to receive subsidies from the government right now?" I asked.

"Yes. I am afraid it can destroy us. There is a big danger that it can do so."

"Without the subsidies you would do better?"

"I am sure that our religious movement can profit from it."

The religious kibbutzim are doing better financially than the secular ones. Only three of the 17 religious communes are debt-ridden. A part of the explanation is that "our approach to public money has been different. We are not so close to the public...cash...trough, yes?" (English had not come easily to him.) At Yavne, fiscal conservatism is the rule. The religious kibbutzim do not have the same political clout as those affiliated with the Labor Party, and therefore are less confident of being bailed out. This has encouraged prudence.

There might be a more specifically religious reason for the better performance of the religious kibbutzim, Gadish thought, and he had read Max Weber on the Protestant ethic. A few very ideological, socialistic kibbutzim have also managed to stay in the black, he said. Joel Dorkam's "hidden assumption" of self-sacrifice can probably be sustained over a long time only by people driven either by ideological conviction of the need for selflessness or by a belief in God.

"You know," Gadish said, "there is a big discussion in economics about whether aid is useful. We know that only once in recent history was it profitable, and that was the Marshall Plan. Otherwise I don't know one country that received money where the economy was helped. You become dependent—addicted." It was clear that he had the country in mind as well as the economically dependent kibbutzim.

As for linking individual pay and performance: "The moment there is a connection between contribution and compensation, at that moment the kibbutz system is finished." The kibbutz system, he said, is in conflict with human nature, "the statistical meaning of human nature." But "we are speaking of the 3 percent on one side of the Gauss distribution," he said. "There are some people who are willing to live in such a system. You cannot force anyone. It is contrary to individualism, yes. But we have to improve ourselves. That is the idea! The idea is to be a little less materialistic and to be ready to share your ability with people of less ability."

The next day I drove to Granot, about 30 miles northwest of Tel Aviv. Granot is a kind of central buyer and manufacturer of agricultural products for 45 area kibbutzim. There is an avocado packing house, a cotton gin, a slaughterhouse, and so on. About 500 people work there, among them Yochanan Blumenfeld, who is a member of the central board of Granot and an accountant. I arrived at Blumenfeld's office in mid-afternoon, by which time almost everyone seemed to have gone home; my footsteps echoed in the deserted corridors.

Blumenfeld, a cheerful man of 44, said that the kibbutzim were being managed much more cautiously these days. He candidly recalled "what we used to call the good days of Aridor," referring to Israel's former finance minister, "when the inflation was high and you could do what you wanted and nobody knew what your real financial position was." Now everybody was on his best behavior, he said, and I took his word for it.

I knew that his job—"coordinating the balance sheets of the regional kibbutz industries"—would be indecipherable, and he didn't seem terribly excited about it either, so I asked him about his own kibbutz, Givat Hashlosha, east of Tel Aviv. He was glad to change the subject to that. He discussed the problems of the kibbutzim more candidly than anyone else I met. He was also younger than the others.

Givat Hashlosha was founded in 1925, he said, all its early members coming from Eastern Europe. His parents had come from Poland. Half the children born on his kibbutz subsequently left it, he said. Today, 30 percent of the members are age 70 or over.

"The crisis of the kibbutz movement is a crisis of motivation," he said. "And I am not sure that this is clear yet to the leadership of the kibbutz movement. My parents' generation had an ideology that they were going to build 'the world of tomorrow.' They believed that the kibbutz was going to be the dominant way of life not only in Israel but in all the world. This faith gave them a strong motivation, and so did the Zionist dream. They knew that if they were to achieve this they would have to work hard. And they did work very hard, compared with today. They were ready to sacrifice. The problems began after 1948. In the first place, the real state of Israel wasn't the same as a dream. But even then, people at that time still believed they were doing something very important. But after the second generation took over, we didn't believe so strongly."

The religious kibbutzim are more successful, Blumenfeld said, because "even though they never believed in Karl Marx, they still believe in equality. Religion gives them the ideology that we don't have any more.

"The idea that the socialist system will dominate the world doesn't exist any more," he said. "And if there is no socialism, we will return to traditional motivation around the world. And the main motivation—not the sole one—is economic. If the kibbutz does not solve this problem of providing economic rewards, then it will not survive. Because the kibbutz members will vote with their feet." Blumenfeld then added something that I had not heard before:

"The main idea of the kibbutz is equality among the people. We are all supposed to receive the same reward. But many members now have property outside the kibbutz. They married outside the kibbutz, in many cases. As a result, their situation is much better, because when their spouses joined the kibbutz, they didn't give their outside property to the kibbutz. And today this has become a big problem." Many of these people with outside property are "marginal members," he said, simultaneously enjoying kibbutz privileges and unshared property. But both Blumenfeld and his wife grew up on the same kibbutz. If the kibbutz system collapses, many others will have something to fall back on. He and his wife will have nothing.

He pulled a snapshot out of his wallet and smiled. It was a photo of his only child, a 3-year-old son. For a long time, he and his wife had had no children. But then they were blessed. "Everyone on the kibbutz loves him," he said.

Blumenfeld predicted that there would be a "revolution on the kibbutz" and that it would involve what everyone I had spoken to had tried to disavow: "There will be reward according to work."

Joint ownership of the overall property would remain, he thought, "but it will become more clearly identified—more defined. For example, I will know exactly what part I own. As it is now, a member cannot pass his property on to his son unless his son stays on the kibbutz. I think that this will change too." Moreover, in order to join a kibbutz, people will have to invest money in it.

He was talking about establishing private property rights in the kibbutz and making these rights transferable, at least within the family.

"Everyone I have spoken to says that will be the end of the kibbutz," I said.

He did not deny it. He said: "All around the world now, people work for themselves and for their families. We are not different people. We are the same as everyone else in the world."

He looked again at the photo of his child, and again that made him smile. "He will decide what to do." Blumenfeld said. "I hope he will not have to ask me what to do."

Then he looked off into the distance, thought for a second and said: "He won't have to. The revolution on the kibbutz will come before that time."

Uncle Sam Wants Your VCR

By George Gilder

November 1986

s it Rambo leaping forth from Japanese screens and onto the streets of Tokyo? Or Bruce Springstein in a "Born in the USA" rant?

No, it's just Lee Iacocca again, huffing and puffing his macho American theme and denouncing the "closed society" of Japan—where he has sold more than half a million books and bought tons of autos and engines from Mitsubishi.

Is it a U.S. cast for the Kabuki theater?

No, it's merely the American Chamber of Commerce putting on a show in Tokyo early in 1986.

Is it Conan the Barbarian, bursting out of a Shinjuku billboard?

No, it's just Sen. John Danforth (R) of Missouri, the swashbuckling preacher of "reciprocal trade." With a heavy note of Hollywood menace, he declared at the Chamber's conference: "In 1984, Japan exported more than 80 percent of its entire production of cameras, watches, VCRs, and microwave ovens. These Japanese products have two things in common: They are attractive to consumers everywhere and they are totally unnecessary."

Is it the madman from "Death Wish 3"?

No, don't worry, it's merely Danforth's Missouri colleague, Sen. Tom Eagleton (D), chiming in: "We lost our shoe industry, we are losing our textile industry," and now, he implied, we are losing not only our manufacturing but also our minds. He, too, threatened new barriers to Japanese goods and exalted the noble inanity of a balance of trade.

Everywhere, the trade-balance refrain is repeated. Clyde V. Prestowitz of the U.S. Department of Commerce issued dire warnings about the magnitude of the U.S. trade imbalance—the goods we imported in 1985 were worth nearly $150 billion more than the goods we exported. Without trade restrictions, he concluded, the United States may go bankrupt. Just like that.

Japan is invariably spotlighted as the villain. As Sen. Lloyd Bentsen of Texas (D) puts it poetically: "The Japanese are ripping out the heart of U.S. industry and destroying it piece by piece." Other analysts write of Japan's "deep cultural resistance to foreign goods" and cite polls showing that Japanese citizens prefer to buy products made in their own country. Unlike Americans?

Winston Churchill once wrote, "Man will occasionally stumble over the truth." An American businessman—or even an American politician—disembarking from a Japanese Airlines 747 at Narita and taking a bus into the Shinjuku *Hyatt Regency* across the street from the Tokyo *Hilton* and down the street from *American Express* and *Kentucky Fried Chicken*, passing Japanese offices full of *IBM* equipment and bookstores and newsstands selling diverse *American publications*, and finding friendly Japanese everywhere who speak *English* and an English channel on the TV, might pause to consider for a moment the contrary plight of a Japanese visitor arriving at Kennedy Airport in New York.

Might the American visitor—even the American senator—stumble momentarily in his insular assurance that Japan is hostile to American goods? Of course, Churchill added that having tripped over the truth, "most of the time [the man] will pick himself up and continue on"...perhaps to the auditorium, where he will denounce once again the closed economy of Japan.

A Japanese consumer shaving with his Schick, drinking a cup of Maxwell House before leaving for work, wolfing down honey-dips at Mister Donut or a hamburger at McDonald's, getting a six-pack of Coca-Cola and a box of Kleenex at the 7-Eleven, signing his name with a Sheaffer, walking along the Ginza under a huge Hollywood billboard of Charles Bronson, on his way to Computerland in his new Levis, might be forgiven for wondering what the problem is.

Of course, he might not want Iacocca's overpriced "K" car, with the steering wheel on the wrong side. But he would sympathize with Danforth's assertion that "there is nothing wrong with the steering wheel on our beef." More beef imports would be fine with our Japanese consumer. Nor, he might add, after savoring a thimbleful of orange juice at the Okura for 1,000 yen, would there be anything wrong with access to more California citrus fruits. The Japanese do lead the world in purchases of American agricultural produce, including beef and oranges. But partly because of an island fear of food embargoes—and mostly because of the political clout of farmers (an Oriental peculiarity no doubt hard for Westerners to comprehend)—the Japanese consumer suffers from quotas on these products.

But, coming from a U.S. Congress that keeps Alaskan oil away from Japan and protects sugar beets "for reasons of national security," that imposes a special system of price controls on oranges and frequently acts to restrict beef imports from Argentina and Australia—and plans to subsidize American farmers by tens of billions of dollars during the next five years of supposed budget-balancing fiscal austerity—Sen. Danforth might allow the Japanese their political crotchets. After all, when all is said and done, the average Japanese citizen, in his "closed society," purchases some three times as much U.S. brand-name merchandise in proportion to his income—and two times as much in absolute terms—as the "open-door Americans" buy Japanese.

The fact that Americans are more resistant to foreign goods than the Japanese never penetrates to the precincts of Washington. With American politicians raving about a trade war, with Speaker of the House Tip O'Neill threatening "to get the Japanese and get 'em good," and with the normally genteel author Theodore White, shortly before he died, invoking memories of Bataan and Pearl Harbor in an explanation of Japanese export policy, it is the Japanese—not the Americans—who can plausibly charge xenophobia. But it is the Americans who claim to be aggrieved, losing jobs, suffering the slings and arrows of Japanese industrial policy, crucified for their belief in "free trade."

In a speech in March, economist Lester Thurow depicted the deficit in the trade account in harrowing terms and compared the U.S. economy, in some detail, to Mexico's currently precarious situation. It seems the trade imbalance has made the United States a "net debtor," and soon enough we will slide down a slippery slope, with deputations of grim reapers from the International Monetary Fund trooping over to the U.S. Treasury, demanding adoption of austerity policies: devaluations, higher taxes; a zero-sum society at last. One pictures wetbacks swimming south, led by Sen. Bentsen and Professor Thurow.

Welcome to wonderland: the fantasy world of American politics and economics. It would not be a serious problem but for one uncomfortable fact. The underlying premises of this world of fantasy are accepted in economics classes and political conferences around the globe, from Great Britain to Japan and from MIT to MITI.

Everywhere the dismal science of macroeconomics casts its Keynesian shadow, intelligent people begin babbling in tongues; they prattle in terms of gigantic numbers—gross national products, budgetary deficits, money supplies, and aggregate demand—as if these raw quantities captured the essence of economic life. They speak of balancing exports and imports as if that goal embodied some cardinal virtue in itself, like balancing our diets or our tires, or as if the balance of payments constituted the final scorecard of an international tournament of trade. Beclouded with these illusions, world capitalism is now stumbling toward a gigantic trap of austerity programs, monetary restrictions, protectionist barriers, and tax increases that promise to enforce some fantasy of "balance" but in fact would lead to economic breakdown and decline.

The pursuit of trade balance originated in the dim days of old, when a deficit would dictate a laborious transfer of precious gold bullion on clipper ships across treacherous seas. Today, however, capital bounces off satellites around the globe in split seconds. A country with attractive capital markets, declining tax rates, and rapid economic growth will tend to run a surplus in its capital account (people will want to send it money) and a deficit in its trade account (its people will be able to buy more than they produce).

The new American tax rates, once they are fully installed, will make the United States a mecca for capital and growth. But unless they are copied by our competitors, they may also lead to a continued imbalance of trade. Should we be worried?

The fear for the future of American manufacturing is overwrought. In recent years, the United States has increased its share of world manufacturing exports. The recent economic boom showed a recovery in manufacturing some three times as fast as in services. And while employment in manufacturing, as in farming, has declined as a share of total employment, manufacturing has maintained its share of U.S. economic activity at just below 25 percent for the last 20 years.

In fact, a trade deficit may well be a symbol of a healthy economy. Far from destroying jobs, it may create them. Certainly, on the evidence from the United States, a better case could be made that trade *surpluses* destroy jobs, particularly in manufacturing.

Over the last decade, for example, the United States ran its largest surpluses in manufacturing trade in the years 1979, 1980, and 1981. During this period the country lost a total of 1.43 million manufacturing jobs. Over the following three years, on the other hand, the United States ran a manufacturing trade deficit, largely with Japan, of approximately $160 billion. But overall employment soared by 8 million jobs, and manufacturing employment grew by over a million.

By contrast, Japan, with its 1984 trade surplus of $35 billion, created, proportionate to population, less than 10 percent of the new jobs created in the United States in that year. In 1985, Japan's trade surplus rose again, and this time the United States created proportionately four times as many jobs as Japan. In fact, throughout the entire postwar era in the United States, there has been a strong correlation between trade deficits and employment growth.

Nonetheless, nearly every major economist will tell you that "net exports" contribute to something called "aggregate demand" and thus enhance economic growth and job creation. This Keynesian maxim leads to the idea that industrial policies—specifically, government spending to promote exports or to foster investment in export-oriented firms—are fiendishly effective. Using Keynesian models, government policy makers around the globe—from West Germany to Washington, D.C.—see trade surpluses as a testimony to moral rectitude and job creation.

In order to understand why there is no special virtue in a trade surplus, it is necessary to transcend the idea that economic growth is somehow driven by "demand." A supply-side economist will insist that buying power—"aggregate demand"—is impotent to impel growth. What matters is the willingness and ability of particular workers and entrepreneurs to expand and improve their productive efforts and the willingness of new producers to enter the economy.

On the most basic level, the very concept of people as "consumers" or demanders is deceptive and patronizing. Income cannot long exceed output. Consumption springs not from a willingness to spend money but from a willingness to spend effort. Economic policy must focus first, last, and always on enhancing the incentives and capabilities of producers.

Imports often increase those incentives and capabilities. People do not produce for "money." They work in order to be able to buy goods and services. On the margin, where the economy grows, they very often work to buy foreign goods. Contrary to Sen. Danforth's charge that VCRs and other Japanese imports are "totally unnececessary," they are probably the most motivational items in the U.S. economy today. They increase the marginal value of American incomes and enhance the productivity and incentives of American workers.

Similarly, imports of capital equipment enhance the ability of American workers and entrepreneurs to expand their efforts. In earlier decades, equipment flowed disproportionately from the United States to Japan's semiconductor and automobile industries. Thus a vast imbalance of trade in capital goods made possible the rise of those Japanese industries. Now, the balance has shifted, and the availability of ingenious new capital equipment from Japan enhances opportunity in the U.S. economy.

Far from hurting the sales of U.S.-made capital equipment, imports of capital goods require and enable the use of complementary capital and labor. Economic progress and opportunity in the United States, from Detroit to the Silicon Valley, would slacken drastically without the availability of foreign equipment and other supplies. For example, General Motor's futuristic Saturn project, designed to

94

produce a new generation of cheaper and better automobiles, could not succeed without Japanese machine tools and other devices. From Fujitsu-Fanuc's robots to Kyocera's ceramic chip packages, imports stimulate the use of U.S. capital equipment and enhance the real competitiveness of the U.S. economy.

Equipment producers in this country should not try to "catch up" with Japan. They must try to create *new* capital goods that respond to the needs of the future. If instead they afflict their U.S. customers with second-best gear, they merely spread the problems of the producers of capital goods to the producers of final products.

If the U.S. senators want something to worry about, they should focus not on trade balance but on trade volume—not on the brisk and valuable exchanges of goods and capital between the United States and Japan but on the general stagnation of world commerce, including trade between the United States and Asia. In a recent cover story, *Fortune* magazine actually presented the slowdown of the Japanese economy this year as a "rare opportunity for the U.S." But a slowdown in Japan and Asia *reduces incentives* for real productive effort in the United States. Trade is not a zero-sum game, and its contraction is bad for everyone.

An obvious inhibition on the volume of trade is the widespread resort to protectionism in an attempt to achieve trade balance. Equally destructive is erratic monetary policy based on pursuing deceptive aggregates such as the so-called money supply. At present, with all producer and wholesale price indexes showing worldwide deflation, monetary policy is too tight in all industrial nations. In a perverse effort to refight the war against inflation while prices plummet, government monetary officials in the leading industrial nations are risking a major deflationary crisis.

Not only is the price of money too high around the globe, so is the price of government. The price of government is called the tax rate, and tax rates are the most important single price in any economy. If tax rates are kept too high, the entire system suffers from this extortionate cost of production, and trade volume declines. The upward drift of real tax rates around the world is the chief long-term cause of the decline in global commerce and the chief cause of America's export problem.

A further source of the declining volume of trade is management timidity and myopia. As in a country, so in an industry, leaders must be willing, over time, to push down price and increase value. When prices and profit margins are dropping fast, markets tend to expand as producers pursue high-volume, low-price strategies. With larger volumes, customers improve their knowledge of the good, use it more, and invent more applications for it, and its real value rises as its price drops.

With prices dropping and performance improving in the leading sectors of an economy, real incomes move up and create demand for other products and other industries. Work and investment incentives rise. Workers and entrepreneurs create new jobs and opportunities. Imports surge. This is real economic growth.

But when prices stop dropping—or the critical dimensions of value and quality stop rising faster than price—all these positive trends are reversed. In the end, trade slows and firms turn to politics to achieve what they cannot attain in the marketplace. At business conferences, there is more talk about "industrial policies" than about industrial products.

A key problem at present is automobiles. The industry uses commodity materials whose costs are presently declining, and it is turning to new technologies with rapidly improving ratios of cost and performance. So automobile prices should be following the fast-sinking trajectory of the experience curve, which dictates a 20 to 30 percent decline in costs for every doubling of cumulative unit sales. Instead, in this highly politicized industry, auto prices are coasting along comfortably with the consumer price index, which itself radically exaggerates real monetary inflation. By allowing real prices to drift upward, the auto industry is rapidly becoming part of the problem of international stagnation.

These rules of price and trade apply to all industries. The latest worry is that the United States is suffering from an influx of Japanese semiconductor chips. This is wrong. The Japanese semiconductors can save the industry by giving the American firms a vivid sense of competitive realities and by helping reduce prices in the computer industry, which is the key semiconductor market in the United States.

The semiconductor executives should have learnt from the experience of the automobile industry. The effects of protecting weaker industries cascade through the economy and end up jeopardizing the strongest sectors. Thus "trigger prices" and other devices protecting the steel industry raised the costs of production for American makers of automobiles—as well as machine tools, construction gear, and farm equipment.

Soon, there arose demands for the protection of *these* industries, beginning with the car companies because of their political clout. And so we came to have various quota systems imposed on foreign automobile makers. But the results were not as wonderful as Lee Iacocca and his buddies envisioned.

When Japanese auto producers were prevented by quotas from going for large volumes at low prices, they moved up-market to sell smaller volumes of higher-priced cars. Rather than competing against the Americans at their point of weakness—and thus dramatically improving the range of value in the automobile market—the Japanese moved up to compete with the Americans at their point of strength. American purchasers sent more money to Japan, but they didn't even get more cars.

In addition, since consumers didn't get more value at lower prices, they didn't have more money to spend on other products where U.S. producers excelled. They did not receive new incentives to work and save. Protection unnecessarily weakened the strongest parts of the U.S. economy in an attempt to save the weakest.

It doesn't take too much prescience to predict a similar outcome for chips. The labyrinthine new price-fixing agreement between the United States and Japan on semiconductor memories ironically penalizes the top U.S. memory producer, Texas Instruments, which fabricates its memory chips in Miho, Japan. It also penalizes U.S. computer firms that manufacture in the United States. Commodity memory chips such as DRAMs (Dynamic Random Access Memories) account for up to a third of the cost of computers. The new trade accord allows Japanese computer firms to acquire memory chips at half the cost that U.S. producers must incur. The final irony is that the agreement will fail to help American chip firms in any lasting way.

Diverted from commodity memory chips such as DRAMs, Japanese companies will focus on the less vulnerable parts of the U.S. industry. Not only are the U.S. semiconductor industry's best customers—the computer firms—hurt by such protection, so are the best semiconductor producers.

The preceding, three-year-long surge of chip imports from Japanese conglomerates does partly reflect U.S. inferiority to Japan in manufacturing disciplines. America is still a country that prefers lawyers to engineers, teaches more students social adjustment and sex education than physics or calculus, and double-taxes the returns to savings out of fear of "inequality" between the prodigal and thrifty. But these problems offer no reason for a dismal retreat to protectionism or government subsidies.

Although large companies are crucial to the production of commodity products, the ultimate sources of competitiveness and growth are startups pursuing new technologies. Leading business magazines continue to proclaim that the end of the line has come for small firms in semiconductors and computers, but in fact the last four years have seen more spinoffs and startups than any previous period in the history of electronics.

For example, a young American entrepreneur, Raymond Kurzweil, has started three companies to pursue his amazing inventions in artificial intelligence, including the leading-edge music synthesizer used by Stevie Wonder, a reading machine for the blind, and a revolutionary new voice-actuated word processor. This last device can take dictation at 150 words per minute and recognize a 15,000-word vocabulary. In developing the word processor, which will be sold by Wang and Xerox for around $5,000 late this year, Kurzweil beat out IBM, AT&T, and the entire Japanese electronics industry. Because typewriters cannot accommodate the hundreds of Kanji characters, this technology has long been a supreme goal of leading Japanese conglomerates and government planners at MITI.

As time passes, such inventions and entrepreneurial efforts will revitalize trade between the United States and Japan. First, however, all this U.S. creativity may well *increase* imports rather than reduce them. By generating a stream of new inventions, the new firms will stimulate the import of complementary components and capital goods. This process of American innovation, which leads to increasing trade deficits, was vividly manifest during the recent electronics boom.

The exemplary product in this surge of American growth was probably the IBM personal computer. Introduced in 1981, in a mere three years it grew from nothing to some $7 billion in sales. It enhanced productivity and management resources in businesses, large and small, across the country. As it fed on the creativity of the suppliers of software—chiefly new firms such as Microsoft and Lotus—the PC simultaneously expanded the market for software. It fueled the success of the huge new industry of computer retailing. It provided standards that offered targets and specifications for all other efforts in personal computing. It fostered boom years for many semiconductor firms, starting with Intel and Advanced Micro Devices, the producers of its central microprocessor and peripherals. All in all, it was a dramatic boon to the U.S. economy.

Yet by the standards of Sen. Danforth and others fixated on the trade balance, the personal computer was a catastrophe. It represented a drastic decline in U.S.

competitiveness. Not only did it gorge on Japanese DRAMs, it also used Asian keyboards, disk drives, monitors, power supplies, and other components. In fact, while only a small proportion of total sales went overseas, between 60 and 70 percent of the machine was manufactured outside the United States. The Japanese version of the IBM PC was made by Matsushita. Moreover, by creating a settled hardware standard, it allowed the Japanese to penetrate the U.S. computer market with hundreds of thousands of PC clones.

The IBM personal computer symbolizes a computer revolution in the United States that contributed heavily to U.S. growth, productivity, incentives, and real personal income. It also contributed billions of dollars to the much-feared deficit in the balance of payments vis-a-vis Japan and other countries. Yet the gains to the U.S. economy dwarfed the debts incurred overseas. Similarly, the import of VCRs manufactured abroad is generating a far greater industry of video software and retailing in the United States. And as the debts to foreigners are repaid, every dollar will ultimately be spent on U.S. goods and services or investments. But the single-entry bookkeepers of Congress focus only on the liabilities of foreign trade.

The conventional economics of trade and aggregate demand are simply bankrupt. Nothing they predict is true. A trade deficit does not necessarily destroy employment; it may well increase it. A trade surplus does not necessarily increase national wealth and power; it may deplete it. OPEC nations have had the largest trade surpluses over recent decades, and the United States has recently had some of the largest deficits. What matters in economics is the release of creative energies in productive work and entrepreneurship.

Crucial by this supply-side measure is not aggregate demand but creative supply, not trade surpluses but trade incentives, not capital formation but entrepreneurial quality, not balanced budgets but low marginal tax rates, not national or institutional savings but the disposable personal savings that fuel more than 90 percent of all new businesses. What matters most of all is a nation's success in attracting, educating, and emancipating the most valuable capital in any economy: its human beings.

The United States remains in the world lead in chips and other high-tech products chiefly because it continues to enjoy a massive favorable balance of trade in the single most important area—a category that dwarfs in importance all the numbers that agitate American politicians. That domain is the international movement of human resources, chiefly immigrants.

Immigrants are the lifeblood of U.S. high-tech companies, from the top echelons of management and engineering (for example, Andrew Grove and Masatoshi Shima of Intel) through the design centers and dust-free "clean rooms" of Silicon Valley, and on to its remaining assembly lines. A Japanese immigrant teaching linguistics at Harvard University made critical contributions to Kurzweil's word processor. A Cuban refugee, Juan Benitez, recently became president of Micron Technology, the inventive company that created the world's smallest 64K and 256K DRAMs and is the only domestic producer to survive in that business, selling heavily in the open market. Luckily, the United States still accepts immigrants in large numbers (although Sen. Danforth's colleagues are trying to pass protectionist legislation in this area, as well, and the welfare state is reaching out to destroy the work incentives of the refugees who do make it in).

Foreigners express greater confidence in America and its prospects by importing American bonds (claims on future American goods) than they would by importing more American bulldozers or baseball bats. By immigrating, they pay the United States the ultimate tribute.

The ideal of trade balance springs from a world when national power stemmed from the control of territory or the command of land masses and sea lanes, natural resources and bullion reserves; a time when the balance of power in Europe depended on who ruled the iron and coal mines of the Ruhr basin. In an age of 50-trillion–dollar capital markets that operate far more smoothly and efficiently than the markets for goods and services, however, there is no more reason for imports and exports to be balanced from one country to another than for the flow of immigrants to be in balance, or for a balance of trade between any two American states.

There is no particular relationship between the competitiveness of an entire economy and the pattern of imports and exports it displays. Such a balance is completely arbitrary, its pursuit entirely irrational, and its achievement possible only by ripping and tearing at the fabric of international commerce and inter-dependency.

The world has passed far beyond the economic theories that inspire the world's policy makers today. Failing to comprehend the new technologies that dominate capital markets and that shape the prospects of nations, they retreat to the accounting codes of mercantilism and the zero-sum games of static econometrics. They plunge back into primitive superstitions and numerological symmetries, into nationalist categories that are all but meaningless in a global economy or even to two systems as intimately intermeshed as the United States' and Japan's.

Contrary to the predictions of most modern writers, from George Orwell to Norman Mailer, this is preeminently the era not of nations but of individuals. Against the decisions of entrepreneurs to move themselves and their money, the bureaucracies of the state are increasingly impotent and at bay. The state may confiscate the means of production, manipulate the markets for money, issue orders and guns. It can steal technology but it cannot produce it; it can capture land but can scarcely till it. It can retain power by police controls but it cannot productively use it.

If a nation wishes to increase its wealth and power, it must create an environment that is hospitable to the men and women who populate the intellectual frontiers of enterprise. In this pursuit, what matters is maintaining a surplus in the accounts of liberty.

America's Rising Sun

By Joel Kotkin

January 1989

Over the past year America has become a nation obsessed with forebodings of decline. A perceptible gloom grips the nation's political, corporate, and media elites. We have seen one bestseller, Paul Kennedy's *Rise and Fall of the Great Powers,* chart America's progress down the road to relative insignificance and another, Allan Bloom's *Closing of the American Mind,* paint America's future—its young people—as essentially anti-intellectual, Philistine, and in conflict with the basic values of our civilization.

Yet even as they point out serious deficiencies—the primacy of consumption over production and military spending over the generation of wealth—the apostles of decline are distorting the objective reality of America's actual situation in the world. In their passion to explode the Norman Rockwellesque mythology of Reaganism, the decliners ignore the assets that can help America reclaim its message to the world.

One common fallacy is to compare the United States to the fading empires of the past, most particularly Great Britain. But unlike Britain, or any of the other past empires, the United States remains a relatively young nation, still in the process of establishing its own identity. Even after the debacles of the last 15 years, including the disaster in Vietnam and widespread stagnation on the industrial front, this youthfulness gives us what Fuji Kamiya, a leading social commentator and professor at Tokyo's Keio University, describes as *sokojikara*—a resiliency and ability to recover in new and often unexpected ways.

America's *sokojikara* rests upon three pillars—massive immigration, an entrepreneurial open economy, and vast natural resources. At a time when many critics suggest we refashion our national character to European or Japanese standards, we would be far better served by finding ways to build upon these unique advantages. In the process we can best find the strategy for America's resurgence in our third century of independence.

By changing the very core of America, its people and their racial identity, immigration has the potential to play the most revolutionary role in this resurgence. Since the 1970s the United States has accepted more *legal* immigrants than the rest of the world combined. Due largely to their presence, America by the 1990s will have a younger population than any of our rivals; in Japan, for instance, by the end of the century, the percentage of retirees will be nearly twice ours. In Europe, where anti-immigration sentiment has been growing, some national populations are already beginning to shrink, with Germany's expected to fall nearly 50 percent by the middle of the 21st century.

Perhaps more important than mere numbers, however, is the racial makeup of America's new immigrants, the vast majority of whom hail from Latin America and Asia. Due largely to their presence and to their higher birth rates, by the middle of the 21st century the majority of Americans will no longer trace their ancestry to Europe. We are moving from being a "melting pot" of Europeans to a "world nation" with links to virtually every part of the inhabited globe.

In a world where the economic center of gravity is rapidly shifting away from the Atlantic toward the Pacific Basin, the emergence of the American world nation provides a major advantage in adjusting to the new world reality. As a world nation, the United States can transcend its European identity and emerge as a multiracial role model in an increasingly nonwhite world economic order.

Some may see in this concept of the world nation a contradiction of the traditional America. Yet it rests solidly upon the basic ideological firmament of our republic. Never a racial or cultural motherland in the sense of *La France* or *Dai Nippon,* America at its best represents a universal idea, a conception of humanity that transcends narrow racial classifications.

This idea has its roots in the earliest days of the republic. Thomas Paine, writing in 1776, rejected the notion of America as a purely Anglo-Saxon nation. In revolutionary Pennsylvania, for instance, Germans represented a majority of the population and Englishmen less than a third. In 1790, before the final ratification of the Constitution, Anglo-Saxons constituted slightly less than 50 percent of the population. Far from being merely an offshoot of English civilization, America, in the conception of revolutionaries such as Paine, was destined to be "an asylum for mankind."

Today, Paine's notion has expanded to include not only other Europeans but people of other races as well. The growing appreciation of nonwhite contributions—from the celebration of Martin Luther King's birthday to the academic study of Hispanic and Asian roles in developing the American West—reflects the continuing development of the original revolutionary idea. Today we more fully embody what Walt Whitman wrote over a century ago: "America is the race of races."

The power of this new identity can already be seen in the growing hegemony of multiracial American culture—epitomized by nonwhite stars such as Eddie Murphy and Michael Jackson—throughout various nations of the world. Already the second-largest source of American exports, our entertainment industry dominates virtually every market in which it is allowed to operate. But it is more than movies and music. It is the appeal of our individualist lifestyle that is leading to "the Californianization of the free world," in Japanese consultant Kenichi Ohmae's phrase.

The emergence of the American world nation also has profound ideological implications. The American message—stressing individual rights and private initiative—is gradually becoming universal and less linked to "white" ideology. Nowhere is this clearer than in China, where American cultural and political influence has a powerful appeal, particularly among the young. When 50,000 Chinese students demonstrated in Shanghai's People's Square in December 1986, they waved banners depicting the Statue of Liberty and a dragon bound in chains.

Emblazoned on the banners were calls for such American-style values as democracy, human rights, and freedom.

None of this means to suggest that these foreign movements identify with the defense or foreign-policy positions of U.S. administrations. But it does suggest that our cultural forms and ideals, if not our policies, still possess a revolutionary appeal to those non-Europeans who constitute the overwhelming majority of the planet's inhabitants.

But we do not have to look abroad for the positive impact of immigration. Hispanic influence has transformed Miami into the banking capital of Latin America, while on a smaller scale boosting San Antonio and San Diego into business centers for rapidly industrializing northern Mexico. Asian immigrants have turned Los Angeles and San Francisco into dynamic centers of Oriental capitalism.

Indeed, wherever they have clustered, immigrants have injected new dynamism into local economies. In the Santa Clara Valley near San Francisco, for instance, nearly 70 companies have been formed by Chinese-Americans. And, notes Robert Kelley, president of the Southern California Technology Executives Network, an association of 170 local technology firms, "Without the movement of Asians, particularly Vietnamese, there would not have been the sort of explosion you had in Orange County."

An example of that explosive growth is AST Research, a leading personal computer firm. It was founded in 1980 by a typical group of new American entrepreneurs: Tom Yuen and Alben Wong hailed from the crowded tenements of Hong Kong; Safi Qureshey was the son of a Pakistani foreign service officer, raised in Karachi. Although they had been brought up in the backwaters of Asia's colonial past, their aspirations were American. "My school was British, but it seemed foreign to me," says Wong, who emigrated in 1970. "But America was different. It was our culture; the movies, TV, and Pepsi were everywhere. The Gemini program, Apollo—they were what we talked about back home."

When AST's sales broke $400,000 in 1982, the young company resorted to traditional Chinese methods. Albert Wong called in members of his sprawling family, who in turn recruited their friends. When the production runs got larger than the family could handle, they recruited hundreds of Vietnamese, Chinese, and Latinos who had begun to concentrate in the poorer sections of the county. Today, AST, with sales in excess of $206 million, stands as the world's leading independent producer of add-on boards for personal computers. With sparkling new plants in Hong Kong and Irvine, California, it makes over one-quarter of its sales overseas, mostly in Europe and Asia.

Similarly, Hispanic immigrants play a crucial role in the garment, leather, textile, furniture, and lumber industries in Southern California. During the 1970s, all these California businesses grew by more than 50 percent, while the same industries declined in the rest of the country. Rather than taking jobs from "native" Americans, note RAND Corp. researchers Kevin P. McCarthy and R. Burciaga Valdez, the massive influx of Mexicans into California has actually boosted employment. As Richard Rothstein, former manager of the Amalgamated Clothing and Textile Workers Union in Los Angeles puts it: "Prohibiting employment of immigrants, the only workers willing to labor in minimum and near-minimum garment jobs, will only accelerate the destruction of domestic industry."

The economic contribution by our immigrants reflects a greater source of American strength—the openness of our economic system. This flexibility, allowing for the birth and death of companies on a massive scale, has produced in the past decade a resurgence of entrepreneurial enterprise admired around the world. As Peter Drucker has noted, "America shares equally in the crisis that afflicts all developed countries. But in entrepreneurship—in creating the different and the new—the United States is way out in front."

Drucker's observation, of course, flies in the face of many of the leading economic gurus, such as Harvard's Robert Reich, who reject the entrepreneurial model for the more-closed and controlled corporatist system common in Europe and, to a lesser extent, some Far Eastern nations. It also contradicts the notion advanced by Reich that our addiction to "individualism" and "the myth of the self-made man" lies at the heart of America's economic problems.

In reality, it is precisely this individualism, as expressed in entrepreneurial activity, that provides the economic basis for America's resurgence. Due almost totally to small and mid-sized firms, the United States in the 1980s has created nearly 15 times as many jobs as the more closed and controlled systems of Europe.

In fact, the European model—with its much-ballyhooed stress on cooperation among government, labor, and business—has proved almost totally incapable of meeting the economic challenges of the 1980s. Unemployment rates in these countries, once far lower than in the United States, are now as much as two to three times the U.S. level—despite stagnant or even decreasing populations. Even as the economic gurus urge us to adopt the corporatist model, many European leaders, from Margaret Thatcher to members of France's Socialist Party, are seeking ways to emulate the American model.

Equally important, entrepreneurs are emerging as key players in the reindustrialization of the United States. Falsely linked by such pundits as John Naisbitt with the rise of a "post-industrial" society, entrepreneurs are manning the manufacturing battlements all too often abandoned by our large corporations.

While large firms shed nearly 1.4 million factory jobs between 1974 and 1984, nearly 41,000 *new* industrial companies have offset almost all this loss. As a result, companies employing fewer than 250 employees have increased their share of American manufacturing employment to 46 percent, up from 42 percent a decade ago. If this trend continues, small firms could employ 50 percent of our industrial workforce by the 1990s.

The success of these firms springs from superior execution. For instance, Nucor Corp., based in Charlotte, North Carolina, now produces twice as much steel per hour as its giant U.S. counterparts. From its new Pilgrim, Utah, plant, Nucor is also penetrating the West Coast markets dominated by the Japanese and other Asian steelmakers. In 1986, the company began an assault on the steel-fastener market, at present 90 percent dominated by foreign firms, and in the following year started construction of a technically advanced plant outside Indianapolis to produce flat rolled steel, thus threatening one of the last bastions of the big steel companies.

Nucor president Ken Iverson, who took over the company in its infancy back in 1965, believes in economic *sokojikara,* even in one of the world's most overbuilt, fiercely competitive industries. Convinced that free competition can lead to renewal, he opposes protectionist measures. "Unless you're under intense competitive pressure and it becomes a question of the survival of the business to do it, you're just going to lapse back into your old ways," Iverson says. "There's no other answer. But out of all this will come a lot of things that are beneficial: more of an orientation toward technology, greater productivity, certainly a lot of changes in management structure." Such manufacturing companies, with their internal flexibility and emphasis on niche markets, will become increasingly crucial in America's struggle to regain international competitiveness.

This leads to the most important challenge of all, meeting the competition from Japan and other rising economic powers in Asia. Of course, here again the economic gurus have their European guidebook ready, urging an industrial policy based on close cooperation among organized labor, government bureaucrats, and, most particularly, the *Fortune* 500 corporations—the very forces that have led us to the current abyss.

Fortunately, there are signs that some large U.S. companies—notably Xerox, IBM, and Cummins Engine—are recommitting themselves to the "blocking and tackling" of the production process. Product-oriented executives, such as Ford's Don Peterson and IBM Executive Vice President Jack Kuehler, are emerging as the new corporate role models, replacing the discredited green-eyeshade managers typified by David Roderick of USX and Roger Smith of GM.

But the most significant challenge to the Japanese will likely come not from the renewal of large companies but from a new breed of American industrialists. These executives, hardened by the humiliations of the past 15 years, represent something of a "post-Vietnam" generation. Unlike the prototypical managers of the 1960s and 1970s, they have gained the wisdom not to assume American supremacy. At the same time, these executives—many only in their 20s and 30s—have no desire to hand the keys of the future to Asian competitors.

This post-Vietnam mentality can be seen at work in companies all across the spectrum of American industry. Steel minimills, such as Nucor, now represent over one-fifth of the nation's steel production, winning market share not only from U.S. giants but also from Japanese and Korean steelmakers. And while Japan's vertically integrated electronics houses have "taken over" the high-volume, low-margin DRAM market, smaller American firms—such as LSI Logic, Cypress Semiconductor, and Linear Technologies—have continued to dominate many of the cutting-edge, high-margin parts of the chip business.

But perhaps the most interesting example of the post-Vietnam managers can be seen in the microcomputer field. Several years ago, many analysts predicted that only giant firms, such as IBM and AT&T, would be able to withstand the onslaught of the Japanese and Korean conglomerates. Yet since 1986 the gainers in market share and profitability have been the new breed of entrepreneurial industrial firms—such as Compaq, AST Research, Everex, and Dell Computers—all of whom started within the past decade.

The failure of Japanese companies to win in the personal computer business reflects a growing problem for the island nation. While the Japanese have done well in projecting themselves into already established industries, often with the assistance of their brain-dead American competitors, they have had little success in creating the new growth companies—the modern-day equivalents of the Hondas and Sonys of the 1950s—who tend to provide leadership in cutting-edge industries.

Such trends, of course, rarely impress our politicians, corporate lobbyists, and economic gurus, but the Japanese themselves are profoundly aware of these problems. Although currently buoyed by low oil prices and an orgy of domestic spending, Japan's rate of economic growth, once among the highest in the world, has in recent years been roughly even with that of the United States and below that of such places as California.

Equally important, the current *endaka*, or yen shock, has sent Japan, the prototypical industrial superpower, speeding toward a more service-based and financially driven economy. Over the past few years, new investment in plant and equipment has generally slowed, and the largest source of profits for many Japanese firms last year was not products but *zaitech,* money made through financial and real estate transactions. While American MBAs are rethinking their commitment to Wall Street, Japanese financial institutions, now the world's largest, are becoming "hot" among that nation's top college graduates. And without a pool of immigrants to take up the slack, Japanese industry is having problems finding young motivated workers to man its assembly lines.

If these patterns seem familiar to Americans, they should be—the United States has undergone a similar process in the past 25 years. But Japan's transition from an industrial to a financial paradigm is likely to be more lasting. This is because Japan lacks that third pillar of *sokojikara,* a large continental landmass.

Growing up in a huge country, we Americans often forget the advantages of our natural endowment. Our prime industrial competitors—Japan, the newly industrializing nations of Asia, and Western Europe—are fundamentally land and resource poor. Many of these nations, notably Japan and Germany, spent much of the first half of this century attempting to achieve what the Japanese call *tairiku,* or continental power, ultimately failing at a terrible cost.

Rather than some dark conspiracy to "take over" an America beset with a weak currency, the recent upsurge in foreign investment reflects foreigners' often greater appreciation of our natural advantages, as well as U.S. demographic and entrepreneurial vitality. A poll of Western European executives in 1984—at the height of the strong dollar—found that 45 percent preferred the United States as their first choice for expansion. Similarly, the majority of all capital exported from the cash-rich Chinese diaspora, notably Taiwan and Hong Kong, is flowing toward the United States.

But in the long run, no nation more appreciates America *tairiku* power than Japan. Within its borders the United States possesses 30 times Japan's arable land, 1,300 times its oil reserves, and 327 times its coal deposits. Viewed from the Japanese perspective, the United States simply represents what Max Weber once called "the area of optimal economic opportunities."

Japan's could be a crucial role—in terms both of capital and of technology— in rebuilding our nation's industrial plant. Increasingly, for instance, many of our imports from Japan are in the form, not of consumer products such as cars and

VCRs, but of capital goods, such as machine tools and textile-making machinery, that are used to make products here at home. Sometimes these goods find their way into Japanese-financed industrial expansions—from the car plants in Ohio to cotton mills in California.

Indeed, so great is Japan's role in refinancing America—accounting for roughly 45 percent of that nation's worldwide direct foreign investment in 1986— that some Japanese are afraid it might eventually threaten Japan's own economic position. Capital-rich nations have tended to lay "the secret foundations," in Karl Marx's words, for the next economic ascendancy. As Venice financed Holland, and Holland Great Britain, and Great Britain America, some Japanese fear the new outflows of capital and producer goods could in the long term hand the keys to future ascendancy to its great competitor.

"United States society is very strong, with all your immigration from other countries. You have the scale and the resources that we simply will never possess," Hiroshi Takeuchi, chief economist for the Long Term Credit Bank of Japan, says resignedly. "The Japanese role will be to assist the United States by exporting our money to rebuild your economy. This is the evidence that our economy is fundamentally weak. The money goes to America because you are fundamentally strong."

"The empires of the future," wrote Winston Churchill, "are the empires of the mind." In this context, American greatness does not mean attempting to recreate the artificial, war-induced hegemony of 1945. Nor does it mean bankrupting ourselves for our competitors' sake, most lavishly in the case of Europe, in order to achieve military control of the planet. And most importantly of all, the American empire cannot preserve itself—as Gore Vidal, among others, has advocated—by lining up with the other white powers, including the Soviet Union, to defend European civilization against the rising forces of Asia.

To retain its preeminence, America must instead hasten its transition into a world nation. Rather than submitting to the great angst of the Atlantic world, we must begin to identify ourselves more with the Asians, Latins, and Africans, who every day become a greater part of America. They, together with Americans of European descent, are the true sources of our nation's unparalleled technological, cultural, and economic dynamism—the human basis for our "empire of the mind." Similarly, in our foreign affairs, we must turn from our historical obsession with Europe and shift our prime attention to the Pacific that is our future and to a Latin America with which we share growing economic, cultural, linguistic, and ethnic ties.

Pacific and North American countries now represent our largest markets, while Europe's share of U.S. trade has fallen from 36 percent to 22 percent over the past decade. Today our three leading trade partners and export markets are Canada, Japan, and Mexico. Our fastest-growing export markets are Taiwan and the People's Republic of China. Today we already sell more products in Taiwan than we do in Italy; by the beginning of the 1990s it is likely that Taiwan and South Korea will become bigger markets for U.S. products than France, perhaps even larger than West Germany and the United Kingdom.

But more than economic necessity drives us to the Pacific. It is indeed our national destiny. Some such as Allan Bloom see the embrace of a post-European reality as a denial of our fundamental values. But by extending the nation's mission beyond the confines of the narrowly defined "West," the United States, for the first time, could begin to fulfill the aspirations of the 18th- and 19th-century visionaries who saw our destiny as something greater than the western expansion of European history. "We are the heirs of all mankind," wrote Herman Melville, "and with all people we share our inheritance."

We should never forget that America's revolutionary message—its promise of an open economic and political system based on individuals freely associating— remains as relevant and powerful as in any epoch. In Asia, in Latin America, even the Soviet Union, millions seek those very liberties that Paine, Jefferson, and Adams created from revolution two centuries ago.

For in the end, the greatness of America depends not so much on its force of arms, or even the opulence of its economy, but upon the power of its message to the world. Lacking a sense of mission, the nation will likely continue to flounder, unsure even of its true identity. Only by rediscovering our revolutionary charter and applying it to the realities of the post-European world can the United States in its third century enjoy a renaissance equal to the great vision of its founders and the uniqueness of its people.

PART THREE

PEOPLE

Inside Ronald Reagan

Interviewed by Manuel S. Klausner

July 1975

T hose of us concerned about liberty have had good reason of late to be interested in Ronald Reagan. Increasingly, California's former governor has been turn- ing up in first place among Republican figures in political opinion polls, among independents as well as Republicans. In addition, in recent months Reagan has taken to using the term "libertarian" or "libertarian-conservative" to describe his political philosophy. All of which naturally made us interested in taking a closer look at the man and his ideas. Thanks to the efforts of the late Ned Hutchinson (a former Reagan aide), *Reason* was able to obtain time out of Reagan's busy schedule for him to be interviewed by Editor Manuel S. Klausner.

Ronald Wilson Reagan was born in Illinois in 1911. After a varied career as a radio sports announcer, motion picture actor, and TV host, Reagan became active in conservative politics. After achieving national publicity for his televised speeches for Barry Goldwater in 1964, Reagan went on to win the California governorship in 1966 and was re-elected to a second four-year term in 1970. Throughout his eight years in office, Reagan stressed the idea of holding down the size and cost of government; nonetheless, the state budget increased from $5.7 billion to $10.8 billion during his time in office.

Reagan did institute property and inventory tax cuts, but during his tenure the sales tax was increased to 6 percent and withholding was introduced to the state income tax system. Under Reagan's administration, state funding for public schools (grades K-12) increased 105 percent (although enrollment went up only 5 percent), state support for junior colleges increased 323 percent, and grants and loans to college students increased 900 percent. Reagan's major proposal to hold down the cost of government was a constitutional amendment to limit state spending to a specified "slowly declining" percentage of the gross income of the state's population. The measure was submitted to the voters as an initiative measure, Proposition One, but was defeated when liberal opponents pictured it as a measure that would force local tax increases.

Reagan instituted a major overhaul of the state welfare system that reduced the total welfare caseload (which had been rapidly increasing) while raising benefits by 30 percent and increasing administrative costs. He encouraged the formation of HMO-like prepaid health care plans for MediCal patients, a move that has drawn mixed reactions from the medical community. His federally funded Office of Criminal Justice Planning made large grants to police agencies for computers and other expensive equipment and funded (among other projects) a large-scale research effort on how to prosecute pornographers more effectively. He several times vetoed legislation to reduce marijuana possession to a misdemeanor and signed legislation sharply increasing penalties for drug dealers.

Thus, Reagan's record, while generally conservative, is not particularly libertarian. But one's administrative decisions, constrained as they are by existing laws, institutions, and politics, do not necessarily mirror one's underlying philosophy. We were therefore curious to find out more about the real Ronald Reagan. Looking relaxed and healthy despite his 64 years and a hectic schedule, Reagan welcomed us to his Los Angeles office on Wilshire Boulevard and talked political philosophy with us for over an hour. Here is what we learned.

REASON: Gov. Reagan, you have been quoted in the press as saying that you're doing a lot of speaking now on behalf of the philosophy of conservatism and libertarianism. Is there a difference between the two?

REAGAN: If you analyze it I believe the very heart and soul of conservatism is libertarianism. I think conservatism is really a misnomer just as liberalism is a misnomer for the liberals—if we were back in the days of the Revolution, so-called conservatives today would be the Liberals and the liberals would be the Tories. The basis of conservatism is a desire for less government interference or less centralized authority or more individual freedom, and this is a pretty general description also of what libertarianism is.

Now, I can't say that I will agree with all the things that the present group who call themselves Libertarians in the sense of a party say, because I think that like in any political movement there are shades, and there are libertarians who are almost over at the point of wanting no government at all or anarchy. I believe there are legitimate government functions. There is a legitimate need in an orderly society for some government to maintain freedom or we will have tyranny by individuals. The strongest man on the block will run the neighborhood. We have government to insure that we don't each one of us have to carry a club to defend ourselves. But again, I stand on my statement that I think that libertarianism and conservatism are travelling the same path.

REASON: Governor, could you give us some examples of what you would consider to be proper functions of government?

REAGAN: Well, the first and most important thing is that government exists to protect us from each other. Government exists, of course, for the defense of the nation, and for the defense of the rights of the individual. Maybe we don't all agree on some of the other accepted functions of government, such as fire departments and police departments—again the protection of the people.

I don't believe in a government that protects us from ourselves. I have illustrated this many times by saying that I would recognize the right of government to say that someone who rode a motorcycle had to protect the public from himself by making certain provisions about his equipment and the motorcycle—the same as we do with an automobile. I disagree *completely* when government says that because of the number of head injuries from accidents with motorcycles that he should be forced to wear a helmet. I happen to think he's stupid if he rides a motorcycle without a helmet, but that's one of our sacred rights—to be stupid.

But to show you how these gray areas can creep in, the other day I was saying this to a man who happens to be a neurosurgeon, and who has treated many cases of this particular kind of injury and accident, and he disagreed with me on this issue. He disagreed with me on the basis of the individuals who become public charges as a result of permanent damage—he has pointed to an area where it *does* go over into not just hurting the individuals directly involved but now imposes on others also. I only use this extreme example to show that when we come down to government and what it should or should not do for the good of the people and for protecting us from each other, you do come into some gray areas, and I think here there will be disagreements between conservatives and libertarians.

So, I think the government has legitimate functions. But I also think our greatest threat today comes from government's involvement in things that are *not* government's proper province. And in those things government has a magnificent record of failure.

REASON: Could you give some examples of what areas you're talking about?

REAGAN: Well, many of them in the regulatory fields of our private enterprise sector. We've noticed, for example, that for half a century the railroads have been saying that they could take care of themselves and would have no problems—if they could be freed from a great many government regulations and the ICC. Finally their plight was such that the government had to take over the passenger traffic with Amtrak, and one of the first things that Amtrak did was ask to be relieved of the ICC regulations!

REASON: Are you in favor of decontrolling the railroads and the other regulated industries?

REAGAN: Yes. Again this comes down to the point at which we get into regulations that are for the protection of the people. I don't think anyone suggests that we should do away with those regulations which insure safety for the passengers in transportation. I don't think that we should do away with those regulations in the field of pure foods and so forth, that make sure that some unscrupulous individual can't sell us canned meat that gives us botulism. But, we start with those legitimate areas and then we go on and regulations just keep spreading like spores of a fungus until we find that they literally are taking away the rights of management to make business decisions with regard to their competition.

REASON: What about higher education? Is there a proper role for government in providing a university education?

REAGAN: Well, I think here there's been an exaggeration. Originally public education was based on the idea that you cannot have our kind of society without a literate citizenry. If you're going to have government of, by, and for the people, then you're going to have a citizenry that is able to read, and to make decisions at the polls. It then extended to higher education because there was a segment of our society that could not get education. Now you wonder why government didn't think in terms of saying, "We will provide an education for the individual that can't provide for himself, but we'll do it by way of the private sector universities." Then they would have expanded and there would be more private universities and they would be far cheaper than they are today.

REASON: These days, most private universities are the recipients of federal funds. Do you think that it's proper to use tax revenue to finance higher education?

113

REAGAN: Well, if I answer that question then I'm answering that we should do away with our state universities and frankly I haven't given enough thought to what could be a counter-system.

At first, there was a great opposition to most of the federal revenues that are going to education on the part of many educators. Once the money was there, however, it was like the farmer who went into the woods and came back with the wagon loads of wild pigs. When they asked him how he had done it—they'd been wild for a hundred years—he said, "I built a fence and I put corn down and fed them, and they got used to eating the corn there, so I extended the fences's sides and finally I had an enclosure and I corralled them." He said, "If I can get them to take food from me, I'll own them." And this is what really happened with federal aid to education. You know, the federal government could have done it differently if the federal government did not at the same time want control.

REASON: Many students at universities are middle class or upper middle class and tax support means that a lot of the lower class/lower income people are paying for that education. Don't you feel that there's something immoral or unethical about redistributing wealth from the lower class up to the middle class?

REAGAN: Yes. And I used that argument in my fight to get tuition in the University of California. I have to tell you about that fight with the University of California—they were very much opposed! They wanted it kept totally free, as it had been. The tuition I was proposing was less than 10 percent of the actual cost of educating the student—which is more than $3,500 now, and at that time was roughly $3,000. I was proposing $300 tuition—and I used the exact same argument you're using. Finally, tuition was instituted.

But, I had always said that tuition should never be a block to anyone getting an education who could not otherwise afford to go to the university. I fought for a plan that would have allowed the financially needy student to defer until after graduation all or part of his tuition. And the same university administration that had fought me and did not want tuition at all, fought me equally hard on deferred tuition and did not want that benefit for the students!

REASON: Let us shift for the moment from education to your Proposition One initiative that you campaigned so hard for. How would you describe the purposes of Proposition One, Governor?

REAGAN: Well, first of all, we realized that at the state level we could not do an awful lot to reduce the vast tax burden that the people of America carry. Right now, virtually half of every dollar earned in the United States is taken by governments—federal, state or local. And governments in the United States are all growing at about the same rate, which is about 2.5 times as fast as the increase in population. We couldn't do anything with the federal rate, which is the big villain. Nor could we impose on local governments. But we said that if the biggest state in the Union can put itself on a basis of establishing a percentage of the people's earnings above which government cannot go in taxation without the consent of the people, and if it works, then it sets an example that makes it almost impossible for the federal government not to follow suit and do the same thing. And hopefully local governments also.

So I appointed a task force and this task force talked to economists like Milton

Friedman who then volunteered to help. The task force report came back with all the facts and figures. We concluded that we could over 15 years reduce the percentage the California state government was taking—from about 8.75 cents out of every dollar down to 7 cents out of every dollar. It doesn't sound like much, but at the end of 15 years the difference would be that you could triple the present budget of California at a 7-percent rate, and you'd have a budget three times the present size of the budget. We thought the growth of the economy was such that people could recognize that you could have this tax rate reduction without doing away with any useful government service.

Now we could have probably passed Proposition One if we had settled for the percentage the state is now taking and proposed freezing the percentage at the present level. But you see, the opposition was very dishonest. (And when I say this, I include the State Employees Association, the whole educational establishment of California that opposed it, and the League of Women Voters, who made it very plain that they were going to oppose anything that limited government's ability to get more money.) These people dishonestly campaigned and convinced the people that to reduce the state's share we were going to dump the load on local government, so that the local property taxes would go up. We couldn't make clear the fact that in our plan there was a distinct prohibition on the state transferring this cost over to local government without lowering the percentage comparably. And so we lost. I *still* think it's an idea whose time has come.

REASON: Governor, given the way that Prop. One was misrepresented in California by these very strong interest groups (which would exist in other states as well), how would you restructure a campaign to sell it to the people, to counteract that kind of misrepresentation?

REAGAN: Well, as I say, it was so complicated. Maybe if we had to do it all over again, I shouldn't be so greedy. Maybe we should have settled for the present percentage, and then just held at the present spending, while waiting for people to realize that maybe you could then reduce spending in the future as you were successful with it. That would have robbed our opponents of their argument. You see, if they hadn't been able to say, "They're going to reduce the money the state's getting—so they must be going to get it from someplace else"—if they hadn't been able to say that, we could have refuted anything else they said by saying, "Wait a minute—if *they* don't want it frozen at the present percentage they must be telling you that they're going to raise taxes if they have their way."

REASON: Governor, isn't it true that in your first year in office there was actually a 24-percent increase in the state budget?

REAGAN: Oh, for heavens sakes, I don't know what the percentage was—but you see, the problem was that the state budget we inherited didn't *mean* anything. We got in and found that to get through the election year, the previous administration had changed the bookkeeping and had a budget that was financed by 15 months' revenue. By changing to an accrual method of bookkeeping, what they really were doing was postponing until after the election what they knew was going to have to be a tax increase. We won and found that out to our surprise—because we were quite unable, even in the period between election and inauguration, to get very much information from the outgoing administration. It was *not* an orderly transition! In fact, the Director of Finance in his briefing said to one of my representatives, "Look, we're spending a million dollars a day more than we're taking in—I've got a golf game—good luck." *That* was our briefing in finance! We had to—much as we objected—institute a gigantic tax increase, and put the state back on a solvent basis. I said at the time that I did not recognize that as permanent—that we were going to try to give the money back to the people, just as we could institute reforms. Over the eight-year period we gave back in the form of one-time rebates, tax cuts, and even bridge-toll cuts $5.7 billion—which comes pretty close to giving back the amount of that increase.

REASON: Let me ask you—still in the area of tax reform, governor—how you feel about the Liberty Amendment, which would abolish the income tax. Is that something you're in favor of?

REAGAN: Well, let me tell you where my doubts are there. I am very critical of the income tax—the progressive features and the complications of it—it's the one instance in your whole fiscal experience in life in which you figure out what you owe and government reserves the right to come back and tell you your figures are wrong. If you're going to have a tax the people should know what the tax is and the government should be able to tell them without the people having to go to the expense of figuring it out themselves.

On the other hand, I have always felt that taxing income is probably as fair a method of raising revenue for government as any. Let's take a simple case. Suppose 100 of us were shipwrecked on an island and we knew there was little chance of release and we established a community to get along—to survive there. In a sense we set up a government. What you'd probably do is ask each individual to dedicate a certain amount of his time to such things as standing guard or hunting and fishing to keep the people alive and providing fresh water and so forth, so you'd probably each one contribute a certain amount of service to the community. You'd basically be on your own except for X amount of time. Well, this in a sense is what you do with your income tax.

REASON: Of course, if you're talking about starting from scratch—the shipwrecked people on the island—you're really talking about a voluntary approach, aren't you—as against taxation?

REAGAN: Well, we're inclined to think that our government here *is* a voluntary approach and that we've set up a government to perform certain things, such as the national protection, etc.

REASON: Aren't we deluding ourselves to talk in terms of consent, though? When we talk about taxation, aren't we really dealing with force and coercion and nothing less than that?

REAGAN: Well, government's only weapons are force and coercion and that's why we shouldn't let it get out of hand. And that's what the Founding Fathers had in mind with the Constitution, that you don't let it get out of hand.

But you say voluntary on the island. Let's take a single thing. Let's say that there was some force on the island, whether it's hostiles or whether it was an animal, that represented a threat and required round-the-clock guard duty for the safety of the community. Now I'm sure it would be voluntary, but you get together and you say look, we're all going to have to take turns guarding. Now what do you think would happen in that community if some individual said "Not me; I won't stand guard." Well, I think the community would expel him and say "Well, we're not going to guard you." So voluntarism *does* get into a kind of force and coercion where there is a legitimate need for it.

REASON: You said earlier that government doesn't exist to protect people from themselves. Let's take the desert island shipwreck situation. Would you be in favor of any laws against gambling in the shipwrecked island situation?

REAGAN: You've named an issue that is one of the most difficult for me to reconcile. I know this gets into the whole area of the sin laws, and here again I think you're in one of the gray areas. There's one side of me that says I know this is protecting us from ourselves; there's another side of me, however, that says you can make the case that it does get into an area in which we are protecting us from each other.

I cannot go along with the libertarian philosophy that says that all of the sin laws can be ruled out as simply trying to protect us from ourselves. You can take the case of the father who gambles his money away and thus leaves his family dependent on the rest of us. You can take surrounding areas—the necessity for protection against dishonest gambling—which requires added government duties and obligations.

REASON: But isn't it really very selective law enforcement when it comes to nonvictim crime areas?

REAGAN: Well, now, you know the nonvictim crimes. Here again I think you're in a gray area that requires certainly more study than I've given it. Prostitution has been listed as a nonvictim crime. Well, is anyone naive enough to believe that prostitution just depends on willing employees coming in and saying that's the occupation they want to practice? It doesn't.

REASON: Well, it partly depends on the options. There are a lot of jobs that people might find distasteful in a free market. I suppose that if you work in a paint shop and you're breathing paint fumes all day, it might not be a very desirable job either.

REAGAN: Yes. But get into the seamy side. Talk to law enforcement people about the seamy side of how the recruiting is done, including what in an earlier day was called the white slave traffic—and you will find that the recruiting for prostitution is not one of just taking an ad in the paper and saying come be a prostitute and letting someone walk in willingly.

REASON: Yes, but, Governor, we really haven't lived in a time when prostitution has been decriminalized.

REAGAN: Yes, we *have* lived in such a time. In many areas of the country in the old days, prostitution operated with local control and there was no problem and they even claimed inspection and so forth. Once, at the beginning of World War II, I asked the medical officer at our post (it was in New Orleans) why they were closing up the brothels with so many military bases there. And he gave me a pretty hard, cold answer. He said the army isn't interested in morals. The army's interested in keeping soldiers healthy. He showed me the difference in the statistics. He said the average girl in a house handled roughly 40 to 50 customers a night. And he said if you give her a five-day week, that's 200 to 250. Suppose the first

117

man infects her and here are 200 to 249 men that follow suit during that week, and he said the most often that you could possibly inspect would be once a week. He said we also know statistically that by putting a girl out on a street because of the difficulty of soliciting and getting to a place and getting back out on the street again, they only handle about 9 customers. Now, he said, the first thing that's done when they're picked up is inspection. So every 10 days she averages inspection—and there's only been 90 customers in between. Now, you stop to think of the public health situation of this. You have to, then, take on certain regulatory chores if you're going to have this.

REASON: Back to taxes, you've been very critical of the People's Lobby and the League of Women Voters' drive to change the [California] Constitution to do away with the two-third majority requirement for raising bank taxes...

REAGAN: If they're really a People's Lobby, why aren't they going to do what we tried to do and were opposed all the time that I was governor? Don't change that part of the law—change the other part of the law that says the rest of us can be taxed by a simple majority. If they really want to put a referendum on the ballot, why don't they go out and say to the people, do you want to change this and make it so that a simple majority can increase that tax or do you want to make it that it requires a two-thirds majority of the legislature to change any tax?

Look—you've got a legislature that takes two-thirds to pass the budget, it takes two-thirds to pass an appropriation bill, a spending bill—so why shouldn't it take a two-thirds majority to say whether you're going to raise the taxes. But these are fools who are circulating this petition, and again the League of Women Voters have explained that they are against any effort on the part of government to restrict government's ability to meet the needs and so forth. In other words, to spend your money.

But they are fools in thinking that business somehow is getting a special break. Who pays the business tax anyway? *We do*! You can't tax business. Business doesn't *pay* taxes. It *collects* taxes. And if they can't be passed on to the customer in the price of the product as a cost of operation, business goes out of business. Now what they're going to do is make it easier for demagogic politicians—and you've got plenty of them in the state legislature—to say to the people, look, we need money for this worthwhile project but we're not going to tax you, we're going to tax business, now that we can do it by a one-vote margin. So they'll tax business and the price of the product will go up and the people will blame the storekeeper for the rise in the price of the product, not recognizing that all he's doing is passing on to them a hidden sales tax.

If people need any more concrete explanation of this, start with the staff of life, a loaf of bread. The simplest thing; the poorest man must have it. Well, there are 151 taxes now in the price of a loaf of bread—it accounts for more than half the cost of a loaf of bread. It begins with the first tax, on the farmer that raised the wheat. Any simpleton can understand that if that farmer cannot get enough money for his wheat, to pay the property tax on his farm, he can't be a farmer. He loses his farm. And so it is with the fellow who pays a driver's license and a gasoline tax to drive the truckload of wheat to the mill, the miller who has to pay everything from social security tax, business license, everything else. He has to make his living

118

over and above those costs. So they all wind up in that loaf of bread. Now an egg isn't far behind and nobody had to *make* that. There's a hundred taxes in an egg by the time it gets to market and you know the *chicken* didn't put them there!

REASON: Governor, how did you develop your philosophy of individualism?

REAGAN: Oh, Lord! I suppose I did it myself and I did it by way of the mashed-potato circuit. I started out in life as a New Deal Democrat, and I campaigned many times for that. In later years—you know if you don't sing or dance and you're in show business as I was, you find that you either wind up as the toastmaster or the after-dinner speaker—there were two or three of us in the business who were used quite widely: The industry would always call on us to represent show business someplace where speaking was to be done. But if you make a speech about Hollywood, for example, and the sorrows and problems of the motion picture industry, you've got to tie it into the people you're talking to and why they should be interested. I used to use the very obvious comparison that if one industry could be discriminated against taxwise and otherwise as ours had been—threats of censorship and all—then how long could it be before this happened to their industry. Pretty soon businessmen were coming to me and saying, "Let me tell you what's *already* happening to our industry!"

Finally after years of this I came back home once from a speaking trip and said to Nancy, "Look, you know it's just occurred to me that I go out and make all these speeches of things that I'm against and then I go out and campaign for the Democrats who are making it happen. I'm going to stop." Now it took me a while to get around to reregistering. But I started campaigning even though I was still a Democrat, for people on the other side; and then finally I didn't want to become one of those professional Democrats who goes all his life saying he's never voted for a Democrat, so I reregistered.

REASON: You said you were speaking out against censorship at that time?

REAGAN: Oh yes, yes.

REASON: Are you still against censorship?

REAGAN: Yes. I believed in the voluntary motion picture code. I think the motion picture industry is destroying itself and I think it is displaying bad taste in its lousy theater.

REASON: Would you allow anything to go by way of hard-core pornography as long as there are willing and consensual buyers?

REAGAN: I didn't want the picture industry doing it. I just think it's bad business. But I'm opposed to outside censorship.

REASON: Now that you're in the minority party how do you feel about other prospects for minor parties or third-party activities?

REAGAN: Well, third parties have been notoriously unsuccessful; they usually wind up dividing the very people that should be united. And then we elect the wrong kind—the side we're out to defeat wins. I have been doing my best to try to revitalize the Republican Party groups that I've spoken to, on the basis that the time has come to repudiate those in our midst who would blur the Republican image by saying we should be all things to all people in order to triumph. Lately, we find that of the 26 percent of the people who didn't vote, more than half of them now say they didn't vote because they don't see any difference between the parties.

I've been urging Republicans to raise a banner and put the things we stand for on that banner and don't compromise, but don't try to enlarge the party by being all things to everyone when you can't keep all the promises. Put up a banner and then count on the fact that if you've got the proper things on that banner the people will rally round.

I'd like to see some of these other parties maybe come to this remnant of the Republican Party which is basically conservative in its thinking and, I think, akin to the philosophy I'm talking—I'd like to see them all come in (and this would include a large segment of the Democratic Party in this country, that certainly proved in 1972 that they do not follow the leadership of the Democratic Party any longer) and be able to say to them, OK we're not saying to you give up what you're doing, but can't we find a common meeting ground in order at least to defeat first of all those who are doing what they're doing to us (and this present Congress is an example)? I think this is the most irresponsible and most dangerous Congress, in my experience, that this country has ever had. I think we're seeing it in the crumbling now of our position worldwide, their attitude in Indochina. Maybe many of the young people that you write for, with their hatred of war and disillusionment with what went on, don't feel this way and any thought of Indochina is going to be a red flag to them; but, for the first time in 200 years, the United States has violated its word, has abandoned an ally that it pledged to help and we're seeing the result. Mr. Kissinger came home from the Middle East empty handed because even the Israelis said, "What? Give up the passes on the basis of your word that you will help us? We now see evidence that maybe you won't help us. You can't guarantee your promise." So the dominoes fall. To me this is what's most important—if we could all make a change in that Congress that now has a two-thirds majority.

I think the Republican Party should take the lead and, as I say, raise that banner and say this is what we stand for. And what we stand for would be fiscal responsibility. I know that you can't get a balanced budget instantly, but at least an end to deficit spending. Then the goal, established as quickly as possible, of a balanced budget, and begin the retirement of the national debt, or the reduction of it certainly. I think that it should be a government, or a party, that has a position that makes it plain that even though there are social faults that may lead to people turning to crime, the individual must be held accountable for his misdeeds. That on the world scene we're going to do whatever is necessary to insure that we can retain this free system of ours; in other words, we will maintain a defensive posture that is sufficient to deter aggression.

REASON: Are you thinking in terms of a Fortress America approach or a world policeman approach?

REAGAN: No. Fortress America is just what Lenin wanted us to have—whether it is world policeman or not. You know, Lenin said the Communists will take Eastern Europe, they will organize the hordes of Asia; he said they will then move into Latin America, and he said the United States, the last bastion of capitalism, will fall into their outstretched hands like overripe fruit. And that's all that Fortress America is. Now, you don't have to come through someone's beachhead—you just go over them with missiles; and one of these days, under the present policies of the Congress, the United States will stand alone as Lenin envisioned it and then face the ultimatum from the enemy.

REASON: Do you think that the war in Indochina represents any real military threat to the security of the United States?

REAGAN: Not in the sense that the North Vietnamese are going to attack the United States. But if anyone keeps asking why we are involved in Vietnam, they also should ask the question, Why is Russia involved in Vietnam? Why is Russia sponsoring the aggression of the North Vietnamese?

REASON: Well, to the extent that you may have wrongdoers or criminals elsewhere in the world, is that a justification for the American government to use conscripts and tax funds to send American boys halfway around the world?

REAGAN: Well, of course, we never should have sent them halfway around the world. You see, the Eisenhower policy had always been one of logistical support—help the South Vietnamese to be able to resist and take care of themselves, maintain themselves as a nation. It was John Kennedy who sent the first division in there. And he had to do it and when he did it he had to know that they were going to be followed by hundreds of thousands of men, that you couldn't do it with just one division. I'm not privy nor is anyone else privy to the information that a president has when he makes such a decision, but then came the mistake. Once you are going to commit yourself to a combat role and you're going to ask young men to fight and die for your country, then you have a moral obligation as a nation to throw the full resources of the nation behind them and to win that war as quickly as possible and get it over with, and this is where we made the mistake: to pour half a million men in there, to kill 54,000 young men in a cause that Washington, that the government was unable or unwilling to win. And don't tell me that we couldn't have licked the North Vietnamese—my God! their gross national product is the equivalent of that of Cleveland, Ohio!

REASON: Let me ask you do you believe in conscription?

REAGAN: Only in time of war.

REASON: What about in the last 10 years?

REAGAN: I disagreed with it, and I'll tell you why: I believe Lenin also on that. Lenin said that he would force the capitalist nations to maintain military conscription until the uniform became a symbol of servitude rather than patriotism.

REASON: Governor, what about the United Nations? Are you in favor of the United States withdrawing from the UN?

REAGAN: Well, I am in favor of certainly a different policy than we've had. I think the United States should have taken a very drastic action; perhaps it should have staged a walk-out at the time of the recognition of Red China. I think that the United Nations today is virtually impotent when you stop to think that countries representing two-thirds of the votes of the United Nations represent less than 10 percent of the world population. It's a funny thing that everybody who wants one-man/one-vote doesn't hold it true for the United Nations!

REASON: Governor, if the Republicans were to nominate a candidate that was unacceptable to you in 1976, could you support a Libertarian third-party candidate?

FREE MINDS & FREE MARKETS

REAGAN: I have to wait and see what you're doing and what you are standing for.

REASON: Are there any particular books or authors or economists that have been influential in terms of your intellectual development?

REAGAN: Oh, it would be hard for me to pinpoint anything in that category. I'm an inveterate reader. Bastiat and von Mises, and Hayek and Hazlitt—I'm one for the classical economists....

REASON: What about Rand or Rothbard?

REAGAN: No. I haven't read Ayn Rand since *The Fountainhead.* I haven't read *Atlas Shrugged.* The last few years, I must say, have been a little rough on me for doing that kind of reading—for eight years I found that when I finished reading the memorandums and reports and so forth, then I found myself digging into nonfiction, economists and so forth, for help on the problems that were confronting me.

REASON: As far as problems confronting us, a quick response if you could, Governor: the pro and con assessment of Jerry Brown. How do you think he's doing so far?

REAGAN: Well, he is an enigma. I am overjoyed, of course, at his budget approach. And I just assume that that probably stems from his Jesuit training—that that has him thinking in terms of property and economy. I think he's going to find that some of his own appointees are not sympathetic to his budgetary approach. They've got their own constituencies and pretty soon they're going to be wanting to do things for those constituents and that's going to call for spending, and then he's going to find that he might be battling the legislature on one side and his own appointees on the other.

REASON: Thank you very much.

The Road from Serfdom: F. A. Hayek

Interviewed by Thomas W. Hazlett

July 1992

F.A. Hayek must have sensed something in the wind at about the time I interviewed him in Los Angeles in May 1977. In the 1930s and '40s, Hayek had been the second most famous economist on the planet, best known as John Maynard Keynes's intellectual sparring partner. On the fundamental questions of economic policy, the debate pitting Professor Hayek of the London School of Economics against Professor Keynes of Cambridge University sparked a memorable confrontation between classical economics and the new-fangled "macroeconomics" of Lord Keynes's 1936 *General Theory.*

The Keynesians swept academic arguments in a virtual shut-out. With Keynes's death in 1945, in fact, Hayek (and the classical trade cycle theory) quickly faded from public view. Economic policy entered a golden age of "demand management" in which the business cycle was rendered obsolete, and Hayek moved out of economic theory altogether. In 1950 he went to the University of Chicago, where he chaired the Committee on Social Thought, finishing his career at the University of Freiberg (1962-68) and the University of Salzburg (1968-77). He embarked upon major contributions in such new fields as psychology (*The Sensory Order,* 1952), political theory (*The Constitution of Liberty,* 1960), and law (*Law, Legislation & Liberty,* Volumes I-III, 1973-79).

He was wise to steer clear of economics. For his quibble with Keynes was not the only humiliation he had suffered in rarefied theoretical discourse. The famous Socialist Calculation Controversy was prompted by the Austrian critique of central planning. From the 1920s until the '40s, Hayek and his countryman Ludwig von Mises argued that socialism was bound to fail as an economic system because only free markets—powered by individuals wheeling and dealing in their own interest—could generate the information necessary to intelligently coordinate social behavior. In other words, freedom is a necessary input into a prosperous economy. But even as Hayek's elegant essay extolling market prices as the signals of a rational economy was hailed as a seminal contribution upon its publication in the *American Economic Review* in 1945, shrewd socialist theorists proved to the satisfaction of their peers that central planning could be streamlined so as to solve, with really big computers, the very information problem that F. A. Hayek had so courteously exposed.

Losing a scholarly debate or two is not the worst that can befall a human being of talent, and Hayek was not destroyed. He went on to publish brilliant work in subsequent years. But within the economics profession it is no secret that Hayek was an academic outcast, a throwback, a marginal character whose ideas had been neatly disproven to all reasonable men in the scientific journals of his day.

But then something bizarre happened. The late 20th century decided to provide a reality check on the academic scribblers. The 1960s and '70s saw post-war prosperity ignite into an inflationary spiral in the very countries that had embraced Keynesianism (mainly the United States and the U.K.). Shocking to the peer-review process, which had rigorously proven otherwise on many occasions, full employment could not be maintained via off-the-shelf Keynesian bromides. The traditional therapy—stimulate consumption and penalize savings with a healthy infusion of government deficit spending—was now being refereed by the real world, and the results were found "nonrobust." The macro models of Cambridge, Harvard, Berkeley, and MIT fell apart, and by the 1980s the very solutions that Keynes had hustled were being painfully thwacked as precisely the root of our troubles. Suddenly the old classical medicine—savings, investment, balanced budgets, competition, and productivity growth—were popularly claimed to be the economic-policy goal of good government. Even the politicians, so bubbly to receive Keynes's prescription for government spending as the magical elixir with which to treat an ailing economy, had publicly abandoned Keynesianism.

And the possibility of rational economic planning under socialism? Yes, we ran that experiment as well. The Third World tried it and promptly dropped to income levels last recorded in the Pleistocene Epoch. The Second (Communist) World tried it in massive police-state doses and... well... dissolved.

The trends away from Keynesianism in the West and from socialism everywhere else were just beginning to assert themselves when Hayek—out of the economics profession for, essentially, 30 years—was surprisingly awarded a Nobel Prize in Economics in 1974. Quickly, he was transformed from goofball to guru. And not without justification. By the late 1970s—with the Labor, Democratic, and Social Democratic parties (oh come on, you remember them: Think, now think!) still in power in London, Washington, and Bonn—Hayek's vision had already spotted global political movements on the horizon. The glacial worldwide policy shifts of the 1980s were cautiously anticipated by Hayek in this (never before published) interview. He seemed to sense that soon it would not be a sign of disrespect to be dubbed the greatest philosopher of capitalism since Adam Smith.

Sometimes you have to live a long time just to be proved right. When Friedrich August von Hayek, born in 1899, died March 23 in Freiberg, Germany, he had outlived both Keynes and Marx. Happily for the human race, so have his ideas.

[Contributing Editor Thomas W. Hazlett interviewed Hayek in 1977, shortly before starting graduate school in economics at the University of California, Los Angeles.]

REASON: Of your bestselling *The Road to Serfdom,* John Maynard Keynes wrote: "In my opinion it is a grand book....Morally and philosophically I find myself in agreement with virtually the whole of it: and not only in agreement with it, but in deeply moved agreement." Why would Keynes say this about a volume that was deeply critical of the Keynesian viewpoint?

HAYEK: Because he believed that he was fundamentally still a classical

English liberal and wasn't quite aware of how far he had moved away from it. His basic ideas were still those of individual freedom. He did not think systematically enough to see the conflicts. He was, in a sense, corrupted by political necessity. His famous phrase about, "in the long run we're all dead," is a very good illustration of being constrained by what is now politically possible. He stopped thinking about what, in the long run, is desirable. For that reason, I think it will turn out that he will not be a maker of long-run opinion, and his ideas were of a fashion which, fortunately, is now passing away.

REASON: Did Keynes turn around in his later years, as has frequently been rumored?

HAYEK: Nothing as drastic as that. He was fluctuating all the time. He was in a sort of middle line and he was always concerned with expediency for the moment. In the last conversation I had with him (about three weeks before his death in 1945), I asked him if he wasn't getting alarmed about what some of his pupils were doing with his ideas. And he said, "Oh, they're just fools. These ideas were frightfully important in the 1930s, but if these ideas ever become dangerous, you can trust me—I'm going to turn public opinion around like this." And he would have done it! I'm sure that in the post-war period Keynes would have become one of the great fighters against inflation.

REASON: Was the Keynes thesis that government spending is needed to bolster aggregate demand in times of unemployment correct at one time?

HAYEK: No. Certainly not. But, of course, I go much further than this. I believe that if it were not for government interference with the monetary system, we would have no industrial fluctuations and no periods of depression.

REASON: So trade cycles are caused solely by government monetary authorities?

HAYEK: Not that directly. As you put it, it would seem that it results from deliberate mistakes made by government policies. The mistake is the creation of a semi-monopoly where the basic money is controlled by government. Since all the banks issue secondary money, which is redeemable in the basic money, you have a system which nobody can really control. So it's really the monopoly of government over the issue of money which is ultimately responsible. Nobody in charge of such a monopoly could act reasonably.

REASON: You have written that the period from about 1950 to 1975 will go down in history as the Great Prosperity. If the Keynes thesis is incorrect, why the tremendous economic success? Why, for instance, haven't we experienced a hyperinflation on the order of Germany in 1922?

HAYEK: Because the inflation in Germany was not for the purpose of maintaining prosperity but was forced upon them due to financial difficulties. If you inflate for the purpose of maintaining prosperity you can do so at a much more moderate rate.

The prosperity did last longer than I anticipated. I always expected its breakdown, but I thought it would come much sooner. I was thinking in terms of the collapse of the inflationary booms during past trade cycles. But those collapses were due to the gold standard, which put a brake on those expansions after a few years. We never had a time where a policy of deliberate expansion was unlimited by any framework of monetary order. We've come to an end only when it has been seen we cannot accelerate inflation so fast that we can still maintain prosperity.

REASON: The United States has cut inflation from 12 percent to 4.8 percent, Britain from 30 percent to 13 percent—both without Depression-type setbacks. Doesn't this offer hope that economic adjustments can be made without massive unemployment?

HAYEK: I don't know why you suggest this. It has been accomplished, very much, through extensive unemployment. I think it is certainly true that ending an inflation need not lead to that long-lasting period of unemployment like the 1930s, because then the monetary policy was not only wrong during the boom but equally wrong during the Depression. First, they prolonged the boom and caused a worse depression, and then they allowed a deflation to go on and *prolonged* the Depression. After a period of inflation like the past 25 years, we can't get out of it without substantial unemployment.

REASON: How does inflation cause unemployment?

HAYEK: By drawing people into jobs which exist only because the relative demand for the particular things is temporarily increased, and these employments must disappear as soon as the increase in the quantity of money ceases.

REASON: Yet, if the United States, for example, went through a period of temporarily high unemployment—say we have double the current rate of unemployment for one to two years—wouldn't all the automatic income-maintenance programs, such as unemployment insurance, welfare, etc., run up such an enormous bill as to bankrupt the federal government, which already runs a deficit of $50 billion or $60 billion in a so-called recovery period?

HAYEK: Yes, they probably would. There would be an enormous political struggle on the question of whether social-security benefits ought to be adapted to inflation or cut down. I don't think that you can effect a permanent cure without a substantial alteration of the social-security system.

REASON: Will the horror of financing this colossal welfare bureaucracy prove the stimulus to "shock" us into a more rational government framework?

HAYEK: No. My only hope really is that some minor country or countries which for different reasons will have to construct a new constitution will do so along sensible lines and will be so successful that the others find it in their interest to imitate it. I do not think that countries that are rather proud of their constitutions will ever really need to experiment with changes in it. The reform may come from, say, Spain, which has to choose a new constitution. It might be prepared to adopt a sensible one. I don't think it's really likely in Spain, but it's an example. And they may prove so successful that after all it is seen that there are better ways of organizing government than we have.

REASON: To avoid inflation, your prescription has been to advocate that monetary policy be pursued with the goal of maintaining stability in the value of money. Is it necessary to trust the politicians to regulate the money supply? Can't market forces adjust to correct for a gradual deflation?

HAYEK: Yes, they do occasionally. The trouble is, in the mechanical system what forces politicians is the gold standard. The gold standard, even if it were nominally adopted now, would never work because people are not willing to play by the rules of the game. The rules of the game that the gold standard requires [say] that if you have an unfavorable balance of trade, you contract your currency. That's what no government can do—they'd rather go off the gold standard. In fact, I'm convinced that if we restored the gold standard now, within six months the first country would be off it and, within three years, it would completely disappear.

The gold standard was based on what was essentially an irrational supersti-tion. As long as people believed there was no salvation but the gold standard, the thing could work. That illusion or superstition has been lost. We now can never successfully run a gold standard. I wish we could. It's largely as a result of this that I have been thinking of alternatives.

REASON: You have, at various times, championed a commodity-reserve monetary system and competition in the money supply. Are these practical alter-natives to a government controlled central banking system?

HAYEK: Yes. I have been convinced that while the idea of the commodity-reserve system is a good one, practically it is unmanageable. The idea of accumu-lating actual stocks of commodities as reserves is so complex and impractical that it just cannot be done.

Then I came to the conclusion that the necessity of actual redemption of the real commodities is only necessary if you have to place a discipline on an authority which otherwise has no interest in keeping its currency stable. If you place the issue of money in the hands of firms whose business depends upon their success in keeping the money they issue stable, the situation changes completely. In that case, there is no necessity of depending upon their obligation to redeem in commodities; it depends on the fact that they must so regulate the supply of their money that the public will accept the money for its stability. This is better than anything else.

REASON: The Keynesian economic formula seeks out a nearly perfect symbiotic relationship with the political forces of the modern welfare state. At what point can this marriage be broken? How can the Keynesians be politically defeated?

HAYEK: I really should begin with Keynes himself. Keynes despaired in the 1920s of the possibility of again making wages flexible. He came to the conclusion that we must accept wages as they are and adjust monetary policy to the existing wage structure. That, of course, forced him to say, "I don't want any restriction on monetary policy because I have to adjust monetary policy to a given situation."

But he overlooked that, at that very moment, the trade unions knew that the government was under an obligation to correct the effect of the trade-union policy, and so we get a hopeless spiral. The unions push up wages, and government has to provide enough money to keep employment at these wages, and this leads into the inflationary spiral. This came out of the practical considerations of Keynes in the short run—that we can't do anything about the rigidity of wages.

In fact, the British in the 1920s were very near success. The very painful, and silly, process of deflation was very nearly successful at the end of the '20s. Then they got frightened by the long period of unemployment. I think if they had lasted a year or two longer they probably would have succeeded.

REASON: Gunnar Myrdal, your co-winner for the Nobel Prize in 1974, recently published an article advocating the abolition of the Nobel Prize for economics, apparently as reaction to the awarding of the prize to Milton Friedman and yourself. His most remarkable statement is his reference to you regarding your "lack of concern." Specifically, that you have "certainly never been much troubled by epistemological worries."

Not only does the statement summon shock on the basis of your numerous writings on the very question of epistemology (in economics as well as in other fields), but your Nobel speech, delivered into Myrdal's own ears, centered on the subject of the methodology of economics. Is Myrdal's misstatement prompted by ignorance or malice? And is this a fair sampling of the general academic environment throughout Europe?

HAYEK: No, it is certainly a rather extreme case combined with an intellectual arrogance that, even among economists, is rare. Myrdal has been in opposition on these issues even before Keynes came out. His book on monetary doctrines and values and so on dates from the late 1920s. He has his own peculiar view on this subject which I think is wrong. His book couldn't even be reproduced now. I don't think he has ever been a good economist.

REASON: So Myrdal is not typical? The intellectual and academic environment is, on the whole, much more hospitable to your ideas?

HAYEK: Oh, much more than Myrdal, yes. And, of course, the younger generation is coming around to my sort of view. In a sense, I would say that the great problem is still a methodological one but not the one Myrdal has in mind. I believe that economics and the sciences of complex phenomena in general, which include biology, psychology, and so on, cannot be modeled after the sciences that deal with essentially simple phenomena like physics.

Don't be shocked when I call physics essentially simple phenomena. What I mean is that the theories which you need to explain physics need to contain very few variables. You can easily verify this if you look into the formula appendix to any textbook on physics, where you will find that none of the formulas which state the general laws of physics contain more than two or three variables.

You can't explain anything of social life with a theory which refers to only two or three variables. The result is that we can never achieve theories which we can use for effective prediction of particular phenomena, because you would have to insert into the blanks of the formula so many particular data that you never know them all. In that sense, our possibility both of explaining and predicting social phenomena is very much more limited than it is in physics.

Now, this dissatisfies the more-ambitious young men. They want to achieve a science which both gives the same exactness of prediction and the same power of control as you achieve in the physical sciences. Even if they know they won't do it, they say, "We must try. We ultimately will discover it." When we embark on this process, we want to achieve a command of social events which is analogous to our command of physical affairs. If they really created a society which was guided by the collective will of the group, that would just stop the process of intellectual progress. Because it would stop this utilization of widely dispersed opinion upon which our society rests and which can only exist in this very complex process which you cannot intellectually master.

REASON: In 1947 you founded the Mont Pelerin Society, an international group of free-market scholars. Has its progress pleased you?

HAYEK: Oh yes. I mean its main purpose has been wholly achieved. I became very much aware that each of us was discovering the functioning of real freedom only in a very small field and accepting the conventional doctrines almost everywhere else. So I brought people together from different interests. Any time one of us said, "Oh yes—but in the field of cartels you need government regulation," someone else would say, "Oh no! I've studied that." That was how we developed a consistent doctrine and some international circles of communication.

REASON: *U.S. News & World Report* did a special cover story last year in which they interviewed eight leading social scientists from around the world, including yourself, on the question: "Is Democracy Dying?" What I found most interesting was that several of the other thinkers seemed to be reciting passages out of *The Road to Serfdom* in identifying the current crisis as a result of the involvement of the welfare state in vast areas of our formerly private lives. Do you see this thesis gaining academic adherents? Are more intellectuals beginning to understand the fundamental conflict between liberty and bureaucracy, so to speak?

HAYEK: No doubt, yes. That the ideas are spreading, there is no doubt. What I cannot judge is what part of the intelligentsia has yet been reached. Compared with what the situation was 25 years ago, instead of a single person in a few centers of the world, there are now dozens wherever I go. But that is still a very small fraction of the people who make opinion, and sometimes I have very depressing experiences. I was quite depressed two weeks ago when I spent an afternoon at Brentano's Bookshop in New York and was looking at the kind of books most people read. That seems to be hopeless; once you see that you lose all hope.

REASON: You currently carry the torch for the Austrian school of economics, representing a great tradition from Carl Menger to Bohm-Bawerk to Ludwig von Mises to yourself. What is the most important way in which the Austrians differ with Milton Friedman and the Chicago School?

HAYEK: The Chicago School thinks essentially in "macroeconomic" terms. They try to analyze in terms of aggregates and averages, total quantity of money, total price level, total employment—all these statistical magnitudes which, I think, is a very useful approach and even quite impressive.

Take Friedman's "quantity theory." I wrote 40 years ago that I have strong objections against the quantity theory because it is a very crude approach that leaves out a great many things, but I pray to God that the general public will never cease to believe in it. Because it is a simple formula which it understands. I regret that a man of the sophistication of Milton Friedman does not use it as a first approach but believes it is the whole thing. So it is really on methodological issues, ultimately, that we differ.

Friedman is an arch-positivist who believes nothing must enter scientific argument except what is empirically proven. My argument is that we know so much detail about economics, our task is to put our knowledge in order. We hardly need any new information. Our great difficulty is digesting what we already know. We don't get much wiser by statistical information except in gaining information about the specific situation at the moment. But theoretically I don't think statistical studies get us anywhere.

REASON: You have written that the main reason that the Keynesian explanation of unemployment was accepted over the classical explanation was that the former could be statistically tested while the latter could not.

HAYEK: From that point of view, Milton's monetarism and Keynesianism have more in common with each other than I have with either.

REASON: You met Alexandr Solzhenitsyn at the Nobel ceremonies in Stockholm. How did you find him?

HAYEK: I was strongly confirmed in my very high opinion of the man. He is a very impressive figure in addition to his works. But I had no chance to argue with him because he had just come out of Russia and his capacity for communicating orally was very limited.

REASON: What validity is there in his thesis concerning the collapse of the West?

HAYEK: I think he is unduly impressed by certain superficial features of Western politics. If he believes, as he does believe, that what our politicians do is a necessary consequence of opinions generally held in the West, he really must come to that conclusion. Fortunately, I think, what the politicians do is not an expression of the profound belief of the more intelligent people in the West, and I hope Solzhenitsyn will soon discover that there are people who can see further than seems to be shown by the policies of the West.

REASON: Your teacher, Ludwig von Mises, wrote *Socialism* in 1920. It became the opening round in a controversy that is still brewing over whether a socialist economy was even logically possible. Socialist economists, particularly in Eastern Europe, have thanked Mises for his thoughtful criticisms and have generally engaged in a thought-provoking discourse with Mises, Lord Robbins, and yourself for the past half-century. What is the present state of the debate?

HAYEK: I've always doubted that the socialists had a leg to stand on intellectually. They have improved their argument somehow, but once you begin to understand that prices are an instrument of communication and guidance which embody more information than we directly have, the whole idea that you can bring about the same order based on the division of labor by simple direction falls to the ground. Similarly, the idea [that] you can arrange for distributions of incomes which correspond to some conception of merit or need. If you need prices, including the prices of labor, to direct people to go where they are needed, you cannot have another distribution except the one from the market principle. I think that intellectually there is just nothing left of socialism.

REASON: Could socialist economies exist without the technology, innovations, and price information they can borrow from Western capitalism and domestic black markets?

HAYEK: I think they could exist as some sort of medieval system. They could exist in that form with a great deal of starvation removing excess population. It's all a question of why should an economy not continue to exist? But whatever economic advance Russia has achieved was, of course, achieved by using the technology developed by the West. I know that the Russians would be the last ones to deny it.

REASON: A very interesting part of your social philosophy is that *value* and *merit* are and ought to be two distinct qualities. In other words, individuals should not be remunerated in accordance with any concept of justice, whether it be the Puritan ethic or egalitarianism. Do you find many free-market advocates falling into this thinking, that value and merit should be equated in a "truly moral society"?

HAYEK: I think there is a little shift recently as a result of my outright attack on the concept of social justice. It is now turning on the problem of whether social justice has any meaning at all and, of course, social justice is essentially based on some concept of merit. I'm afraid I have shocked my closest friends by denying that the concept of social justice has any meaning whatever. But I haven't been persuaded that I was wrong.

REASON: Well, then, why isn't there any such thing as social justice?

HAYEK: Because justice refers to rules of individual conduct. And no rules of the conduct of individuals can have the effect that the good things of life are distributed in a particular manner. No state of affairs as such is just or unjust; it is only when we assume that somebody is responsible for having brought it about.

Now, we do complain that God has been unjust when one family has suffered many deaths and another family has all of its children grow up safely. But we know we can't take that seriously. We don't mean that anybody has been unjust.

In the same sense, a spontaneously working market, where prices act as guides to action, cannot take account of what people in any sense need or deserve, because it creates a distribution which nobody has designed, and something which has not been designed, a mere state of affairs as such, cannot be just or unjust. And the idea that things *ought* to be designed in a "just" manner means, in effect, that we must abandon the market and turn to a planned economy in which somebody decides how much each ought to have, and that means, of course, that we can only have it at the price of the complete abolition of personal liberty.

REASON: Is Britain irrevocably on the road to serfdom?

HAYEK: No, not irrevocably. That's one of the misunderstandings. *The Road to Serfdom* was meant to be a warning: "Unless you mend your ways, you'll go to the devil." And you can always mend your ways.

REASON: What policy measures are currently possible to reverse the trend in Britain?

HAYEK: So long as you give one body of organized interests, namely the trade unions, specific powers to use force to get a larger share of the market, then the market will not function. And this is supported by the public because of the historic belief that in past the trade unions have done so much to raise the standard of living of the poor that you must be kind to them. So long as this view is prevalent, I don't believe there is any hope. But you can induce change. We must now put our hope in a change of attitude.

I'm afraid many of my British friends still believe, as Keynes believed, that the existing moral convictions of the English would protect them against such a fate. This is nonsense. The character of a people is as much made by the institutions as the institutions are made by the character of the people. The present British institutions contribute everything to change the British character. You cannot rely on an inherent "British character" saving the British people from their fate. But you must create institutions in which the old kinds of attitudes will be revived which are rapidly disappearing under the present system.

REASON: So there is really nothing the government can do prior to a change in public opinion?

HAYEK: You can distinguish between positive and negative moves. The government should certainly cease doing a great many things it does now. In that sense it depends upon the government ceasing to do things, and then that would open the possibility for other developments which you cannot guide and direct. Take the general complaint about British entrepreneurs being inefficient, lazy, and so on. All of this is a result of institutions. You would soon drive out the inefficient entrepreneur if there was more competition. And you would soon find that they would work hard if it was in their interest to do so. It is the set of institutions which now prevails which creates the new attitudes which are so inimitable to prosperity.

REASON: If big government is really the culprit, why do Sweden and many Scandinavian welfare states seem to be prospering?

HAYEK: Well, we mustn't generalize. Sweden and Switzerland are the two countries which have escaped the damages of two wars and have become repositories of a large part of the capital of Europe. In Switzerland, there is still some traditional instinct against government interference. Switzerland is a marvelous example where, when the politicians become too progressive, the people hold a referendum and promptly say, "No!"

REASON: Yet Sweden is reasonably successful...

HAYEK: Yes. But there is perhaps more social discontent in Sweden than in almost any other country I have seen. The standard feeling that life is really not worth living is very strong in Sweden. Although they can hardly conceive of things being different than what they're used to, I think the doubt about their past doctrines is quite strong.

REASON: From 1948 until about a decade ago, West Germany pursued pointedly free-market policies and experienced an economic recovery so vital as to be judged a "German Miracle." Yet, the Social Democrats are firmly in power today, and some American analysts have suggested that this indicates a basic flaw in the philosophy or strategy of the so-called Freiberg School, the group of free-market economists that led the "German Miracle." What mistakes did they make and what can we learn from their example?

HAYEK: First, the idea that the Germans are now governed by a socialist government is just wrong. The present German chancellor admits—perhaps not publicly, but in conversation—that he is not a socialist. Secondly, until recently, the German trade unions were led by people who really knew what a major inflation is. And, until recently, all you needed to tell German trade unionists when they made excessive wage claims is that "this will lead to inflation," and they would collapse.

The German prosperity is due, to a very high degree, to the reasonableness of the German trade-union leaders which, in turn, was due to their experience with inflation.

REASON: A fellow Austrian great, the late Joseph Schumpeter, wrote *Capitalism, Socialism and Democracy* in 1942. In that book, Schumpeter predicted the collapse of capitalism due, not to its weakness (as Marx had predicted), but due to its strengths. Specifically, the tremendous economic abundance that would flower from the capitalist seed would produce an age of bureaucrats and administrators, displacing the innovators and entrepreneurs that had made it all possible. This, in turn, would undermine the social fabric upon which capitalism rested: a widespread acceptance and respect of private property. How does Schumpeter's thesis concerning the inherent political instability of capitalism fit in with your own theories on our road to serfdom?

HAYEK: Well, there is some similarity in the nature of the prediction. But Schumpeter was really enjoying a paradox. He wanted to shock people by saying that capitalism was certainly much better but it will not be allowed to last, while socialism is very bad but it is bound to come. That was the sort of paradox he just loved.

Underlying this is the idea that certain trends of opinion—which he correctly observed—were irreversible. Although he claimed the opposite, he had, in the last resort, really no belief in the power of argument. He took it for granted that the state of affairs *forces* people to think in a particular manner.

This is fundamentally false. There is no simple understanding of what makes it necessary for people under certain conditions to believe certain things. The evolution of ideas has its own laws and depends very largely on developments which we cannot predict. I mean, I'm trying to move opinion in a certain direction, but I wouldn't dare to predict what direction it will really move. I'm hoping that I can just divert it moderately. But Schumpeter's attitude was one of complete despair and disillusionment over the power of reason.

REASON: Are you optimistic about the future of freedom?

HAYEK: Yes. A qualified optimism. I think there is an intellectual reversion on the way, and there is a good chance it may come in time before the movement in the opposite direction becomes irreversible. I am more optimistic than I was 20 years ago, when nearly all the leaders of opinion wanted to move in the socialist direction. This has particularly changed in the younger generation. So, if the change comes in time, there still is hope.

Charles Murray

Interviewed by Thomas W. Hazlett

May 1985

ast year, Charles Murray was not a household name. Today, *Newsweek* columnist Meg Greenfield suggests that if you haven't yet been "Charles Murray'd" in a political conversation, you're about the last person in the country who hasn't.

It's all because of his book *Losing Ground*. Its powerfully documented thesis is that poor blacks made rapid progress from 1950 to 1965, but these gains were halted—even reversed—during the Great Society and affirmative-action period that followed, from 1965 to 1980.

Losing Ground goes on to link a renaissance of lower-class despair to the federal interventions ostensibly on behalf of the poor, and it even suggests abolishing all welfare for able-bodied Americans of working age.

Murray's credentials lend credibility to his argument. For seven years, he was with the American Institutes for Research, a respected think tank, where he conducted program evaluations in urban education, welfare, child nutrition, adolescent pregnancy, and other social services. He is a Peace Corps alumnus with a Ph.D. from the Massachusetts Institute of Technology.

No one thought his book would have much impact; his publisher reportedly expected it to have a limited academic market. Yet *Newsweek*'s Robert Samuelson warned that Murray's haunting questions deserve hard answers. William Raspberry wrote a sympathetic *Washington Post* column called "Is the Best Welfare No Welfare?" Even in the liberal *New Republic*, a reviewer comparing *Losing Ground* with socialist Michael Harrington's *The New American Poverty* concluded that Murray's analysis "is, for better or worse, much more compelling—it has a feeling of horrible authenticity about the social and economic fortunes of poor Americans."

Murray was interviewed by *Reason* contributing editor Thomas Hazlett.

REASON: Your book *Losing Ground* is very hot right now. Why did you go into this analysis of social welfare policy?

MURRAY: My professional background consisted of evaluating specific programs the government was sponsoring in education or social services or, when I was in Thailand, rural development. So few programs accomplished anything like their ambitions, despite a lot of effort, and I just kept seeing patterns and reasons why they didn't accomplish what they were supposed to accomplish, and that led to the spin-off.

REASON: I'd like to go into some detail about the conclusions of your book. You spend a lot of time looking at three points—1950, 1965, and 1980—in your trend analysis. Could you briefly summarize your findings there?

MURRAY: There are separate chapters in the book on poverty as officially measured, unemployment, wages, occupations, education, crime, and the family. In one of these areas, namely, wages and occupations among those who have jobs, I paint a very positive portrait of blacks with jobs getting white-collar work, which they had not done before, and achieving in effect wage parity for equivalent years of education and experience. But with that single exception, the trend lines show sudden and mysterious changes for the worse, mostly in the mid-1960s. In some cases you actually had advances turn into retreat. I would argue that in education, for example, we had been seeing marked improvements for minorities and poor people up through about 1964 and suddenly that just flipped. Similarly, there is a lot of evidence that among poor people—again, especially blacks—crime had been getting lower in the 1950s and that then there was a surging rise in the 1960s. Summarizing the data, I say to the reader: You need to explain this; you have to recognize that in many important aspects of life things got worse for the poor, starting precisely when we kicked into high gear in the effort to help these people.

REASON: In 1965 you had been an architect of the Great Society programs of President Lyndon Johnson and had been very interested in solving the problems of the poor, particularly the black poor. As you note in the book, you were very optimistic about future years. What went haywire starting in the mid-1960s?

MURRAY: We had, first, a change in our attitude toward who the poor are and why they are poor or why they are ill-educated or why they commit crimes. That change consisted very simply of deciding that the system is to blame. It was logically appropriate for us to do the things we did with the Great Society programs once you granted the basic premise that the system is to blame, that it's not the fault of the people we're trying to help. Unfortunately, in the process of making those changes, we sent a terrible message to all people, but especially the young people. We said, "You don't need to feel any sense of chagrin at the situation you're in. Even if you do make an effort to try to improve your situation, it's not at all clear that it's going to do any good, because the system is so locked in against you."

REASON: You say that the rules changed between 1960 and 1980 for some people, particularly the young and particularly the poor, but not for the affluent members of society. How was it that these people on the bottom of the economic totem pole got a different message?

MURRAY: Well, let's take the classic example of welfare. In the book, I take a pair of youngsters, Harold and Phyllis—they aren't necessarily black, Oriental, or Caucasian. They don't necessarily live in the slum, but they come from low-income parents and they have average ability, average education, and average skills. In 1960, if Phyllis finds herself pregnant, her only real option is to convince Harold to marry her or give the baby up for adoption. I mean there is AFDC (Aid to Families with Dependent Children), but that's a lousy life, because it's a very small payment. There are no other sources of support. She can't get a job, because then she'll lose her benefits; and she can't live with Harold or else she will lose her benefits. Just from a very commonsense point of view, she has to do something about that situation and not try to bring up the baby herself. By 1970, 10 years later, the situation has changed drastically. She can get the equivalent of a minimum-wage income by putting together a package of AFDC, Medicaid, food stamps, subsidized housing, and the rest of it. She may now live with Harold without losing her benefits, which is an extremely important change. In all of these ways, what made sense in 1960 no longer necessarily makes sense. If she wants to be with Harold, one thing is quite clear: It would be disastrous for them to be married, because once they're married then she will lose many of these benefits. So the same young couple that very likely would have gotten married in 1960 won't get married in 1970. And a woman who very possibly would not have kept a child is now raising the child. They are responding to the reality of the world around them.

REASON: One of the most striking aspects of your book is your very meticulous outlining of the process by which one set of poor people is dispossessed in favor of another set of poor people. How did this develop, and why is it allowed to go on?

MURRAY: We decided in the mid-1960s that all poor people are the same: They are all poor. We know they're poor because we have defined a poverty line, and they're all underneath it. So that's one aspect of it. The other aspect is, if it's not your fault that you are a student who is constantly assaulting the teacher, then it becomes very awkward to *credit* the student who is sitting there and studying hard. If you give that student credit, aren't you implying that the good student has something to do with his goodness, and doesn't that force you to admit the bad student has something to do with his badness?

We simply did not think about the very large population of poor people out there who are holding down jobs and trying to raise their kids right and hate crime and think people ought to obey the law and support themselves and do well in school. They just became invisible.

REASON: This sounds like an incredibly elitist notion—I mean, to look at a block of people and to say that they are simply victims and that there are no self-reliant individuals who will or can work their way out of poverty.

MURRAY: Is it elitism or is it racism? In the mid-1960s we also had the civil rights movement, and white America was confronted with a real dilemma. In 1964 we had passed the Civil Rights Act; in 1965 we had the Voting Rights Act. We were also making available a variety of other opportunities, educational and otherwise. Yet we were confronting riots in the street, and we were also confronting an extremely violent rhetoric in which white America was being accused of still falling far short of what it owed black America.

Now don't misunderstand me. I think the civil rights movement was an extraordinarily positive development, essential and positive. But white America's reaction when we failed to satisfy black America with the Civil Rights Act was to come up against a choice. On the one hand we could say to blacks, "Look, just because you ought to have equal rights doesn't mean you can burn down cities. You try that, and we're going to throw people who do it in jail. And if your kids are failing in school, we're going to flunk them. We'll make the schooling available, but if they flunk, they flunk." Theoretically, we could have said that. Or we could say, "It's much worse than we realized. We cannot in good faith make demands on this population of people." It was also racism in the sense that there are many whites who pay lip service to programs, pay lip service to values and behaviors and other things in blacks they completely disdain when they appear in whites. We've got to recognize that and ask ourselves, "White people, just what are we up to?"

REASON: I'd like to give you a chance to respond to some critics of your central thesis. First of all, there's the argument that the economy in general took a tailspin starting in the mid to late '60s, and the downward trends you note simply followed the economy at large.

MURRAY: The changes in the indexes of unemployment occurred not at the end of the '60s, when the economy started to go bad. They occurred in 1965-67, '68, when the economy was overheated, when the overall unemployment was under 4 percent and for males in particular was under 3 percent. So it's kind of hard to appeal to a disintegrating economy to explain those trends.

REASON: What about the idea that the work force experienced a massive increase, that you had all these young people coming into the work force and crowding out people for jobs? You also had an enormous increase in the 15-25 population, which caused the great bulk of crime and overload of the schools during that period and what not. What's your response to this sort of a "demographic argument"?

MURRAY: For the economic indicators, part of the response is the same comment I made earlier. You're talking about an economy which was showing no signs of being unable to absorb people in the '60s. And on the question of crime, the increases in crime are seen even after controlling for the changing age and other demographic statistics.

REASON: Still another comment on your book is that you were attacking sort of a generic welfare, when in fact it's not welfare that's bad—it's the sort of programs we have put in place under social welfare. How do you deal with that criticism?

MURRAY: When I got to the end of the book and was trying to put together my ideal system, I was not philosophically opposed to installing a federally run system that tried to correct these things, but I could not construct a system that I believed in myself. Any system I could concoct for myself and try to imagine what would happen if it were actually put in place ran into the problem that the downward-pulling incentives were greater than the upward-pushing ones. The 19th-century British intellectuals of whom Gertrude Himmelfarb writes so fascinatingly in her book *The Idea of Poverty* were right when they dealt with the true difficulties of trying to give something to somebody and at the same time do good for them. It's ironic that we pass off as being sort of a pop-wisdom notion that you do more harm than good by trying to help people. A little bit of intellectual history would help us a lot here.

REASON: There does seem to be some realization among social-policy experts that we really have some negative incentives and some negative effects coming out of these programs, yet these programs seem totally resistant to reform. Why don't bureaucrats themselves take the initiative to reform the policies so that we're not destroying incentives for the poor?

MURRAY: They see themselves as doing precisely that. They see themselves as having evaluations of their programs and taking those evaluations and trying to improve them and so forth. I, as a person who wrote those evaluations, know that the recommendations are very seldom implemented. Even if they are implemented, however, they are recommendations within a rather narrow range of possibilities. For example, one very seldom gets recommendations to just scrap a program.

Another reason that the programs don't get changed as the evaluations go on is that people see success where I see failure—for example, in the jobs programs. The evaluations of the jobs programs do not generally show no effect at all. What they show is, on the average, about $200 per year more income for those on the program. These effects are extremely tenuous and bear no relationship to the expectations of policymakers when they started the program. But they are statistically significant and can be shown to be cost-effective if you stretch out your time horizon far enough in the future and make certain assumptions about the permanence of these changes. Policymakers look at the glass which I consider to be about an eighth full and say, "Look at this glass of milk." I look at that glass and I say, "You've only got an eighth of a glass of milk in there, and that's a failure." So there's a strong impulse on the part of these designers of programs to sustain their faith on the basis of very slender gains.

REASON: What are your specific policy suggestions in welfare, education, and crime?

MURRAY: I will begin by saying that the tenor of the last part of the book is: I'm going to lay out some moral problems for you. In the very last chapter I do this in terms of proposals. The first one has to do with affirmative action. I think we ought to strip our laws and regulations of everything that rewards or recommends or requires preferential treatment by race. I think that is one of the single most unfortunate changes of the 1960s and it is one that we can change at no cost. Then I could take on two other proposals. The first is in education, and I'd say let's give vouchers or some other form of aid to parents which enables the free market to work in education. I probably have gotten more instead of less radical on this one since I wrote the book. I am increasingly ready to junk the public school system. The reason for doing this in terms of poor people is that you have lots of parents out there who, given the opportunity, would go out and interview teachers and select schools just the way middle-class parents do when they send their kids to private schools, and they would do a very good job of it and they would finally get schools that operate on the same principles they do. Some parents won't behave that way, but my response is, how have you lost?—because the schools right now are not educating our children in the inner city.

The other proposal was the most interesting and the one that's gotten the most attention. I simply say this: I have a plan that would unquestionably make steady workers out of most people who are now considered not job-ready, which would make the numbers of illegitimate children to single teenagers plunge, and would do a number of other good things—including, by the way, restoring status to that working class that most deserves it. That proposal consists of scrapping the whole thing, getting rid of everything in the whole social welfare system. Having done that, let's look around and see what the world looks like and see what we can do to even make further improvements. And I say, well, I'll put back unemployment insurance. But once I've done that, my argument is: Just what kinds of people are left that need help that can't expect to get it through locally funded services? I would say that in this proposal perhaps the punchline comes at the end, where I've offered the choice to my readers that they would make if they knew their own children were going to be orphaned. Would they put their own children with a family that was so poor that their children would be ragged and some days would be hungry, but they would be sent to school and would be taught to value independence? Or would they put their children with parents who would not send them to school, would not teach them such values, but would have plenty of food and clothing given to them by others? To me the answer is obvious, and I'm trying to get readers to realize the ways in which they are making the other choice for other people's children.

REASON: When you refer to local services, do you mean local government services or private agencies?

MURRAY: I'm not too specific about that in the book, because I figure I antagonize people enough already by getting rid of the federal system. My own feeling is that it is very difficult even to have good municipal services because of the inherent problems in deciding who gets help and who doesn't. I believe in the free market in lots of different ways, and one of the ways I believe in the free market is that it throws forth services that are most badly needed more or less to the extent that they are needed. It also is pretty good in calibrating how to deliver those services. I don't have much faith in governments to do that.

REASON: When you say, "Throw out the whole system," you're talking everything but unemployment insurance and Social Security?

MURRAY: Yes, I don't deal with the elderly in the book, so I don't deal with Social Security. Otherwise you've stated it correctly—the whole shebang, from food stamps to AFDC and the rest.

REASON: What about the hungry children?

MURRAY: The hungry children? Well, let's talk about hungry children, if you don't like it when I say that I'd get rid of food stamps. Let's back off a minute and think about hungry children. If it is true that malnourished children in this country are predominantly youngsters who are malnourished because their parents cannot afford to give them an adequate diet, then food stamps make sense. If, however, malnourishment of children in this country is predominantly a problem of a parent who is feeding a baby on soft drinks and potato chips, to take an example that unfortunately is not drawn out of thin air—if that is the nature of the problem, then food stamps are not going to help. I submit to you as an empirical statement that the vast majority of malnourished children in this country are of the latter type. So don't talk to me about hungry children unless you are prepared to ask why they are malnourished, which is a better word than hungry, and what "generous" programs will do for them.

Furthermore, can you imagine in the absence of federal programs that a hungry child in this country is going to go on without anybody being willing to help? I'm willing to accept the responsibility that you are always going to have problems in coverage, as indeed you have problems in coverage of food stamps. But the notion that there are not going to be people ready and eager to feed hungry children is absurd and ahistorical.

REASON: The reaction to *Losing Ground* has been phenomenal. This must surprise you in terms of the depth of the commenting, but what about the tone?

MURRAY: There are some things that bother me a lot about the reactions. Those which have been critical bother me because of the number of times that reviewers have simply either not read the book or, if they have read it, have been unwilling to come to grips with what it says. For example, there is a strong impulse on the part of many of the critical people to say, well his numbers are wrong, and then to advance examples which are simply not accurate and which could be seen to be inaccurate by a careful examination of the book itself. On other grounds, occasionally I get a conservative who agrees with the book so fast, for the wrong reasons, that it scares me. I think they are agreeing because this looks like a good way of lowering their tax bill, and they really aren't that interested in the welfare of the poor and disadvantaged. The heartening reaction is among sort of the neoconservative, neoliberal, and libertarian groups who are ready to argue about a lot of these issues. I keep hearing a dialogue going on that I say to myself could not possibly have occurred five or six years ago. Right now, I think too much attention is being devoted to the final chapter and to the technical debate about whether the trends have really been that bad. But I think the guts of the book, which may have reverberations down the road defining social-policy lines, are in the chapters discussing the role of status and noneconomic rewards and the constraints that we really face in trying to develop policies that help people.

REASON: I think for me the most remarkable thing in all this reaction is that you, to my knowledge, have not been called a racist and you've been taken seriously even by the left.

MURRAY: I've been very surprised that I have not been called a racist. I expected that, and it has not happened.

REASON: So the times they are changing?

MURRAY: Maybe. I think, however, that I won't let you end on such an optimistic note. There is still a lot of inertia that says, "Let's just more or less keep on doing the same thing because it's really no skin off our nose, and it gives the feeling of doing good." So I think that when change comes, it's not going to come as a result of the Reagan administration pushing for it. It's going to come probably because people on the left, with the moral fervor they have brought to almost everything, become attached to what I see as the real problems of the poor.

REASON: Now we're going to finish up on a philosophical note here. What do we owe the poor?

MURRAY: A chance. Let me put it another way. When I am trying to decide what kind of social policy I want, I say to myself, "What would I want if I were a parent with little money trying to raise kids." I would want them to have a chance at an education. I would want there to be a job out there if I went out and looked for it hard enough. I would want to be safe in my person. I would want my children to be safe. I would want to be secure in my possessions—I guess rights of property, even though I would have very little property. After that, I really find a lot longer list of things I *wouldn't* want if I were poor. I don't want somebody coming down into my neighborhood and telling my daughter that it's okay for her to have a baby—not when I'm telling her the opposite. I don't want someone to come into the school and tell my son that it's not his fault that he's not doing well on the test. There's a whole list of things like that I look around right now and see I *would* get if I were poor.

So, what do we owe the poor? We owe them a chance, we owe them opportunities that they can make good on, with no guarantees, but most of all with no penalties for success.

REASON: Finally, you say as a general rule that compulsory transfers from one poor person to another are uncomfortably like robbery. Is there a moral element in government welfare programs?

MURRAY: Yes, I see a morality problem, but one on which I'm willing to compromise. It is my own personal view that the government has very limited rights in what it can do to me, including taking my property to use on behalf of others. And even if I'm in the middle class, for them to take money that I have earned and spend it on these programs is wrong. They don't have that right. On the other hand, when I say I'm willing to compromise, it is because, yes, I've paid too much taxes, but I still get along okay. So I'm not going to go to the barricades for that. I hope that sooner or later I can address these issues in more clearly philosophical terms. I explicitly avoided doing that in *Losing Ground,* because as soon as I do that, I am too easy to dismiss. I'm just another nut from whatever political viewpoint. If you're a liberal, you don't have to take Charles Murray seriously, because obviously he's one of those people who thinks it's like robbery if you tax people to do good. In the book, I try very hard to say to some people whose good intentions I respect, "I'm going to deal with this issue on the same terms you use and try to lead you to see that what you're doing is wrong *even as you define right or wrong."*

REASON: Your next project is going to go into this, if my inside information is correct here. What is your next step?

MURRAY: I quit the American Institutes for Research, where I formerly worked, with an idea of exploring the role of some of the noneconomic aspects of the quality of life. I want to go out there and look at how we can capture the other extremely important aspects of life, including perhaps the most elusive of all, the value of freedom. Where that will lead me, I do not know. But it ought to be interesting.

Clarence Thomas

Interviewed by Bill Kauffman

November 1987

larence Thomas, the chairman of the Equal Employment Opportunity Commission, is that Washington rarity: a genuinely independent thinker. Thomas's character was sculpted by his fierce, proud grandfather, Myers Anderson of Savannah, Georgia, who raised Clarence and his brother during the twilight years of segregation. Thomas went on to Holy Cross, where he was an angry black militant, then to Yale Law School, the Monsanto Corporation, and finally the staff of Missouri Republican Sen. Jack Danforth.

Thomas emerged as a leading critic of civil-rights orthodoxy at the Fairmont Conference of black conservatives in late 1980. He caught the Reagan administration's eye; a short stint as assistant secretary of education was followed by his 1982 nomination to head the EEOC. (He was reconfirmed in 1986.)

Under Thomas's direction, the agency—which is charged with overseeing enforcement of the panoply of job discrimination laws—has shifted its emphasis from imposing hiring goals and quotas toward protecting individual victims of discrimination. And Thomas has come under heavy fire from civil rights leaders for his heterodox views.

The liberal and conservative establishments have never quite known what to make of the man.

He is not your typical Reagan appointee: He flirted with the Black Panthers; he still respects Malcolm X; he cites the angry novelist Richard Wright and his laborer grandfather as major influences.

In a much-discussed profile in *The Atlantic,* Juan Williams recently painted Thomas as "something of a black nationalist, as well as a sad, lonely, troubled, and deeply pessimistic public servant." Thomas disagrees.

And it is true that any melancholia lies beneath a friendly, engaging disposition. His candid conversation is punctuated by loud, hearty laughs; he is reputed to be a kind boss given to philosophical discussions with his colleagues.

[Clarence Thomas was interviewed in his Washington office by Assistant Editor Bill Kauffman.]

REASON: Every Clarence Thomas profile I've ever read begins with a discussion of your grandfather.

THOMAS: We're not going to start this one that way, right?

REASON: Do you view your professional career as a vindication of his life?

THOMAS: It is a vindication of the way I was raised. Thank God I have had the opportunity to attempt to vindicate it. The thing that bothered me when I was in college was that I saw myself rejecting the way of life that got me to where I was.

REASON: What were you rejecting?

THOMAS: We rejected a very stable, disciplined environment. An environment with very strict rules, an environment that put a premium on self-help, an environment that did not preach any kind of reliance on government—there was a feeling that you had an obligation to help other people, but it didn't come from the government. For example, we lived out in the country during the summer, and so we'd shop once a month. We had chickens and hogs and corn and beans on the farm, but the staples we had to go to the grocery to get. When we came back my grandfather would go by people's houses, and he would just drop groceries on the porch. Or if we harvested something, he'd just put it there and leave. Somebody's house burned down, he'd go and start marking it off and we'd start building another house.

We rejected all of that—it was gauche. You weren't supposed to think that old-fashioned people who couldn't read and write had anything to offer.

REASON: Isn't there a danger of idealizing his environment? He felt the sting of racism, I assume, quite often.

THOMAS: Sure, there is a danger of idealizing everything. I think unfortunately we've idealized the bad, particularly about the South. The myths that are created about the South, about the way we grew up, about black people, are wrong. The things that worked have nothing to do with the things that are being offered today. We've talked more about civil rights *after* the Civil Rights Act of 1964 than we talked about it before 1964. I grew up in the midst of all that. My grandfather was very active: He put his property up to bail the protesters out. And all of us were members of the NAACP—the *local* NAACP. But my grandfather was more interested in raising a family. He had two little boys to provide for. Maybe there is a danger in idealizing. But I am defending what I know occurred, and what was important to us and what worked.

REASON: A number of scholars over the last decade or so have also been trying to revive that sort of ethos. The gray eminence of it all is Thomas Sowell. When did you first become acquainted with Sowell, and did you agree with him right away or did you think he was nuts?

THOMAS: I think initially I thought he was nuts. I was just starting Yale Law School, and someone had given me *Black Education: Myths and Tragedies*—"God, you've got to read this crazy book. This guy is out of his mind." I picked it up and flipped through it. It really went against all the things we'd been indoctrinated to believe about the radical movement and the peace movement when we were in college. So I threw it in the trash.

I went on my merry way, challenging all sorts of things but not really aligning myself with anybody or any idea. I went out to Jefferson City, Missouri—if you ever want to be deprogrammed from any kind of a cult, go to Jeff City—and I just rethought everything. A friend of mine, I'll never forget it, called me up and said, "Clarence, there's another black guy out here who is as crazy as you are. He has the same ideas that you have. There are *two* of you!"

REASON: Better not get on the same plane, right?

THOMAS: "I can't remember his name," he said. "It's Sowl or Sool or Sail or something." I said, "Oh my goodness." He said, "I've got the review of a book that he just wrote." So I immediately dropped everything I was doing and got the review of his book, *The Economics and Politics of Race.* It was like pouring half a glass of water on the desert. I just soaked it up. Then I tried to get ahold of him. I called UCLA, where he was—the word I got was nobody knew who he was. So I didn't contact him. A friend of mine noticed that he was speaking at Washington University, so I left work and went over there. He was really great. I went up to him and begged him to autograph my book.

Then he moved on to Stanford, and I bugged him. I know I bugged the man. When I got to Washington I used to hold court every morning with some of the other black staff assistants and give lectures about these things.

REASON: How were they received?

THOMAS: Let's just say it was a mixed reaction. At a point, both in Monsanto and on the Hill, there were some people who when they saw me tried to evade me: at 12:15 they were trying to catch a 12:00 plane! At any rate, I consider him not only an intellectual mentor, but my salvation as far as thinking through these issues. I thought I was absolutely insane. His book was manna from heaven.

REASON: Did you talk to him before taking the job at the EEOC? Did he have any advice?

THOMAS: Oh, I don't think Tom Sowell would tell anybody to join the administration. That's not his style. But I think his attitude has always been if it had to be done he'd prefer me to do it than somebody else.

REASON: I suspect that he might think that the EEOC ought not to exist. Why do you think that this agency should exist in a free society?

THOMAS: Well, in a free society I don't think there would be a need for it to exist. Had we lived up to our Constitution, had we lived up to the principles that we espoused, there would certainly be no need. There would have been no need for manumission either. Unfortunately, the reality was that, for political reasons or whatever, there was a need to enforce antidiscrimination laws, or at least there was a perceived need to do that. Why do you need a Department of Labor, why do you need a Department of Agriculture, why do you need a Department of Commerce? You can go down the whole list—you don't need any of them, really.

I think, though, if I had to look at the role of government and what it does in people's lives, I see the EEOC as having much more legitimacy than the others, if properly run. Now, you run the risk that the authority can be abused. When EEOC or any organization starts *dictating* to people, I think they go far beyond anything that should be tolerated in this society.

REASON: Although the EEOC does issue mandates to private employers.

THOMAS: No, not really. To some extent in the past there has been what I consider a social engineering phase of the agency. But what I believe is that if a person's individual rights or right to be a part of our economic system is violated under statute, we aggressively go after it. But we don't issue mandates to businesses that you've got to do this and you've got to do that.

REASON: Say I'm a private employer and I'm a racist, and no matter how qualified a black candidate is I won't look at him. Isn't it my right to hire whom I choose? Should the state force me to hire somebody?

THOMAS: I guess theoretically, you're right. You say, it's my property and I can do as I damn well please. I'm able to choose my wife, I can choose my employees. I can choose where I live, I can choose where I want to locate my business, the whole bit. I think, though, that we've embodied the principle of nondiscrimination because we don't have a homogeneous society. And the problem is that we had state-imposed racism in our society. We had segregation and slavery that was state-protected, state-imposed, state-inflicted. The state can't undo the harm that was done, but I feel very strongly that if there is any role for the state, it is to protect us from others.

Let's look at it from the other side. When you prevent somebody from participating in our free society and the economics of our free society, I have some real problems. That's a *right* to me.

REASON: Well it's clearly immoral to do that, but should it be illegal?

THOMAS: I'm torn. If I were to look at it theoretically, as you say, I would have to say I'd like the state out of my business. Putting it back in the context of reality, I can't say that. I have seen the devastating impact of the denial of economic opportunities to certain groups, including my race. For example, my grandfather— here was a man who worked really hard. He owned his own business 'cause he didn't want to work for anybody, and the state and other individuals ganged up to conspire against him. It sounds really nice and convenient to say that if he were in an equal bargaining position, if he possessed other options, he could have pursued those options. But when a group of whites who are not a part of government conspire to deprive him of that, what does he do?

REASON: You've said that quotas are basically for the black middle class. What do you mean by that?

THOMAS: When you look at where the real problems are among minorities in our society, particularly blacks, it's at the bottom. It's the people who are in school systems that don't educate, neighborhoods where there is a lot of crime, drugs, the whole bit. You don't see *them* being affected by a quota system at IBM or Xerox or the *Fortune* 500. They're not going to have those jobs. They're not going to be the people who go to Yale or Harvard or Princeton. They don't even come up to the line to be included. To the extent that you should have any kind of efforts, it should be for those individuals who are on the bottom. Help the people who need help most, and don't just feed them this pablum of welfare and leave them in neighborhoods that are riddled with crime, where nobody would start a business or would go to try to live. Don't shuttle them off into public housing, which in some instances amounts to concentration camps.

REASON: Is that the nub of your criticism of the establishment civil rights movement today—that it's essentially upper-middle-class blacks who've made it, presuming to speak for people on the bottom?

THOMAS: I would not characterize it as the nub of my criticism. I think it's really out of touch with reality. I came from the people that they're leading; I didn't come from the leadership ranks. I came from among the people I'm most concerned about. So did Thomas Sowell, so did Jay Parker, so did Walter Williams. We lived in the neighborhoods that they've created myths about. My grandfather—that's the guy that got me out. It wasn't all these people who are claiming all this leadership stuff.

It really bugs me that someone will tell me, after I spent 20 years being educated, how I'm supposed to think. That is offensive to me; it was offensive to me in the second grade, so you *know* it's offensive to me now, almost 39 years old. And I don't think that government has a role in telling people how to live their lives. Maybe a minister does, maybe your belief in God does, maybe there's another set of moral codes, but I don't think government has a role.

REASON: So would you describe yourself as a libertarian?

THOMAS: I don't think I can. I certainly have some very strong libertarian leanings, yes. I tend to really be partial to Ayn Rand, and to *The Fountainhead* and *Atlas Shrugged.* But at this point I'm caught in the position where if I were a true libertarian I wouldn't be here in government.

REASON: In the early days the Black Panthers seemed to be very much decentralists, power to the neighborhood, and all that. You were sympathetic to them, weren't you?

THOMAS: I was sympathetic to virtually all groups that wanted to get away from the old system. And I thought that the NAACP and the Urban League and CORE and the rest of those groups were not aggressive enough. The Panthers offered, for some of us who were young and hot-blooded and ill-tempered, another way.

REASON: In retrospect was there something good about the Panthers?

THOMAS: I really don't know. At that time, 19, 20 years old, we thought there was a lot. The positive was that it did keep us thinking about change. The unfortunate thing was that it wrapped up a lot of Marxist-Leninism and a lot of violence. But I was also partial to the Black Muslims, primarily because of their belief in self-help.

REASON: It's odd that Malcolm X is not a conservative hero, isn't it? He was very good on self-help.

THOMAS: Yes, but he had some very strong things to say about whites. I've been very partial to Malcolm X, particularly his self-help teachings. I have virtually all of the recorded speeches of Malcolm X.

REASON: Then you still see him as a hero?

THOMAS: Let's say I'm a little bit more discriminating in what I accept and what I reject. There is too much sometimes of the antiwhite rhetoric. There is a lot of good in what he says, and I go through it for the good.

REASON: Any writers who were really influential to you when you were young and still are?

THOMAS: Richard Wright. I would have to put him number one, numero uno. Both *Native Son* and *Black Boy* really woke me up. He captured a lot of the feelings that I had inside that you learn how to suppress. His novel *Outside,* which is his autobiographical flirtation with communism, was really good for me, because when I got to college you had a lot of radical groups that were trying to attract black students who were upset—and I was *really* upset—and that novel sort of prepared me to not be swept away by this kind of recruitment.

REASON: There was a very interesting article—I'm not sure if you thought it was interesting—by Juan Williams in *The Atlantic* where he called you a black nationalist. Do you agree with that?

THOMAS: Nah. I think Juan stopped short—he got halfway to the destination and got off the train. He is certainly an excellent writer and a good person, but

I'm not a nationalist. I have been angry enough in my life, and there are some points where I'm sure my attitudes approached black nationalism. I'm certain you could say the same thing about Malcolm X. But again, a lot of that grows out of that anger and that frustration and the feeling that you've got to do something, and you hear certain groups beckoning you on. You heard the Panthers beckoning you on. You heard the socialists or communists beckoning you on. You heard the radical students and the anarchists beckoning you on. The conservatives really didn't make an effort—they were hoarding the status quo.

REASON: Are there any areas where you think today that the civil rights establishment is doing really good work? By that I mean NAACP and...

THOMAS: No.

REASON: None?

THOMAS: I can't think of any. I'm the wrong person to ask, because of the malice with which they have treated me. There were grand opportunities for them to focus on the proper education of minority kids, the kids who are getting the worst education, and instead they're talking about integration. God—I went to segregated schools. You can really learn how to read off those books, even if white folks aren't there. I think segregation is bad, I think it's wrong, it's immoral. I'd fight against it with every breath in my body, but you don't need to sit next to a white person to learn how to read and write. The NAACP needs to *say* that.

You've got a situation recently where the president of the NAACP or one of his spokespersons is defending a kid who punched out a teacher. Give me a break! How in the hell are the kids going to learn, if they can punch out the teacher? I would have *died* if I'd done something like that and I went back home to my grandfather—literally died. You've got to have some standards of morality, some strong positive statements about expectations—and those organizations could do that. Instead, they spend their time telling minority kids that it is hopeless out here. Why is it hopeless? Because Ronald Reagan is making it hopeless.

When Ronald Reagan is gone, why are you going to tell them that it's hopeless? Because the government isn't spending enough money. It will always be hopeless if that's the reason. You don't have any control over that. What you do have control over is yourself. They should be telling these kids that freedom carries not only benefits, it carries responsibilities. You want to be free, you want to leave your parents' house? Then you've got to earn your own living, you've got to pay your own mortgage, pay your own rent, buy your own car, and pay for your own food. You've got to learn how to take care of yourself, learn how to raise your kids, how to go to school and prepare for a job and take risks like everybody else.

REASON: Why do you think the NAACP has never really picked up on any of the opportunity themes that Walter Williams sketched in *The State Against Blacks,* like taxicab regulations? Why do you think they seem uninterested in things like that?

THOMAS: They are pro-government. It's simple. My grandfather had an opportunity to make a lot of money during the building boom after the Korean War and World War II. He couldn't get the license. These are things that I didn't have to read *The State Against Blacks* to know. We saw it. A black person could not obtain an electrician's license. So what they would do is wire an entire house and then pay maybe $100 to a white electrician to connect the wire from the post to the box—about a two-minute job.

REASON: I guess it's dangerous to speak about people as a block or a monolith, but do you think a large number of black Americans share your instinctive aversion to government?

THOMAS: I think that a lot of black Americans have a lot of different opinions on a lot of different things. But I know that the vote of 9 out of 10 black Americans for the Democratic Party or for leftist kinds of policies just is not reflective of their opinions. The Republican Party and the conservatives have shown very little interest in black Americans and have actually done things to leave the impression among blacks that they are antagonistic to their interests. Even as someone who's labeled a conservative —I'm a Republican, I'm black, I'm heading up this organization in the Reagan administration—I can say that conservatives don't exactly break their necks to tell blacks that they're welcome.

REASON: Is the solution for guys like you to assume really public profiles, maybe not as Republicans, but as independents or something and run for office?

THOMAS: I don't think we'd ever win. Certainly the blacks won't vote for you—at least not now. And whites...I'd have to say there is still racism in our society, and there are still attitudes based on race. So I wouldn't expect that that would work anytime soon. We've gotten beyond the point where we were totally ignored—"They're just pimples on the horizon. They'll disappear and everything will be all right. It's a passing fad, like hula hoops or pet rocks." We *haven't* gone away. And I think the best thing we can do is not to go away. One of the things that it's forced us to do is to think through everything. I don't know one of my friends who is considered a conservative who has not had to go back and thoroughly think through everything. You do a lot of soul-searching—'cause we are not going to win any popularity contests.

REASON: You seem uncomfortable with the label "conservative."

THOMAS: I'm willing to accept it for the sake of discussion, so I don't have to spend a whole lot of time on definitions, etc. But I'm just Clarence Thomas. I'm an individual. Some people say, well, you're something. Well, I'm Clarence Thomas, okay? I'm black, I know it. I'm a male, I know that. I know my biography up to a point, and these are my beliefs now. If that adds up to your view of what a conservative is, fine.

REASON: You took this job in government, and all of a sudden people are saying terrible things about you—are you used to that now? Does it bother you when you go home at night?

THOMAS: It doesn't bother me when I go home. Early on—you have to remember I was thrown on this scene. After we got back from the Fairmont Conference in 1980, it was the first time I'd had any kind of articles written about me. All of a sudden my views, or at least the journalistic synopsis of my views, are in a major paper, *The Washington Post*. I wasn't used to this kind of thing. I never ran for office. I rarely raised my hand in college. And suddenly, my name is in the paper. And to hear the things they said about me—Carl Rowan and some of the others. It does affect you. But it is so bad and so off-base that you just have to shake your head.

Winston Churchill was asked, Why did you become prime minister? He said, "Ambition." Well, why did you stay so long? He said, "Anger." That's one of the reasons I went back up for reconfirmation. You're not going to run me out of town. I'm going to stay right here. If I'm not reconfirmed, I'll drive a truck. I'll work in a gas station. I'll work at McDonald's.

REASON: I guess it was at the Fairmont Conference that you said, "If I ever went to work for the EEOC or did anything directly connected with blacks, my career would be irreparably ruined. The monkey would be on my back to prove that I didn't have the job because I'm black." I assume you've changed your mind?

THOMAS: No. I haven't changed my mind.

REASON: The monkey on your back, is it?

THOMAS: I'll be honest with you. When I was asked to go to the Department of Education as well as come here, you're dang right I was insulted. What other reason besides the fact that I was black? But then I had to ask myself, if you don't do it, what are you going to say about these issues in the future? If you had an opportunity to get in there and you didn't do it, what standing do you have to complain? As one friend put it to me, "Clarence, put up or shut up." And I wasn't going to shut up. [Laughter] There is no way anybody was going to shut me up.

And since I've been here, I've thought a lot about the rights of the individual. If the things that are being done to the individual in this city were being done by one person, we'd all think that we were living under a dictatorship. We'd all be thinking in a rebellious way about how we were going to get out from under this dictatorship. The erosion of freedoms is incredible.

REASON: Should we be thinking about rebellion?

THOMAS: Well, I'm not an anarchist. But I tell you what—we should all be thinking about going to Sears and getting ourselves a tent and a survival kit! [Laughter]

I do think that our freedoms are at risk. There are very few people in the private sector and the public sector who are talking about freedoms. We're talking about interest groups, we're talking about issues, we're talking about your piece of the action, my project, this building, that building. What about freedom? What about the system or the environment that allows us to mind our own business? To live our lives, raise our families? There isn't a whole lot of talk about that.

REASON: This isn't really a big-picture city, is it?

THOMAS: Ultimately somebody has to think about that. What is there about this country that will lead people to crawl through sewers, get on innertubes and float across miles of water, to sneak out in the middle of the night, to cram in under trucks and buses and other things, risk their lives going across mountains, etc.— what is it about this country that people will do all those things to come in, and what is it about the Soviet Union or Cuba or the Eastern Bloc countries that would force people to do those same things to get out?

It's not so much that we're not asking ourselves the big-picture questions— we're not asking ourselves the simple questions about what is good about our society. And whether or not we are preserving the health of our society. Are we going to wait until we lose that health to be concerned about it?

PART FOUR

THE MARKETPLACE OF IDEAS

The Viewer Is the Loser

By Thomas W. Hazlett

July 1982

Nobody thinks of drawin' the distinction between honest graft and dishonest graft....There's an honest graft, and I'm an example of how it works. I might sum up the whole thing by sayin' "I seen my opportunities and I took 'em."

Just let me explain by examples. My party's in power in the city, and it's goin' to undertake a lot of public improvement. Well, I'm tipped off, say, that they're going to lay out a new park at a certain place. I see my opportunity and I take it. I go to that place and I buy up all the land I can in the neighborhood. Then the board of this or that makes its plan public, and there is a rush to get my land, which nobody cared particular for before.

Ain't it perfectly honest to charge a good price and make a profit on my investment and foresight? Of course, it is. Well, that's honest graft.

—George Washington Plunkitt, circa 1905

Look at that pathetic prefabricated cube sitting there in your living room. All those wires, transistors, electrodes—and to what high purpose? BJ and the Bear chasing CHiPs for a glimpse of Farrah Fawcett's hair or Donahue's smirk or Loni Anderson's "profile" or Tom Snyder's haw-haw-haw-haw so Real People can Be a Pepper and say Hello Larry on the Love Boat. Is this the *best* substitute for a little dose of some late-night sleep-inducer?

Perhaps your mind has wandered to a far-off land, where a dapper Latino and his pint-sized deputy sit you before what looks in every respect like your television set—until you turn it on. "Wow!" you say (but not, "That's Incredible"). For you find, not two to seven channels of the kind of programming that gave the boob tube its name, but scores of simultaneous program choices, of programs that only a *few thousand* people are expected to watch; and you discover at your fingertips a mysterious two-way communication capability to use this machine as a home security system or to shuffle money out of your savings and into your checking or to pick up a few shares of IBM or to vote some rascals into office. Only on *Fantasy Island?*

If you're one of America's 18 million cable-television subscribers, you know better. But what you, and the three-quarters of the nation's television victims who do not get cable, might not know of is the enormous battle over cable television *off*stage. Because every facet of cable—who provides it, who gets it, what you see, and what you pay—is the prize in a frantic scramble by big-time political interests

153

in every city hall in America. From Pittsburgh to Houston to Los Angeles, the cable-television business is proving that a brilliant consumer-pleasing innovation is only as good as the political system it serves.

The Shape of the Era to Come

When one samples the delicious menu cable is cooking up, it is easy to see the records being made in the race to feed. The cable technology bonanza has ignited the creation of whole networks to deliver nonstop sports (ESPN and USA Network); 24-hour news (Ted Turner's interesting Cable News Network will soon be challenged by Westinghouse Broadcasting); first-run movies (by several firms, including Home Box Office, Showtime, and Movie Channel); la-di-da cultural events on no less than five ritzy networks (including CBS Cable, ABC Arts, and Bravo) that have already swiped, by outbidding, half of PBS's national programming (including the highly acclaimed BBC menu); a batch of old-movie stations; exotic/erotic programming stations; an educational all-children's service without sex or violence (Nickelodeon); an Italian-American network that broadcasts movies starring Marcello Mastroianni, Sophia Loren, and Gina Lollabrigida; Black Entertainment Television; Spanish-speaking networks; and even channels where representatives of consumer product manufacturers are invited to demonstrate and discuss their goods for 5 to 30 minutes at a time.

And entertainment is but the opening volley in the cable revolution. As *Fortune* magazine notes, "The television set will eventually do other things besides sit there passively, waiting to be watched. Companies are already testing data-transmission devices and energy-load management systems that will all be hooked up through the TV set by cable. If properly instructed, your set may soon be capable of turning on your washing machine at 3:00 AM, when the demand for power is low. Indeed, as the expansion of television continues, these last thirty years may be nostalgically remembered as those days when the television set was just a television set."

Two-way transmissions now in production will permit thousands of voters in a community to cast ballots simultaneously on local referendums or other issues, and systems now in limited use bring home security service, in conjunction with a private security firm in the neighborhood, into a new generation altogether. The "electronic cottage" hi-tech world will, as reported in *Business World*, "fundamentally change the way people shop, bank, work and communicate, since it will permit them to do all of these things without leaving their living rooms. They will be able to call up on their video screens the news on any selected topic, as well as a wide variety of continuously updated information on such subjects as airline schedules, and stock and commodity prices."

Cable-TV systems require wires to be strung throughout the audience area from hub receiving stations that capture signals from satellites. These cables connect individual television sets to the cable system just as phone lines connect your telephone to Ma Bell's circuits. Traveling either below the ground or above, often utilizing existing telephone or utility poles, these lines ordinarily deliver the customer between 30 and 110 channels.

(Over-the-air pay television, on the other hand, emits signals from a transmitter placed in the locality and "descrambled" by an electronic receiver that plugs into the television set and must be bought or rented from the local "subscription television" (STV) company. Pay television channels are sold one at a time and are generally limited by regulation to only one or two channels in each market area. And finally—if we can ever use that word in *this* industry—there is the ultrarevolutionary, super-space-age, mega-hip innovation just now peeking around tomorrow's corner: the direct broadcast satellite (DBS), whereby the individual customer can purchase a parabolic dish antenna for a couple of hundred bucks and tune in *hundreds* of television channels (perhaps more?), direct from where only space shuttles roam.

It is regulatory manipulations, however—a complicated labyrinth of incentives and disincentives—that will, when all is said and done, steer the course of the era to come. This direction will not be *planned* by but will definitely be *influenced* by the political agencies: While changing the course of the technology, the "authorities" still have little idea where their hands-on policy will take the industry and even less appreciation of the forces of science and consumer demand that will compete with their wishes in determining this unknowable outcome.

Popping the Chains at the FCC

There are two broad layers of regulation in the cable TV industry: local and national. Each cable franchise must gain the approval of the local jurisdiction in which it operates; on a national scale, the Federal Communications Commission (FCC) must decide what the various communications services will be allowed to do and not to do.

The national market is subject to the actions of Congress and federal regulatory agencies. The FCC has territorial "rights" to regulate the emerging technologies and has acted with characteristic energy and foresight in exercising those rights. Their first move in this field was to throttle pay TV for a decade. Between 1968 and 1972, for example, the FCC buried cable (or prohibited companies from burying *their* cable) in the 100 largest metropolitan markets and slapped on such burdensome requirements (including a ban on movies that were less than three years old) that cable was grounded almost everywhere else, as well.

In a delicious irony, however, the FCC now has taken the lead, along with that great political fundraising group, the U.S. Congress, in *pushing* cable deregulation and television competition. In an FCC study released in late 1980, the agency found that efforts to introduce higher-quality programming and greater diversity through direct federal regulation of television had failed. The two-year, 3,700-page investigation conceded that FCC policies had "served effectively to limit television to a system dominated by three over-the-air advertiser-supported networks." Commission Chairman Charles Ferris responded enthusiastically: "We should actively use these findings as mandates to encourage more competition and new services; in short, to create more choices for the viewing public."

Ferris, a Carter appointee, has since been replaced by Mark Fowler, a Reagan appointee. And it is Mr. Fowler's concurring opinion that, where his predecessors began the task of "deregulating," he will finish the job by "unregulating." The FCC has recently loosened the rules governing over-the-air pay television, for example;

is beginning to license low-power TV stations; and is talking, over network opposition, of unleashing direct broadcast satellite.

The great lure for the national deregulators is the rich cornucopia of product that awaits. Considering solely the entertainment aspects of the medium, television has long been the turf of none but the most subterranean of intellects. Nothing intrinsic to the electronic box as television set mandates this, however. What has short-circuited your TV set's foray into the world of high drama has been the FCC soldering of the wires.

TV critics often mistakenly attribute the forum's antisophistication to the commercial ownership of the companies who provide the offerings. But Shakespeare sells well in the book stores, as do lesser literary virtuosos, and these saints of the homogenized aesthete simply burst forth in every other *commercial* medium that has escaped regulatory strangulation: newspapers, magazines, movies, plays— even AM/FM radio, which the FCC has grasped, but not completely gagged.

The Great Leap Forward taken by cable technology is to expand our number of programming options radically beyond the point where FCC restrictions on VHF, or even UHF, channels can have much impact. The difference between 3-channel service under the FCC's restrictions and 50 channels under cable's New Possibilities technology is nothing other than a dramatic reduction in the *opportunity cost* of using up any one channel. When consumers have but three choices, a network that broadcasts Luciano Pavarotti at the Met is throwing away the opportunity to keep tens of millions of customers watching some lesser, more broadly appealing fare. Big audiences are still important with the 50-channel option, and the most production money will characteristically be spent on the highest-rated shows, but *opportunity* costs are a fraction of what they were. Using one station for opera becomes feasible when it does not have to outbid all but *two* competitors; now it only has to outbid all but 49. *Reader's Digest* is top 3; *Psychology Today*, top 50—deregulation *is* diversity.

Science, in short, has de-FCC'd television. As one city official familiar with the new technology puts it, "Cable TV's success lies in its ability to provide steak and specialty foods to smaller numbers of people in numerous categories," as opposed to the "McDonald's and Jack-in-the-Box" fare of the network big three. The message is so compelling that the federal regulators—always the last to know—have caught the spirit and now rush to pop the chains and free the competition.

Competition the Political Way

Yet, with the future so well received by the feds, the dividends from this space-age fantasyland on the end of your TV's "on" switch are being pilfered at the *local level*. The very opportunities that offer an explosion in consumer choice offer local authorities—and those who have pull with the authorities—a chance to snare a prime-time piece of the action. Just as the FCC has abandoned its restriction of output, local governments have jumped in to fill the "void" with their own.

The cable franchise permit is the *how*. While most localities do not issue "exclusive" franchises, they do issue only one. They call it a nonexclusive franchise so that they have the option to issue another "nonexclusive" cable license should the first company not perform to specifications, but the understanding, always implicit, is that no other will be issued unless a serious breach occurs. The reason, incidentally, that one must have a city or county permit to put in a cable system is that such a project entails digging below public streets or stringing cable on utility poles. It is from their jurisdiction over government-owned streets and rights-of-way, not by any authority over the provision of television services, that the locals are permitted to permit.

It is only recently that a tiny shadow of a doubt has been cast over this power to regulate. In January the Supreme Court threatened to upset the applecart with a decision that the city of Boulder, Colorado, may be sued under federal antitrust laws for holding up a cable firm's planned expansion. But the last word is not in yet: A lower court is still to decide whether the Boulder city council actually winked at the antitrust edifice in this instance.

The cable industry has been mute about the decision—but not the city *pols*. Within days, the National League of Cities had raised cries of outrage and promised to run straight to the state capitals or even to the U.S. Congress to obtain relief from the Supreme Court position.

Why the fuss? All the uninitiated bystander need do, in order to understand the locals' panic at the idea of having the regulatory rug snatched from under them, is to look at the "competitive" process by which franchises are awarded.

Let's listen in on one such award hearing: for the Scottsdale, Arizona, cable franchise ("nonexclusive," naturally), October 17, 1981. Held at the Scottsdale Senior Center, the hearings pit eight fierce competitors against one another. They have all submitted their bids to the city council, and the council staff has made its ratings and recommendations. Today, the task for each competitor is to respond to these findings and to sell the cable committee on the merits of the best proposal.

There are a lot of blue suits in this room, and, as could be expected, where you find blue suits you find lawyers, lots of lawyers. Most of these lawyers come from far away, but they all seem to know the local community, and to know—and work with—a lot of people who *are* the local community. In fact, the *Scottsdale Pilot*, only two days prior, boasts a big advertisement for Capital Cities Cable: "Meet Our Local Stockholders," it beams.

The public is invited and, as always, the "public" is in attendance, sort of. *Representatives* of the public are in attendance, that is, and they can ravage an applicant. To wit:

QUESTIONER: You show [in the franchise application] only six hours of local programming per week, which is considerably lower than any of the other applicants.

APPLICANT (Times-Mirror Cable): Yesterday [a city official] told us that nobody watches it. Times-Mirror says that the demand just isn't there right now. If the demand were to rise, we would up our local programming.

QUESTIONER (different from before): Do you mean that you would increase your programming if it would help sell more subscriptions?

APPLICANT (Times-Mirror Cable): Yes. If there were an interest in this, we would be right there to expand our coverage.

Times-Mirror did not win the Scottsdale franchise. And how could they?

They weren't even playing in the ballpark. Scoring in the cable-monopoly game works just as in any other in the economic marketplace: goods go to the highest bidder. But make no mistake about the difference between bidding for consumers with actual product on the barrelhead and bidding for a franchise monopoly with a "proposal for community service." In the former, consumers view the competition and volunteer their dollars for the selection that they believe fulfills their own needs. The political franchise authority, however, gets to make quite a different choice: What company's offer *should* the citizens of my community want to pay for?

And so it is that local government regulation does not eliminate competition in the cable business; it simply shifts the competitive battleground. Instead of outdoing one another to entice customers, firms fight to lure the politically powerful. The rivalry is just as intense, but it leads to a vastly different set of demands being satisfied.

A Not-So-Natural Monopoly

Before viewing the high drama of the political competition for a monopoly franchise, an intermission is in order. For it might occur to the mere and actual consumers of television services to ask *why* they must settle for one and only one cable company. Must the coming of cable be as a monopoly franchise?

While the important word in this question appears to be *monopoly*, the key word is, in fact, *franchise*. The presumption of local regulators is that cable is, by its technical circumstances, a "natural monopoly"—the high capital investment makes it uneconomic for a second cable company to compete in an overlapping market. Even if this is so, however, it does not automatically mean that a *franchise* should be granted to the monopolist. The industry argues for such a grant on the grounds that, absent an exclusive entitlement, the necessary investment capital would not be forthcoming. On the other hand, the same industry sources claim that, for a second firm, the costs are not justified by the returns from being number two, meaning that the market would only support one cable firm per area, and a de facto monopoly is assured. So why must we enforce a monopoly where monopoly is a certainty?

If the logic appears shaky, the empirical test of the proposition is devastating. The necessary and sufficient counterexample to the hypothesis is visible for viewing in the metropolis of Phoenix, Arizona. Dissatisfied with the one "nonexclusive" cable franchise it had issued in 1976 to American Cable Television—the firm had failed to connect more than a small percentage of the city to the cable—the city council voted in June 1980 to allow two more firms into the market. Cross Country Ltd., and Camelback Cablevision eagerly jumped in to compete head-to-head with American—established with a four-year head start. ("Natural monopolies" are presumably immune to such upstart rivalry.)

Another nearby city, Paradise Valley, also dissatisfied with American Cable's progress and service, decided to invite Camelback Cablevision to compete in offering subscriber service, and it has now laid cable there on the very *same* streets as American Cable. Nationwide, better than 25 cities have head-to-head cable competition. Must cable companies be given monopolies to induce them to lay cable?

158

(One need not be a ruthless cynic to understand why local officials would argue in favor of their regulating cable-TV content, prices, service, and the rest, but the industry argument for monopoly franchising is a thinly veiled plea for protectionism. Regulation is the ever-popular quid pro quo for acquiring monopoly rights. One particularly brassy cable company executive told me that he favors "deregulation" of cable television. When I asked if he thought such open competition would be good for the industry, he unabashedly corrected me: "No, I'm talking about removing the ability of local governments to *regulate*; I am not talking about repealing our monopoly franchises." Quite a "deregulation.")

Bruce Merrill, president of American Cable Television in Phoenix, remains bitter, outspoken, and angry over the city's decision to allow competition within the franchise area. Two city council members championed competition on the theory that monopoly is bad for consumers. Merrill, however, claims that, even though he received a "nonexclusive" franchise, allowing two more cable companies in the market is ill-conceived. "It's destructive and nonproductive," he feels, "and eventually there will be only one cable system anyway." He boasts that his firm is sure to outperform the others and, ultimately, buy them out. So why not determine this winner-take-all contest by open, market competition? "Do you use swords or pistols?" rejoins Merrill.

The question is anything but rhetorical. For, while the eventual winner of the bloody cable-fest may be the same under either the exclusive franchise arrangement or the free-market rivalry method, the means to the end will be diametrically different. In fact, the essential reason why Mr. Merrill lost his "understanding," as he puts it, that his 15-year franchise would be exclusive is that the permit, issued in 1976, was close to a no-strings agreement. American did make minor concessions to the city of Phoenix, including provision of a two-way energy communications system; but the firm had little incentive to offer more because there had been *no competition* to *obtain* the franchise. It was Merrill's misfortune that, because he was so far ahead of his competition, the city was unable to force him to promise much in the way of politically demanded cable services. The monopoly he got was not one he shared. That was Mr. Merrill's sin.

Divvying Up the Dividends

Do not waste time scrounging the cable industry for those who "ideologically" favor open competition. Any such rotten eggs have long since been sorted out by the selection process of the market. (One can imagine the amazing number of successful franchising operations such a matador would bag, lecturing city councils on the need for competitive enterprise and the supremacy of consumer demand.) What all local politicians who regulate cable and all firms who provide cable "believe" in is: The Community. The proud advertising display of the U.S. Cable corporation (not to be confused with the equally patriotic American Cable Television), provides but one example:

In every neighborhood, town, or village—where U.S. Cable is granted the franchise—the community is all. The company reserves channel after channel for strictly local programming, welcoming the participation of the best talents around—community leaders, artists, entertainers, educators, newscasters. What-

ever is happening nearby—a high school band concert or track and field event, a students' play, local council meetings, a holiday parade, every kind of civic event—is wired right into our subscriber's living room.

But, while The Community may be all, the important citizens who get to decide *on behalf* of that community have some definite ideas about who all is to count as The Community. The "average citizen" (you know the sop) is denounced at franchise hearings as "one of the 99 percent who only care about their movies and sports," and the chosen representatives, of course, are out to get something quite distinct. The Scottsdale hearings show what "Community" means to them.

Take, for instance, the proposal of Camelback Cablevision. Camelback was not chintzy. An "executive summary" of its proposal runs to 22 pages and is elegantly produced in glossy, multicolored artistry on the outside and slick, well-groomed copy on the inside. The presentation is smooth and professional, explaining the proposition of cable monopoly so surefootedly that even a city council member could comprehend it. Beginning with a citation from Alvin Toffler, the pitch wastes little time on what Camelback's 104 channels might serve the *viewers*; by page five, we embark on the section, "Camelback and the City of Scottsdale in Partnership." At this point, were this presentation transmitted via cable, we'd be ransacking the other 103 channels for a program of interest.

Here the would-be monopolist dishes out huge portions to The Community. The kitchen will be "a fully equipped $400,000 local origination studio in North Scottsdale" and a "$140,000 mobile production unit with 2 color cameras [and] a staff of 27 operational and technical personnel." And the menu—what a meal! "Programs on Scottsdale history...candidate debates during [local] election campaigns...local news shows...fire prevention and safety programs...musical programs presented by Scottsdale musical groups and societies." Who will do the cooking? A board of directors with, as Camelback puts it, *representatives from various segments of the Scottsdale community as follows:* Religion, Education (Two), Social Service, Health, Business-manufacturing/retail/service, Hospitality-tourism-motel/hotel, City Government, Public Service (fire/police), Chamber of Commerce, Arts, Members at Large (Two).

Their budget? A cool $26 million over the course of the 15-year franchise, as compared to a 3-year capital cost of $31 million to build the whole system.

Don't turn the channel, because there's so much more! A "professional arts/cultural channel" will broadcast all the culture occurring in Scottsdale. In case of any lulls in activity at the Scottsdale Center for the Arts, roving minicams—blessed with $225,000 in supersonic videotronics courtesy of the Camelback philanthropists—will be aimed at local art galleries to stir up those pesky little cultures residing in The Community.

Beyond this, way beyond, stretches Camelback's 104-station commitment (although, it may fairly be noted, this is strictly conditional, for the deal's all off if Camelback loses its *monopoly* interest in The Community). They take us to new, oxygen-thin heights with such contributions as whole channels checked for Public Library Access, Senior Citizens Access, Cultural Interconnect, Youth Access, Business Access/Professional Arts, Health Access, Public Schools (2 channels), Community College (2), Arizona State University (not even in Scottsdale), Educational Access (2), Women, the Christian Broadcasting Network, and Local Government—with "interviews of City staff explaining their various department functions, services and office hours" or "Mayor/Council Breakfast programs" or "Question & Answer 'call-in' talk shows with the Mayor, Council Members, and City staff members." Is the reception getting clearer? Is the picture coming into focus?

Now no one will seriously argue that *none* of the foregoing services are without justification from the perspective of those consumers who will shoulder the burden of subsidizing them. Indeed, some of the above (particularly the Christian Broadcasting Network) have proven their ability to accrue revenues in excess of their costs (also known, somewhat more earthily, as "profits").

Yet the undeniable pattern that takes shape under cable regulation is that, taken as a whole, breathtakingly vast harvests of plump cable fruit are being plopped on the tables of the politically ravenous. In an almost divinely created conspiracy against the public interest, a very private "public interest" is being decided by a triumvirate of the potential cable monopolists who must offer the fruit if they are to go from potential to actual, the political decisionmakers who may choose the recipient of the franchise monopoly gift, and those well-placed, well-connected individuals who desire to be an active part in The Community. The politicians have their own tastes and preferences, naturally, and would try to indulge them, but they do not operate in an isolation chamber. They have their constituencies to accommodate, such as the movers and shakers in Religion, Education (Two), Social Service....

Anticonsumer Coalition

Cable TV may have lowered the costs of television air time; it has not reduced the costs of television air time to zero. Each channel sliced and diced from the community for The Community is one less by which the paying viewers will be treated to what they would in fact pay for. The regulations prompting cable systems to shift resources to political pressure groups that are unwilling to bear the costs by outbidding competing consumers for the use of such resources is clearly a wealth transfer. It is a tax, in the first part, on those who pay to support the cable's profitable services. It is a tax in the sense that consumers are prevented from patronizing other firms that might offer, in their view, better cable services at a more reasonable price. This is a monopoly tax. Some of the "tax" revenues are deposited by the cable operator, and the rest are sent right over to The Community via provision of the very services that they would like to utilize but aren't quite willing to pay for (at least not so long as they can get someone else to do that for them). Confusing as the game becomes, that is all there ever is to the joust of cable television franchising: who promises the biggest buffet on the other guy's tab.

So rock-solid is the sympathy and support for the abstract concept of "programming for senior citizens" or free air time for the "Chicano Orphans Association" that one cable regulator claims she has "never heard anybody stand up and say we didn't need public access channels." At the very same time, she paradoxically observes that "I have heard people say that they've had public access in their town for five years, and nobody has come in to use it."

161

Recent franchising battles have seen political pressure to "correct" this situation by increasing the franchise's ante in the form of more-expensive, more-sophisticated production equipment. Cable franchisers now "bid" against each other with all kinds of fancy studio and "roving" television production units to make local origination/public access easier. But keep your eye on the bouncing ball. Those production facilities *will* be paid for, not by viewers of the channels they create programming for (else the firm would offer these services in the absence of any franchise approval process, which they do not), and not by those who receive the facilities for the asking (taking?), but by those who pay monopoly rates for other programming.

The coalition thus established to press for the massive cross-subsidy from those who pay for movies and sports to those who perform on the "local origination talk-shows" is a coalition made in politico-heaven. The cable industry solidly supports the system: With a commitment to lose money on services the political interests demand, the cable corporations receive a monopoly rate of return on the profitable services that the overwhelming majority of television viewers desire. The local pols love the offerings laid at their door: channels devoted to the county tax collector explaining his appraisal techniques, thousands of dollars of "free" TV equipment to publicize (incumbent) legislators' activities, putting politicians in front of television cameras.

Top this coalition off with the third, and perhaps decisive, link in the chain of consumer bondage: the "community activists." The fabulous thing about this obscure phrase is that while you may have a dickens of a time figuring out who speaks for your community, the cable operators have achieved an absolutely fool-proof way of deciding *precisely* who they are. They go out into the community and offer to put certain groups on the tube for free; the ones who volunteer, *they* are the community activists. (And if they weren't particularly active before, why they'll become really active now, as lobbyists—er ah, *concerned citizens*—to encourage the council to approve your franchise.)

Nothing much is subversive about this procedure, and nothing whatsoever is in the least bit mysterious. If your firm is attempting to lay claim to a gold-mine cable franchise, what better way than to buy off all the local pressure groups with bountiful promises of much of the product you lust to deliver? The one small catch is that someone will pay for your largesse.

Tuning Out the Customers

While virtually every major market in the nation that has cable has only one cable firm per geographic area, one may search the industry high and low for anything approaching a coherent *pro-consumer* explanation as to why. Merrill, the president of the lost-monopolist American Cable in Phoenix adamantly insists that "I don't have to defend that [monopoly logic]. It is almost universally accepted that there be only one cable franchise." When asked to explain this in his own words, he responds, "It would take too much time."

Yet Merrill did find time to discuss his competitors' inconsistency on the topic: Camelback Cablevision is a warm proponent of competition in Phoenix, where they've broken ground in competition with Merrill's American; but when

Merrill went into Mesa, Arizona, in 1978 to obtain a second franchise to compete with Camelback, Merrill says, "They opposed me bitterly." (It is also curious that Merrill, who argues for the impossibility of competition, was himself attempting such an impossibility in Mesa.)

Just how prominently consumers figure in the great franchising game can be seen in the reaction to several recent events. In Boston, a bitter franchising competition was won last summer by Cablevision Systems Development Corp., which promised to offer 52 channels to 240,000 Boston TV sets for a bargain-basement $2.00 per month, far less than the $8.00, approximately, that most systems charge for the basic monthly service. The firm openly hopes to sell lots of extra entertainment and news channel subscriptions to recoup its $93-million, 3 1/2-year capital investment.

The franchise award has been attacked, however, as a gimmick: Cablevision Systems, it is charged, will be able to hold up the city for higher rates once they've established themselves as the sole cable operator (the low rates are only guaranteed for the first 5 years of the 15-year franchise). "The low offer was just so that they could get one of the last remaining urban franchises," says industry analyst Anthony Hoffman of A. G. Becker, Inc. "Five years down the line, the people of Boston will be paying as much as they would have paid Warner-Amex (a competing applicant). But Cablevision will have the last laugh, because it got the franchise." The odd note here is, if the consumers save lots of money but it only lasts for five good years, after which they pay what they would have to someone else, why are they seen to be suckers preyed upon by the low-ball bidder who sneaks the "last laugh"?

In Indianapolis, too, consumers have been dropped from the picture. After two "nonexclusive" franchises were awarded for nonoverlapping sections of Marion County, Indiana, in 1981, one of the competitors who didn't get a franchise decided to lay down big bucks on a bet that it's not economically impossible for a second cable company to compete once the first company is established. Robert Schloss, general partner of Omega Satellite Communications, approached the owner of a large apartment complex in Indianapolis who had the option of hooking up with the approved cable firm. Schloss offered the owner a competitive cable package delivered via an on-site earth station.

Schloss figures he can profitably install such a receiver for a building of 300 units or more. High-density neighborhoods where a row of apartment buildings of even modest size are bundled together offer exciting competitive possibilities with just this technology, because cable firms can compete for business *one building* or row of buildings at a time. Soon, Omega had 2,000 cable customers.

As usual, the snag to competition was city hall. After city workers last December discovered a secret cable that Omega had inserted through a drainage culvert to connect the systems of apartments across the street from each other, Omega was slapped with an order to back off. Schloss was told to "disconnect his cable," as one newspaper put it, "or the city would save him the trouble." Schloss is now challenging in the courts the city's power to enforce the cable franchise monopoly agreements.

In its own defense, the city charges that firms like Omega simply want to come into the area and "cream-skim" by offering competitive services at low prices to the cheaper service areas (the high-density apartment complexes). The line of reasoning becomes all too transparent. If apartment dwellers find themselves cheaper to serve with cable, why should they be forced to pay higher prices to subsidize the relatively affluent homeowners? With this argument, the city is baldly supporting a cross-subsidy wealth redistribution scheme to prevent poor renters from taking advantage of the benefits of competitive cable.

But this is simply the underlying rationale for *all* of cable's misguided franchise finagling. When Federal Judge Cale J. Holder ruled in March that he would not grant a preliminary judgment in Omega's favor, it was a victory for the politicians of Indianapolis and a grand defeat for the cable customers who live in apartments, who don't partake of city council meetings for cable broadcast, who would just like to use the cable at a reasonable price for their *own* purposes.

The only thing approaching a real proconsumer argument among the forces in favor of monopoly franchising is the claim that the "workmanship" on competitive systems, such as those being constructed in Phoenix, will suffer and, the story goes, will make everyone very disappointed several years from now when they deteriorate to the unserviceable. While this contention's ingenious impregnability to any actual test of the facts is to be admired, what we can say about the experience in competitive Phoenix contradicts it.

Competitors were licensed to enter the market against American because the latter firm was thought to have "dragged its feet" on constructing its system. One city councilman, Jim White, claims that because American Cable had both the Phoenix cable and Home Box Office over-the-air pay-television franchises, the firm was in no particular hurry to build a cable system to compete with its already-established monopoly. Complaints of sloppy construction, a prime concern of local governments, have overwhelmingly been about American Cable, the established firm, rather than the upstart competitors. According to Terry Parker, cable communications officer for the city of Phoenix, "American gets a tremendous number of complaints," while "Camelback's work is excellent."

Parker views the competitive market, after the city's practical experience with the system, as a reasonable way to do business. "When I first heard of us letting new companies into Phoenix to compete with American," she admits, "I thought, 'Why would anybody want to go against an established cable TV company?' But these new firms are out to make money, and they're not stupid—they're coming here because there's a market."

As for the chaos of competition, Parker really hasn't seen any. "There have been no gunfights in the streets," she remarks. "The newspapers ran headlines like 'range wars,' but that has not happened." Crews from rival firms have actually laid cable on opposite sides of the street—without firing a single shot.

For the most part, Phoenix cable construction, which has still reached only a small portion of the city's 270,000 households, is proceeding in nonoverlapping sectors. While no one knows what will take place when the entire city is wired with cable, one cable per neighborhood, it is too early to rule out head-to-head competition. Limited areas have already seen this, in a half-mile-square section of Phoenix and in suburban Paradise Valley. So strong is the industry presumption that overlapping competition is economic disaster that both Cross Country and Camelback, in gaining their Phoenix licenses, assured the city that they would *not* "overbuild," as it's called in the industry. A Los Angeles cable consultant, Carl Pilnick, however, cites a recent trend for aggressive companies to challenge existing franchise holders, especially the older companies that received their licenses before the big cable boom in competitive clashes. But some just cannot conceive of this, including American's Bruce Merrill, whose heart will always and forever belong to monopoly, at least in the long run: "I think we will remain dominant and buy the others out."

If we may take him at his word, then, there is no *economic* reason to keep competition limited to hearings before city council operatives and a great number of *political* considerations for avoiding this intense sort of "opportunity-seeking behavior." While Merrill cries that "there's no way they'll ever get the politics out of it," he ignores the underlying reason for the politics in it: *Politicians* do the choosing. Consumers, who will pay the tab, get stuck with the choice.

The procedural shenanigans around the nation in awarding these franchises have often reached the point of outright scandal. More than one politician is on the line for damages over conflict-of-interest charges, one cable operator is in jail for bribing city officials, and more socially acceptable forms of bribery—like a potential franchiser in an eastern city flying the city council out West to see its other franchise, with a "pit stop" in Las Vegas tossed in—are nearly the order of the day. In Los Angeles, a current franchising battle illustrates the byzantine politics called forth by cable à la monopoly.

Will the Future Be Unleashed?

The silliest shame of all, the catch that will make the more enlightened generations far in the future howl with delight when told of our folly, is that there is no "cable monopoly"— not in any *economic* or *technological* sense. The "cable monopoly," even where only one firm wires a region. is a figment of the regulatory imagination of the Federal Communications Commission. For *if* the FCC were simply to license a few thousand more commercial television stations for "low power" use (meaning local, not to interfere with distant signals), *if* they were to license 5 or 10 STV channels in each city, *if* they were to allow DBS broadcasters to compete for a share of the electromagnetic band, *if* they were to allow telephone companies to compete with cable firms in the cable business (isn't this a controversial one), and if cable franchises were to face actual or potential sources of competitive entry—then one *could* talk of a "cable monopoly." But one can also *talk* of unicorns.

Before the lynch mob riles the entire cast of FCC villains out of their government shrines and onto the gallows, however, it may be interesting to probe the depths of the FCC's conscience. If the press releases are to be taken seriously, the FCC has decided to throw its chips down on competition but is getting some mighty fierce stare-downs from the champions of regulation. Item: When the FCC proposed to drop almost all STV regulation, "public interest groups," according to the *Los Angeles Times*, jumped in with the complaint that it "would make it much more difficult to monitor the performance of individual stations." Item: When CBS and NBC applied for DBS permits, ABC ran to Washington with a formal complaint. Item: When AT&T announced an experiment in offering an electronic version of its Yellow Pages, sports news, weather forecasts, a community bulletin board, and other services, a group of newspaper publishers geared up to block the test. Then there is the National League of Cities, whose spokesman in a *New York Times* interview derided Sen. Robert Packwood's telecommunications deregulation bill as "a meat ax for cutting local government out of any effective regulatory role in present or future cable franchises."

And why, indeed, not? For reasons of consumer choice, for reasons of depoliticizing the Wunderkind of modern telecommunications, and—let us break the thunderous silence—for reasons of freedom of speech. Where, oh where, are the civil-libertarian howls for the First Amendment? Where are the blue-blooded Constitution wavers on the most blatant and appalling freedom-of-the-press issue in the New World since Gutenberg? At the local level, they're all down at city hall, extorting "amendments" for "public interest broadcasting" in special clauses of the cable monopolists' contracts. Michael Gatzke, a San Diego attorney who deals in cable franchise litigation, says no more than the stark, raving apparent: The cable franchise is "no different than if you granted a franchise to the *Los Angeles Times* to be the sole distributor of newspapers in the city of Vista." But the American Civil Liberties Union has just gotten around to "reviewing its position" on cable TV—a position in favor of monopoly franchising, although on the telephone/common carrier model.

Meanwhile, in one of the many ironies of the cable revolution, it is a "conservative" group—the Mountain States Legal Foundation, famous for its defense of property rights and for once having been presided over by James Watt, now of Interior secretary fame—that has taken up the cudgels for the First Amendment. After the Supreme Court in January sent the case of *Community Communications Company v. Boulder* back to a lower court to determine whether the city regulators of Boulder had violated the antitrust statutes in denying CCC's request to expand its existing cable services in that city, the Mountain States Legal Foundation (MSLF) petitioned the court to intervene in the case on First Amendment grounds.

City officials, notes the MSLF, view cable TV as a natural monopoly that must be regulated by the award of exclusive franchises "pursuant to express conditions established by the City including program content review." And so it is arguing that such an award violates the First Amendment rights of Boulder residents by denying them the opportunity "to receive the widest possible spectrum of programming and communication from competing cable operations."

The First Amendment has also been raised by Robert Schloss of Omega Satellite Communications, challenger to the right of the city of Indianapolis to bar cable competition. While the court refused to grant a preliminary judgment in Omega's favor, the judge did set a September date for a full hearing on what he labeled "numerous constitutional issues and alleged statutory violations." Yet he did not personally appear impressed with the modern imperatives of the Bill of Rights. "When a television operator uses the public ways to deliver his message, disruption of the streets, alleys and other public ways necessarily occurs," he wrote. "Accordingly, some form of local government permission must precede such potentially disruptive use of the public way."

It may legitimately be asked how governments are allowed to assume such enormous power over the *content* of television programming with such pedestrian encroachments on public resources as Omega's underground cable—undetected for months and only discovered by city workers by accident. Should local commercial television stations be licensed by cities if their camera news crews drive on public streets? Should newspapers be licensed because they are delivered via the sidewalks?

The opportunities appear so vast and the constitutional imperatives seem so clear that one can very easily get caught up in the fantasy of our rich cable future, of Toffler's "cottage industry," of the Met on nightly, of unheard-of improvements in the "quality of life," of security systems that make crime problems just another nostalgia trip, of environmental goods and energy savings. But as the *idea* of cable entices, the wolves of politics growl.

Every current proprietor of monopoly privilege will fight to the bone to keep tomorrow's world from destroying today's special license. Should the FCC and the Supreme Court rule in favor of free and open communications competition next Tuesday, the stock value of great corporations would plummet; the stock-in-trade of powerful political empires would evaporate. Cable, as opposed to over-the-air or satellite technologies, may have one super monopolistic advantage: It requires construction crews to chip at our streets and staple our poles and to apply to local governments for permission to do same. Could so trivial a fact hold one enormous technology up for ransom?

If the past is any guide, we must be brave with the answer. "As viewers of American television flip across their dials in search of something they would like to see," observed economist Robert Crandall of the Brookings Institution a few years ago, "they are silently mocked by seventy-five or more channel demarcations where their sets do not respond. Instead of many choices of program, they must reconcile themselves to three, four, or perhaps, five." Is this a bitter scarcity imposed by the technical limitations of man's grasp of nature's forces? "The real reason," noted Crandall, "has little if anything to do with electronic phenomena— with either a shortage of channels or, as some would have it, the inherent inferiority of UHF. Rather, the limitation exists because of the FCC's desire to make sure that viewers are offered a big dollop of edification with each swallow of entertainment no matter how edifying the edification or how entertaining the entertainment." By artificially limiting the number of broadcast licensees, the FCC has intentionally "created substantial monopoly power—monopoly power which is by no means inevitable given the available spectrum and the technology that can be applied to use it." To what noble purpose, you ask? "To provide the FCC with considerable leverage for requiring licensees to cross-subsidize programs that the commissioners believe reflect the 'public interest.'"

The technology of cable television has given us one more opportunity to accelerate beyond the constraints of those who would trample the First Amendment and deny the desires of the great mass of consumers in favor of a regime of entirely civilized, socially acceptable "honest graft." The challenge of cable television, then, is whether we will once more allow the astonishingly advanced technology of tomorrow to be stifled by the ruthlessly predictable politics of the past.

Subverting the First Amendment

By Michael McMenamin and William Gorenc, Jr.

January 1983

Since the 1960s an agency of the federal government has been engaged in flagrant suppression of the First Amendment rights of a small group of publishers. In direct contravention not only of the First Amendment but of explicit instructions from Congress, this agency has imposed a requirement that these publishers secure a printing license—something that English-speaking democracies have not seen since the 17th century, when England's licensing laws for publishers were abolished. When, to avoid the risk of a felony conviction, publishers comply and obtain a license, they become subject to regulatory demands showing blatant disregard for freedom of the press—for example, censorship of the publication's content, forced disclosure of subscribers' names, and restrictions on the sale of the publishers' assets.

That federal agency is the Securities and Exchange Commission. The publishers it is aggressively drawing into its regulatory net, in spite of several adverse court decisions, are the publishers of financial newsletters offering investment information to the public. And what is the agencies rationale for actions that subvert the First Amendment? Protection of the investing public.

Ordinarily, one would not expect that people were in any particular need of "protection" from those who want to offer for sale their opinions on the merits of various investments. As consumers of such information, investors can quickly determine for themselves what the advice is worth. And so, for the same SEC that has, without blinking an eye, registered astrologers as investment advisers, cases such as that of Christopher Lowe must seem particularly important.

Papers filed by the SEC in June 1982 in U.S. District Court in New York indicate that Lowe (or corporations with which he is associated) currently publishes such newsletters as the *Lowe Investment & Financial Letter*, the *Lowe Stock Advisory*, and the *Lowe Stock Advisory Service*, for which he has, altogether, 4,000-5,000 subscribers. But, notes the SEC, Lowe pled guilty in 1977 to appropriating $2,200 of an advisory client's funds, pled guilty in 1978 to stealing $764 from a bank, and pled guilty in 1978 to writing bad checks on various accounts in an amount in excess of $27,000. And so, says the SEC, Lowe should be muzzled—barred for the rest of his life from putting out newsletters offering his opinions about investments.

But should possession of a criminal record disqualify one from publishing investment information and opinion—any more than from publishing a newspaper or a book? And, more generally, should publishing investment commentary require

168

a printing license (the SEC prefers to call it a "registration requirement") from the government?

The SEC claims its power to license financial newsletters from the Investment Advisers Act of 1940, which requires a money manager, investment counselor, pension fund adviser, or anyone else who gives investment advice "either directly or through publications or writings" to register with the SEC as an investment adviser. In passing this legislation, Congress was mindful of the First Amendment's provision that it "shall make no law...abridging the freedom of speech, or of the press." Congress specifically exempted from the coverage of the act "the publisher of any bona fide newspaper, news magazine or business or financial publication of general and regular circulation." Yet the SEC has adamantly refused to recognize the applicability of the publishers' exemption to financial newsletters.

True, these newsletters are fairly small-time operations. But the Supreme Court has long held that the protection against government restrictions on freedom of the press afforded by the First Amendment "is the right of the lonely pamphleteer who uses carbon paper or a mimeograph just as much as the largest metropolitan publisher who utilizes the latest photo composition methods." Nor is there anything in the legislative history of the Investment Advisers Act to suggest that Congress intended to protect only the "largest metropolitan publishers" rather than "the lonely pamphleteer."

The key phrases in this exemption are *bona fide* and *regular and general circulation*—phrases that appear designed to keep a genuine investment adviser with individual customers or with responsibility for other people's funds from using the publishers' exemption to avoid registration. There are no similar phrases in the exemption, however, to warrant the SEC's conclusion that it does not apply to persons who are solely engaged in regularly publishing investment advice and commentary in a pamphlet or newsletter format available to the general public by subscription.

There are no indications that anyone at the SEC has carefully thought through the First Amendment implications either of its efforts to shut down Chris Lowe's printing press or of its efforts to license and regulate publishers of financial newsletters generally. Why this is so has a lot to do with the nature of the SEC, an independent regulatory agency, and the way it has exercised its statutory authority. Roberta Karmel, a former SEC staff attorney and an SEC commissioner during the Carter administration, recently wrote an insightful, albeit sympathetic, critique of the agency, *Regulation by Prosecution*. The SEC, she says, "became so enamored with law enforcement as an adversary sport that it lost sight of the need to justify its programs politically at the same time as it overstepped the boundaries of its statutory authority."

Long before there was an SEC or an Investment Advisers Act, there were financial newsletters. *Babson's Reports*, generally recognized as the first newsletter, was founded in 1904 by Roger W. Babson, "the father of the newsletter industry." During World War I, the federal government was also involved in the newsletter business, publishing financial information in the *United States Bulletin* right alongside casualty reports. Babson worked for the *Bulletin* during the war and in 1919 assumed private control of its publication, which soon became the *United Business Service,* and began weekly distribution on a subscription basis. Babson continued to publish *Babson's Reports*, and in 1924 his cousin, Paul T. Babson, purchased the *United Business Service*. The Babson family is still prominent in both enterprises, which are among today's larger newsletter operations.

Many others, including *Standard & Poor's*, began publishing newsletters during the bull markets of the 1920s. Many newsletter publishers went out of business in the years following the crash of 1929, most suffering from a terminal case of lost credibility. *Babson's, United, Standard & Poor's*, plus a handful of others, however, survived both the crash of '29 and the Great Depression.

During the depression in the 1930s, Congress passed extensive reform legislation designed to eliminate certain practices in the securities industry that were thought to have contributed to the stock market crash. The Securities Act of 1933 required (with a few exceptions) filing with the SEC a registration statement for initial investment offerings. The Securities and Exchange Act of 1934 governed secondary distributions of securities, including regulation of proxies and "insider trading." The Investment Advisers Act of 1940 required registration of all broadly defined "investment advisers." In commenting on these laws, the Supreme Court has held that their fundamental purpose was to substitute the rule of full disclosure for the existing one of *caveat emptor*.

Following passage of the Investment Advisers Act, the SEC made little effort to compel newsletter publishers to register as advisers. While some did, many did not and were likely unaware that the SEC even maintained a registration requirement. Starting in the early 1960s, however, the SEC began to zero in on financial newsletter publishers. It promulgated regulations under the 1940 act prohibiting advertisements by investment advisers containing "testimonials" or reference to former recommendations that would have been profitable to the potential investor-subscriber.

At the same time as it was issuing these regulations on "testimonials"—which, when applied to newsletter publishers, are a form of prior restraint—the SEC was in the process of litigating *SEC v. Capital Gains Research Bureau*. This is the only case under the Investment Advisers Act involving newsletters ever decided by the Supreme Court.

Capital Gains Research Bureau was the publisher of a newsletter with a circulation of 5,000 subscribers at an annual fee of $18. Capital Gains was accused of "scalping" by the SEC when, on six occasions over an eight-month period in 1960, it recommended a particular security in its newsletter as an excellent long-term investment, purchased it for its own account, and then within 5-10 days after publication sold the security at a higher price (allegedly caused, in part, by the Capital Gains recommendation). The total income from these transactions was approximately $20,000, or about 3 percent of the company's annual gross income of $570,000.

Although the SEC offered no evidence that the securities were not worth their appreciated value, it claimed that Capital Gains was involved in a conflict of interest. The Supreme Court upheld the SEC, and Capital Gains was subsequently ordered to disclose the "scalping" technique to its subscribers.

The First Amendment implications of licensing and regulating financial newsletters were not considered or ruled upon by the Supreme Court in the *Capital Gains* decision. Nevertheless, the SEC thereafter commenced a campaign focused not on the supposed evil of scalping but on unregistered financial newsletters generally. During the '60s and '70s and continuing into the '80s, it has engaged in an open and frequently arrogant suppression of First Amendment rights of financial newsletter publishers under the guise of its otherwise unsupported interpretation of the Investment Advisers Act.

The SEC's mistreatment of these publishers and their First Amendment rights is largely a sideshow, ancillary to its primary role of overseeing the nation's securities markets. For example, when we queried the SEC, we were told that only $58,000 of its annual $7.8 million budget is spent on registration and compliance for "investment advisers" who only publish newsletters. This is an unrealistically low figure. It does not include the hidden costs of litigation and compliance investigation in the field. Nevertheless, it is still a sideshow, and the victims are for the most part small operations. As a consequence, the SEC's suppression of their rights has been conducted outside the glare of publicity.

Why does the SEC show such insensitivity to one of our most important freedoms? As Roberta Karmel observes, regarding the agency's performance generally, "Staff members sometimes forgot that they were public servants and lapsed into an arrogance...intolerable in a democratic government."

The SEC gets away with its edict requiring the licensing of financial newsletters by intimidation. Failure of an investment adviser to register as such with the SEC is a felony punishable by up to five years in prison and a $10,000 fine. The SEC made it well known in the 1960s and thereafter that it considers publishers of financial newsletters to be investment advisers. The commission knows that many financial newsletters have material resources more akin to the lonely pamphleteer than to the large metropolitan publisher. It is not surprising that most newsletter publishers capitulate and register. The course of resistance and litigation to assert basic freedoms granted by the Constitution is not a popular one when your lawyers charge you by the hour and you started a newsletter with the purpose of making a profit.

When it comes to actual litigation regarding its interpretation of the Investment Advisers Act vis-à-vis financial newsletters, the SEC is a paper tiger that has been living off its reputation for years. The one time the SEC actually received a court ruling on the issue of whether a financial publication must register as an investment adviser, it lost.

The SEC's defeat, in a suit that it pursued for over 10 years, involved Richard A. Holman and the *Wall Street Transcript*. The *Transcript* was a weekly tabloid newspaper mailed to its 8,000 subscribers and sold on a few newsstands. It consisted of verbatim reports of various brokerage houses previously circulated and relating to particular securities, news on offerings of stocks and bonds, speeches by corporate managerial personnel, notices of executive promotions and transfers, and occasionally an editorial. By far, most of the *Transcript* was written by people it did not employ. Holman was its principal operating officer.

In 1965, in matters unrelated to his publication of the *Transcript*, the SEC revoked Holman's broker-dealer registration, ordered his expulsion from the National Association of Securities Dealers, and enjoined him from further securities law violations. Two years later, without possessing any evidence or having received any complaints of wrongdoing, the SEC suddenly launched an investigation of the *Transcript* and subpoenaed virtually every piece of paper maintained in its publishing operation. The ostensible purpose of the subpoena was to secure evidence to help the SEC determine whether the *Transcript* was an investment adviser.

Holman and the *Transcript* claimed the subpoena was harassment and a sham, refused to comply, and attacked it in federal court on First Amendment grounds. In 1968, the district court judge summarily threw the SEC out of court and held the *Transcript* to be a "bona fide newspaper" and thus exempt from the Investment Advisers Act. But the SEC pursued its case in the court of appeals, which ruled that the SEC should be allowed to gather evidence and make an initial determination on investment adviser status before the courts reviewed the validity or constitutionality of that decision. Dismissing fears expressed by the district court, the court of appeals asserted (too optimistically, as we shall see) that the SEC was "fully aware of the importance of First Amendment considerations."

The case was remanded to the district court, where in 1978 the *Transcript* was found to be "clearly involved in the business of publishing investment advice (in return for) subscription fees." But, just as happened 10 years earlier, the *Transcript* was also clearly found to be a bona fide newspaper and financial publication and hence exempt from registration. The SEC did not appeal.

Despite its loss to the *Transcript*, the SEC has not changed its policy of licensing and regulating financial newsletters. The SEC continues to maintain that the publishers must register as investment advisers. And if they do register, the SEC moves in with regulations and demands from which other publishers are immune under the First Amendment.

Examinations. The SEC regularly conducts unannounced examinations of registered brokers and investment advisers—including financial newsletters—both on-site and by phone, to determine their financial status. The examiners are typically unfamiliar with the publishing business. Consistent with the SEC's fiction that newsletters are investment advisers, they apply to the newsletters (many of which are small operations run out of the publishers' homes) the same standards that the SEC has established to ensure the solvency of investment advisers and brokers who actually have custody of clients' funds.

More chilling for freedom of the press is the door opened to harassment. The SEC admitted in congressional testimony in March 1980 that it only examines investment advisers of all types on an average cycle of once every 12 years. Yet some members of the Newsletter Association of America (NAA) who are registered with the SEC report that they are examined every two to three years. Glenn Parker, chairman of the NAA's Freedom of the Press Committee, has been examined three times in the past six years, most recently after being identified as a potential expert witness for the defense for Christopher Lowe, whom the SEC wants to put out of business because of a criminal record.

Restrictions on Financing and Sale. According to the SEC, a subscription to a financial newsletter is an "investment advisory contract" and cannot be "assigned" without the subscriber's consent. Since the SEC views the sale of a newsletter publishing company as an "assignment" of the firm's subscriptions, the company cannot be sold without the consent of each individual subscriber. A newsletter publisher is even forbidden to pledge the stock of his company for a bank loan without the consent of his subscribers, on the rather specious grounds that such a pledge represents a potential assignment.

This policy, which restricts the freedom of a newsletter publisher to sell his business, is supposedly intended to protect readers against unannounced changes in editorial staff or policies. This constitutes control of a publisher that is patently inconsistent with the First Amendment.

But then, the SEC contends that financial newsletter publishers who register with it—to avoid the expense of litigation and the risk of a felony conviction—thereby forfeit their First Amendment rights. As the SEC argued before the court, in response to First Amendment objections to one of its demands of the publishers of *Smart Money*, "[Publisher] *Has no constitutional privilege* to relinquish with respect to records that it is required to keep in the course of its business *as a registered entity.* (Emphasis added.)

Smart Money is a monthly eight-page newsletter published by the Hirsch Organization. It has a circulation of approximately 9,000 and is directed to "potential investors and readers who are interested in small, emerging growth companies, many of which have been overlooked by other publications." In April 1981 the SEC commenced an investigation of possible securities violations in connection with a public offering of shares of Entertainment Systems Inc., a previously private company. *Smart Money* had published two articles about Entertainment Systems prior to the effective date of the public offering. Stating that its interest was "piqued," the SEC promptly subpoenaed both Yale Hirsch, the president of *Smart Money*'s publishing company, and George Brooks, the *Smart Money* staff writer who wrote the two articles.

Hirsch and Brooks testified, produced many documents, and generally answered all relevant questions. Hirsch refused, however, to respond to a portion of the subpoena requesting the names and addresses of all of *Smart Money's* subscribers. In an action in federal court to enforce the subpoena, the SEC claimed it needed the subscription list so it could ascertain whether the Hirsch Organization "solicited" investors to purchase the Entertainment stock and whether the *Smart Money* articles played any role in the decision of those investors who did purchase the stock.

Yet the SEC knew, based on evidence submitted to it by Entertainment's underwriter, that no one connected with *Smart Money* either asked for or received anything in return for publishing the articles. Moreover, Hirsch's attorneys proposed a compromise whereby the list of *Smart Money* subscribers would be made available to SEC staff for the limited purpose of determining who among them had purchased Entertainment stock (the SEC already had the purchasers' names and addresses). And although arrangements like this to protect confidential business documents are quite common in federal litigation, the SEC rejected the compromise offer out of hand.

Did the SEC have ulterior motives, then, in seeking to compel the production of all the names and addresses of *Smart Money*'s subscribers—motives not revealed to the court? Intimidation of financial newsletters generally could have been one of them. Another likely motive was to establish a new legal precedent to overcome a comment in the *Wall Street Transcript* decision by the appellate court which suggested that the SEC does not have authority to cast a "dragnet...for lists of all subscribers," which would necessarily "go to the jugular of...a publishing firm."

Evidence of ulterior motives came in the fall of 1982. The SEC entered into a consent decree settling the underlying suit against the underwriters of the Entertainment System stock offering. Yet it continued its attempt to enforce the subpoena against *Smart Money*. Why? The SEC is not talking. Neither Michael Berenson, chief of the SEC's Investment Advisers Study Group, nor the SEC trial attorneys would comment on the matter. Late in October 1982, U.S. District Court Judge David Edelstein issued a decision refusing to enforce the subpoena. The SEC, he noted, had failed to "demonstrate that the need for the information outweighs the First Amendment protection accorded it." But the SEC could come back to the court to attempt a demonstration, added the judge.

The SEC staff is neither naive nor innocent. They know that subscription lists *are* the jugular of a publishing firm. They know that if they can persuade a court to ratify their self-proclaimed right to possession of the names and addresses of all newsletter subscribers, their power over newsletters will be well-nigh absolute. They know, as Justice Douglas wrote in his 1953 concurring opinion in *U.S. v. Rumely*, that:

A requirement that a publisher disclose the identity of those who buy books, pamphlets, or papers is indeed the beginning of surveillance of the press....The finger of government leveled against the press is ominous. Once the government can demand of a publisher the names of the purchasers of his publications, the free press as we know it disappears. Then the spectre of a government agent will look over the shoulder of everyone who reads. The purchase of a book or pamphlet today may result in a subpoena tomorrow....If the lady from Toledo can be required to disclose what she read yesterday and what she will read tomorrow, fear will take the place of freedom in the libraries, book stores, and homes of the land. Through the harassment of hearings, investigations, reports, and subpoenas, government will hold a club over speech and over the press.

Even without the right to cast a dragnet for subscribers' names, the clubs the SEC holds over newsletters are still quite heavy. One of them is the ever-present threat of baseless litigation designed to force a publisher out of business.

One victim of this particular tactic was Phillips Publishing Company. In 1974, Phillips published three newsletters, including the *Retirement Letter*, which offers investment advice to retired persons and had registered with the SEC as an investment advisor. In 1975 the SEC filed an action against Phillips seeking to permanently bar the firm from publishing the *Retirement Letter* unless it agreed to convey to the some 15,000 subscribers false information about the financial condition of the company. Specifically, the SEC wanted Phillips to tell its subscribers that it was "insolvent." Since this was not true and would have amounted to signing its death warrant as a publisher, Phillips refused.

When the case came to trial, the judge laughed the SEC out of court. It turned out that all the SEC was complaining about was that Phillips was using income from new subscriptions to fund its current operations and that it was not treating the full cost of unfilled subscriptions as a current liability. As anyone in the publishing industry can attest, almost all periodicals follow these accepted accounting principles in publishing, and the judge so held, finding "credible and persuasive evidence of...solvency—illustrating rather than an insolvent company, a young expanding company merely following the widely adopted financing practices employed in the contemporary publishing industry."

As with its loss to the *Wall Street Transcript*, the SEC never appealed this defeat. For Phillips Publishing, the price of liberty was $25,000 in attorneys' fees (Phillips' gross income for the previous year being only $135,000).

The SEC is determined that the price of First Amendment freedoms for financial newsletters will continue to be high. Censorship is part of that price. Although the SEC has denied to both Congress and the White House that it engages in censorship of the contents of financial newsletters, the facts do not support its denial. Censorship by the government is nothing more than the power to direct and control the content of a publication.

Case: The *Bowser Report*, a financial newsletter published by R. Max Bowser, was examined by the SEC in April 1982. In May, the SEC sent a letter directing Bowser to make "revisions of certain practices...to comply with the Act and its rules and regulations"—or lose his printing license. Two of these "practices" involved the *content* of publications by Bowser. One of the offenses was a piece that he sent to all new subscribers. Entitled "Brokers Familiar with the Bowser Plan," it listed brokers throughout the country who get the *Bowser Report* each month "and are aware of the stocks we recommend and our philosophy." Bowser's other offense was to print unsolicited letters from satisfied subscribers that, noted the SEC, "praise your publication, your rating system or your investing philosophy."

Case: In its newsletter, *Money Fund Safety Ratings*, the Institute for Econometric Research evaluates money market mutual funds on a scale ranging from a high of AAA to a low of D. The institute requests, from time to time, current portfolios of the many funds it rates, most of which readily respond. Not all do so, however, and for those funds, the institute suggests in its newsletter that "as a matter of public policy, money funds should publicize their portfolios at all times, and that funds which fail to do so should be avoided by cautious investors."

In the October 1981 issue of *Money Fund Safety Ratings*, the John Hancock Cash Management Trust, managed by John Hancock Mutual Life Insurance Co., received an "avoid" recommendation based, in part, on its secretive portfolio policies. The fund was also given a BBB safety rating by the newsletter based on the institute's evaluation of what the fund chose to release regarding its portfolio, that is, "the minimum diversification restrictions set forth in the fund's own SEC filings and prospectus." The fund was not happy with its BBB rating and on November 4, 1981, through its attorneys, demanded that the institute retract the rating. Its attorneys claimed that the institute had committed criminal violations of the Investment Advisers Act by its BBB rating of the fund and threatened to file a complaint with the SEC unless the retraction was promptly forthcoming.

The threat was not an idle one. The institute knew that a former law partner of the fund's attorneys was, at the time, an SEC commissioner. But it ignored the fund's heavy-handed attempt at intimidation and did not publish a retraction. In December 1981 the institute received a threatening letter from an SEC staff attorney advising that a complaint had been filed with the SEC about BBB ratings and "avoid" advice given with respect to certain unidentified funds. The SEC attorney echoed the claims made by the fund and concluded that it was "improper" for a financial publication "to provide a low rating rather than to state that it has insufficient information available upon which to base a rating."

The institute's attorneys promptly responded that the "avoid" recommendation was based only in part on the secretive nature of the fund's portfolio, that the BBB rating derived from the institute's evaluation of what information was publicly available regarding the portfolio, that there was no evidence to support the tortured inference of the fund's attorneys (unquestioningly adopted by SEC staff) that either the recommendation or the rating was designed "to force funds into providing...(more) information," or that any of this constituted a "conflict of interest." The SEC has not responded.

The SEC has never produced any verifiable evidence to prove that there are abuses inherent or peculiar to the newsletter industry that SEC licensing requirements and regulations are specifically designed to prevent or discourage. Nor has it produced evidence to demonstrate why antifraud provisions under SEC Rule 10(b)(5) are somehow inadequate to police newsletter publishers.

Recently, the SEC suggested in a letter to a U.S. senator that Rule 10(b)(5) does not apply to newsletter publishers. But the court cases it cited did not limit the SEC's authority to bring an action for violation of the rule. Of course, senators do not usually have federal case reports sitting in their offices. Federal judges, however, are known to keep them around, and hence the SEC regularly claims in its lawsuits that Rule 10(b)(5) *does* apply to newsletter publishers.

When we interviewed Michael Berenson, chief of the SEC's Investment Advisers Study Group, he confirmed that the SEC does believe that the rule applies to newsletter publishers. So we asked him why anything more than this rule is needed to police any fraudulent securities conduct by newsletter publishers. Mr. Berenson declined comment.

Inconsistency is not infrequent in the SEC's responses to criticism of its long-standing disregard for the First Amendment rights of newsletter publishers. In its brief in the *Hirsch* case involving a subpoena for subscribers' names, the SEC's response to the First Amendment issues raised by Hirsch was, in effect: "First Amendment? Trust us. We're the SEC." As the SEC brief intoned:

[Hirsch] posits that compulsory production of the subscriber information may potentially inhibit publication of articles about "small, emerging, growth stocks," intimidate subscribers and result in the disclosure of subscription information to competitors. This apocalyptic scenario derives from Hirsch's apparent fear or belief that the Commission cannot be trusted....This unattractive contention is belied by the Commission's reputation for thoroughness, tempered by fairness, and if given credence will, not may, impose unreasonable shackles upon the Commission's broad investigatory mandate....Ultimately, one is led to conclude

that, in this instance, "freedom of the press and speech" is a subterfuge, designed to shield [Hirsch's] possible culpability from disclosure.

Conspicuous by its absence from the brief, dated March 3, 1982, was any claim that *Smart Money* was engaged in "commercial speech" and subject as such to regulation. Yet only two months later, in May 1982, the SEC in a letter to Sen. John Warner (R-Va.) based its entire First Amendment defense of regulation of financial newsletters on the ground that the newsletters are allegedly engaged in "commercial speech."

The letter, signed by Richard W. Grant of the SEC's Division of Investment Management, incredibly cited the court of appeals decision in the *Wall Street Transcript* case without mentioning that the SEC, after 10 years of litigation, had finally lost the case, that it had not attempted to appeal the loss, and that it had yet to find a court that approved of its strained interpretation of the bona fide publisher exemption in the Investment Advisers Act. As if that omission were not deceptive enough, the SEC also falsely told Sen. Warner that the Supreme Court had "affirmed" its authority to regulate "newsletter publishers," when in fact the issue has never been ruled on by the Supreme Court at all.

The SEC soon discovered that some senators are more easily mollified than others. When the SEC sent the same response to Sen. Alfonse D'Amato (R-N.Y.), he promptly expressed his dissatisfaction at such a disingenous position and demanded a further response. The SEC is still working on it.

Sen. D'Amato's reaction is not difficult to understand. Aside from the dubiousness of the current dogma that commercial speech is not fully protected by the First Amendment, the Supreme Court has held that commercial speech is "speech which does no more than propose a commercial activity"—that is, sales advertising. Clearly, as Michael Schoeman has argued in the *Business Lawyer* (the official publication of the American Bar Association's Business and Banking Law Section, which is not particularly known as a bastion of First Amendment zealotry), financial newsletters are *not* advertising vehicles but rather "are more akin to traditional press publications in that they contain information and opinion...about the merits of products (in this case, investments) sold by others, often mixed with traditional news about economic events." Supreme Court decisions support this view and have granted First Amendment protection in numerous cases to consumer or news accounts on goods and services, including commentaries on resort hotels, medical testing labs, and osteopathic physicians. As the Supreme Court held in *Buckley v. Valeo*: "This Court has never suggested that the dependence of a communication on the expenditure of money operates itself to introduce a non-speech element or to reduce the exacting scrutiny required by the First Amendment."

Late in July 1982, the SEC filed a case in federal court seeking to permanently shut down *Stock Market Magazine* ("The Voice of the Small Investor") unless it secures an SEC printing license. According to the SEC papers filed with the court, *Stock Market Magazine* is a monthly publication with approximately 50,000 mail subscriptions and newsstands sales in major metropolitan areas throughout the country. The essence of the four-count SEC complaint was that the magazine publishes "analyses and reports concerning securities...without being registered as an investment adviser." Other charges are that the magazine published certain unspecified articles on companies written by their public relations firms (without attribution) as well as running certain unspecified articles on companies by free-lance writers who were paid $250-$500 by the companies featured (without disclosing by whom the writers were paid).

Questionable journalism? Possibly—if true. Sufficient cause to shut the magazine down? Never—unless the SEC has become immune from any obligation to honor the First Amendment. But that is what one must begin to wonder.

And then one must begin to wonder about the fate of the free press generally in the United States. Financial publishers and their editors and writers are a small minority among members of the media. They have in their midst an occasional Christopher Lowe. No doubt there are a few skeletons in closets throughout the publishing world, but in this case there is an agency of the government that has arrogated to itself the power to ride roughshod over the First Amendment—first with the requirement that permission be obtained and requirements be met before access to a printing press be allowed; then, once its foot is in the door, with demands pursued via lawsuits and censorship of editorial content.

It is indeed only one government agency waging war on the rights of only part of the press. Yet it is the government and it is the press, and as Justice Douglas warned in 1953, "The finger of government leveled against the press is ominous." If the SEC can continue with impunity its disregard for freedom of the press, which publishers are next? From which finger of government? For the seemingly benign protection of which group of consumers?

The First Shall Be Last?

By Charles Oliver

October 1990

For 70 years, the First Amendment has been the American Civil Liberties Union's chief client. In case after case, ACLU lawyers have argued for absolute free speech, for a press unfettered by government restrictions, and for the strict separation of church and state. Outside the courtroom, ACLU leaders have been among the most eloquent defenders of the libertarian principles embodied in the First Amendment.

Now those principles face their strongest opposition in years. Public and politicians alike appear increasingly intolerant of free speech—whether the lyrics of The 2 Live Crew, the anti-abortion pronouncements of the Catholic church, the art of Robert Mapplethorpe, the advertisements of tobacco companies, or the posters of antigay college students. There is abroad in the land a sentiment that many, many ideas are too dangerous to be expressed and that these ideas must be shouted down or, where possible, forbidden by law. The ACLU, it would seem, has plenty of work to do—both in the courtroom and out.

So what is the ringing battle cry of ACLU President Norman Dorsen? "We are the American Civil Liberties Union, not the American First Amendment Union."

In recent years, the ACLU has adopted an expansive definition of "civil liberties" that dilutes its absolutist commitment to free speech. The ACLU, critics say, is now more committed to goals such as comparable worth, government aid to the homeless, and nuclear disarmament than to defending the First Amendment.

In 1988, attorney Mark S. Campisano documented the shift from the ACLU's "old agenda," which he describes as "the rights of free speech, free press, free exercise of religion, freedom of assembly and association, and freedom from official acts of racism." In 1948, he reported, this agenda encompassed 94 percent of the ACLU's cases; by 1987, it accounted for only 45 percent.

Critics complain that greed and left-wing ideology have corrupted the union. The ACLU, they fear, has diluted its message, compromised its mission, and, in some instances, abandoned its commitment to the First Amendment.

"America needs a civil liberties union," says Harvard law professor Alan Dershowitz, a 25-year member of the ACLU who once sat on the group's national board of directors. "It no longer has one."

Dershowitz notes that the ACLU didn't get involved in one of the most important pornography cases in years: *Osborne v. Ohio,* which involved a sweeping Ohio statute aimed at child pornography. This spring, the Supreme Court upheld the law, in the process greatly expanding the states' ability to ban pornography.

179

Civil libertarians blasted the decision for enunciating a new theory of censorship—a theory that says that the government can ban possession of child pornography not because the material itself generates crime but because allowing people to own it creates a market for material that grows out of crime.

"And the ACLU wasn't in that case at all," says Dershowitz. "And yet, it's in every abortion case, and it's in every feminist case, and it's in every fetal rights case, and it's in every racial case defending the most extreme forms of quotas and affirmative action."

The ACLU has also taken heat from libertarians for some of the cases that it *does* take. Perhaps the most famous example began over a decade ago, when teenage immigrant Walter Palovchak decided that he did not want to return to the Soviet Union with his parents. The ACLU went to court on behalf of his family to force Walter to return to Russia.

"It still strikes me as strange," says Palovchak's attorney, Henry Mark Holzer. "The ACLU has a children's rights project. Their attorneys argue that teenage girls are competent to have an abortion without parental consent, but a teenage boy can't choose the United States over a totalitarian state. The only answer that makes sense is that their decisions aren't based on civil liberties but liberal politics. The ACLU likes abortion, and it likes the Soviet Union."

More recently, the ACLU actually sued an editor over the contents of his newsletter. In 1984, the ACLU's Southern California affiliate won a $1.8 million settlement against the Los Angeles Police Department. The ACLU had sued the police department on behalf of 144 left-wing organizations and individuals who complained that they had been the targets of illegal surveillance.

But the litigation didn't stop there. Some of the information in the files had allegedly been funneled to the conservative Western Goals foundation and printed in the foundation's newsletter. Shortly after settling with the police, the ACLU sued Western Goals; John Rees, the editor of the newsletter; and the estate of Western Goals' chairman, Rep. Larry McDonald, (D-Ga.). "It's not the business of law enforcement to furnish information to individuals, even reporters," said Southern California ACLU attorney Mark D. Rosenbaum, according to *The Wall Street Journal*.

"I can understand why the ACLU was concerned about the police keeping records on people who aren't connected with any crime. I can understand the suit against the LAPD," says Rees's attorney, Manuel Klausner (who is a trustee of the Reason Foundation). "But under what interpretation of the First Amendment could they sue the journalist? The ACLU took the position that Rees and other journalists don't even have the right to receive a newspaper clipping or other article in the public domain from the police. The implications of this position would undermine the ability of journalists to use the police as sources. In my judgment, we were defending the First Amendment against the ACLU." (Western Goals' insurance company eventually forced the organization to settle out of court.)

No issue more clearly demonstrates the new thinking within the ACLU than the group's reaction, or differing reactions, to recent attempts by some universities to ban sexually or racially insensitive speech on their campuses.

Last year, the Michigan affiliate of the ACLU brought the first lawsuit against one of these college codes. A federal district judge overturned the University of Michigan's speech restrictions on First Amendment grounds. The ACLU has now taken more than 20 cases across the country challenging student conduct codes that prohibit offensive speech.

But two of the ACLU's largest affiliates aren't so sure about such challenges. In September 1989, the University of California revised its student conduct code to ban racial or sexual epithets on the university's nine campuses. The Northern and Southern California affiliates—which account for more than one-fifth of the ACLU's total membership—didn't challenge the code.

Instead, they endorsed a policy that recognizes that colleges can prohibit speech that creates "a hostile and intimidating environment which the speaker knows or reasonably should know will seriously and directly impede the educational opportunities of the individual or individuals to whom it is directly addressed."

Campus speech codes divided the Massachusetts affiliate for months. *Village Voice* writer Nat Hentoff reports that the debate was heated. One proponent of speech codes "accused some of his opponents of giving free rein to white racists," writes Hentoff. "He claimed the real issue is not speech, but white power." Another advocate of speech codes "wondered whether the position of the First Amendment absolutists 'has something to do with who the victims of this kind of speech are.'"

Finally, this summer the board approved 16-14 a policy that called for colleges "to minimize and eliminate attitudes and practices that create a hostile educational environment, but these measures must not include rules which prohibit and punish speech on the basis of its content." It was not exactly a resounding victory for free speech.

Because of the differing policies adopted by affiliates, the national board has appointed a committee to study the issue and decide on how to deal with campus speech codes. "I think the fact that they even appointed this committee forces one to question whether the national board is as committed to the First Amendment as it used to be," says Hentoff.

Advocates of speech codes see the issue as a conflict between equality, embodied in the 14th Amendment's Equal Protection Clause, and liberty, protected by the First Amendment. The ACLU, they say, should defend the entire Constitution, including their interpretation of the 14th Amendment.

"Properly framed, there is generally no conflict between equality and free speech," says ACLU National Legal Director john powell, who spells his name without capital letters. But certain types of speech may create an atmosphere that makes minority students feel unwelcome on campuses and keeps them from exercising their freedom. When that happens, he says, minorities have been denied the equal protection promised by the 14th Amendment. Restricting offensive speech guarantees minorities and women equal protection.

"It's not simply a First Amendment issue; it's an equality issue," says powell. "Sometimes we get confused and say that if something is a verbal utterance, then it's protected, but that's not what the First Amendment is about." Since "verbal utterance" is pretty much the dictionary definition of *speech*, the ACLU's national legal director is in the curious position of interpreting the First Amendment out of existence.

Others argue that a commitment to expansive free speech has always been *the* core principle of the ACLU and that there is no legitimate reason to abandon that commitment. "The ACLU's position has been, and should be, that speech should be met by more speech. Students should speak out against racism on campus, meet the arguments of racists with their own arguments," says Hentoff. "But that takes time, effort, and initiative. I guess that it seems much easier to erect these codes."

For the moment, Hentoff's view still holds sway. At the ACLU's 1989 national conference, delegates defeated a resolution recognizing that speech "can be regulated in the interest of protecting the fundamental rights of equal opportunity guaranteed by the Fourteenth Amendment."

But the delegates did approve 130-60 a resolution that the ACLU "should undertake educational activities to counter incidents of racist, sexist, anti-semitic and homophobic behavior (including speech) on school campuses."

"Next we'll be required to give presentations on the evils of pornography when we defend sexually explicit material," says Mark Lambert, former legislative director of the Iowa Civil Liberties Union.

"I think the changes started when the ACLU got involved in the civil rights movement," says Lambert. "That opened the door for all of these other issues that have nothing to do with the First Amendment. Today, when someone says that homelessness or comparable worth is not a civil liberties issue, the common retort is 'Well, 30 years ago some people didn't think civil rights was a civil liberties issue.' Well, maybe it wasn't."

Civil liberties have usually been conceived as freedom from government coercion, including government-enforced segregation. But once Jim Crow laws began to fall, civil rights leaders started to demand government coercion—from antidiscrimination statutes to racial quotas—to ensure racial equality. That quickly created tensions between the ACLU's commitment to civil liberties and its involvement in civil rights. And in nearly every debate, civil liberties lost.

In 1960, for example, the ACLU's national board opposed the inclusion of questions about race, color, or national origin on the nation's census forms. But once Congress passed the 1964 Civil Rights Act, the board changed its mind. Census data, it held, provide the basis for programs "to combat discrimination in education, employment, and housing." At first, the ACLU supported only voluntary answers to questions about race; now it says the census may make such questions mandatory. The group does, however, request that the government store the racial information apart from the personal items.

To further racial integration, the ACLU even supports bans on certain kinds of speech. In response to white flight, many cities have passed "antiblockbusting statutes" aimed at real estate agents who try to get white homeowners to sell out by telling them that the neighborhood is "going black." Ironically, these "civil rights" protections actually harm blacks who would like to enter these neighborhoods.

They also, of course, restrict free speech. But in 1972, the ACLU adopted a policy, still in its manual, supporting "antiblockbusting statutes which prohibit false or deceptive statements concerning changes in the racial, religious, or national origin character of a neighborhood and/or the effect of those changes." Although the ACLU does limit its support to laws against "false or deceptive" statements, "deceptive" is in the eye of the beholder, and an absolutist position on the First Amendment should lead one to oppose any such laws.

In *The Politics of the American Civil Liberties Union*, William Donahue reports that in 1975 the national board considered amending the housing policy to explicitly oppose any attempts to combat discrimination by means that are "offensive to the constitutional guarantee of free speech." This amendment was defeated when someone pointed out that it "would rescind, in effect, the board policy on antiblockbusting ordinances."

Perhaps the most important result of the ACLU's plunge into civil rights was the change in its attitude toward quotas. Throughout the 1940s and 1950s the group opposed racial quotas. In the 1970s the ACLU reversed its stand and came out in favor of quotas. In fact, in 1977, it adopted its own quota system.

Under this policy, the ACLU's national board must be 50 percent female and 20 percent minorities. Thirteen years after adopting the policy, however, the ACLU— which frequently goes to court to force such systems on other employers—hasn't filled its quotas. According to minutes of the ACLU executive committee's March 10, 1990 meeting, this failure is of great concern to committee members and ACLU staff:

"Several [Executive] Committee members pointed out that there are no Asian Americans or Arab Americans on the Board....We let affiliates send us non-minorities over and over without requiring any serious affirmative action by them, and then we try to make it up with the at-large members. But this is inefficient because at-large members represent only 30 of 83 members and also because it has allowed us to ignore the responsibility of affiliates in this matter."

The committee went on to consider two nominations to fill a vacant slot: a black male political science professor who had worked hard to gain affiliate status for the San Diego ACLU and an Indian (Asian-American) woman who is executive director of the National Gay and Lesbian Task Force. While members praised the work of both nominees, the minutes indicate that debate soon centered on crude gender and ethnic generalizations:

"Paul Meyer said that in light of her record, the need for women, and the lack of Asian Americans on the Board, [the woman] should be submitted to the Board as the sole recommendation. Gwen Thomas disagreed, saying that because Indians are not a sufficiently numerous minority in the country and have not been commensurate victims of discrimination, we should not be as concerned with their representation on the Board." Committee members proceeded to add a black woman and two white women to the list of possible nominees. They considered and rejected a motion to limit the search to women. Finally, they voted to nominate the original two suggestions and "a white woman who is an important feminist and First Amendment lawyer."

Some believe that racial and gender quotas changed dramatically the nature of the boards and the nature of the ACLU. "Election to the board used to be based on one's dedication to civil liberties. Members were elected because they had demonstrated an effective commitment to free speech and separation of church and state," says Dershowitz. "But affirmative action changed all that. Some people were elected *because* they were women and *because* they were minorities. And they were told that they were there to represent women and minorities. Inevitably they formed caucuses for women's rights and minority rights within the ACLU....What the ACLU needs now is a civil liberties caucus." (ACLU President Norman Dorsen, who has presided over national board meetings for the last 14 years, responds, "I don't think our minority and women members are any less committed to free speech than others on the board.")

While quotas may have speeded up the changes taking place within the ACLU, there is a more basic explanation for what has happened to the organization over the last two decades: self-interest, even greed.

The central goal of business is to increase profit. For the ACLU, the equivalent goal is to get more dues-paying members. One way to do this is outreach programs into new markets. Hence, the ACLU's adoption of quotas may be seen as a way to expand its customer base.

Offering a more diverse selection of products will also attract new customers. If some people don't like Big Macs, McDonald's tries to get them to buy Chicken McNuggets. If some people aren't interested in the First Amendment, the ACLU offers civil rights or comparable worth.

In the last 25 years, the ACLU's membership has sky-rocketed from around 70,000 to almost 300,000. But many long-time members worry that recent recruits are mainly interested in the group's liberal politics, rather than civil liberties. "They were advertising for members. *Period*. They weren't trying to get members who were necessarily committed to civil liberties," says Hentoff.

Former Iowa legislative director Lambert argues that the ACLU's stands on economic issues turn off promarket libertarians and conservatives who would support First Amendment rights. "To recruit new members," he complains, "the ACLU buys the mailing lists of other liberal groups. They have more and more people joining who are just liberals, not civil libertarians. You have to worry that someday there'll be no one there whose top commitment is the First Amendment." A spokeswoman for the national office says that the ACLU rents the lists of "like-minded" groups. When pressed for examples, she cites Greenpeace and Amnesty International.

The danger of this strategy was exposed in Skokie, Illinois. In 1977, the ACLU defended the rights of Nazis to march through this predominately Jewish suburb. Although some civil libertarians regard this as the ACLU's finest moment, many of its members disagreed. Because of Skokie, the ACLU, which had been steadily gaining members during the 1970s, lost over one-fifth of its national members. The resulting financial crisis almost destroyed the group.

The message to the ACLU was clear: Liberals are not necessarily First Amendment absolutists. Some of the ACLU's products repel some of its potential customers and must be repackaged. The result, some hold, is that the group compromises its commitment to the First Amendment.

Lambert sums up the new philosophy of the ACLU: "Let's do whatever will raise the maximum amount of money to support the organization and ignore any loss in philosophical integrity. Some liberals don't like the fact that we defend racist speech. Fine, develop a new policy that says we must balance the First and 14th Amendments."

"The ACLU has become too crassly commercial," concurs Dershowitz. "It's too concerned about its pocketbook. The national board in particular is too worried about whether a stand will help or hurt membership and fund raising. It's increasingly afraid to take stands that are unpopular with its constituents." President Dorsen and other board members deny that financial considerations affect policy decisions.

Still, the First Amendment is not the group's number-one priority anymore. Asked to name the most important issue for the ACLU today, powell—whose office most closely tracks the cases taken by the group—first cites abortion, followed by civil rights. (*The New York Times* reports that the group litigates 80 percent of the abortion cases in the country.) He lists the First Amendment third. The national board members interviewed for this article emphasized the same issues but didn't imply any order of priority.

Abortion may indeed be a civil liberties issue, but it seems strange to make it the ACLU's top priority. After all, Planned Parenthood, NOW, and the National Abortion Rights Action League ably fight for abortion rights. Only the ACLU speaks for the First Amendment. But defending abortion rights may seem like a much more lucrative venture than defending the speech rights of Nazis. Or of anti-abortion protesters.

The federal Racketeer Influenced and Corrupt Organizations law represents one of the most potent, and potentially abusive, weapons for silencing dissent. In 1970 the ACLU opposed the passage of RICO, and the group recently urged Congress to reform the law because of its chilling effect on free speech.

But three years ago the Pennsylvania affiliate chose not to speak out against the use of RICO against abortion protesters in Philadelphia. Nat Hentoff asked why. "The legislative director, Stefan Presser, told me that the board of directors had decided on silence," he wrote, " 'I'm not saying,' Presser said, 'that the debate was not influenced by who the parties were.' "

In principle, the ACLU officially opposes certain private protests. "Defending the right of all to advance their points of view by whatever nonviolent methods they may choose," says the ACLU policy guide, "does not mean that the ACLU should refrain from objecting when the likely consequence of pressure group activities would be...to restrict a free and diverse marketplace of ideas."

This exception leaves some civil libertarians puzzled. "Isn't the purpose of every protest to restrict certain ideas?" asks Hentoff.

In practice, it seems that right-wing protests are the ones that the ACLU finds restrictive. Consider the conflicting signals the ACLU has sent in its handling of a racketeering suit filed in Florida against the American Family Association. The AFA's Florida chapter threatened to boycott bookstores that wouldn't remove *Playboy* and *Penthouse* from their stands and to ask prosecutors to consider legal action against such stores. In response, the American Booksellers Association, *Playboy*, and Waldenbooks filed a civil RICO suit against the AFA, alleging extortion.

Florida Civil Liberties Union Executive Director Robyn Blumner has announced that she will file a friend-of-the-court brief on behalf of the AFA. "We are opposed to the use of RICO to suppress protests," she says. But some reports indicate that the national office doesn't support her stand. Asked if her position has the approval of the national office, Blumner says only, "This is a local matter, and it is not their decision to make." So she has national cooperation? "It isn't their decision."

Reason tried numerous times over a three-month period to interview ACLU Executive Director Ira Glasser. We were always promised that he would try to work us into his schedule. When asked if Glasser or the national office had taken a stand on the AFA case, a spokeswoman promised to look into the matter and call back. That never happened.

As the ACLU seems to be backing away from its traditional commitments, it has bestowed the title of "civil liberties" on a host of left-wing policy prescriptions. No longer content to defend homeless persons against police harassment, imprisonment under vagrancy laws, or being confined to a mental institution, many in the ACLU demand taxpayer-provided housing as a constitutional right.

Led by the California affiliates, the campaign for a "right to housing" has encountered some opposition within the ACLU. "There's nothing mentioned in the constitution about a right to housing," says Florida's Blumner. "If we start demanding that government provide housing, what's next? A right to health care? A job?"

Well, yes, say some activists. People have a right, not merely to housing, but to some subsistence level of income. And if they can't achieve that income on their own, taxpayers must be compelled to provide it.

In a debate at the 1989 national convention, law professor Peter Edelman argued, "People who lack a subsistence income lack effective political liberty....it is undeniable that people who are deeply worried about how they will pay next month's rent or buy food for the last week or two of the month are unlikely to vote, let alone participate in more active forms of political advocacy about their situation." Of course, this argument confuses political participation with political liberty, but such fine distinctions would inconvenience Edelman's redistributive agenda.

Edelman continued, "So when I talk about subsistence income in a policy sense, I am talking about multiple policies that include employment, wage supplementation, education, health care, housing, and child care as well as cash payments of various kinds."

His opponent, national board member Martin Margulies, countered that there is nothing in the Constitution that guarantees a subsistence income to anyone. He says that advocating Edelman's "multiple policies" would violate the ACLU's own constitution, which prohibits the group from engaging in partisan politics. If the ACLU backs specific economic policies, Margulies worries, then it becomes a group of "social activists rather than principled civil libertarians." Perhaps because of Margulies's arguments, the 1989 convention was the first in almost 20 years that didn't pass a resolution endorsing the concept of "economic rights."

But three months later, the national office endorsed the Housing Now! march on Washington, D.C. Its press release declared that as long as any American gets a rent subsidy or capital-gains tax break, equal protection requires the government to provide "permanent housing, not simply temporary shelter" for the homeless.

The ACLU has also used the banner of civil liberties to intrude in private employer/employee relationships. It has established a National Task Force on Civil Liberties in the Work Place. Implicit in each item on the task force's agenda is the notion of a "right to a job."

Perhaps the most controversial, and revealing, item on the agenda is the push to abolish employment at will. Currently, an employer can, except under certain specified circumstances, legally fire an employee at any time, just as the worker can quit. Task force Director Lew Maltby says the ACLU wants to abolish the at-will doctrine and replace it with a new rule "that employees have a right to keep their job" unless the employer can demonstrate that their performance was deficient.

Of course, each person has a different idea of what constitutes deficiency. This radical shift in the burden of proof could turn every termination into a procedural nightmare. Maltby wants to apply the deficiency standard very narrowly. He grants that "certain infractions, such as assaulting coworkers" are serious enough to warrant firing on the first offense. But for others, "such as lateness and absenteeism," he argues that "the behavior must continue in the face of warnings before a discharge is just." Why Maltby thinks a person has this sort of right to a job—and not, for example, a right to a girlfriend—is problematic.

Since freedom of contract has been all but written out of the Constitution, civil libertarians who object to the ACLU's workplace policies have suggested that using government power to force employers to retain workers erodes freedom of association. In response, Maltby argues that managers in large organizations should enjoy no such freedom: "Within the context of a small business, where everyone knows each other and works together on an intimate basis, this is a legitimate position. Attorneys and other professionals certainly have the right to choose (and change) their partners freely. This model, however, bears little resemblance to a typical American corporation....To maintain that management has a free association right to terminate these people is simply not defensible."

The ACLU's workplace policies assume there is no essential difference between government and a corporation, between political power and economic power. Glasser writes in *Liberty at Work* that some companies have powers that "rival, and in some cases exceed, government power." So the ACLU wants government to assume new powers, to force employers to behave in approved ways.

"Government has a duty to ensure access to public institutions," says john powell. "And business by its nature in our society is a public concern....when a company starts having an impact on people's lives, then we say that civil rights principles should be applied." So, for instance, an employee dismissed by a large corporation is entitled to the same due process protections as a person accused of a crime.

Some in the ACLU would go even further. In the 1984 book *Our Endangered Rights: The ACLU Report on Civil Liberties Today*, law professor Sylvia Law argues that "property rights are not natural, immutable, or inherent, but only grant such power as the courts and legislatures choose to recognize. Property, whether in the form of land, wages, welfare, or a license to practice law, is what society defines it to be." Of course, the same could be said of equal protection, freedom of speech, and other civil liberties. The Constitution was supposed to enshrine the "natural" definition of these rights, not the most popular or most convenient definition.

ACLU leaders realize that such views are not those of the Framers of the Constitution. Indeed, Glasser has noted, with seeming regret, that the Bill of Rights does not apply to the private sector. He brushes off this unpleasant historical fact by saying that the Framers could not have foreseen the enormous power modern corporations have.

But this is really a straw man. Being fired has always been a traumatic, perhaps financially devastating, experience: The Constitution's Framers must have known that. If they had really wanted safeguards against arbitrary dismissals, they could have written them into the Constitution. Contrary to Glasser, this was not an oversight.

The men who drafted the Constitution realized something that the ACLU does not. Government is a unique creature—it holds a monopoly on physical force. It is fear of this coercive power that caused the Framers to put explicit limits on it in the Constitution.

In the classical-liberal tradition, liberty meant one thing: freedom from physical coercion. No matter how the ACLU frames it, the relationship between an employer and an employee is a voluntary one. If someone doesn't want to take a drug test, she can quit. (When this was pointed out to Robyn Blumner, she replied. "Well, if you don't want to take a government drug test you can move to Canada." No, Ms. Blumner, I can go to jail.)

Indeed, the Framers believed that a private sphere was necessary to exercise one's freedoms. That is why they wrote protections for property into the Constitution. But because the ACLU does not distinguish between economic power and physical force, it ends up calling for more government involvement—more coercion—to restrict the power, or freedom, of business managers and owners.

And it isn't just economic liberties that this view endangers. Three years ago, the ACLU joined a suit to overturn a federal law that allows religious groups engaged in nonprofit activities to restrict their hiring to members of their own faith. Apparently, religious freedom goes out the window when economic "rights" are at stake.

Law seems to speak for many ACLU members when she writes, "Civil libertarian values cannot be realized by focusing exclusively upon the real threat of abusive government power." But there was a time when focusing on the threat of abusive government was the ACLU's *raison d'être*.

The ACLU's views on the distinction between the public and private sectors, or the lack of such a distinction, warp its policies on free speech. For example, the group actively tries to force private malls to grant access to speakers and petitioners.

Even Martin Margulies, the opponent of economic rights, opposes the right of malls to reject speakers. He told delegates at last year's national convention, "Freedom of speech is useless unless the speaker has access to an audience—and the audiences today are at the malls, not in the publicly owned urban downtowns and village greens of old." This is, he admits, a break with the traditional liberal view that free speech means only freedom from government restrictions. (Catholic churches are full of potential audiences. Why not force them to accept speakers for abortion rights?)

In fact, the ACLU's position is tantamount to a requirement for *listening*. The traditional notion of free speech assumes that in the absence of government coercion speakers will create their own platforms and find their own audience. As anyone who has ventured through a government-owned airport can attest, the mall owner is most likely acting as the agent of the customers, who don't want to be bothered by LaRouchies.

The idea that free speech is meaningless without access to an audience informs the ACLU's policy guide positions on mass media. The group supports reinstituting the government-mandated "fairness doctrine" for broadcasters. It demands that cable systems provide open, public-access channels. And it recommends voluntary guidelines to increase access to the print media. These include a policy of accepting virtually all noncommercial advertising and a policy of printing unedited news and opinions from members of the public.

While the policy guide holds that there is no enforceable right to access to the print media, it is easy to see how the ACLU could come up with one. If there is little substantive difference between the private sector and the public sector, there is no reason (except tradition) why government cannot subject print media to a fairness doctrine. If speech is meaningless without an audience, and malls must open their doors to speakers, why shouldn't newspapers have to give writers access to their readers? If, because of their monopoly nature, cable systems have a duty to provide public-access channels, then shouldn't the government force monopoly newspapers to provide similar access? And if all the ACLU cares about is expanding the marketplace of ideas, then a fairness doctrine for the print media could be said to do that.

Indeed, the thought has at least crossed the mind of the ACLU's executive director. Glasser writes in *Our Endangered Rights*, "If speech is inaudible, what matters that it is free? Effective communication requires access to the mass media, but unpopular views often cannot gain access. Some have therefore suggested that in order to fulfill the purposes of the First Amendment under modern conditions, we should establish a right of access to newspapers and television....Twentieth-century conditions have created a conflict within the First Amendment that was not possible to contemplate two hundred years ago."

Such waffling inspires doubts about the organization's future as a First Amendment defender. "I'm still a member, and I still make my contribution because the ACLU still does some good," says Dershowitz. "But if things don't change, in 10 years, it may not be doing any good. In fact, it could become an enemy of free speech."

PART FIVE

BODY POLITICS

Drug Prohibition

By Thomas Szasz

January 1978

Americans regard freedom of speech and religion as fundamental rights. Until 1914, they also regarded freedom of choosing their diets and drugs as fundamental rights. Today, however, virtually all Americans regard ingesting certain substances—prohibited by the government—as both crimes and diseases.

What is behind this fateful moral and political transformation, which has resulted in the rejection by the overwhelming majority of Americans of their right to self-control over their diets and drugs in favor of the alleged protection of their health from their own actions by a medically corrupt and corrupted state? How could it have come about in view of the obvious parallels between the freedom to put things into one's mind and its restriction by the state by means of censorship of the press, and the freedom to put things into one's body and its restriction by the state by means of drug controls?

The answer to these questions lies basically in the fact that our society is *therapeutic* in much the same sense in which medieval Spanish society was *theocratic*. Just as the men and women living in a theocratic society did not believe in the separation of church and state but, on the contrary, fervently embraced their union, so we, living in a therapeutic society, do not believe in the separation of medicine and the state but fervently embrace their union. The censorship of drugs follows from the latter ideology as inexorably as the censorship of books followed from the former. That explains why liberals and conservatives—and people in that imaginary center as well—all favor drug controls. In fact, persons of all political and religious convictions, save libertarians, now favor drug controls.

Liberals tend to be permissive toward socially disreputable psychoactive drugs, especially when they are used by young and hairy persons; so they generally favor decriminalizing marijuana and treating rather than punishing those engaged in the trade of LSD. They are not at all permissive, however, toward nonpsychoactive drugs that are allegedly unsafe or worthless and thus favor banning saccharin and Laetrile. In these ways they betray their fantasy of the state—as good parent: Such a state should restrain erring citizens by mild, minimal, and medical sanctions, and it should protect ignorant citizens by pharmacological censorship.

Conservatives, on the other hand, tend to be prohibitive toward socially disreputable psychoactive drugs, especially when they are used by young and hairy persons; so they generally favor criminalizing the use of marijuana and punishing rather than treating those engaged in the trade of LSD. At the same time, they are permissive toward nonpsychoactive drugs that are allegedly unsafe or worthless and thus favor free trade in saccharin and Laetrile. In these ways, they too betray their fantasy of the state—as the enforcer of the dominant ethic: Such a state should punish citizens who deviate from the moral precepts of the majority and should abstain from meddling with people's self-care.

Viewed as a political issue, drugs, books, and religious practices all present the same problem to a people and its rulers. The state, as the representative of a particular class or dominant ethic, may choose to embrace some drugs, some books, and some religious practices and reject the others as dangerous, depraved, demented, or devilish. Throughout history, such an arrangement has characterized most societies. Or the state, as the representative of a constitution ceremonializing the supremacy of individual choice over collective comfort, may ensure a free trade in drugs, books, and religious practices. Such an arrangement has traditionally characterized the United States. Its Constitution explicitly guarantees the right to freedom of religion and the press and implicitly guarantees the right to freedom of self-determination with respect to what we put into our bodies.

Why did the framers of the Constitution not explicitly guarantee the right to take drugs? For two obvious reasons. First, because 200 years ago medical science was not even in its infancy; medical practice was socially unorganized and therapeutically worthless. Second, because there was then no conceivable danger of an alliance between medicine and the state. The very idea that the government should lend its police power to physicians to deprive people of their free choice to ingest certain substances would have seemed absurd to the drafters of the Bill of Rights.

This conjecture is strongly supported by a casual remark by Thomas Jefferson, clearly indicating that he regarded our freedom to put into our bodies whatever we want as essentially similar to our freedom to put into our own minds whatever we want. "Was the government to prescribe to us our medicine and diet," wrote Jefferson in 1782, "our bodies would be in such keeping as our souls are now. Thus in France the emetic was once forbidden as a medicine, the potato as an article of food."

Jefferson poked fun at the French for their pioneering efforts to prohibit drugs and diets. What, then, would he think of the state he himself helped to create, a state that now forbids the use of harmless sweeteners while encouraging the use of dangerous contraceptives? that labels marijuana a narcotic and prohibits it while calling tobacco an agricultural product and promoting it? and that defines the voluntary use of heroin as a disease and the legally coerced use of methadone as a treatment for it?

Freedom of religion is indeed a political idea of transcendent importance. As that idea has been understood in the United States, it does not mean that members of the traditional churches—that is, Christians, Jews, and Mohammedans—may practice their faith unmolested by the government, but that others— for example, Jehovah's Witnesses—may not. American religious freedom is unconditional; it is not contingent on any particular church proving, to the satisfaction of the state, that its principles or practices possess "religious efficacy."

The requirement that the supporters of a religion establish its theological credentials in order to be tolerated is the hallmark of a theological state. In Spain, under the Inquisition, there was, in an ironic sense, religious tolerance: Religion was tolerated, indeed, actively encouraged. The point is that religions other than

Roman Catholicism were considered to be heresies. The same considerations now apply to drugs.

The fact that we accept the requirement that the supporters of a drug establish its therapeutic credentials before we tolerate its sale or use shows that we live in a therapeutic state. In the United States today, there is, in an ironic sense, pharmacological tolerance: Approved drugs are tolerated, indeed, actively encouraged. But drugs other than those officially sanctioned as therapeutic are considered worthless or dangerous. Therein, precisely, lies the moral and political point: Governments are notoriously tolerant about permitting the dissemination of ideas or drugs of which they approve. Their mettle is tested by their attitude toward the dissemination of ideas and drugs of which they disapprove.

The argument that people need the protection of the state from dangerous drugs but not from dangerous ideas is unpersuasive. No one has to ingest any drug he does not want, just as no one has to read a book he does not want. Insofar as the state assumes control over such matters, it can only be in order to subjugate its citizens—by protecting them from temptation, as befits children; and by preventing them from assuming self-determination over their lives, as befits an enslaved population.

Conventional wisdom now approves—indeed, assumes as obvious—that it is the legitimate business of the state to control certain substances we take into our bodies, especially so-called psychoactive drugs. According to this view, as the state must, for the benefit of society, control dangerous persons, so it must also control dangerous drugs. The obvious fallacy in this analogy is obscured by the riveting together of the notions of dangerous drugs and dangerous acts: As a result, people now "know" that dangerous drugs cause people to behave dangerously and that it is just as much the duty of the state to protect its citizens from dope as it is to protect them from murder and theft. The trouble is that all these supposed facts are false.

It is impossible to come to grips with the problem of drug controls unless we distinguish between things and persons. A drug, whether it be heroin or insulin, is a thing. It does not do anything to anyone unless a person ingests it or injects it into himself or administers it to another. Obviously, a drug has no biological effect on a person unless it gets into his body. The basic question—that is logically prior to whether the drug is good or bad—is, therefore: How does a drug get into the person's body? Although there are many ways that that can happen, we need to consider here only a few typical instances of it.

A person may take an accepted nonprescription drug like aspirin by way of self-medication. Or, he may be given an accepted prescription drug like penicillin by way of medication by his physician. Neither of these situations disturbs most people nowadays. What disturbs the compact majority is a person taking a drug like LSD or selling a drug like heroin to others.

The most cursory attention to how drugs get into the human body thus reveals that the moral and political crux of the problem of drug controls lies, not in the pharmacological properties of the chemicals in question, but in the character properties of the persons who take them (and of the people who permit, prescribe, and prohibit drugs).

The true believer in conventional wisdom might wish to insist at this point—not without justification—that some drugs are more dangerous than others; that, in other words, the properties of drugs are no less relevant to understanding our present-day drug problems than are the properties of the persons. That is true. But it is important that we not let that truth divert our attention from the distinction between pharmacological facts and the social policies they supposedly justify.

Today, ordinary, "normal" people do not really want to keep an open mind about drugs and drug controls. Instead of thinking about the problem, they tend to dismiss it with some cliche such as: "Don't tell me that heroin or LSD aren't dangerous drugs?" Ergo, they imply and indeed assert: "Don't tell me that it doesn't make good sense to prohibit their production, sale, and possession!"

What is wrong with this argument? Quite simply, everything. In the first place, the proposition that heroin or LSD is dangerous must be qualified and placed in relation to the dangerousness of other drugs and other artifacts that are not drugs. Second, the social policy that heroin or LSD should be prohibited does not follow, as a matter of logic, from the proposition that they are dangerous, even if they are dangerous.

Admittedly, heroin is more dangerous than aspirin, in the sense that it gives more pleasure to its user than aspirin; heroin is therefore more likely than aspirin to be taken for the self-induction of euphoria. Heroin is also more dangerous than aspirin in the sense that it is easier to kill oneself with it; heroin is therefore more likely to be used for committing suicide.

The fact that people take heroin to make themselves feel happy or high—and use other psychoactive drugs for their mind-altering effects—raises a simple but basic issue that the drug prohibitionists like to avoid, namely: What is wrong with people using drugs for that purpose? Why shouldn't people make themselves happy by means of self-medication? Let me say at once that I believe these are questions to which honest and reasonable men may offer different answers. Whatever the answers, however, I insist that they flow from moral rather than medical considerations.

For example, some people say that individuals should not take heroin because it diverts them from doing productive work, making those who use the drugs, as well as those economically dependent on them, burdens on society. Others say that whether individuals use, abuse, or avoid heroin is, unless they harm others, their private business. And still others opt for a compromise between the total prohibition of heroin and a free trade in it.

There is, however, more to the prohibitionist's position than his concern that hedonic drugs seduce people from hard labor to happy leisure. If prohibitionists were truly motivated by such concerns, they would advocate permission to use heroin contingent on the individual's proven ability to support himself (and perhaps others), rather than its unqualified suppression. The fact that they advocate no such thing highlights the symbolic aspects of drugs and drug controls.

The objects we now call "dangerous drugs" are metaphors for all that we consider sinful and wicked; that is why they are prohibited, rather than because they are demonstrably more harmful than countless other objects in the environment that do not now symbolize sin for us. In this connection, it is instructive to consider the cultural metamorphosis we have undergone during the past half-century, shifting our symbols of sin from sexuality to chemistry.

196

Our present views on drugs, especially psychoactive drugs, are strikingly similar to our former views on sex, especially masturbation. Intercourse in marriage with the aim of procreation used to be the paradigm of the proper use of one's sexual organs; whereas intercourse outside of marriage with the aim of carnal pleasure used to be the paradigm of their improper use. Until recently, masturbation—or self-abuse, as it was called—was professionally declared, and popularly accepted, as both the cause and the symptom of a variety of illnesses, especially insanity. To be sure, it is now virtually impossible to cite a contemporary medical authority to support the concept of self-abuse. Expert medical opinion now holds that there is simply no such thing: that whether a person masturbates or not is medically irrelevant, and that engaging in the practice or refraining from it is a matter of personal morals or life style.

On the other hand, it is now impossible to cite a contemporary medical authority to oppose the concept of drug abuse. Expert medical opinion now holds that drug abuse is a major medical, psychiatric, and public-health problem; that drug addiction is a disease similar to diabetes, requiring prolonged (or life-long) and medically carefully supervised treatment; and that taking or not taking drugs is primarily, if not solely, a matter of medical concern and responsibility.

Like any social policy, our drug laws may be examined from two entirely different points of view: technical and moral. Our present inclination is either to ignore the moral perspective or to mistake the technical for the moral.

An example of our misplaced overreliance on a technical approach to the so-called drug problem is the professionalized mendacity about the dangerousness of certain types of drugs. Since most propagandists against drug abuse seek to justify certain repressive policies by appeals to the alleged dangerousness of various drugs, they often falsify the facts about the true pharmacological properties of the drugs they seek to prohibit. They do so for two reasons: first, because many substances in daily use are just as harmful as the substances they want to prohibit; second, because they realize that dangerousness alone is never a suffficiently persuasive argument to justify the prohibition of any drug, substance, or artifact. Accordingly, the more they ignore the moral dimensions of the problem, the more they must escalate their fraudulent claims about the dangers of drugs.

To be sure, some drugs are more dangerous than others. It *is* easier to kill oneself with heroin than with aspirin. But it is also easier to kill oneself by jumping off a high building than a low one. In the case of drugs, we regard their potentiality for self-injury as justification for their prohibition; in the case of buildings, we do not. Furthermore, we systematically blur and confuse the two quite different ways in which narcotics can cause death: by a deliberate act of suicide and by accidental over-dosage.

I maintain that suicide is an act, not a disease. It is therefore a moral and not a medical problem. The fact that suicide results in death does not make it a medical problem any more than the fact that execution in the electric chair results in death makes the death penalty a medical problem. Hence, it is morally absurd—and, in a free society, politically illegitimate—to deprive an adult of a drug because he might use it to kill himself. To do so is to treat people like institutional psychiatrists treat so-called psychotics: They not only imprison such persons but take everything away from them—shoelaces, belts, razor blades, eating utensils, and so forth—until the "patients" lie naked on a mattress in a padded cell, lest they kill themselves. The result is one of the most degrading tyrannizations in the annals of human history.

Death by accidental overdose is an altogether different matter. But can anyone doubt that this danger now looms so large precisely because the sale of narcotics and many other drugs is illegal? Persons buying illicit drugs cannot be sure what they are getting or how much of it. Free trade in drugs, with governmental action limited to safeguarding the purity of the product and the veracity of labeling, would reduce the risk of accidental overdose with so-called dangerous drugs to the same levels that prevail, and that we find acceptable, with respect to other chemical agents and physical artifacts that abound in our complex technological society.

In my view, regardless of their dangerousness, all drugs should be "legalized" (a misleading term that I employ reluctantly as a concession to common usage). Although I recognize that some drugs—notably, heroin, amphetamine, and LSD, among those now in vogue—may have dangerous consequences, I favor free trade in drugs for the same reason the Founding Fathers favored free trade in ideas: In a free society it is none of the government's business what ideas a man puts into his mind; likewise, it should be none of its business what drug he puts into his body.

Clearly, the argument that marijuana—or heroin, methadone, or morphine—is prohibited because it is addictive or dangerous cannot be supported by facts. For one thing, there are many drugs, from insulin to penicillin, that are neither addictive nor dangerous but are nevertheless also prohibited: They can be obtained only through a physician's prescription. For another, there are many things, from poisons to guns, that are much more dangerous than narcotics (especially to others) but are not prohibited. As everyone knows, it is still possible in the United States to walk into a store and walk out with a shotgun. We enjoy that right, not because we do not believe that guns are dangerous, but because we believe even more strongly that civil liberties are precious. At the same time, it is not possible in the United States to walk into a store and walk out with a bottle of barbiturates or codeine or, indeed, even with an empty hypodermic syringe. We are now deprived of that right because we have come to value medical paternalism more highly than the right to obtain and use drugs without recourse to medical intermediaries.

I submit, therefore, that our so-called drug-abuse problem is an integral part of our present social ethic that accepts "protections" and repressions justified by appeals to health similar to those which medieval societies accepted when they were justified by appeals to faith. Drug abuse (as we now know it) is one of the inevitable consequences of the medical monopoly over drugs—a monopoly whose value is daily acclaimed by science and law, state and church, the professions and the laity. As formerly the church regulated man's relations to God, so medicine now regulates his relations to his body. Deviation from the rules set forth by the church was then considered heresy and was punished by appropriate theological sanctions, called penance; deviation from the rules set forth by medicine is now considered drug abuse (or some sort of "mental illness") and is punished by appropriate medical sanctions, called treatment.

The problem of drug abuse will thus be with us so long as we live under medical tutelage. That is not to say that, if all access to drugs were free, some people would not medicate themselves in ways that might upset us or harm them. That, of course, is precisely what happened when religious practice became free. People proceeded to engage in all sorts of religious behaviors that true believers in traditional faiths found obnoxious and upsetting. Nevertheless, in the conflict between freedom and religion, the American political system has come down squarely for the former and against the latter.

If the grown son of a devoutly religious Jewish father has a ham sandwich for lunch, the father cannot use the police power of American society to impose his moral views on his son. But if the grown son of a devoutly alcoholic father has heroin for lunch, the father can, indeed, use the police power of American society to impose his moral views on his son. Moreover, the penalty that that father could legally visit on his son might exceed the penalty that would be imposed on the son for killing his mother. It is that moral calculus—refracted through our present differential treatment of those who literally abuse others by killing, maiming, and robbing them as against those who metaphorically abuse themselves by using illicit chemicals—which reveals the depravity into which our preoccupation with drugs and drug controls has led us.

I believe that just as we regard freedom of speech and religion as fundamental rights, so we should also regard freedom of self-medication as a fundamental right; and that, instead of mendaciously opposing or mindlessly promoting illicit drugs, we should, paraphrasing Voltaire, make this maxim our rule: "I disapprove of what you take, but I will defend to the death your right to take it!"

Sooner or later we shall have to confront the basic moral dilemma underlying the so-called drug problem: Does a person have the right to take a drug, any drug—not because he needs it to cure an illness, but because he wants to take it?

The Constitution and the Bill of Rights are silent on the subject of drugs. That would seem to imply that the adult citizen has, or ought to have, the right to medicate his own body as he sees fit. Were that not the case, why should there have been a need for a constitutional amendment to outlaw drinking? But if ingesting alcohol was, and is now again, a Constitutional right, is not ingesting opium or heroin or barbiturates or anything else also such a right?

It is a fact that we Americans have a right to read a book—any book—not because we are stupid and want to learn from it, nor because a government-supported educational authority claims that it will be good for us, but simply because we want to read it; because, that is, the government—as our servant rather than our master—hasn't the right to meddle in our private reading affairs.

I believe that we also have a right to eat, drink, or inject a substance—any substance—not because we are sick and want it to cure us, nor because a government-supported medical authority claims that it will be good for us, but simply because we want to take it; because, that is, the government—as our servant rather than master—hasn't the right to meddle in our private dietary and drug affairs.

It is also a fact, however, that Americans now go to jail for picking harmless marijuana growing wild in the fields, but not for picking poisonous mushrooms growing wild in the forests. Why? Because we, Americans, have collectively chosen to cast away our freedom to determine what we should eat, drink, or smoke. In this large and ever-expanding area of our lives, we have rejected the principle that the state is our servant rather than our master. This proposition is painfully obvious when people plaintively insist that we need the government to protect us from the hazards of "dangerous" drugs. To be sure, we need private voluntary associations—or also, some might argue, the government—to *warn* us of the dangers of heroin, high-tension wires, and high-fat diets.

But it is one thing for our would-be protectors to *inform* us of what they regard as dangerous objects in our environment. It is quite another thing for them to *punish* us if we disagree with them.

Whatever Happened
to Human Body Glue?

By David A. Mathisen

May 1980

S uppose someone developed a revolutionary surgical technique that could save tens of thousands of lives every year. Suppose also that the technique required the use of a specific new chemical.

Although a doctor can employ any new surgical technique he finds useful, involvement of a chemical throws the entire procedure into the lap of the Food and Drug Administration (FDA). And since the substance cannot by law be used without FDA clearance, it becomes automatically illegal to use the *surgical technique* without FDA approval. Thus, in our scenario, the revolutionary surgical technique could not lawfully be used, regardless of its lifesaving possibilities, until the FDA had approved at least an Investigational New Drug Exception (IND)—and later a New Drug Application (NDA)—for the chemical involved.

Now suppose that for some ill-defined reason concerning potential undesirable side-effects—already disproven many times by leading medical investigators and taken seriously by few outside the agency—the FDA refused to issue the needed NDA. What could anyone do about it? What could even the most renowned surgeon do to get around FDA refusal to license the chemical even in the light of abundant evidence indicating that its qualms were unfounded? The answer is *nothing*.

Unfortunately, this scenario is not hypothetical at all. It is exactly what has happened in the case of a group of chemical bonding agents known in technical terminology as cyanoacrylate tissue adhesives.

Put simply, these chemicals glue body tissues together in much the same way model-airplane glue binds plastic. Cyanoacrylate is a monomer glue that rapidly polymerizes (forms long chains of molecules much like the intertwining of short fibers of wool or cotton to form thread) upon contact with body fluid and adheres firmly to bleeding tissue. There, it forms a flexible temporary seal beneath which natural healing takes place. The substance erodes gradually and is eliminated from the body.

Over the past 25 years, cyanoacrylate glue has been effective in saving lives in a staggering variety of cases. Used primarily as an aerosol sprayed on open wounds, the glue proved itself as the most significant surgical breakthrough of the decade during the Vietnam War, when Army doctors were able to save hundreds of lives in the field and in military hospitals at home.

Since then, the substance has been perfected for application through an endoscope, a sophisticated long, flexible tube run through a patient's nose or mouth and down the esophagus to gain direct access to the esophagus, stomach, and intestines. In this way it can be used to seal bleeding internal abrasions and cuts—primarily ulcers—in seconds, enabling them to heal rapidly without interference from digestive acids.

With a green light from the FDA, there is no reason why endoscopically applied cyanoacrylate couldn't render the treatment of ulcers a problem of the past. In terms of the alleviation of human suffering, the implications of this use alone are inestimable. And this is only the beginning.

More recently, techniques have been perfected for applying cyanoacrylate almost anywhere in the body through micro- and macro-catheters—fine, flexible plastic tubes inserted directly through veins and arteries to reach specific parts of the body far inside. The aim? To block malfunctioning blood vessels—without surgery.

Again, further applications are just beginning to be realized: control of malignant tumors, for example, or destruction of all or parts of malfunctioning organs (such as the appendix or spleen) where surgical intervention is impossible or difficult. Cyanoacrylate has also been used successfully since 1965 for reinforcing and preventing rupture of aneurysms (tiny blood vessels whose weakened walls threaten to burst and cause fatal hemorrhaging), particularly in the brain.

There are conventional agents similar to cyanoacrylate, such as methacrylate, the synthetic agent used most often for sealing aneurysms. But cyanoacrylate has a big advantage: Because it can form its protective coating in the presence of water, it can be used while bleeding is still active. All other agents require that bleeding be stopped *first*. In wet tissue, the liquid glue congeals into a bleeding-stopping film in about 90 seconds.

Considering these and other available applications, even the most casual observer must wonder where this medical "miracle" is today. Why aren't there spray cans of it on the shelves of every American emergency room or operating room and in every ambulance, ready to save lives in otherwise hopeless situations? It's easy to spell out the answer: F-D-A.

Since the years of the Thalidomide panic and the subsequent Kefauver congressional hearings, the Food and Drug Administration has consistently refused to license cyanoacrylate glue for any medical use, including dental work. And it has done so in the face of 27 years of use in laboratories in American medical schools and research institutions and in the U.S. armed forces and despite 10 years of intensive general surgical use overseas, in nations where drug regulatory agencies have long considered cyanoacrylate innocuous.

For the uninitiated: The FDA licensing procedure involves the reluctant issue of Investigational New Drug exceptions to specific doctors and their research groups, who are then enabled to use a drug or substance in specific clinical situations—but only on patients who are almost certain to die anyway or are unacceptable candidates for conventional surgery. The burden of proving the drug's safety for general use, along with the expense of financing the detailed studies necessary to convince the FDA, falls on the medical community and private corporations. In the case of cyanoacrylate, even the large numbers of specialists convinced of its safety and efficacy have found that mustering evidence sufficient to satisfy the FDA is a formidable, costly, and slow process.

American surgeons familiar with the tissue adhesive and aware of its amazing healing capability are anxious for the FDA to license it for general surgical use. It could, they believe, become a hospital mainstay, saving countless lives by enabling the rapid sealing of hemorrhaging in accident victims or providing instant fluid-loss protection over large areas of the bodies of burn victims.

But these researchers remain powerless. Be it out of simple ignorance or out of a desire to play it safe and protect its image and its track record—a record of few errors of commission despite countless fatal errors of omission, usually from doing nothing—the FDA's stance on licensure of cyanoacrylate is so typically and tragically haphazard that the glue may never be widely—and legally—available.

The earliest form of cyanoacrylate was developed by Eastman Laboratories, which in 1955 first reported its remarkable ability to glue ruptured body tissue until natural healing processes could take place. This form of the glue, called Eastman 910, was perfected for a wide variety of uses during the late '50s and early '60s at Walter Reed Army Institute of Research (the Defense Department's center for medical research and treatment of VIP Defense personnel). The Walter Reed work was done under the direction of Dr. Teruo Matsumoto, then chief of experimental surgery, with the G. Barr Company cooperating in development of the aerosol delivery system for use on open wounds. As the story of cyanoacrylate unfolds, it will become clear how important it was that, as part of the military, both Matsumoto and the institute were exempt from FDA controls.

The Eastman glue was used extensively during the war in Vietnam—at Walter Reed and at the Third Surgical Hospital in Bien Hoa—under the direction of Capts. John Collins and Paul James. Its performance in the field was nothing short of miraculous. *Medical World News* reported on it in July 1967: "Military surgeons have developed a novel technique to stop bleeding....A small aerosol bottle that delivers a fine spray of adhesive has saved the lives of critically wounded U.S. infantrymen in Vietnam. The spray put an end to massive hemorrhages of the kidney or liver that could not be controlled by any other technique. Within seconds after the adhesive was sprayed onto the ruptured organs, a crust formed and bleeding stopped." The article quoted Col. Robert M. Hardaway III, then director of Walter Reed's surgery division. "So far, follow-up studies on the men treated for massive bleeding have not revealed any unfavorable side effects."

Other significant advances had been made using cyanoacrylate outside the military—largely without benefit of INDs from the FDA, which was much less strict in the years before Thalidomide. Between 1956 and 1973, for example, 45 terminal patients at the University of Minnesota and affiliated hospitals were successfully treated with the glue. But because civilian researchers could not find corporations wealthy enough to underwrite their battles against FDA intransigence—a problem the military didn't have to bother with—these advances have seen little publicity.

Much of the early pioneering work was done by Dr. Shelly Chou, head of neurosurgery at the University of Minnesota, and Dr. Charles Carton of Cedars-Sinai Hospital in Los Angeles. In the mid-60s, Dr. Chou and his group worked with a version developed in Japan, testing it on cats to determine whether there are any long-term effects in the brain. After three years the animals showed *no* effects. At autopsy, no brain or nervous system effects from the glue were found, and it was pronounced totally innocuous—that is, to have *no* side effects.

Overseas, applications of cyanoacrylate proliferated rapidly. By the early '60s it was already in general clinical use in Japan for sealing wounds, mending torn intestines and broken bones, neurosurgery, and gynecological surgery. It was also gaining wide acceptance in clinical surgery in Germany, France, Switzerland, and Canada.

SAFE—OR NOT. A glance at *Index Medicus*, the "bible" of current American medical research, for any year since 1970 reveals at least a half-page of cyanoacrylate citations for uses ranging from hemorrhage control to eye surgery. In the United States, most of these applications have been developed on lab animals, only to be forbidden for human use by the FDA. The October 26, 1973, issue of *Medical World News* reported the sad situation: Despite its numerous uses, manufacturers of cyanoacrylate adhesives "evidently feel it is not worth their time, money, and effort to win FDA approval."

It's not that they haven't tried. In the early '60s several companies were working on perfecting cyanoacrylate. But when the FDA found signs of tissue toxicity (tendency to cause inflammation in surrounding tissue and to activate the body's rejection mechanisms) in one of the three types under investigation, licensure was refused for all three until the companies developing the other two were able to submit proof that the toxicity was not common to theirs as well.

A few years later, American industry again tried to break through FDA blockades. In the late '60s several major drug firms, including Eastman, Ethicon (now owned by Johnson & Johnson), and the Surgical Products Division of Minnesota Mining and Manufacturing (3M), focused on potentially lucrative dental applications of cyanoacrylate tissue glue. This, they thought, was an area in which they might be able to commercially justify use of the time and money needed to meet FDA standards.

Unfortunately, FDA tests revealed tissue toxicity in the Ethicon type, and the toxicity bogeyman was again foisted on all three companies. Later, Eastman and 3M were able to prove independently that their versions of the glue were not toxic, and dental INDs, allowing use only in the mouths of humans already dying from some other malady, were approved for Eastman 910 and 3M's version, MBR 4197.

But then, in 1972, FDA tests showed that large aggregations of the adhesive implanted in lab animals sometimes caused malignant fibrosarcomas (cancerous masses of scar tissue). At that point, the agency indicted cyanoacrylate as "possibly carcinogenic," ordered an immediate halt to any use of the glue, and rescinded all outstanding INDs.

Although convinced that their products were not carcinogenic and that the FDA's results were insignificant, Eastman and Ethicon dropped out. They simply could no longer bear the financial burden of proof. That left only 3M, which held on and undertook another costly series of carcinogenicity tests to prove the safety of MBR 4197.

Even at that time, however, the fibrosarcoma test—long the most popular test with the FDA and AMA for determining the propensity of a substance to cause cancer—had been discredited. The FDA's labeling of cyanoacrylate as "possibly carcino-genic" was taken seriously by few nongovernment investigators outside the AMA.

And long before the FDA's questionable reports of carcinogenicity and the industry's expensive "counterstudies," the experience with cyanoacrylate had given no indication that it can cause cancer. At the top of the list was the 15-year use of the glue at Walter Reed Army Institute of Research.

In 1977 I asked Lt. Col. Arthur Fleming, director of surgery at the institute, to make a complete search of all records of soldiers treated with cyanoacrylate. After receiving the necessary clearance from Walter Reed security headquarters to release the information, Fleming reported: "My evidence is that there was no carcinogenesis associated with the cyanoacrylates that were being used at Walter Reed....The man who did the original histo-chemical studies [of effects on the body's normal biochemical activity] was with Walter Reed in the 1960s and found no evidence of carcinogenesis."

It has, unfortunately, proven impossible to learn the name of that man. According to Lt. Col. Fleming, "He is with the FDA now, and could not comment due to 'conflict of interest.'"

Dr. Larry Johnson, chief of gastroenterology at Walter Reed then and now, had this to say about the FDA's unilateral action of 1972: "I hadn't...seen any patients treated with the cyanoacrylate who had any side effects from the glue. In 1972 we had substantial evidence that it was not carcinogenic, and no results suggesting that it might be."

With the wealth of evidence prior to 1972 indicating that cyanoacrylate is not carcinogenic, with all the use it had seen before 1972 among civilians in Europe without even the suspicion of carcinogenicity, and with American researchers involved since 1955 unanimous in their conviction of its safety, the FDA's 1972 shutdown of all work on cyanoacrylate adhesive applications is difficult to make sense of. My own search for an explanation, via calls to the head of the FDA department responsible for the fibrosarcoma tests, has been fruitless. The department head claims that he cannot comment without clearance from the FDA's public relations officials, and that office has refused to grant a clearance—and refused to give any reason for its refusal.

Outside of the FDA, there is no such unwillingness to discuss those tests. William Walsh is a senior specialist with the clinical research group of 3M's surgical products division. His comment on the 1972 research shutdown and the FDA's continued lockup of cyanoacrylate? "The rodents used in these [fibrosar-coma] studies are very prone to develop these tumors—much more so than humans. It is simply an innate characteristic of the animals. They will develop fibrosarcomas when practically any foreign body is implanted in delicate tissue.

"Even in Germany, when the cyanoacrylates first came on the market, the German Ministry—the analog of our FDA—raised the same questions raised by the FDA here. But German toxicologists had little trouble convincing the German Ministry that it was due to a trait in the lab animals. In the United States it isn't nearly so easy...but we have to deal with the political reality that the FDA has absolute authority to keep *any* drug—no matter how life-giving its primary action and no matter how unlikely the possibility of untoward side effects—*off* the market."

Dr. Stephen Silvis has worked with cyanoacrylate at the Minneapolis Veterans Administration Hospital. His comment? "The FDA became concerned...when they got some fibrosarcomas in lab animals. But these fibrosarcomas didn't prove it was carcinogenic. In their tests, they formed a hard ball with the glue and, when implanted in the lab animals' tissue, it gave a typical foreign-body reaction. Fibrous tumors surrounded them. But this reaction is not necessarily specific to the material implanted."

Dr. Gerald Shklar, head of the department of oral medicine and oral pathology at the Harvard University School of Dental Medicine and a foremost cancer study expert, was retained by 3M to do further carcinogenesis tests on MBR 4197 after the FDA revoked 3M's IND in 1972. The results?

"Our model was very good," reported Dr. Shklar. "We used the cheekpouch of the Syrian hamster—a very delicate mucous membrane. We painted this tissue with 3M's cyanoacrylate homologue three times a week for six months. If the cyanoacrylate was carcinogenic, it would have caused cancer in the hamster. It did not. There was not a single tumor. The results were completely negative."

"We also applied the glue to open wounds in the hamster's mouth," added Shklar, "with the same conclusively negative results. We did not observe even any precancer stages. I would be quite confident that the glue would prove equally innocuous in any part of the body."

I asked Shklar what he thought of the FDA's 1972 fibrosarcoma studies. "I'm not familiar with their particular studies, but the only way I could foresee that you could get a tumor would be if you built up a bulk of the material in an implantation [exactly what the FDA did]. You could then get a physical irritant and a fibrosarcoma could result. But by this method, you could get a tumor with practically any foreign substance, including glass and sugar."

The FDA is, of course, aware of the ambiguities of the fibrosarcoma test. While outside experts maintain that the test is irrelevant in this case, the FDA stands by it as a statistical indicator of degree of carcinogenicity related to the number of tumors produced. What the outside experts have in their favor is that cyanoacrylate is simply never used in a manner that would permit sizable deposits to develop. Autopsies performed on thousands of lab animals since 1955 have shown no tendency in the adhesive to concentrate in body tissues. The glue is so effective, and is used so sparingly, that it would be a rare case indeed in which the amount applied would be sufficient to form an aggregation even close to the size of the FDA test implants.

Put bluntly, then, it appears that the test that halted work with a chemical substance known since 1955 to be effective and *safe* was one that virtually *forced* lab animals to develop tumors—as a nonspecific reaction to an implanted foreign body. And because the foreign body happened to be a cyanoacrylate aggregation, the FDA ignored all evidence to the contrary and banished a miraculous lifesaver to confinement in the bowels of its labyrinthine bureaucracy.

It took three years for 3M to rescue cyanoacrylate from the FDA's questionable verdict. In 1975 it won approval of a second IND for oral applications of MBR 4197.

Later in 1975 Dr. Stephen Silvis, then chief of gastroenterology at the Veterans Administration Hospital in Minneapolis and professor of medicine at the

University of Minnesota, secured an IND for the 3M glue applied with an endoscope for gastrointestinal (GI) problems. Silvis soon became the leading—in fact, the only—researcher *legally* using cyanoacrylate to save human lives. (Several others elsewhere continued to use it without FDA approval. Had they been caught thus saving lives, they could have been prosecuted and found guilty of a federal felony and jailed.)

One striking example of cyanoacrylate's efficacy in GI cases concerned a man admitted to the Minneapolis VA Hospital in 1976, after attempting suicide by swallowing Drano. The man was hemorrhaging massively from lesions (lacerated tissue) throughout his esophagus and upper GI tract. By conventional medical standards, he was as good as dead. Luckily, under the existing IND, Dr. Silvis and his colleagues were able to use an endoscope to spray the lesions with cyanoacrylate. Eighty percent of the bleeding was stopped within minutes, and a second application took care of the rest. There was no further bleeding and the man was discharged a week later. Now, after more than three years, the patient is still healthy and has displayed no side effects from either the glue or the lesions, which have healed completely.

Two other advanced methods to stop bleeding—electrocoagulation and lasers—are now under investigation. But cyanoacrylate, again, has an advantage: It causes no further tissue damage, whereas both electrocoagulation and lasers can cause extensive damage to surrounding tissue.

In 1977, Dr. Silvis's studies were expanded into a multicenter investigation involving several hospitals across the nation. Walter Reed Institute became involved in the use of the glue for the first time since Dr. Teruo Matsumoto left in the mid-60s, putting an end to his research. (Matsumoto, now at Hahnemann Medical College, has refused comment on his own cyanoacrylate work—or anyone else's.) Under this study, 100 patients received cyanoacrylate treatment, with results similar to those obtained by Silvis in his earlier research.

An IND has also been granted to researchers to try one other application of tissue glue: blocking of blood vessels by applying the glue through a fine tube fed through the vessels to the appropriate spot (transcatheter embolization). Dr. Martin L. Goldman, director of vascular research at the Albany (N.Y.) Medical Center Hospital, has had considerable success using the glue for "medical splenectomies" (killing a lethally infected spleen in place—without surgery—by blocking the blood vessels feeding the spleen and its infection). Again, cyanoacrylate is not only successful but superior to alternatives. More than half of all conventional nonsurgical destruction of infected spleens (done with Gelfoam or other particle embolizers) lead to abcess of the organ, notes Dr. Goldman. Cyanoacrylate, on the other hand, has shown no tendency to promote abcessing.

At the Mason Clinic in Seattle, Dr. Patrick C. Freeny has used this material to block malfunctioning blood vessels in some 40 patients made "legal" subjects under FDA doctrine because they were high surgical risks. He too concludes that the glue has significant advantages over conventional methods. "With particle embolization," he reports, "you inject into the blood stream, and the particles go where the blood stream carries them—you hope, where you want them. Sometimes they can go off and fatally block an artery you *don't* want blocked, such as one bringing blood to the heart. But with the cyanoacrylate we can use a silicone micro-catheter to go way out in the peripheral circulation and plug the vessel exactly where we want to."

And Dr. Freeny's work has turned up still more evidence of the safety of cyanoacrylate. Autopsies of patients who died of the terminal condition that made them legal for use in the study have shown that the glue has about the same, negligible, tissue toxicity as nonabsorbable silk suture. And, notes Freeny, the vessel blockages have proven permanent enough to achieve the desired lifesaving result.

There is some hope that the FDA is coming to the realization that its longstanding suspicion of cyanoacrylate may be unfounded. In early 1979, in a guarded and unpublicized letter to William Walsh of 3M, the agency allowed that, for oral applications, it seems likely that the glue is not significantly carcinogenic.

Yet the outlook for cyanoacrylate is still bleak. Even if the FDA made an across-the-board declaration that the substance is not carcinogenic, the time-consuming and stringent tests required for licensure constitute an undeclared war of attrition against the glue, its manufacturers, and its long-time proponents. And even if the FDA could be convinced to approve a New Drug Application, the road to approval for general surgical use remains long. If 3M obtained a cyanoacrylate NDA for gastrointestinal use, notes Dr. Silvis, "doctors would be able to use it only for the gastrointestinal applications specified in the detailed restrictions circular qualifying the NDA. All other uses would require a step-by-step process similar to the one we've gone through. First, extensive studies of *that* specific use on lab animals; then, approval of an IND; then, more extensive controlled studies on terminal patients under the IND."

Absurd as it may seem, *each specific use* of tissue glue—as with all new medical chemicals and drugs—must fight its own lonely battle through the bureaucracy. For each, a corporation must be found that is willing and able to bear the financial portion of the burden of proof.

And, as one researcher notes, "In dealing with the FDA on these carcinogenesis tests, it's extremely expensive to convince them that a substance has no serious side effects. A drug company must justify enough economic return from estimates of potential sales markets in order to sink so much money into it. These economic constraints are probably the major thing that differentiates between the advance of modern medical breakthroughs into wide-scale public use in the United States from the advances in other nations, where the regulatory agencies are not nearly so difficult to satisfy—or where the regulatory agencies must assume the burden of proof that a substance *does* have harmful side effects before they can refuse to allow it on the open market."

The sizable potential sales needed to offset the costs of maneuvering the FDA course put cyanoacrylate in a particularly bad position. The very nature of the glue requires that it be used in only limited amounts. And since repeated applications are unnecessary, it appears that no matter how many uses of the glue are approved, it would still sell in very small quantities. A single *drop* goes a long way.

And so even 3M, which continued for so long to work on a promising new product in spite of uncertain returns, late in 1979 finally put cyanoacrylate "on the back burner," in the words of a disappointed William Walsh. Like the other

American companies that have done cyanoacrylate work in the past, 3M has turned instead to the nonmedical arena, producing thousands of gallons of a nonmedical form of the glue for sale in department and dime stores as the household "super glues." Eastman markets its 1955 version under the original name, Eastman 910; 3M has resorted to selling MBR 4197 under the commercial name Super Glue; other companies produce brands like Krazy Glue.

The simple fact that these household adhesives are in such wide use today further discounts one of the FDA's reasons for keeping it off the medical/surgical supply lists: that it is allegedly "too dangerous to apply," that physicians might accidentally get it on tissue other than that for which it was intended, with disastrous results. When household cyanoacrylate first came on the market in the early '70s, Consumers Union expressed similar misgivings, worrying that consumers might inadvertently bind their fingers together and "require surgery to separate them." The Consumer Product Safety Commission responded by recalling 10 brands of the glue, but tests quickly satisfied both Consumers Union and the CPSC that their fears were unfounded. An acetone like simple nail-polish remover will quickly dissolve the glue if it accidentally binds to fingers or other tissue.

The history of cyanoacrylate at the hands of the FDA leaves us with the hypothetical question posed earlier—and now carrying the urgency of reality: What can a doctor do for a patient who is bleeding to death or who has another condition that cyanoacrylate can alleviate *without* significant risks of deleterious side effects? If the physician is to obey FDA regulations, he or she can still do nothing. The evidence marshaled here, however, makes a strong case for another response—civil disobedience. This would solve the patient's problem; it would provide no remedy for the larger problem at the root of cyanoacrylate's sad history: the untenable position medical research has been placed in by the FDA.

To render the Food and Drug Administration more sensitive and humane, to increase its understanding of the risk/benefit analysis individuals would *themselves* make when faced with new drugs and unforeseen side effects, to speed up its response to escalating rates of technological and medical progress, would require total reorganization under congressional supervision. Yet this too would offer only superficial relief. The same forces that turned the FDA into the monolithic morass of self-justification it is today, and which *all* federal regulatory agencies tend to become, would ensure that in a decade or two we would be right back where we started.

The problem with conservative "reform" of the FDA is that, like many regulatory agencies, its "crime" is inherently passive. It need do nothing to withhold new drugs from the public. They are assumed a priori to be dangerous and remain illegal until the FDA gives its blessing. Potential developers of cyanoacrylate, along with countless other miracle medicines, are presumed guilty until proven innocent. And so the products they could be offering remain buried in *Index Medicus* and reports on investigators' shelves.

But this is not a fluke reflecting FDA arrogance or anachronism. This question of burden of proof is at the heart of setting up regulatory agencies as guardians of the public welfare. It is the only way the FDA—or the CPSC, EPA, or OSHA—can play the regulatory game. But in the FDA it is far deadlier than in other agencies. Each flaw and inefficiency translates more or less directly into an unnecessary loss of life or increase in human suffering.

And the patients at risk, and the doctors involved, have no recourse. That's what protection by regulatory fiat means. Guilt is assumed, innocence must be proven, and there is no court of appeals. Neither individual patients nor their doctors have any place to argue in their own behalf, to appeal even for one-shot exceptions based on the suffering that could be alleviated or death that could be averted.

Evidently, simply because a new drug is involved, Congress and the FDA consider doctors and patients unqualified to weigh the risks and benefits. And so the right to informed consent, held inviolable in all other domains of medical treatment, is withheld.

The paternalistic role of regulatory agencies can sound very nice in theory. Fatherly Uncle Sam is to look out for our interests, protecting us from undue risks and, in popular parlance, from greedy capitalist robber barons who may be negligent or, at best, mistaken about safety. All of our lives are thus to be made easier. This parental image of government is the only conceivable justification for the immense, unilateral powers that the FDA and other regulatory agencies exercise over individual liberties. But it is the very antithesis of the free choice necessary for democracy.

And, to add insult to injury, the idea of paternalistic regulation doesn't even work out in practice like it is supposed to in theory, as the story of cyanoacrylate and any number of other case studies make crystal-clear. But as long as people delude themselves into believing that picture of an all-protective government, they absolve themselves of any responsibility for taking the trouble to think and become educated about the various aspects of modern life that have come under government control. Ironically, regulatory agencies monopolize the protection business, severely reducing the incentive for agencies in the private sector—such as Consumers Union—to come forward to do a better job. *Informed* consent is thus not only prohibited but made nearly impossible.

How have we become a nation in which nearly everything we do is regulated to our disadvantage by some government agency? The evolution of the FDA illustrates how those agencies turn out to be, not the well-intentioned bodies Congress may well have in mind when it creates them, but Frankensteins over whom the individuals they are meant to serve have no control.

The only reason the FDA exists today is that Congress, via the Constitution, was given the power to enact laws to protect the "health, safety, and general welfare" of the public. Congress, one would assume, had this mission firmly in mind from the time of the original Food and Drug Act of 1906 right through 1931, when the FDA became an independent regulatory body under the Agricultural Appropriations Act.

Since that time, Congress has added various amendments to the FDA's enabling legislation, but the agency was not allowed to become the truly repressive force it is today until the great Thalidomide panic of the early '60s. Out of the resulting congressional hearings came a vast increase in the FDA's regulatory powers.

Unfortunately, the wave of hysteria and journalistic sensationalism inspired by Thalidomide was quite out of proportion to the actual number of deformed infants born. Drug companies were characterized as nothing but money-hungry capitalists anxious to increase profits by shoving all manner of untested drugs down American throats. They needed firmer regulation by fatherly Uncle Sam.

Of course, those congressional hearings did reveal pharmaceutical industry cover-ups and irresponsibility regarding possible drug side effects. But could that justify an automatic presumption of guilt for all firms and all new drugs? Does it change the fact that it may well be unconstitutional for any regulatory agency to have such powers over individual choice?

While Congress might be forgiven for not understanding then the implications of bestowing such powers upon a hard-line bureaucracy, those implications should be obvious by now to anyone who has the courage to face them. The overreaction of Congress was immense—and tragic. There is little excuse for Congress not to take prompt action to remedy its constitutional error.

The public today has demonstrated, in fact, that it does not want the FDA dictating its choices just because risky matters are involved. The reaction to the saccharin controversy is a fine example, and the message could not be more clear if a national referendum were taken. Clearly, modern Americans believe that they can make responsible assessments of risk independently of government.

Vast changes have taken place in the level of public awareness of medicine and medical advances since 1906, 1922, and 1931, when the FDA was taking shape. Even if at those times most people were too far from understanding the risks and side effects to be able to give reasonably informed consent regarding treatment with new drugs, in today's climate of an enlightened, educated public, FDA paternalism is undesirable and unjustifiable. It is, in fact, detrimental to the health, safety, and general welfare of the American public, as the cyanoacrylate experience makes abundantly clear.

If cyanoacrylate tissue adhesive is finally approved by the FDA for general surgical use, it will be interesting to see who will be called to account for the thousands of lives lost and the suffering prolonged during the years that it was withheld—years during which available methods were wholly inadequate to the tasks doctors faced. And it would be enlightening to see what the response of the Supreme Court would be if a citizen ever sued the FDA on behalf of a relative who died in an emergency room or ambulance for want of a lifesaving cyanoacrylate adhesive application. It would be interesting, indeed, to see how anyone could justify *that* as being helpful or effective in promoting anyone's health, safety, or general welfare.

A Calm Look at Abortion Arguments

By Roger Bissell

September 1981

The abortion issue in our time has been likened to the slavery issue in the 1800s: Emotions run high, and the citizenry is deeply divided over what is universally acknowledged to be more than a superficial issue. In fact, there is a more fundamental similarity: In both cases an important underlying issue is, *What is a human being?*

Many who supported the continuation of slavery did not favor the violation of human rights; they simply did not believe that the black man was quite human. And although some people would not prohibit abortions even if the fetus is a human being (for example, because the woman or society would benefit more from the abortion than would the fetus from being left to develop), most people would agree that *if* the fetus is a human being, then abortion is wrong (except perhaps if the mother's life is threatened). For if a living being is a human being, then it has a right to life and cannot rightfully be aborted or otherwise killed except in self-defense.

Where the disagreement enters, though, is precisely on the issue of whether, or at what stage, the fetus is a human being. Emotionalism on both sides of the abortion debate has tended to obscure this fundamental point of contention. So have appeals to religious teachings, tradition, opinion polls, women's independence versus men's domination, and so on.

All of these tactics are designed to make a point about abortion; they do very little to address the real disagreement over the tough question, When does a human being come into existence? But until the air is cleared of emotionalism, and solid arguments and the available facts are brought to bear on that question, it will be impossible to settle the debate over abortion legislation in a manner consistent with the American political tradition, to which individual rights for all human beings are central. So, where do reason and the facts lead us?

Those who oppose abortion altogether are agreed on the premise that existence as a human being begins with conception. Given the human right to life, abortion is thus murder and must be outlawed. (Some allow an exception if the woman's life is endangered by continuation of the pregnancy; others add pregnancy by rape or incest.)

Why do they claim a link between conception and human existence? Although some anti-abortionists (or pro-lifers) refer to religious teachings or make emotional pleas, there are others who make their case with logic and facts. The strongest argument offered by the rational anti-abortionists is based on certain facts of biology pertaining to the nature of life and the nature of the fetus.

I myself was at one time such an advocate. Like some other rational anti-abortionists, I rested a good part of the argument on the essay "Man's Rights" by Ayn Rand, who is, however, a staunch defender of the pro-choice position on abortion. This anti-abortion argument, quoting from and expanding on Rand, goes like this:

As Ayn Rand argues, "Life is a process of self-sustaining and self-generated action." Such a process begins when an egg and sperm cell unite. Thus, a new living human being comes into existence at conception. All human beings have the right to life, so even a newly fertilized zygote (being a living human being) has the right to life. And "the right to life," explains Rand, "means the right to engage in self-sustaining and self-generated action." For a zygote, embryo, or fetus, this means the right to continue receiving sustenance and shelter from its mother. Therefore, abortion is murder.

This is a powerful argument—it gets to the heart of the matter; it is consistent; and it appeals to relevant facts. It can withstand a number of stiff objections.

The first pro-choice challenge is to deny that the fetus even qualifies as a being, a separate and distinct organism, before it is born. It may be separable or viable at some point, they concede, but until then it is simply a parasite or a part of the woman's body.

In reply, anti-abortionists point out that the fetus carries out digestion, excretion, and a number of other functions and, from at least 28 weeks after conception, perceives via its sense organs and nervous system. The fetus thus has centers of organismic activity separate and distinct from those of the woman harboring it. Reliance upon the uterus for shelter and the placenta for nourishment no more makes the fetus a nonindividual or parasite than does the dependence of an infant (or an adult, for that matter) upon someone else's house for shelter and someone else's food for nourishment make *it* a nonentity.

The second pro-choice challenge to the rational anti-abortionists' case is to deny that the fetus qualifies as a *living* being engaged in self-sustaining, self-generated action. It is clearly *dependent*.

Those on the anti-abortion side point out, however, that by this standard a child is not "alive" either, since he or she is unable to provide for himself or herself. They further correctly observe that this line of argument betrays a gross misunderstanding of Rand's concept of life.

Although Rand defines "life" as "a process of self-sustaining and self-generated action," "self-sustaining action" does not mean providing one's own sustenance through one's own efforts. It means something much more fundamental biologically: an action *directed*, either by choice or automatically, toward the organism's own continued action—regardless of the source of the materials necessary to sustain that action.

Similarly, "self-generated action" means an action *initiated*, either by choice or automatically, by the organism itself. Even the simple energy conversions of a plant qualify as life, since they are initiated by the plant and directed toward the plant's own continued conversion of energy. Clearly, the fetus—which is the center of increasingly complex processes of metabolism, locomotion, and consciousness, separate and distinct from those of the woman—is an actual, living being.

The pro-choice people have but one move left: to deny that the fetus is a *human* living being; that is, to deny the claim that there is no essential difference in a fetus's nature at any two points in its development from conception onward. If correct, this denial would be entirely adequate to refute the anti-abortion position.

There is no unanimity among pro-choice people, though, as to *when*, and *how*, the fetus does in fact *become* human. Unless it can be established at what point in its growth, and because of what developments, a fetus—or baby or child—changes in its essential nature from not-yet-human to human, any stance in favor of leaving women free to choose an abortion should be regarded with suspicion. The question is: Can this gap in the pro-choice position be filled?

A defensible argument for the pro-choice position requires, first, an adequate conception of what it is to be human and, second, facts about fetal development.

Aristotle defined man, or the human being, as *the rational animal*. The point was not that human beings always behave sensibly or logically. What he meant was that humans are the only creatures with a rational *faculty* that makes possible and explains all the *other* activities and accomplishments that distinguish humans from the lower animals.

Even within the vastly greater context of all of mankind's knowledge to date, Aristotle's definition still seems to have captured what it is to be human. As Ayn Rand, a 20th-century Aristotelian, explains:

"One could observe that man is the only animal who speaks English, wears wristwatches, flies airplanes, manufactures lipstick, studies geometry, reads newspapers, writes poems, darns socks, etc. None of these are essential characteristics: none of them explains the others; none of them applies to all men, omit any or all of them, assume a man who has never done any of these things, and he will still be a *man*. But observe that all of these activities (and innumerable others) require a *conceptual grasp* of reality, that an animal would not be able to understand them, that they are the expressions and consequences of man's rational faculty, that an organism without that faculty would *not* be a man—and you will know why man's rational faculty is his essential distinguishing and defining characteristic." (This passage is from Rand's *Introduction to Objectivist Epistemology*.)

If possessing this rational faculty is what sets humans apart from other creatures, then the point at which that faculty comes into play is the point of development at which a *human being* may be truly said to have made its appearance.

This rational faculty, however, involves much more than the complex levels of abstraction generally associated with "rationality." As Aristotle observed, the conclusions derived from reasoning are sound only when they rest on the evidence of the senses, only when tied to perceptual awareness of reality. So reason is not some abstract, freely floating ability separate and apart from perception but instead, to quote Rand, is "the faculty of perceiving, identifying, and integrating the evidence of the senses." In other words, the rational faculty that is a defining human characteristic is the ability to perceive *and then* conceptualize about reality.

It seems plausible to conclude that this faculty begins its functioning when the living being develops beyond the undifferentiated chaos of pure sensations and actually distinguishes objects of perception. But exactly when does perception begin? When is the brain sufficiently developed?

Much earlier than previously suspected, according to recent findings. Neurophysiologists have made EEG measurements of developing fetuses and prematurely born babies and discovered that the patterns of electrical brain activity prior to the 28th week of development are radically and fundamentally different from those occurring *after* the 28th week.

In *The Conscious Brain*, Steven Rose, a British neurophysiologist, observes that "before 28 weeks the patterns are very simple and lacking in any of the characteristic forms which go to make up the adult EEG pattern." Then, between the 28th and 32nd weeks, the theta, delta, and alpha waves of the adult make their appearance—at first only periodically, "occurring in brief, spasmodic bursts; but after 32 weeks the pattern of waves becomes more continuous, and characteristic differences begin to appear in the EEG pattern of the waking and sleeping infant."

American neuroscientist Dominick P. Purpura concurs with Rose. In a recent interview, Purpura defined "brain life" as "the capacity of the cerebral cortex, or the thinking portion of the brain, to begin to develop consciousness, self-awareness and other generally recognized cerebral functions as a consequence of the formation of nerve cell circuits." Brain life, said Purpura, begins between the 28th and 32nd weeks of pregnancy.

To summarize: The pre–28-week fetus—while indeed a living organism—cannot be regarded as *human*, since it does not yet possess a functioning rational faculty. It is a potential human being. It becomes an *actual* human being only when the faculty that makes it distinctively human begins operating—at about the 28th week of pregnancy.

It follows then that until at least the 28th week of pregnancy, the fetus has no human rights that might be violated by abortion. So there should be no legal impediment placed in the way of a woman who seeks to abort such a fetus.

From the 28th week on, however, the fetus *does* have the right to life. Abortion past this point should be permitted only under two conditions: when the woman's life is threatened by the pregnancy (in which case, a fetus that survives the abortion must not be killed or allowed to die) or when the fetal brain is so defective that it will never function on the human level of awareness.

Otherwise, abortion after the 28th week is equivalent to murder and should be treated as such under the law. The same legal protection presently given to normal children should be extended to normal post–28-week fetuses. This includes full recognition and implementation of their rights to life, liberty, property—and support.

In contrast to the case I have presented above, the mainstream pro-choice argument says that "heart-lung viability"—which happens around the third trimester, or last three months, of pregnancy—should be the dividing line between the woman's right to an abortion and the fetus's right to life. This is the view that anti-abortion forces are trying to defeat through legislation or a constitutional amendment.

But as Purpura has pointed out, the concept of viability at 24 weeks only makes sense if the heart is the central organ of human life. In fact, he notes, it is the brain that should be so regarded. The essence of human life rests, not in having a heart and lungs that permit one to survive outside the woman's body, but in having a brain that functions on the perceptual level and is normal enough eventually to function on the conceptual level, as well. So the viability of a fetus—its ability to survive *as a human being*—should properly be placed at around the 28th week instead of the 24th week, as presently maintained by most of those arguing for the pro-choice position.

This new definition of viability in terms of brain development is not vulnerable to a rather serious anti-abortionist objection to the heart-lung criterion: making the right to life dependent upon technology. Ten years from now, physiological viability may be possible as early as three months, instead of six months, because of certain medical advances. So, they ask, how is it moral to deny a three-month fetus the right to life *now*, since its *nature* would be identical in the technologically advanced future? But, by the neurological standard based on brain development and function, the three-month fetus would not qualify as human even if technology made possible physiological three-month viability.

Another competing pro-choice argument is drawn from the common law. As expressed by Lord Coke in the 17th century, the common law held that "wilful murder" was the unlawful killing of "any *reasonable* creature *in being* and under the king's peace with malice fore-thought—either express...or implied." And it had a strikingly simple standard for establishing what was "a reasonable creature in being": one separated from the mother's body and sustained by an independent circulation. In other words, one was born, and that was that!

While some pro-choice advocates maintain that we should stick with the common-law criterion, we now know more about the nature of the fetus. It makes sense to conclude that a normally developing fetus past the 28th week is also a "reasonable creature in being." It is viable, capable of being born from its mother's body; and while not yet separate, it is certainly *separable*. So to extend the concepts of murder and manslaughter to include unjustifiable termination of the post–28-week fetus is not a travesty of the common law but is instead a reasonable modification of it in the light of the best knowledge available to us now.

Another error avoided by the neurologically based argument is that made by an extremist minority in the pro-choice camp who equate the functioning of the rational faculty with full-blown conceptual thought. While this group agrees with the definition of "man" as the rational animal, they would reject the claim that the rational faculty begins functioning in the womb with the onset of perceptual awareness (at about 28 weeks). Instead, they say that the rational faculty doesn't operate until the child is capable of *reasoning* and *willing*—that is, of conceptual thought and moral choices, of directing its own life independently. Thus, they say, infanticide—and even the killing of perfectly normal older children—while perhaps *morally* monstrous in some cases, should not be legally regarded as murder.

Despite the overwhelming emotional horror with which most people react to this position, it cannot be dismissed out of hand. There is a serious concern here with preserving the doctrine of human rights. It *cannot* be the correct definition of "rational" or "human" to claim that the fetus's rational faculty begins functioning in the womb, they say, for it makes it impossible to apply human rights consistently.

Why? Because if the parents are unwilling to support the child and can find no one else to do so, doesn't it violate the parents' rights if they are forced to support another human being—even their own child? Isn't this tantamount to involuntary servitude?

Clearly, the problem here is not just whether abortion is ever justifiable. The broader question is whether any child has a right to be supported by its parents—

rather than killed, abandoned, or simply neglected—until it becomes an independent person capable of surviving by its own effort and initiative.

In fact, though, there is no conflict between parents' and children's rights. The right to child support—including during the last 12 weeks of fetal life—springs from the same basic source as the right to compensation for disablement when caused by someone else. A person who is responsible for causing the helpless state of another human being is appropriately responsible for that person's care until he is capable of caring for himself (unless another person is willing to assume the responsibility).

In the case of pregnancy and childbirth, a woman who refuses or fails to abort at some point prior to the 28th week has allowed the fetus to become no longer just an embryo, a potential human being, but an actual, helpless, human being. By continuing to nourish and shelter the fetus past the 28th week, the woman has *caused* it to become a helpless human being for which she ought to be responsible from that point onward. She had sufficient time to abort the fetus while it was still nonhuman, and once it does become human, the decision and the rights involved are no longer hers alone. (Again, we are assuming that the fetus is neurologically normal and that the woman's life is not threatened by continued pregnancy.) Thus, the same statutory protection currently accorded normal children ought to be extended to post–28-week fetuses. This includes full recognition and implementation of their rights to life, liberty, and property—and support until they are capable of independence.

The pro-choice case I have defended may well leave some anti-abortion supporters unmoved. But there is a significant group for whom it should be conclusive: those who espouse logic and facts in arguing that the fetus has a right to life from conception.

Rational anti-abortionists make it clear that they are not out to impose on others their personal opinions or religious views about when human life begins. Instead, they want to make the law conform to *facts*—specifically, the facts of biology—rather than to someone's *wish* to obtain an abortion.

Given their commitment to facts, in particular to biological facts, the rational anti-abortionists must seriously consider my argument, for it appeals to some recent and singularly relevant scientific findings. They must either deny that the neurological data are scientific or offer a different interpretation of them. Short of that, they are bound by their own ground rules to accept this argument and join the pro-choice ranks.

Anti-abortionists may be worried, however, that defining human beings in terms of anything other than the product of the union of a human egg cell with a human sperm cell would lead to horrible consequences. Wouldn't it open the door to all the terrors of Nazi Germany: genocide, mercy killing, extermination of misfits and other undesirables, on the grounds that they are "inferior," not human, and thus not worthy of the right to life?

But according to the neurological data and the understanding of human nature offered here, the only candidates for being considered nonhuman are: pre–28-week fetuses; babies born without a cerebral cortex or who would otherwise never be able to function conceptually; and individuals who, because of severe brain damage, will never again be able to function conceptually—the Karen Ann Quinlan types. In each of these cases, it is feasible to determine when the neurological standard applies medically and thus to apply the definition of "human being" consistently. There is nothing in the logic of the case that would allow these criteria to be extended to include the senile, "slow" children, Jews, infidels, or redheads over 6 feet, 4 inches in height!

So totalitarianism is by no means a consequence of the pro-choice position. In fact, as Leslee J. Newman pointed out in *Libertarian Review* in December 1979:

"The Nazis were anti-abortion, yet they were not 'pro-life' in their feeling towards certain minority groups. Today in many countries where abortion is outlawed or severely restricted by the state, thousands of persons might be randomly imprisoned, tortured, or shot, as in many of the nations in Central and South America. Thus, it would appear that there is no correlation between the outlawing of abortion and a general respect for the human rights of a populace."

On the other hand, the anti-abortion position *does* usher in horrendous consequences. Newman wrote in an article in September 1979:

"If a Human Life Amendment made fetal life sacred, any abortion could thus be considered murder or manslaughter. Since 15 to 25 percent of all pregnancies naturally end in miscarriage, our already crowded courts would be required to hold hundreds of thousands of inquests to determine the cause of 'death.' Since in addition miscarriage is by its nature a private occurrence, we might even find the traditional presumption of innocence reversed: a high percentage of formerly pregnant women could become suspect as murderers and might be criminally charged if they could not prove otherwise. Women might even be arrested if it were feared that there was probable cause to believe that they might try to obtain an abortion. Suspicion of pregnancy might be used to justify forced examination. Pregnancy in some cases might result in incarceration or straitjacketing."

These are a few of the consequences of legislation outlawing abortion. Nor would they result only from a perverted misapplication of the law; they would be necessary for its *enforcement*. Nazi-like, fascistic control over the lives of women would be the outcome of such legislation.

The anti-abortionists are not the only ones to run into serious trouble once they abandon their fundamental argument and argue instead in terms of consequences. The pro-choice position fares no better. Claims often heard on the pro-choice side may all be true, but without a fundamental argument to give them support, they fall to the criticisms of the anti-abortionists.

Here are a few examples:

➤ "Abortion is a humane remedy for the problem of unwanted children being brought into the world." The anti-abortion reply: These children may be unwanted by their parents, but there are many other couples who would love to have them.

➤ "Don't women have the sole right to control what happens to their bodies and thus have the right to seek an abortion?" Reply: True enough, a woman does have the sole right to control *her* body; but she has no right to control *her child's body* by choosing to terminate its life.

> "How can a man, who does not have to bear an unwanted child, dictate to a woman that she must do so?" Reply: President Lincoln didn't himself treat other human beings as though they were nonhuman, yet he validly argued for abolition of slavery against those who *did* treat them in this manner. The issue is not whether Lincoln could or couldn't have personally experienced slave ownership; the issue is human rights, which slavery violates. Ditto abortion.

> "For hundreds of years the law never recognized the fetus as a human being, worthy of legal protection. The abortion laws of the 19th and 20th centuries were passed, not to protect the fetus's right to life, but as public health laws, because the medical establishment was concerned that the abortion operation was too dangerous to the woman." Reply: What you say is true, but this doesn't mean that the failure to recognize the slave's right to liberty prior to abolition was justified. The law has been derelict in protecting certain rights for far too long, and it is high time that sensitive people demand that the wrong be righted, as did the abolitionists of the 1800s.

> "Many of us believe seriously and sincerely, as a matter of our moral or religious convictions, that human life begins not at conception but at birth, or at viability at the earliest. What right do you have to force *your* moral or religious views upon us?" Reply: The beginning of human life is not determinable by religion or morality but by observable biological fact. It is not a matter of competing beliefs but of scientific fact: Biologists agree that life begins at conception; the union of the egg and sperm cells result in a new organism. Killing such an organism is murder.

These quite plausible pro-choice arguments can be demolished by anti-abortion objections because they don't have any fundamentals behind them. What *is* it to be a human being? What is the *evidence* about when a human being comes into existence? These questions are sidestepped. Yet it is on this fundamental ground that the pro-choice people must take their stand.

Much harm has resulted in the abortion debate from a rejection of reason and science. The religious community opposes abortion by appeal to the notion, which cannot be demonstrated, that the soul enters the fetus at conception. And many pro-choice advocates favor abortion by appeal to their very strong feelings, say about women's control over their bodies. So advocates and opponents of abortion legislation end up on *fundamentally* the same side, wherein the available facts and the need to define key terms are ignored.

It is unlikely that what I have said here represents the last word on the abortion controversy. However, its principal argument, and the other considerations introduced along with it, should help to polarize the many-faceted debate by reducing it to two clear-cut factions: those who reject reason and reality and those who accept these as the best route to understanding and guiding our world and our conduct. These are, in fact, the only two fundamental positions on the abortion controversy. This polarization, more than anything else, may enable us to discuss the issue clearly enough to resolve it once and for all in a way acceptable to all reasonable men and women.

Up Against the Birth Monopoly

By Sarah E. Foster

September 1982

SANTA CRUZ, CALIFORNIA; MARCH 6, 1974. It was nearly noon on a Wednesday morning when a man phoned the Birth Center, a volunteer community home birth service. "Please send a midwife quickly," he begged. "Terry is in labor." With feelings of misgiving, Linda Bennett, a midwife, and Jeanine Walker, an apprentice, drove to the address given. They knew the pregnant woman, Terry Johnson, and her husband, Peter, but not well. She had made only a few visits to the center and was not due to have her baby for two or three months. It was unlikely she was in labor.

At the apartment they were greeted by men dressed like hippies. Terry didn't seem to be there, but the men said she was in the shower. As Bennett tells it, one of the men tried to press a 50-dollar bill into her hand. She refused to take it and laid it on the table, but it was slipped into her purse.

The rest can be guessed. The "husband" and his "friends" were really undercover investigators and cops: agents of the California Attorney General's Office, the Bureau of Medical Quality Assurance, and the local police. When Bennett started toward the bathroom to speak to Terry, she and her assistant were arrested. The charge? "Practicing medicine without a license"—a violation of the California Business and Professions Code.

Two policemen took them away for booking. The other agents proceeded to the Birth Center and broke in on a meeting of pregnant women and mothers with newborn babies. They had come for the regular weekly "rap session" and found themselves in the middle of a police raid.

Kate Bowland, director of the center, was arrested and hauled off to join Bennett and Walker in the Santa Cruz jail, though not before the local media had been alerted and she had given interviews to reporters. To substantiate the charge of practicing medicine, the agents seized such "incriminating evidence" as notebooks, blood pressure cuffs, stethoscopes, and even diapers.

It was the beginning of an all-out attack by the medical establishment on the growing home birth movement, which had begun in the late 1960s and was in full swing by the mid-1970s—as evidenced by such developments at the Birth Center.

The center had been founded in a spirit of enthusiasm, defiance, and hope. A number of couples in and around Santa Cruz were arranging to have their babies born at home even though no physicians in the area would attend a home birth. Although at first these couples were from the "counterculture," by 1970 they were being joined by middle-class couples—people who ordinarily went to hospitals and paid a good price to have an obstetrician deliver their babies. They were willing to pay for the best, but that was not what they felt they were getting, and they began to drop out of the system.

In January 1971, according to natural childbirth educator Raven Lang, a group of Santa Cruz obstetricians and public health officials decided that the doctors should refuse to give prenatal care to any woman known to be planning a home birth. Since prenatal care is a major factor in assuring a safe delivery, home birth proponents sought an alternative.

Led by Raven Lang, a small group of lay midwives (midwives who are not nurses), childbirth educators, and sympathetic nurses organized the Birth Center, using part of a suburban house for their headquarters. The center provided counseling, classes, and discussion groups—and, compliments of the nurses, prenatal examinations. Within three years, beginning in 1971, the eight-woman staff had attended nearly 300 births in Santa Cruz County. The center was a success—entirely too much so from the point of view of the doctors who enlisted the state to put it out of business.

California regulators developed an elaborate scheme that culminated in the events of March 6, 1974, at Terry Johnson's home and later the Birth Center. It involved an assortment of government agencies, 13 undercover agents, one pregnant accomplice (a clerk in the Department of Consumer Affairs), and untold tax dollars. Not since the early decades of this century, when in cities like New York the public health officials made great "sweeps" to round up immigrant midwives, had a group of unlicensed midwives been subjected to such investigation, entrapment, and arrest. And why were they unlicensed? Because in one of the Catch-22s of the regulatory state, the California legislature decided in 1949 that lay midwives could no longer be certified in that state.

The three women from the Birth Center did not give up readily. In court, their defense argued that assisting at a birth does not constitute the practice of medicine as defined in the Business and Professions Code, since childbirth is not a disease. The defense also challenged the constitutionality of the state's interpretation of the code, arguing that enforcement abridges a woman's right to choose her birth attendant, thus violating the right to privacy.

The case went through several appeals, finally reaching the State Supreme Court, which ruled against the women in 1976. Argued the court in its decision:

> *"...normal childbirth, while not a sickness or affliction, is a 'physical condition' within the meaning of the Business and Professions Code....it is clear that the practice of midwifery without a certificate is prohibited."*

The argument about a right to privacy was summarily dismissed:

> *"the right of privacy has never been interpreted so broadly as to protect a woman's choice of the manner and circumstances in which her baby is born....*
> *"It is true that the Legislature has never attempted to require women to give birth in a hospital, or with a physician in attendance....But the state has a recognized interest in the life and well-being of an unborn child."*

Having won their point, the district attorney's office decided not to prosecute after all. The midwives could have appealed to the U.S. Supreme Court, but if they lost there it might impose the definition of midwifery as the practice of medicine upon the rest of the country. They did not want to risk losing the case for midwives elsewhere.

The Birth Center was no longer a threat to Santa Cruz obstetricians, but women continued to look for alternatives to hospital delivery and found people to help them. Although out-of-hospital births account for only 3.6 percent of the births in California, in some counties the percentage is 10-20 percent, and in Mendocino County, north of San Francisco, it's 50 percent. The California Association of Midwives estimates that there are about 600 lay midwives in practice in the state, some with such good reputations they're booked ahead for months.

With justification, California has been credited with being the fountainhead of the home birth movement. Nationwide, of the 3.3 million births a year, 2 percent are out-of-hospital, and the number is increasing. We don't know what percentage of these are deliberately planned, however, just as we don't know how many hospital births reflect willing acceptance of hospitalization or resignation because no other options are readily available.

As the idea of home birth caught on throughout the country, it attracted not only enthusiastic supporters but the kind of opposition faced in Santa Cruz, characterized by harassment and the use of political power and force. There's an all-out war being waged in every part of the country—directed against parents who want a particular experience of which the medical establishment does not approve, and against anyone who will help them. From Alaska to Florida, from New York to California, there's not one state where midwives, or even doctors, can without difficulty of one kind or another provide home birth services to parents who request it, and not one state where parents are free of possible intimidation and censure for choosing this alternative. Some have even been threatened with charges of child abuse! *And all this despite the fact that in no state is home birth illegal, and in no state is it illegal for a doctor to do home deliveries.*

If couples are planning a home birth, they may, like the women in Santa Cruz, find themselves denied prenatal or postpartum care. Helen Burst, president of the American College of Nurse Midwives, says she quit her job in disgust when the South Carolina hospital where she was working ordered her to refuse prenatal care to parents whom she knew were planning a home birth. To provide such care is to condone home birth, she was told—and this is an "unprofessional" attitude.

Lay midwives (those without institutional training) face the possibility of arrest for practicing medicine without a license in those states where lay midwifery is illegal—and it is legal in only 14. There have been a number of trials and hearings and some convictions. So far, none have actually done jail time. Dee Burns, a midwife in southern California, will probably be the first. She was convicted in March 1981. Her appeals have been unsuccessful, and she is resigned to spending 30 days in the Ventura County Jail.

Sympathetic physicians stand to lose hospital privileges or malpractice insurance if they back a midwife (provide consultation or admit her patients to the hospital in case of emergency) or if they provide prenatal care to a "known" home birth parent. As with Helen Burst, this is called "condoning home birth."

Doctors who are willing to attend home births are few and far between, and a number of them have had their licenses suspended or revoked on charges of malpractice. Usually, such tactics as hearings and court proceedings against home birth doctors are unnecessary. Errant doctors are brought into line merely with a threat of loss of hospital privileges or insurance.

At the legislative level, the game is played fast and loose. Perhaps there's an old law on the books permitting lay midwifery. Then an effort may be made to repeal the law—but secretly, attached to a bill or at the end of a session. That was tried in Maryland in 1976, but midwives heard about it, showed up at the hearing, and managed to defeat it—to the consternation of doctors and the Department of Public Health.

But most states have no provisions for licensing lay midwives, and the medical community intends to keep it that way. Any attempt to legalize lay midwifery is fought tooth and nail. In California, where a strong faction within the Department of Consumer Affairs wants to see midwifery legalized, the California Medical Association has given a Priority 1 status to three recommendations: to continue opposition to lay midwives and home birth; to set up a task force for collecting "statistical and other material" to corroborate this opposition to mid-wives and home birth; and to obtain an attorney general's opinion on whether registered nurses are legally permitted to deliver babies and, if so, to "seek means by which such practice can be terminated." (Presently in California there are two RNs doing home deliveries.)

In Ohio, a bill nearly passed that would have made practicing midwifery without a license a felony carrying a five-year prison sentence and fine. (It also granted subpoena power to the Ohio Medical Board and granted that board the right to suspend a doctor's license without a hearing.) The bill lost by one vote in the lower house, having cleared the senate unanimously. Recent legislation in Ohio would restrict the hospital privileges of certified nurse midwives.

The recent experience in Alaska is unique. A bill sponsored by Democrat Bryon Rogers and cosponsored by Libertarian Dick Randolph has been approved. It legalizes lay midwifery and sets up a system of voluntary certification. (Certification is not a mandated condition for practice, and lack of certification is not a criminal offense.)

Even *teaching* about childbirth in ways not approved by the medical profession can be subject to state action. A Bakersfield, California, home birth physician, Carrie Teasdale, was planning to hold a class in natural childbirth through the Adult Education Department of the University of California, Santa Barbara. It was to be held on a weekend and carry one unit of credit. Local doctors objected, and the university withdrew its support. "So much for academic freedom," Dr. Teasdale told the press.

All these actions by doctors and their allies are in one way or another reaffirmations of the official position of the American College of Obstetricians and Gynecologists (ACOG), a 23,000-member trade association. According to ACOG's 1975 statement of policy on home deliveries: The "potential hazards" of labor and delivery "require standards of safety which are provided in the hospital setting and cannot be matched in the home situation." Warren Pearse, M.D., executive director of ACOG, editorialized in the organization's newsletter in July 1977: "Home delivery is maternal trauma—home delivery is child abuse!"

There are many people who plan never to have children, or, if they do, will go straight to the nearest hospital. They find it difficult to appreciate fully the problems faced by home birth parents. "Yes, a woman has the right to a choice, and yes, the doctors are behaving abominably, but what's that to me?" they ask.

It matters because the right to choose where to have one's child, and under what conditions, is a little-recognized but important issue in the area of civil and individual rights. Historically, the political and legal developments in matters surrounding childbirth have been illustrative and often predictive of political and legal developments in health care in particular and government control in general—a distinction it shares with institutionalized psychiatry.

For over 500 years, beginning in the Renaissance, the medical profession has been consolidating its power base and is so involved in our lives that its influence goes virtually unchallenged. This has been accomplished in large part through enlistment of the state to enforce various controls. Medicine and government are interlocked as closely today as were church and state during the Middle Ages. Psychiatrist Thomas Szasz has aptly labeled this present institution the "therapeutic state," as distinguished from the "theocratic state" of the Middle Ages.

Now while the dependence of the medical establishment on the state has often been noticed, the converse is not generally realized. Without the cooperation of the medical profession, the state would not be as powerful as it is. It was largely through demands from medical organizations and from influential physicians—for everything from licensing of "approved" practitioners to health codes—that regulatory agencies came into being. Doctors were the first to lobby successfully for mandatory controls, monopolistic privileges, and other "reforms" of their profession.

Control over childbirth (who could attend, where it could take place, what practices were permitted or outlawed) established the precedents for other kinds of controls. State licensing of midwives was the first licensing of any class of health care provider. Originating in Germany in the late 15th century, just as the old guild system was breaking down, it led to licensing of other classes of practitioners and ultimately to the licensing ("professionalization") of trades and services as diverse as CPAs and car mechanics.

Midwives, during the colonial period and at other times, were required to report all births to the authorities and to give testimony in cases involving suspected illegitimacy or infanticide. Doctors, bound by the Hippocratic Oath, were under no such obligations. Nor were doctors under state mandate to provide care to anyone who needed it or to limit the amount charged for their services—requirements that were imposed on midwives.

Today there are at least 70 federal programs, administered by several agencies, that concern themselves with pregnancy outcome. The blunt wording of the *Bowland* decision handed down by the California Supreme Court presents the general rationalization: "The state has a recognized interest in the health and well-being of an unborn child."

A number of people, including many doctors, foresaw what would happen and tried to give warning. They were ignored. After all—how could anyone object to helping newborn babes and their mothers? Laws were passed, agencies established—all in the name of health, the "public good," and "a recognized interest."

Anyone concerned about the lack of freedom in our lives today should be aware of the issues involved in the home birth movement. If you want to know what's to come in our "therapeutic state," watch developments on the home birth front.

"When I first heard about home birth, I thought, my god—why would anyone want to have a baby in a manger!" This reaction of attorney Gail Roy Fraties is typical of many upon learning that there are women in this country who are taking what seems to be three steps back into an abyss of ignorance and superstition. But Fraties, as a trial lawyer, has now handled the defense of several home birth practitioners, examined the evidence, and changed his mind.

Couples seeking this alternative do so for a variety of reasons that together spell "control"—control over their birth experiences, the kind of control that cannot be guaranteed in a hospital setting, where even obstetricians who reject medical intervention in normal childbirth are often subjected to censure from hospital boards. Home birth proponents view childbirth not as a sickness, nor as a pathological condition, but as a natural process in which the rule is, the less intervention the better. They want to avoid certain hospital procedures—"prepping," IVs, "nothing by mouth" orders, and the use of medication to relieve pain. They want to choose who is to be present—husband, friends, other family members; to move about during labor; to be unrestricted during delivery; and to be able to choose the most comfortable position for giving birth. (This may mean being on one's hands and knees or standing, in contrast to the customary hospital position, in which a woman lies flat on her back with her legs up in stirrups.)

Above all, these women believe it best to deliver at their own (or rather, the baby's) time and not to have labor induced or augmented by drugs or mechanical means. The possibility of a Caesarean section (C-section) is a major concern, and with the C-section rate skyrocketing, it's easy to understand why. It was 5.5 percent in 1970; now it's averaging 20 percent nationwide and rising every year.

"I didn't see why we should pay a lot of money to have them do a lot of things to me that I didn't want them to do," is how a Los Angeles attorney sums up the reasons for her choice. She succinctly expresses the attitude of countless other women.

What type of parents are choosing alternative births? Those interviewed by anthropologist Lester Hazell in a 1975 study (nearly 300 couples in the San Francisco Bay area) were white, middle-class, and often college-educated. They were homeowners and had one or two cars, and the husband was employed in any one of a dozen occupations from law and teaching to farming and truck driving.

Home birth is not just a white, middle-class phenomenon, however. It is also coming to be chosen by middle-class blacks, for example. In Los Angeles, two black, certified nurse midwives have established practices to meet this demand.

There is also evidence that if the market were opened up, the demand for this kind of service would be startling. In an article published in 1971, Ellen Steckert, professor of folklore at Northwestern University, reported on her investigation of attitudes toward childbirth, doctors, and medical care in general among poor Appalachian white women who had moved to Detroit. Their responses were very similar to those so often evident among wealthier women: a belief that childbirth is a "natural process" and not a disease, a concern about intervention by doctors, a fear of surgery, etc. "The women interviewed," reported Steckert, "often expressed a desire to have their children at home, and probably would have, had it not been for the fact that the doctors they contacted refused to make home calls and that without a doctor attending, birth certificates became a legal problem."

It's always there—the possibility that the rate of nonhospital births, currently at 2 percent, might become 5 percent, then 10 percent—and then what would happen? The medical profession predicts disaster, a return to the days of high infant and maternal mortality. In 1900, when nearly all babies were born at home, the maternal mortality rate was 60 deaths per 10,000 live births. Today it is less than 3/10,000. The neonatal mortality rate (NMR—from birth through one week of age) is approximately 12.5/1,000.

There are several reasons for the rapid decline in birth mortality, however, that have nothing to do with hospitalization. One is the enormous improvement in nutrition, another, improved sanitation and greater attention to personal hygiene. We're simply better fed and cleaner than folks were 80, or even 50, years ago, and that's reflected in our mortality statistics. Another factor was the discovery of sulfa drugs (1936) and penicillin (1940), which brought the problem of infection, which was far more prevalent in hospitals than in home settings, under some kind of control.

The fact is that there have been a number of studies, sponsored by different health departments and other government agencies, that have evaluated the performance of midwives and compared their outcomes with those of physicians or hospitals. In virtually every study back to 1895, midwives were found to have results equal or superior to physicians' and hospitals'. This is especially surprising as the mothers whom midwives attended were often poor and thus undernourished and ill.

On January 4, 1978, the American College of Obstetricians and Gynecologists issued a press release claiming that data from eleven state health departments for the years 1974-76 show that "out-of-hospital births pose a 2 to 5 times greater risk to a baby's life than hospital births." But a press release is not a study—the raw data have never been released. Critics were quick to notice that the nonhospital births included not only those carefully planned and attended but unattended births, late spontaneous miscarriages, births in taxicabs on the way to the hospital, etc.

Precisely these factors were taken into account in a more thorough analysis of some of the data prepared by Claude A. Burnett III, M.D., of the Center for Disease Control in Atlanta, and colleagues from the center and other institutions. Their findings appeared in the *Journal of the American Medical Association* (Dec. 19, 1980).

Dr. Burnett and his colleagues had compiled the statistics from North Carolina for the ACOG press release. But they didn't stop there. They dug beneath the surface data, examining all the nonhospital births that had occurred in that state from 1974 through 1976. There were 1,296. The neonatal mortality rate (NMR), at 30 deaths per 1,000, was two and one-half times the hospital NMR of 12/1,000.

When Burnett and his colleagues classified the out-of-hospital (OOH) births according to planning status and attendant present, however, "a different picture emerged." The NMR among *planned* OOHs dropped to 6/1,000, while for *unplanned* OOHs it jumped to 120/1,000.

And that's not all. There were really two subdivisions of planned OOHs—

226

those attended and those deliberately unattended by a physician or midwife. Of the 100 births in this latter category, there were three baby deaths (NMR—30/1,000). There were 768 births attended by lay midwives, with three baby deaths. The authors of the study found that all three were attributable to congenital anomalies incompatible with life. Even counting these deaths, the NMR for births attended by lay midwives was 4/1,000—or *one-third of the hospital NMR of 12/1,000.*

These lay midwives are "grannies." They are licensed and work mainly with poor, black women—women who are, the authors of the report noted, demographically defined as high-risk. No licenses have been issued since 1964, and only a few grannies are left. In view of these statistics, however, it would seem worthwhile to follow the suggestion of the authors and not be too quick to phase out midwifery.

The doctors in North Carolina didn't see it that way. Shortly after this article appeared, a bill was introduced into the state legislature—An Act to Abolish the Practice of Lay Midwifery. It didn't pass, but only because of the lobbying of home birth proponents. However, a substitute bill, for the study and regulation of midwifery in North Carolina, did get approved.

A few years earlier the Arkansas State Board of Health had decided to make midwifery illegal. Letters were sent to the few grannies still practicing. Minnie Mae Farr, a woman with 20 years' experience and an excellent record, received one that began: "Dear Ms. Farr: The time honored profession of 'permitted' midwifery has ended and will become illegal on January 1, 1979 if a fee is accepted for services." She was advised that if she continued her life's work after that date she would face "problems of a legal nature."

The action by the North Carolina legislature and of the Arkansas Board of Health are part of a larger effort being carried out in southern states to eliminate "pockets" of midwifery by grannies. Granny midwifery was an effective low-cost system of providing a health service. The midwives had received basic instruction and were registered with the state. A woman wanting to be attended by a granny had to have a card signed by a local doctor certifying that she was in good health and could deliver at home. Since these women had little money, doctors were willing to let midwives have that tiny corner of the market. Then, during the 1960s and even more during the '70s, large sums of federal money became available for health care and the construction of huge medical centers. It then made sense to try and pull every woman they could through the doors of the hospitals to justify their existence and expense. As the letter to Ms. Farr in Arkansas exclaimed, "The future, which is not too distant, will bring modern protective obstetrical services within easy reach of *all* our state's citizens."

Where it is legal for lay midwives to attend home births, lay midwifery is being "phased out." Where couples who want a home birth have little choice but to turn to unlicensed lay midwives, occasions to haul the midwives into court are seized upon. One of the more-publicized attempts to solve "the midwife/home birth problem" in this way took place in the small agricultural community of Madera, California. Many of the residents are from Mexico, having come to work in the fields. On November 28, 1979, three young women of evident Mexican background brought a newborn baby boy to the emergency room of the local hospital. They said he had been born about 10 minutes earlier. The parents, Graciella and Eugenio

Villa, were undocumented aliens who lived in Fresno, 20 miles south. It was their first child.

Although he appeared dead, a nurse attempted mouth-to-mouth resuscitation, and an electrocardiogram (ECG) picked up a heartbeat. Adrenalin and sodium bicarbonate were administered intravenously, and the heartbeat became strong and regular. Suddenly the ECG indicated critical distress, then nothing. Twelve minutes later he was pronounced dead.

It was learned this had been a planned home birth and that the birth attendant was Rosalie Tarpening, a licensed physical therapist who lived on the outskirts of Madera. Her home was adjacent to the office and examination rooms she shared with her husband, Donald Tarpening, a chiropractor. The doctors at the hospital knew of Mrs. Tarpening. She had delivered 350 babies over the preceding eight years.

Two days later a 15-man SWAT team surrounded their property, entered the house, and took Mrs. Tarpening away for questioning. Then they tore apart the house, her office, and her husband's office, looking for drugs and other "evidence." No illegal substances were found. She was charged with grand theft, practicing medicine without a license, and first-degree murder.

Rosalie Tarpening was not the first midwife in California to face a murder charge. A year earlier, Marianne Doshi had been arrested after a baby she delivered had died in a hospital where it had been taken due to complications during birth. The basic charge was practicing medicine without a license— "bumped" to a felony (second-degree murder) because a death had occurred. At a pretrial hearing the judge threw the case out, declaring that in his opinion, parents have a constitutional right to have their babies at home.

Mrs. Tarpening was not so fortunate. There was a lengthy preliminary hearing, then, in August 1981, a three-week jury trial. Her trial attorney, Gail Roy Fraties, managed to have all the charges dismissed except one: "practicing medicine without a license in such a way as to endanger mother and child." In his client's defense on that charge, Fraties contended that, according to the California statute governing physical therapy, she was permitted to treat "a physical condition" and so was practicing within the limits of her license.

One of the expert witnesses at the trial (and the only defense witness called during the pretrial hearing) was Edith Louise Potter, M.D.—a world-renowned pathologist and authority in the field of infant and fetal death. Her textbooks are the standard reference works on that subject. Her testimony, based on the autopsy report, was directed toward establishing the cause of death.

When Potter took the stand during the pretrial hearing, she made it known that the emergency room doctor had ordered that oxygen be administered through a flexible tube inserted down the baby's windpipe. Although the attending physician and the coroner claimed that the baby died from lack of oxygen, "There's no doubt in my mind that the cause of death was air put into the baby's trachea at too great a pressure," Dr. Potter told the jury during the trial. *"That baby had its lungs blown out!"*

"Did Mrs. Tarpening do anything, in your opinion, that would endanger the mother or child?" asked Fraties.

"Absolutely nothing." Then she thought a minute. "Yes, she did one thing wrong. She sent the baby to the hospital. She should have left it with its mother. It would be alive today."

Fraties built an excellent defense and presented a moving summation. Yet when the jury returned after several days of deliberation, Mrs. Tarpening was found guilty.

I wanted to know how they had arrived at such a verdict and phoned some of the jurors. "Let me tell you, " said one man. "If she had been facing a homicide charge, she'd be completely free today. It was the hospital that killed the baby." I asked if he favored an investigation of the hospital—which had been suggested following the hearing. "*Absolutely.* There's no question the doctors killed the baby—and then they turned the light on Rosalie."

"But if that's so, why did you find her guilty?" I asked.

"Well, she shouldn't have been using an instrument to examine the mother. That was dangerous."

"An instrument?"

"Yeah—one of those things doctors use in examinations."

It turned out that in one of the photos taken by police during their search was a speculum, a device used in gynecological exams but *not* during labor. It was from a kit of obstetrical and gynecological instruments that Dr. Tarpening had acquired during his training as a chiropractor 35 years earlier. Neither he nor Mrs. Tarpening ever used it in their work, and he had forgotten about it until it was dumped out of a storage drawer.

Calls to several other jurors confirmed what the first had said. Although neither prosecution nor defense had referred to it, the jury assumed the speculum had been used during the delivery and constituted "endangering mother and child."

Evidently, Judge Clifford Plumley did not approve of the verdict. He sentenced Mrs. Tarpening to a year in jail, then suspended the sentence. The prosecuting attorney was furious and claimed that "the people" had been robbed.

The reasons for Graciella Villa's choice of birth attendant are obscured by the sensational aspects of the case, but they deserve mention. Mrs. Villa specifically wanted a woman to deliver her baby and did not want to go to the hospital, as she had heard "stories" about hospitals. From friends she learned of Mrs. Tarpening, a woman willing to help other women have their babies. Mrs. Tarpening's profession was physical therapy and nutritional counseling, and although she had delivered 350 babies, midwifery was a small part of her practice. She was responding to a demand in the community—one which doctors ignored. Rather than meet the demand, the doctors used the courts.

It is not only lay midwives like Rosalie Tarpening, and Linda Bennett of the Santa Cruz Birth Center, who face the fury of the medical establishment. Certified nurse midwives (CNMs) are having their own problems, even though *these* midwives are part of "the establishment." CNMs are registered nurses who have completed a program in midwifery at a recognized institution and are certified by the American College of Nurse Midwives (ACNM). Their training is intended to prepare them for handling uncomplicated births, working "under the direction of" an obstetrician-gynecologist. At least that's the position of the American College of Obstetricians and Gynecologists (ACOG), to which ACNM agreed in a joint policy statement in 1975. Some hospitals have interpreted "direction" as meaning an ob-gyn must be in the room with the CNM during a delivery, although ACOG literature says this is not required.

There are some 2,500 CNMs in the United States, with approximately 220 graduating each year. They try to find work in hospitals, but very few will hire them; or they may work for doctors who have birth centers. Some open their own birth centers, in cooperation with sympathetic physicians who provide hospital back-up in case of complications. There are about 100 birth centers in 28 states, staffed by 200 or so CNMs. Some are freestanding centers (not in or attached to a hospital) where women can go to have their babies; some offer home birth services; and some are in hospitals. All this is legal.

But CNMs have met resistance from physicians, hospitals, and government officials in at least 12 states and the District of Columbia, according to Sally Tom, CNM, a spokesperson for ACNM. When nurse midwifery and out-of-hospital births come together, the resistance can be particularly virulent, as illustrated in the case of the Maternity Center Association of New York City.

For 60 years the MCA has been involved in maternity care in that city, especially among immigrant women. In 1917 it established a program for prenatal care and maternal education and in 1931 founded the first school of midwifery in the United States. For the next 20 years the MCA provided a midwifery service for women in low-income neighborhoods, which was phased out in the 1950s during the great push for hospital delivery.

In 1973 MCA began developing another new, equally innovative program under the leadership of Ruth Lubic, CNM: the Childbirth Center (CbC), an out-of-hospital maternity center for low-risk patients, with the aim of "attracting back to the system families engaged in do-it-yourself home birth." The center was the first of its kind in the country. Set up in a former townhouse, it offers a complete maternity service, including prenatal care, childbirth preparation classes, accommodation for labor and delivery, and nearby hospital back-up. By August 1981, nearly 1,000 births had taken place there, at a cost of about half the hospital fee.

In testimony before a congressional subcommittee, in December 1980, Lubic described the difficulties encountered as they tried to get the CbC under way: opposition from ACOG, the state and national American Academy of Pediatrics, the New York State Medical Society, the chairmen of obstetrics and gynecology at six of New York City's seven medical schools; trying to prevent commercial and medicaid reimbursement; interfering with hospital back-up; discrediting the CbC with nurses, foundations, and health insurers; attempting to have its license revoked; harassing families who consulted individual obstetricians; and "falsely alleging maternal, fetal, and neonatal mortality." The city's Health Department made "unwarranted demands for data" and at one point threatened to have the police barricade the MCA's doors.

C. Arden Miller, M.D., who worked with Dr. Burnett compiling data for the study on out-of-hospital births in North Carolina, described the situation as he saw it to a group of professionals:

"The splenetic passion which the medical establishment, and particularly the obstetric community of New York City, attaches to the risks of the

Maternity Association's Childbearing Center is spectacular to behold. Efforts to force closure of the center, depriving it of consultation and back-up supportive service, have been thwarted only by the most heroic perseverance by Ms. Lubic and her Board of Directors. Why does this molehill of a demonstration project attract all the lightning deserving of an Olympus?"

But there were people in high places on the MCA's side, some even in the Health Department and on hospital staffs. They supported the center and guided it through the bureaucratic and professional quagmire. And last year the MCA was awarded a grant of nearly $256,000 from the John Hartford Foundation of New York City, and its plans are to promote "wider public understanding of the birth center concept."

Of all the organized opposition to the home birth movement, probably the most dangerous is legal action against the Association for Childbirth at Home, International (ACHI). It strikes at the life-line of the movement—teaching about childbirth and dissemination of information—and raises the constitutional issues of free speech, free assembly, and the right to be secure against unreasonable search and seizure.

ACHI, a grassroots teaching organization, was founded in 1972 by Tonya Brooks, herself a home birth mother and lay midwife, in response to parents' demand for more information on the birth process than is available in childbirth education classes. For couples in areas where there are no free-standing birth centers, lay midwives, or doctors or CNMs willing to do home births, the only alternative to going into a hospital is to stay home and have an unattended birth, which as the North Carolina statistics show, can be risky. ACHI does not approve of unattended births per se but attempts to narrow the margin of risk by providing couples with what Brooks describes as "essential and accurate technical obstetrics." It is the largest home childbirth education organization in the world; 40,000 couples have taken the basic eight-week course.

ACHI's greatest strength is in the Midwest, so perhaps it was not purely coincidental that their troubles began in southern Illinois. In early May 1978, ACHI instructor Cathryn Feral, who was living in the small community of Harrisburg, gave a brief talk on a local public TV channel—telling about the organization and announcing she'd be available for classes. She describes her talk as "real conservative," but that's not how two Harrisburg obstetricians perceived it, and they requested an investigation.

In October Feral received two subpoenas, for herself and ACHI, ordering her to appear within 10 days in Springfield, the state capital, "to testify...in regard to matters relating to your business transactions with consumers of Illinois since September, 1976, concerning ACHI's series of childbirth classes in violation of the Illinois Consumer Fraud and Deceptive Practices Act."

She was instructed to bring 71 pieces of information, including the names, addresses, and phone numbers of all parents anywhere who had taken the course; a complete list of doctors, CNMs, midwives, and others who were helping ACHI; a list of all ACHI instructors; information regarding insurance; information about compensation for assisting at a birth; and on and on. There was even a request for Feral's driver's license number.

In a letter to the editor of the *Illinois Times* in February 1979, Richard Cosby, first assistant attorney general, tried to assure readers "that we are treating this case with the same approach as the 27,000 others that move through our office each year." But in a phone interview, Wayne Wiemerslage, the original investigator for the Department of Consumer Affairs, admitted that the list of 71 items was "a little longer than usual." But, he explained, "This is a very important case." When pressed, he further admitted that the number of items ordinarily requested in an investigation is 15, *or at most 25 or 30.*

There was a strong likelihood that turning over everything demanded would result in punitive measures against supportive doctors and other professionals and the harassment of many parents. Brooks and Feral decided to fight and began a long journey through the courts. ACHI won at both the trial and the appellate level. The Appellate Court ruled that under *Alabama v. NAACP* (1958), no organization can be forced to turn over its membership and furthermore that the Illinois Consumer Fraud and Deceptive Practices Act was not intended to include educational organizations in its scope. The Illinois Attorney General's Office appealed.

In May 1981 the case was heard by the Illinois Supreme Court. ACHI's attorney, Mary Lee Leahy, argued that "the defendants are engaged in activities protected by the First Amendment: teaching and advertising regarding that teaching." Enforcement, she noted, would have a "chilling effect on free speech."

Following the formal presentations, one of the judges asked Joseph Keenan, counsel for the Attorney General's Office, if he had any public relations material from ACHI to include as evidence to justify the investigation. He hadn't—not one brochure or pamphlet. "It seems to me," the judge remarked, "that you're on a fishing expedition."

"No, your Honor," Keenan protested. "We're not just fishing."

"Well, what are these people supposed to have done? Have they requested money be sent in? Have they made any special claims?"

"No, your Honor, but this is an organization which deals with matters of health. They're teaching about childbirth, and in matters of health and childbirth the state has a compelling interest."

This line of reasoning prevailed. In November the court handed down a verdict. ACHI had lost badly. Concerns about a possible "chilling effect" on the exercise of free speech were tossed into the judicial waste basket: "...the State does not lose its power to regulate commercial activity deemed harmful to the public whenever speech is a component of that activity."

But no "harmful speech" had even been entered as evidence, so the court drew upon the case of *United States v. Morton Salt* (1949) for jurisdiction of any and all investigation by government agencies:

> *"The only proper power that is involved here is the power to get information from those who best can give it and who are most interested in not doing so....Even if one were to regard the request for information in this case as caused by nothing more than official curiosity, nevertheless law-enforcing agencies have a legitimate right to satisfy themselves that corporate behavior is consistent with the law and the public interest."*

This decision should be very sobering to anyone who believes in the Bill of Rights and assumes that the principles embodied in it are somehow inviolate.

Although ACHI would like to carry the case to the U.S. Supreme Court, the cost is prohibitive. Also, as with the litigation involving the Santa Cruz midwives, there's a danger that if they lost at the federal level, every childbirth education organization in the country would be affected. They may be anyway. In May, ACHI was notified that the Illinois Department of Consumer Affairs would be filing an injunction prohibiting their advertising or teaching in Illinois. Tonya Brooks fears that consumer affairs departments in other states may follow suit. It's already rather chilling.

There's a tendency for observers of the medical profession to explain the actions of its members as motivated essentially by a desire for great financial remuneration. The reason, therefore, that obstetricians are behaving as they are toward midwives is to keep them off their professional turf—which is a very bright green. Obstetric is a high-earning medical specialty.

But the matter is not simply reducible to economic concerns. If money were the only consideration, why don't more sharp ob-gyns open birth centers and go directly after the market? Some do—but they face a lot of peer pressure. Also, the opposition to home birth is not limited to doctors. Law enforcement officials and others in government are part of it. What inspires investigators to set traps to catch midwives? What motivated Terry Johnson, a clerk in the California bureaucracy, to use her body, and her baby's body, against other women who had done her no harm? It's not enough to say, "Doctors have power." The question then is, "How did they get that power—who gave it to them?"

We live in a society where attainment of physical and mental well-being has replaced spiritual salvation as the dominant cultural value. A significant number of people accord it an importance above wealth, love, justice, or liberty, and they expect government to secure to them its blessings.

But that's not all. Although there is a common shared interest in health and well-being, there are differences of opinion about how these can best be attained. Current medical practices and theories are of two sorts—"orthodox" and "unorthodox." Orthodox medicine is merely the winner that emerged from a long struggle between several schools of medicine that flourished and competed with each other during the 19th and early 20th centuries. It was then called "allopathy": "a system of medical practice which combats disease by the use of remedies producing effects different from those produced by the disease itself" (*Webster's Collegiate Dictionary*, 1951). Then as now, drugs and surgery were the chief means by which allopathic physicians combated disease and tried to alleviate suffering. They relied heavily on "the heroics" (bleeding, purging, and induced vomiting).

It was the allopaths (also called "the regulars") who fought for government licensing and the regulation of medicine. They were eventually successful. By means of political maneuvering, and with financial assistance from Andrew Carnegie and John D. Rockefeller, they established a monopoly over health care in this country and made the word *allopathic* synonymous with *medicine*.

What today is called "unorthodox" medicine is based on an entirely different approach: stimulating and helping the body to strengthen and utilize its own resources, innate healing powers, and immune systems. Great emphasis is placed on nutrition and the taking of supplemental nutrients. Unorthodox practitioners, even those who are M.D.s, often claim they aren't practicing medicine at all—meaning they don't rely on drugs and surgery—but are simply helping the body regain or maintain a normal state of health.

The home birth movement is an outgrowth of the natural childbirth movement of the late 1950s and 1960s. Both are part of the broader movement in unorthodox medicine. The debate between the medical establishment and the home birth advocates is one of competing ideologies. In every argument, whether in a doctor's office or before a legislative committee, the rhetoric on both sides reflects and expresses these fundamentally opposing points of view about the nature of health and disease, the capabilities of the human body, and the role of the health care practitioner.

Doctors *believe* that hospitals are the safest place to have a baby; that's why they can ignore study after study to the contrary. They "know" the studies are "inconclusive." That is why the California Medical Association is now impelled to collect data against home birth and midwives; it is necessary to "prove" these a danger, thereby justifying the opposition to them. That is why the medical profession dismisses as "anecdotal" all reports and accounts by parents, and even by physicians, extolling the benefits of home delivery.

That is why doctors could look at the autopsy report in the Rosalie Tarpening case and not see that it was their bungling that killed a baby. And when Dr. Potter held it before their faces, they sought some other explanation, as though to say, "We *know* hospitals don't kill babies—we *know* home birth does."

And that is why Dr. Potter's testimony was so devastating. It was the testimony of a person who could step out of the belief system that she shares with the doctors, look at the evidence, and say, as she did: "I don't believe in home birth but I *know* midwives don't kill babies. In this case the hospital was to blame."

There is something more powerful than money that motivates men and women: a conviction that they are right and that they're doing the right thing. Not only are doctors convinced they are right; they have convinced many others that they are. Policemen, government agents, district attorneys—as upholders of the social order in the "therapeutic state," they follow doctors' orders. When they go "red lights and sirens" all over town to arrest a midwife, they look on this as part of their responsibility to "the public." When they launch an investigation into an organization that is teaching about childbirth, they don't see it as trampling on the Bill of Rights. They're stamping out heresy. *They consider it their duty.*

It is impossible to predict the outcome of the struggle. The fundamental issue is not whether home is a "better" place to have a baby or whether a midwife can do a "better" job than a doctor or whether unorthodox medicine has more demonstrable validity than orthodox as a way of dealing with sickness and pain. As expressed by Dr. Edith Potter to an audience of home birth supporters following the preliminary hearing in the Rosalie Tarpening case:

> *"I think that your feeling about home delivery is determined in part by your general outlook on life—your general philosophy. How paternalistic do you think the government ought to be? How much pressure should the*

government put on us to do what it wants us to do?...If you think we ought to have a free choice in our lives...we have to decide as we do in a presidential election....I think this is a matter of free choice, and nobody ought to tell us what we're going to do."

To the question, How did doctors get power? Who gave it to them? the answer is: *We did, and we're still giving it to them.* Until many more people decide that liberty is the primary value, that it is more important than health or anything else, the situation for the midwives, the home birth doctors, the home birth parents—or the rest of us—is not really going to change.

The Missionary's Position on Sex

By David Brudnoy

December 1982

I consider women's liberation and gay liberation to be part of the same thing: a weakening of the moral standards of this nation. It is appalling to see parades in San Francisco and elsewhere proclaiming "gay pride" and all that. What in the world do they have to be proud of? They're immoral, perverted and disgusting .... Men and women who allow themselves to be led blindly by the philosophies and teachers involved with gays, feminists and abortionists are courting their own destruction. Anyone who goes up against his or her God-centered nature invariably destroys himself in the long run.

These aren't the words of the Rev. Jerry Falwell, though Mr. Falwell would approve them. They appeared under the byline Nancy Reagan, in a newspaper called *The Globe* in March 1981. This isn't the same *Globe* that dominates journalism in my home town, Boston; it's something of a tabloid, and until a conservative friend sent it to me, I hadn't known of its existence. You can find it in selected supermarkets next to the *National Enquirer*. It sells for 40 cents a copy, and no home is complete without it.

I don't quote the paragraphs attributed to Mrs. Reagan because of her standing in the philosophical community, nor because I have any reason to think that her husband necessarily shares her every view, nor even because I don't have some doubt about their authenticity. There is at least some reason to wonder just how the article came to *The Globe* and whether, if they *are* the words of Nancy Reagan, they are as current as the publication date suggests. I quote them, however, to demonstrate the pervasiveness in some sectors of the populace of views that we might once have thought, and that some people might still hope, are confined to the rantings of the backwoods preachers and Moral Majority pamphleteers. That no vehement denial of the remarks attributed to Mrs. Reagan has come from the White House indicates either that they are properly attributed *or* that the White House clipping service is inadequate *or* that nobody with the authority to do so thought them bizarre enough to warrant some official distancing from them.

Whoever wrote the article attributed to Nancy Reagan is a recruit, whether consciously or not, to a mighty and some would say holy crusade: a war against sex. This war is waged now by an informal but increasingly harmonious coalition of organizations like Moral Majority, Christians for Reagan, the National Coalition for Decency, Phyllis Schlafly's Eagle Forum, Religious Roundtable, Evangelism Explosion, Christian Women National Concerns, the National Pro-Life Political

236

Action Committee, the National Conservative Political Action Committee (NCPAC), Intercessors for America, and the like.

The targets of this war are selected political candidates and various "immoral" groups, people, and thoughts. What for simplicity's sake we call the New Right is committed to a political strategy for seizing America. It is moved by a complex of attitudes, fears, hatreds, and highly emotional crusades, and it is energized by sex and sex-related matters.

Not that the New Right opposes all sex, else there would be no future generations of Moral Majoritarians to impose their will on everybody else. But outside of heterosexual relations within marriage, all sex is bad. Let us call such sex Sinful Sex. Sinful Sex is worse than murder, at least according to the executive director of Moral Majority, the Rev. Robert Billings, who served as liaison between Mr. Falwell and the Reagan campaign in 1980. At present, Mr. Billings is well-situated within both the Christian Right and the Reagan administration. According to the Fall 1980 issue of *Record*, a publication of Evangelicals Concerned, which has the remarks on tape, Mr. Billings said: "I know what you and I feel about these queers, these fairies. We wish we could get our cars and run them down while they march."

I am not an attorney, though I am deputy sheriff of two Massachusetts counties, and if I remember the law correctly, running people down with automobiles with malice aforethought is a crime in every state in the union. Perhaps God has dictated to Mr. Billings that He, or She, will look the other way if we get in our cars and run down these queers, these fairies.

The Rev. Mr. Billings is not alone among Moral Majority officials in championing the cause of virtue against gay people. Greg Dixon, Moral Majority's national secretary, preached a sermon at the Indianapolis Baptist Temple on August 8, 1977, in which he said of homosexuals, "I say either fry 'em or put them in the pen. Don't unleash them on the human race....I don't know how in the world you can get a society that won't even put their murderers to death, I don't know how you can ever get them to put these homosexuals to death but God's word would uphold that. They which commit such things are worthy of death."

Mr. Dixon reiterated his remarks in March 1981 on a WIND radio program in Chicago, speaking then as a representative of Moral Majority, which hadn't been formed in 1977. In the more recent statement, in response to the question, Would God's word allow a society to execute homosexuals? Mr. Dixon said, "Absolutely correct." But he appeared vexed to be pressed on the execution proposal and indicated that he would settle for something less: "I believe that homosexuals ought to be in jail, I certainly do."

Homosexuality is just one of the monstrous sins against which the New Right-Christian Right missionaries rail. The Rev. Dan Fore, head of the New York State chapter of Moral Majority, who has expressed exceedingly sanguinary views about homosexuals, also acknowledged that he is now giving serious thought to working for the execution of women who have abortions; these women are "murderesses," said Fore at a meeting of the National Coalition Against Censorship.

We have all heard the views of Mr. Falwell and his comrades, and extensive quotation is unnecessary though blood-curdling. The "conservatism" that emerges

237

from an analysis of the writings and preachments of these people is of course not the type of conservatism that Russell Baker of *The New York Times* has called "conservative chic...the ideology where the fun is...an ism whose time is here." It is authoritarian conservatism, not libertarian conservatism or fusionist conservatism; it is the conservatism not of the Grand Old Party but of those who have already leaped off the Reaganite ship in search of a new savior to press the social agenda on a supine America.

Authoritarian conservatism stresses order and the binding fabric of society: home, family, church, constitutional government (so long as the First Amendment isn't taken seriously)—a matrix of stability within which liberty, or at least its hamstrung interpretation of liberty, can function. Authoritarian conservatism preaches hot and heavy against the monster state in matters economic; it opposes the cancerous spread of bureaucracy; it dwells on the necessity for firm military action to oppose Communist dictatorships and to bolster non-Communist dictatorships; it fights forced busing and abortion and deficit spending and SALT treaties and the ERA and sex education in the schools and sex at all on television and radio and in movies and books, all of which media are assumed now to be solidly in the hands of "pornographers."

In their war against today, the authoritarians take on yesterday, as well. Tim LaHaye, another Moral Majority official, wrote in his 1980 book, *The Battle for the Mind*, that "the giant replica of Michelangelo's magnificent David stands nude, overlooking that beautiful city [presumably Florence]. Quite naturally, this contradicts the wisdom of God, for early in Genesis, the Creator followed man's folly by giving him animal skins to cover his nakedness....The Renaissance obsession with nude 'art form' was the forerunner of the modern humanist's demand for pornography in the name of freedom. Both resulted in the self-destructive lowering of moral standards."

From Michelangelo to Moynihan: In the March 5, 1982, issue of *National Review*, George Gilder, house theorist to the Reaganauts on matters of wealth and poverty, explained why he does not number himself among the neoconservatives. You see,

> *"They are willing to palter over quotas while wives and daughters are drafted into the military. They stay fastidiously aloof while a flood of pornography—propaganda for degradation and viciousness that must be seen to be believed—engulfs our nation's youth. I have no doubt that at some future date, when these trends have reached some climax sufficiently catastrophic, the Neo-Conservatives will...finally grant, in essence, that Ernest van den Haag and Billy Graham were right about pornography; that Anita Bryant knows more about homosexuality than does the American Association of Psychiatrists; that Phyllis Schlafly is better at defining national priorities than is Daniel Patrick Moynihan; that the Moral Majority is a more valuable and responsible movement in our politics than is the Coalition for a Democratic Majority.*
>
> *"Until then, though, the Left will maintain the initiative. Millions of*

American boys will be told in sex-education classes that their adolescent lusts may signify a homosexual fixation, that pornography and promiscuity provide a healthy release of tensions, that contraceptives and abortions have removed the constraints of conventional morality, that families are outmoded in an overpopulated world, that religion is a form of bigotry and superstition. Only the New Right understands the urgency and extremity of these issues."

So the graceful prose artist of supply-side returns, in the pages of the leading journal of mainstream conservatism, to the themes he enunciated years ago in *Sexual Suicide—and* apologizes in his "Why I Am Not a Neo-Conservative" for having once written a book that "bitterly denounced the New Right and Phyllis Schlafly as well." The know-nothingism that typifies the New Right is now, if not totally mimicked, then at least vigorously defended by the leading lights of the responsible right.

No better instance of this comes to mind than the illuminating case of Sen. Barry Goldwater, once "Mr. Conservative." When Goldwater expressed his disdain for the Moral Majority's desire to "dictate their moral convictions to all Americans" and said that "every self-respecting Christian ought to give Jerry Falwell a kick in the ass," those who once stood most enthusiastically for Goldwater abandoned him, with lesser or greater degrees of disgust.

Patrick Buchanan, the most vicious of the New Right columnists with an audience beyond his own true believers, took to his column to remind Goldwater that the senator's use of the term "uncompromised idealism of religious groups" comes ungracefully from the man who in 1964 allowed for extremism in the defense of liberty. William F. Buckley, Jr. urged Goldwater to "retreat from the line he has taken" on the religious Right, and William A. Rusher reminded his readers that Goldwater has always had "grave doubts about the so-called social conservatives."

So the leading light of the Moral Majority, Jerry Falwell, and those who float around him in the New Right-Christian Right axis are now to be defended, even championed, by people in the center column of conservatism who once upon a time would have considered Falwell a swamp rat and his adulators primitives. It is not accidental, I think, that the most important journals of the mainstream conservative movement have increasingly taken to writing of sexual matters in terms virtually indistinguishable from those employed by Mr. Falwell. Sexual matters are mighty energizers in the rhetoric of today's conservatism.

Sexual *behavior* is to be regularized such that only heterosexuality within marriage can be approved. Moreover, writing *about* sex, or broadcast material containing sex, is to be suppressed. The Rev. George A. Zarris, Illinois chairman of Moral Majority, calls for book burning, while the kindred souls of the Joelton Church of Christ in Nashville, Tennessee, organize themselves to punish the advertisers of "morally offensive" programs like *Saturday Night Live* and *Dallas* and *The Newlywed Game*. The Rev. Donald Wildmon's Coalition for Better Television singles out for attack *Real People*, *Diff'rent Strokes*, *Love, Sidney*, *Fame*, and *Gimme a Break.*

239

What the networks are trying to do, knows Wildmon, is inflict homosexuality and other horrors on America. In his column in *Conservative Digest*, we learned last year that the networks "think if they keep trying, they can get something on which makes the homosexual lifestyle funny and therefore acceptable." In the next month's issue of the same magazine, Mr. Wildmon shared his mail with us, including letters criticizing a PBS broadcast of a Masterpiece Theatre program wherein, "with no warning whatsoever, a scene showed a man and woman totally naked in an explicit act of fornication." Not only that, but Wildmon reprinted part of another shocked response, this "from a PhD: 'There was actual, visible nudity and passionate bedroom scenes.'"

You must understand what is happening, as Jerry Falwell told us in one of his mass mailings. What's happening here in America:

> *"Known practicing homosexual teachers have invaded the classrooms, and the pulpits of our churches. Smut peddlers sell their pornographic books—under the protection of the courts! And X-rated movies are allowed in almost every community because there is no legal definition of obscenity. Meanwhile, right in our own homes the television screen is full of R-rated movies and sex and violence....Our grand old flag is going down the drain....I believe that the overwhelming majority of Americans are sick and tired of the way the amoral liberals are trying to corrupt our nation from its commitment to freedom, democracy, traditional morality, and the free enterprise system."*

Accompanying this particular mailing was a petition on "Moral Issues," with five questions, on: abortion, pornography, homosexuals, school prayers, and military strength. In that order. In case you missed the point, we're falling behind the Commies because *Love, Sidney* is allowed to remain on TV.

The censors have virtually no opposition on the right, save possibly James Jackson Kilpatrick. Joining Jerry Falwell's Moral Majority and Phyllis Schlafly's Textbook Censorship Committee, along comes the Educational Research Analysts, which amounts to Mel and Norma Gabler, who have boasted of their success in banning, altering, restricting, or challenging over 250 books, among them *The Diary of Anne Frank*, *The Grapes of Wrath*, and *Future Shock*. The Gablers have received extensive press coverage for their national campaign to ban books, but they are only the tip of the iceberg.

Add to the Gablers:

➤ the Pro-Life Action League, which has attacked Ann Landers as a "lethal threat to the unborn" and an "ill-informed, secular-minded commentator misleading the public."

➤ the New Life Interfaith Chapel in Udall, Kansas, which burned hundreds of books, records, magazines, and paintings, among them *Brave New World* and *The Hobbit*.

➤ the Eagle Forum, Lafayette, Georgia, which sued to forbid the county board of education to use a supplemental high school sex education text, even though the book is used for only two weeks, in sex-segregated classes, and is taught to students who have their parents' consent, not to others.

➤ the Eagle Forum in St. David, Arizona, which banned a series of reading books as "anti-family" and succeeded in removing every book from one high school literature class, including classics by Conrad, Hardy, Hawthorne, Hemingway, Homer, Poe, Steinbeck, and Twain.

The world is turning against the good folk. Bob Jones III, president of the school that bears his family name, not only called for divine retribution on Secretary of State Haig but also preached to the congregation at Bethel Baptist Church in Schaumburg, Illinois, that President Reagan "broke his promise to us when he took on Mr. Bush, a devil, for his vice-president....Mr. Reagan has become a traitor to God's people....This is fast becoming a God-hating, devilistic country that I can't be loyal to any more."

The chosen of God know that America is going to the devil, and to alert us to that fact, they have found that sex works best as the catalyst to action and as the key to unlock the door to contributions. They wage the war on many fronts, against perversion, evil, communism, anti-Americanism, satanism, secular humanism, promiscuity, pornography, homosexuality, obscenity, and other incarnations of Sin. The Rev. Robert G. Grant, head of Stop Gay Power/National Action Center, part of American Christian Cause, is typical of the current approach. In a flyer sent out last year, complete with endorsements of American Christian Cause from Pat Boone, Sam Yorty, Lawrence Welk, Art Linkletter, and former Los Angeles police chief Ed Davis, Reverend Grant explained what's eating at him, this, as he asked for a donation.

"I'll do my Christian duty! YES, Rev. Grant—you can count on me to help you stop ABC's homosexual series and defeat the militant homosexuals and other immoral, anti-God forces in our country. So the American Christian Cause National Action Center can launch the mass-media Christian counter-attacks needed to restore Biblical morality and Godliness, I'm contributing my tax-deductible gift of...." Such examples are legion.

And the point is simple. Specific political issues may or may not bring out the troops and bring in the dollars, but so-called family issues almost certainly will do both. Ideally, the New Right-Christian Right combine likes to wed sinful sex to sinful politics. *The New Right Report*, a newsletter put out by the Richard Viguerie organization as an adjunct to its monthly, *Conservative Digest*, makes the connection explicit. In the last issue of 1979 we learned of the "45 specific communist goals taken from communist sources," among them: "Eliminate all laws governing obscenity by calling them 'censorship' and 'a violation of free speech and free press'" and "present homosexuality, degeneracy, and promiscuity as 'normal, natural and healthy'" and "discredit the family as an institution," not to mention that undying passion of Lenin, "internationalize the Panama Canal."

As *Inquiry* magazine calls them, the "moral imperialists" have not only pushed for the so-called Family Protection Act but have supported efforts to legalize unlimited surveillance of citizens to find out what individuals do sexually. As Jere Real, a citizen of Lynchburg, Virginia, Jerry Falwell's home town, has pointed out in several articles in recent years, the head of the Moral Majority regards any defense of privacy in matters sexual as verification of evil.

Advocates of the Equal Rights Amendment are opposed by the Bible, insists Falwell. Women are "the weaker vessel" to be kept under the "Lordship of Jesus Christ" and their husbands. Leaders of the feminist movement are "blasphemers" and the feminist movement is "a satanic attack on the home" led by "uncaring women who have failed."

The right wing makes war not only against Satan's minions but against its own, with sex as the weapon. The presidential candidacy of Rep. Philip Crane, Republican of Illinois, though probably doomed from the moment Ronald Reagan entered the race, was dealt a blow from which it never recovered, this coming from an attack mounted in the pages of the *Union Leader* of Manchester, New Hampshire, the nation's most prominent conservative daily newspaper. Even though the *Conservative Digest* has frequently offered America a Philip Crane who stood as the epitome of family regularity, the *Union Leader* contended that Crane's wife was a harridan and that both Cranes were and are incorrigible party-goers and hard-drinkers to the point of obnoxiousness and, most important, that Mr. Crane had boasted of his intention to "bed" 1,000 women before he hangs it up.

When Crane bit the dust, the right wing simply shifted gears and used sex against President Carter. *The Review of the News*, weekly magazine of the John Birch Society, chided the incumbent for turning "the memorial to our brave war dead into a Tomb of the Unknown Sodomite." This because the Gay Activists Alliance of the District of Columbia had applied to the Department of the Army for permission to "lay a wreath on the Tomb of the Unknown Soldier at Arlington National Cemetery to honor any sex deviants who might have served in the military." The connecting reed is thin, but when you have sex in hand, you can hit with impunity.

The strategy in almost every single New Right broadside is to align sinful sex, sex that is not sanctified by heterosexual marriage, with bad politics. Rock and disco music are Satan's tunes; the SALT treaties are Beelzebub's sell-out to the Commies. Nudie movies will corrupt America's youth; Justice Sandra O'Connor will sanctify the killing of babies. Billy Jean King has ruined tennis. Marijuana is rotting the brains of our youths; Tony Randall, if allowed to play in *Love, Sidney* on TV, will warp us all.

So along they come, these walking telegrams from Heaven, to clamp a chastity belt on America. They dwell primarily on matters sexual since this is the absolute bottom line in the crusaders' litany of complaints. It's as American as apple pie, this morbid fascination with sex and the attendant effort to wish it away. *Their* Jesus, you see, created only nice people like them; somebody else created all the unspeakables. H. L. Mencken might be amused though not surprised to see these folks reworking for us his definition of neo-puritanism: the haunting suspicion that someone, somewhere, may be having fun.

Those organizations that, collectively, we refer to as the New Right reduce at last to a gang of bully boys pushing their prejudices and masking their self-doubts, parading their self-righteous conviction that they have a direct pipeline to God. The New Right casts everything in the form of a crusade—ostensibly several crusades, but actually one all-consuming crusade to rid America of evil by ridding America of Sinful Sex. Abortion, of course, is anathema, but so are birth control and sex education, which might help cut the growing number of abortions. The ERA is to be defeated not only nor even primarily because it could prove to be a Pandora's box for inane judicial rulings but principally because it could lead to coed toilets and, more bizarre, in some indirect way to the validation of that most terrifying perversion of all, homosexuality.

Whatever minimal restraint is now and again shown in the New Right's incessant rhetorical diatribes against unacceptable sex, it is thrown overboard when *that* subject arises. It arises so often in right-wing literature that anyone coming freshly to the material might assume that the whole nation had succumbed to mass forced conversion to homosexuality. In fact, we know from the sad case of former (and would-be future) Rep. Robert Bauman that demon rum leads directly to homosexual "tendencies." But if you will only join the army of the Lord to save America, the right-wing will save your soul, too.

We are witnessing today the proliferation of crusaders hell-bent on repealing the 20th century, masquerading as good Christians while calling for the blood of others. The movement of people like Jerry Falwell from the backwaters to national notoriety is a vivid symbol of the current American receptiveness to these notions and these propagandists. These people occupy the sacred ground, whence they excoriate the "perverts" and trumpet the message that God has personally delivered into their hands. They arm themselves with divine "truth" to make their case, wrapping themselves in the flag, positioning themselves within The Family, lashing out at anybody who reads what they do not wish to read or who goes to movies that rise beyond the level of latter-day Disney or who otherwise reveals his or her attachment to the sins of the flesh as enumerated by these angels of the Lord.

Some of these people mean what they say; others are tricksters; all are in league to impose a rigid authoritarianism on everybody else. At present, their victory looms as a possibility, though not a remote one. The movement backwards is gaining force and adherents. It has claimed for itself the "moral" ground on sexual matters, from which its other positions flow. One would be suicidal to ignore it or to minimize it or to try to laugh it away. "Kill a Queer for Christ," said the bumper stickers in Dade County, Florida, during the 1977 Anita Bryant crusade. Today it is the same slogan in more sophisticated garb, or, if you will, in polyester drag. The right-wing war against sex is much the larger part of the shadow of Reaction darkening the land, a shadow that grows meaner, bigger, and uglier by the day.

Cold Comfort

By Jacob Sullum

April 1991

Listening to Thomas Donaldson, I'm struck by his intelligence, thoughtfulness, and determination. But I'm also thinking, *This is the guy whose picture appeared in the* Star *under the headline OFF WITH MY HEAD!*

That's a direct, if simplified, version of what Donaldson, a Sunnyvale, California, mathematician and computer scientist, wants the Alcor Life Extension Foundation to do to him before a tumor destroys his brain. The headline does not tell the whole story, of course. Donaldson does not just want Alcor's staff to cut off—or, as Alcor officials put it, "surgically isolate"—his head. He also wants them to pump an antifreeze solution into it, wrap it in plastic, chill it to the temperature of liquid nitrogen, and store it in a metal canister inside an earthquake-proof tank.

The head will remain there until medical science is sufficiently advanced to thaw it and repair the damage done to Donaldson's brain by cancer and freezing. The same technology that will make it possible to revive Donaldson will also provide him with a new body. That's the plan, anyway.

There are a few possible hitches, some of which we'll get to later. The most immediate obstacle is this: In California, as in every other state, what Alcor proposes—causing a person to "move from 'live' to 'dead,'" in the careful phraseology of Donaldson's attorneys—is against the law. Says Deputy Attorney General Kirstofer Jorstad, quoting a famous though fictional detective: "That's murder one, baby." Not only do Alcor members have to worry about prosecution, Donaldson has to worry about the prospect of an autopsy as part of a homicide or suicide investigation. However one views his chances of revival, it's certain that defrosting and cutting up his head would only hurt them.

So last April Donaldson filed a complaint seeking an injunction to prevent local and state authorities from interfering with his cryonic suspension, from trying to perform an autopsy on his remains afterward, or from bringing charges against members of Alcor. In September, Superior Court Judge Ronald C. Stevens refused Donaldson's request. He said allowing premortem cryonic suspension would require taking "a giant step" from existing case law. An appeal is pending.

The Donaldson case is the latest episode in a history of government harassment and obstruction. With only about 500 members nationwide and a not entirely deserved reputation for nuttiness, the cryonics movement is an easy target. The three main cryonics groups are Alcor, the largest, based in Riverside, California; the American Cryonics Society/Trans Time, in Oakland, California; and the Oak Park, Michigan, Cryonics Institute, founded by movement pioneer Robert Ettinger.

Ettinger, a former physics teacher, is the author of *The Prospect of Immor-*

tality, "the book that HAS ALREADY begun the greatest revolution in human history" (according to the jacket). He is not bashful about his accomplishments. "Every single individual now active in the movement can trace his involvement, directly or indirectly, to my influence," he writes. That's because *The Prospect of Immortality* proclaimed way back in 1964 that "most of us now breathing have a good chance of physical life after death—a sober, scientific probability of revival and rejuvenation of our frozen bodies."

Cryonicists freeze the seemingly dead—sometimes whole bodies, sometimes just heads—in an attempt to preserve them until a time, perhaps centuries from now, when they can be restored and revived. It's easy to dismiss such people as fools, ghouls, crackpots, or charlatans. And it's hard to rouse popular indignation when the state disrupts what most people consider a bizarre, hubristic attempt to achieve immortality.

But the struggles of the cryonics movement are not about the merits of cold storage. They're about the right to accept or reject medical treatment, including methods as unorthodox as cryonic suspension; to dispose of your remains, whether in a grave, in an urn, or in a vat of liquid nitrogen; and to hasten your death, or, as the cryonicists would have it, try to postpone it indefinitely. Thomas Donaldson and his fellow enthusiasts do not insist that others join them or applaud them—only that they leave them alone.

Still, as Johnny Carson might say, this is weird, wild stuff. It's hard to sympathize with people you don't understand, especially when they're doing unusual things with severed human heads. To understand cryonicists, you have to get to know them. Hence I find myself, in early December, walking down the winding driveway to Saul Kent's house in Riverside, site of Alcor's annual Turkey Roast, bearing a box of Yum Yum doughnuts.

The door is answered by Kent himself, a tall, heavyset man with a pale complexion and sunken eyes surrounded by dark circles. I half expect to hear him say, "Good eeevening," although it's early afternoon. But no, the longtime and briefly notorious cryonicist just smiles, welcomes me, and directs me to the kitchen, where I deposit my contribution to the potluck dinner.

On the way to the bathroom, I pass through the master bedroom, where two guys are huddled around a computer, talking, I think, in PASCAL. In the bathroom, there's a freezer/refrigerator. Its incongruity makes me uneasy. Still, I'm pretty sure that it's not filled with human body parts. Almost certain, in fact. I check anyway. Just food. After this, I relax.

On the TV in the den they're playing tapes of talk-show appearances by Alcor members. The screen shows a man in his mid-40s with horn-rimmed glasses and a fringe of dark hair that has been further thinned by radiation treatments. *Donahue* identifies him with the tasteful caption, "THOMAS DONALDSON, Ph.D., Wants to Have Head Cut Off and Frozen." Donaldson's speech is generally calm and uninflected, even when he's discussing the brain tumor that has begun to impair his coordination and memory in subtle ways.

I sit down to watch. Most of the 50 or so people at the party are wearing Alcor ID bracelets, indicating that they've signed up for suspension. Some have naked wrists; they're still checking cryonics out. The group is overwhelmingly male, with ages ranging from about 25 to about 65; most appear to be in their 30s and 40s.

The atmosphere is earnestly intellectual. There seem to be a lot of computer specialists, space enthusiasts, science-fiction fans, and libertarians of various stripes. One woman is selling parodies of those little Jesus-in-a-fish emblems you see on the backs of cars. These fish have feet, and the name inside is "Darwin." She says they went over big at the Objectivist meeting last week. The Turkey Roast is sort of a cross between a *Star Trek* convention and an Ayn Rand discussion group.

Cryonics may just be the ultimate Revenge of the Nerds. Say what you might about the Alcorians, it's obvious they have thought this thing through. The group's literature presents the arguments for cryonics clearly and methodically, anticipating objections and carefully distinguishing fact from speculation, plausibility from possibility. Alcor's *Cryonics* magazine explores the topics that cryonicists never tire of discussing: cryobiological research, cloning, genetic manipulation, cures for aging, microbiology, nanotechnology, memory formation and storage, artificial intelligence, the definition of death, the nature of identity and consciousness.

Heavy. But the idea, in a nutshell (albeit a large nutshell), is this: The definition of death has always been arbitrary, varying with circumstance and medical technology. A heart-attack or drowning victim who would have been abandoned 100 years ago can now be resuscitated. It seems reasonable to assume that, 100 years (or so) from now, conditions currently deemed fatal will be completely curable. The trick is maintaining victims of cancer, AIDS, heart disease, or old age until then.

By "maintaining," cryonicists mean preserving the structures of the brain that record your memory and personality. Only when these are lost are you truly, permanently, irrevocably dead. Otherwise, you are merely dormant, awaiting a technology sufficiently advanced to bring you back.

When Ettinger wrote *The Prospect of Immortality*, he was a little vague on just what this technology might be. He talked about installing artificial body parts, transplanting organs grown from cell cultures, and using "fabulous machines" to repair subtler damage. But his point was that it *doesn't matter*. We don't have to anticipate what marvelous advances the future might bring. We just have to be there when they happen.

Since then, however, cryonicists have pretty much decided that nanotechnology will be the way to go. That is, itsy-bitsy, teeny-weeny machines, guided by powerful (but really small) computers, will repair individual cells of the body, curing disease, reversing aging, and fixing any damage done by freezing and defrosting. Don't scoff. This is all in a respectable book called *Engines of Creation*, by K. Eric Drexler, an MIT graduate and a professor of computer science at Stanford University. Published in 1986, it was widely reviewed and became a big hit among futurists and technophiles.

Since nanomachines can manipulate individual atoms, they can build (or fix) virtually anything, given raw material and the right instructions. For example, they could rebuild a new body around your brain, reading out the required information from your genetic code. So preserving your whole body may be unnecessary. Like Donaldson, most Alcor members have opted instead for "neurosuspension," the

246

economy plan. (At Alcor, the minimum fee is $120,000 for a whole-body suspension, $41,000 for a neurosuspension.)

Drexler argues that nanomachines capable of cellular repair will be developed, with the aid of artificial-intelligence programs, during the next century. Thus he does for Ettinger's "freezer program" what the idea of genetic mutations did for Darwin's theory of evolution: He suggests how it might really work.

Might, cryonicists stress, not *will*. Cryonics is a matter of probabilities. There are so many variables involved, however, that many cryonicists won't even hazard a guess on the chances of success. Then again, some do. In the May 1989 issue of *Cryonics*, Alcor member Steven B. Harris estimates that the odds of revival are somewhere between 1 in 7 and 1 in 400.

As Harris notes, coming back from the freezer depends on a number of factors, of which the *least* uncertain is probably the development of those itsy-bitsy, teeny-weeny machines. Other things to worry about: We don't know exactly how the brain stores information (although long-term memory does seem to involve physical changes that persist even when the juice stops flowing). So we don't know which structures are essential to identity.

Even if we did, we wouldn't know whether freezing and defrosting a brain leaves those structures intact enough so that nanomachines could infer the brain's original state. We don't know how long Alcor, Trans Time, and the Cryonics Institute are going to be around to keep their clients frozen. We don't know that nanotechnology will be cheap enough for the cost to be covered by the money they've set aside. Either way, we don't know that future physicians will be curious or beneficent enough to bother reviving people.

In short, there's *a lot* we don't know. The cryonicists are candid about this. In exchange for your fee, "we'll put forth our best-faith effort to keep you suspended as long as we can," says Mike Darwin, a former medical technician who is Alcor's research director. "Beyond that, we give no guarantees." About 25 percent of the fee covers the cost of the suspension procedure. The rest goes into a Patient Care Fund that generates interest to pay for maintenance, which consists mainly of replenishing liquid nitrogen. To improve their chances, most Alcor members leave extra money.

Darwin says this arrangement, which resembles "perpetual care" at a cemetery, is a big improvement on the way early cryonics groups operated. In the years following the publication of Ettinger's book, organizations intent on implementing his vision opened and folded like seats in a crowded theater at intermission. As Darwin describes it, families would come to the groups with recently deceased or nearly dead relatives and agree to pay for their shot at another life. Then, as grief faded and car payments, dental bills, and college tuitions loomed, the customers would decide they had better things to do with their money, and they'd let Granny defrost.

Nowadays, Alcor insists on informed, rational consent. It rarely accepts suspendees on the verge of death, and it gets the money up front, usually from members' life-insurance policies. "I hope and pray we have addressed the key things that have caused other organizations to fail," Darwin says. "But it's still a long shot. It's new, and there are a lot of uncertainties."

Largely because it's new, the cryonics movement has had trouble with the government. Alcor, with about 200 suspension members, has attracted the most attention. Members of the other two major cryonics groups acknowledge this with a mixture of relief and resentment. Asked if Trans Time has had legal problems, its president, Art Quaife, laughs. "No," he says. "We've kept our nose clean. We stay out of trouble....They're paying a lot of attention to Alcor....As long as they basically ignore us, we're happy to be ignored."

There's considerable tension among the three organizations, stemming partly from differences in financial arrangements and suspension procedures. Only Alcor does neurosuspensions, for example. Ettinger's Cryonics Institute charges $28,000 for a whole-body suspension, largely because it doesn't use sterile procedures. He reasons that when medical science can revive frozen bodies, dealing with a little infection will be a snap.

Ettinger says the Cryonics Institute, unlike Alcor, does not plan to attempt premortem suspensions—which improve the odds for victims of Alzheimer's disease or other brain disorders as well as cancer patients like Donaldson—even though Michigan has no law against assisting suicide. "It's a thicket we don't want to get into," he says. "We don't really want to pay out large amounts of money in litigation, even in successful litigation." Darwin estimates Alcor has spent about $1 million on legal fees in its various court battles—money raised from membership dues and contributions.

The litigation has largely been an effort to establish the legitimacy of cryonics. Regulators and law enforcement officials are not sure how to handle a group like Alcor. Is it a bunch of harmless weirdos who deserve toleration? Or is it a threat to law and order, a challenge to authority that must be stamped out?

In the Dora Kent case, Riverside County Coroner Ray Carrillo tried both approaches, settling on the second. In the process, he transformed a paperwork oversight into a symbol of the cryonics movement's resistance against bureaucratic interference. The episode is a source of both alarm and inspiration for those who support Donaldson's fight.

Like her son Saul, Dora Kent was an early cryonics enthusiast. So after she became seriously ill, suffering from osteoporosis and atherosclerosis as well as organic brain disease, Saul placed her in a nursing home near Alcor. On December 9, 1987, Kent received a call from the nursing home telling him his mother was near death from pneumonia. Rather than prolong her suffering with aggressive treatment, he had her transferred to Alcor the next day.

Although his 83-year-old mother had suffered brain damage, Kent was not sure how extensive it was. In any case, he says, "my position is that if someone wants this, it should be done regardless, especially if there's any brain tissue at all left." He acknowledges, however, that "bringing my mother back would be an extreme challenge for future generations."

Shortly after midnight on December 11, Dora Kent stopped breathing; her heart stopped beating a few minutes later. Since she was clinically dead, the Alcor staff proceeded with her neurosuspension, which involves administering protective drugs; opening the chest and attaching a heart-lung machine; running the blood through a heat exchanger to cool it; packing the body in water ice; replacing the blood with a tissue-preservative solution; removing the head—or, as cryonicists see it, removing the body; and gradually cooling the head to minus 196 degrees Celsius, the temperature of liquid nitrogen.

In their rush to preserve Dora Kent's brain, however, the Alcor personnel neglected to have her physician standing by to certify death. Instead, he signed the death certificate the next day. Because of this irregularity, the case was referred to the coroner's office, which performed an autopsy on the body. On December 23, Darwin and Saul Kent met with two deputy coroners, who assured them that the case was closed.

"One of the coroners signs the death certificate, saying she died of pneumonia," Kent says. "Everything is fine. The next day is Christmas Eve, and I'm home. At noon, there's a knock at the door, and it's a camera crew from NBC: 'Could you comment on the fact that your mother may have been murdered?' Out of nowhere."

The autopsy had found metabolites of barbiturates in Dora Kent's blood, possible evidence of foul play. But Alcor had already told the coroner's office that the drugs were administered after clinical death to help preserve brain tissue, part of the standard suspension procedure. Kent suspects that Carrillo, who was at first cooperative and understanding, got nervous. "We had done something which was inviting suspicion," he says. "I think there was a fear that...their superiors would get upset and say, 'How can you just let people get away with this?'"

So Carrillo called a press conference to announce a homicide investigation. At the conference, a deputy coroner suggested that Dora Kent might still have been alive when her head was cut off. This did not quite jibe with the theory that Alcor had killed her by injecting an overdose of barbiturates. Nor did it make sense in light of another assertion by the coroner's office—that she was indeed *clinically* dead when her suspension began, but not *brain* dead. Nevertheless, the news media went wild. True or not, this was a great story.

So on January 7, 1988, the TV cameras were ready when coroner's deputies raided Alcor with a search warrant. The main item on their list: Dora Kent's head. It was nowhere to be found. "They threatened everybody in sight," Kent says. "They threatened to thaw out the bodies. They threatened everything they could imagine to try to get someone to talk, and no one did." So they handcuffed six Alcor members and hauled them away, only to release them later that day. They also seized Alcor's patient records.

On January 12, the coroner's deputies were back, this time accompanied by UCLA police and a SWAT team. They occupied Alcor for two days, stripping it of supplies and equipment valued at tens of thousands of dollars. Alcor had purchased much of the equipment from the UCLA Surplus and Excess Property Department, and it still bore university tags. No one asked for documentation of ownership. The coroner's office also seized prescription drugs, eight computers (with their manuals), all data-storage media (including software), and every computer printer, including the two used to produce *Cryonics*.

On February 1, Superior Court Judge Victor L. Miceli issued a temporary restraining order, later made permanent, enjoining Carrillo from attempting to autopsy Dora Kent's head. Among other things, he found there was "no evidence that Dora Kent was alive when she was decapitated." Virtually all of the seized property was eventually returned. The six Alcor members who were taken into custody during the first raid have sued Riverside County for false arrest; an out-of-court settlement is expected.

(Carrillo, by the way, is no longer Riverside County's coroner. Before the Dora Kent case, he had gained notoriety by ostentatiously publicizing the cause of Liberace's death—AIDS. After the unsuccessful Alcor raids, his office put a swift end to a homicide investigation by mistakenly allowing the body to be cremated. Later it was revealed that two of his assistants, a husband-and-wife team, had been performing autopsies on their backyard picnic table and keeping body parts in their garage. Carrillo lost his re-election bid. The obvious lesson: Don't mess with Liberace fans.)

Even after the coroner's office had been thoroughly embarrassed, the Dora Kent investigation continued. In September 1989 the California Board of Medical Quality Assurance informed Alcor that the Riverside County district attorney's office intended to prosecute the organization, not for murder, but for *practicing medicine without a license*. Alcor sued unsuccessfully for an injunction to prevent this, but the charges were never filed. Last November, Assistant District Attorney Don Inskeep told the *Los Angeles Times* that his office had dropped the case.

I know what you're thinking, but you're too polite to ask. While the coroner's deputies were poking around at Alcor, where was the head? "Until the death certificate is changed, I'm not going to comment on that," Kent says.

Today, Dora Kent's head may or may not reside in a cramped building in a Riverside industrial park, along with seven other human heads and six bodies. (The Alcorians won't say.) If you happen to be in L.A., and Universal Studios is too crowded, you can see these and other attractions on the Alcor tour, which is free and available by appointment. The Alcor facility also includes an operating room with a lot of secondhand medical equipment and a row of supply cabinets against one wall. Just outside the operating room is a big chest that contains the silicone-oil bath used to cool suspendees to the temperature of dry ice. The same room serves as a laboratory for research aimed at improving suspension techniques. Ultimately, Alcor would like to achieve true suspended animation, which does no additional damage to the body or brain.

The tanks—or dewars, as Alcor calls them (as in Dewar flask, a kind of thermos used to store liquefied gases) are in a small room off the laboratory. Darwin says the dewar lying on its side contains the body of James H. Bedford, the first person to be cryonically suspended. Bedford has been sealed in there since 1967, and he's had an even more eventful journey (probably) than has Dora Kent's head. He was frozen by the now-defunct Cryonics Society of California, and he was moved from place to place, including at least one garage, before finding a home at Alcor. They're not sure what kind of shape he's in.

Darwin opens another dewar, this one upright, and invites visitors to climb up a ladder onto a platform and peer in. Beneath the fog of nitrogen vapor are two bodies wrapped in blue plastic sleeping bags (presumably rated for low temperatures), floating with heads downward. Nearby is a tank that resembles a hot tub covered by concrete. It holds nine metal canisters containing heads and tissue samples. Thomas Donaldson has reserved similar accommodations.

"I believe there are only eight patients in there, because we have some pets in there as well," Darwin says.

I've heard about this, but I wasn't sure whether to believe it. I ask the obvious question. "The whole pet?"

"No. We do have a whole dog in that unit over there and another whole dog in that unit there. My childhood dog is in here."

"Just the head?"

"Just the head. Thomas Donaldson's cat, Daisy, is in there, too. So...some have pets." (It costs about $7,500 to suspend a pet.)

"Couldn't you buy another pet in the future?" I suggest—tactfully, I hope.

Darwin, who until now has been mild-mannered and friendly, gets a bit testy. "I love my dog. That was my childhood dog. That dog spent a lot of time with me. I thought the world of her. I thought more of her than I do of a lot of people." After a pause, he is cordial again. "Look at it this way: If I make it into suspension, at least that's one person I'm going to know—someone who'll be glad to see me."

The 12-year-old daughter of Alcor's accountant, who has come along for the tour, won't let the matter drop. She has viewed the frozen bodies and heads with equanimity, but this upsets her. "That's gross," she says. How, she asks, did these pet owners know their dogs and cats *wanted* to be suspended?

"You should keep in mind that those people who die and have pets, their pets end up getting put to sleep," Darwin notes.

"That's sick," she says.

The city zoning authorities have different concerns about the Alcor facility. "We are technically here illegally, because the city of Riverside requires a conditional use permit," Darwin says. "When we came here, we told them what we were doing. We said we were freezing people. And they said, 'What's that like?' We said, 'Well, it's biomedical research.' You don't need a CUP for biomedical research, but you do need one for storing body parts...like a mortuary. And that's what they've decided we're most like. But we haven't been able to get a CUP because the state of California has been telling everyone that we're illegal."

Without the permit, Alcor cannot expand; the current facility is designed to serve only about 80 people. The zoning controversy may be resolved, however, as a result of a court decision last fall. Superior Court Judge Arelio Muñoz ruled that people have a right to dispose of their remains however they wish. He found that California's Uniform Anatomical Gift Act applies to cryonics, which therefore constitutes "scientific use," a recognized way to dispose of bodies. He instructed the state Department of Health Services to register death certificates and issue body-disposition permits for Alcor members, which it had been refusing to do since May 1987. The state has appealed the ruling.

"The people running the health department really believe, as do many government officials, that if something isn't [explicitly] permitted by law, it's illegal," Kent says. "They feel that unless people like them are overseeing an activity, it shouldn't be permitted."

In light of Alcor's regulatory problems—and, especially, in light of the Dora Kent case—Thomas Donaldson has good reason to fear that his prospect of immortality is in jeopardy. If the government obstructs Alcor's attempts to suspend people *after* clinical death, it's not likely to look kindly on premortem suspension, which is probably Donaldson's only chance of preserving the essential structures of his brain. Indeed, the state has made it clear that it would consider the procedure to be assisted suicide at the very least, and perhaps murder.

At least one judge thinks otherwise. In 1989, when Alcor sought a court order to prevent the district attorney from charging the organization with unauthorized practice of medicine, Superior Court Judge Robert J. Timlin said he could not oblige. But he made a remarkable concession: "This court concludes that the adherents...under Article I, Section 1 of the California Constitution and the Fifth and Ninth Amendments to the United States Constitution, have a right to privacy, which includes the right to exercise control over his/her own body and to determine whether to submit his/her body, or any portion thereof...to *premortem* cryonic suspension."

Donaldson would be surprised to hear such a ruling from California's Second District Court of Appeals, where his case went after he lost in Superior Court last fall. "I'm basically pessimistic about the lawsuit, although I think it's a good thing to pursue," he says. There is some cause for hope. California's constitution explicitly protects a right to privacy, and the Second District Court of Appeals has applied that right to euthanasia cases. In 1983 the court ruled that physicians who follow family instructions to remove feeding tubes from comatose patients cannot be prosecuted for murder. In two later cases, the court upheld the right of seriously ill (but not necessarily terminal) patients to have feeding tubes disconnected.

Donaldson's attorneys, David Epstein and Christopher Ashworth, also cite the cases of Karen Quinlan and Nancy Cruzan, in which the U.S. Supreme Court held that, where the patient's wishes are clear, families may disconnect life support from comatose relatives. They note that the highest courts of 10 states have upheld the right of terminally ill patients to hasten their deaths.

Epstein argues that there is no principled distinction between "passive" suicide by starvation or dehydration and the "active" suicide that Donaldson seeks. He quotes Justice Antonin Scalia's concurring opinion in *Cruzan v. Missouri*: "It would not make much sense to say that one may not kill oneself by walking into the sea, but may sit on the beach until submerged by the incoming tide; or that one may not intentionally lock oneself into a cold storage locker, but may refrain from coming indoors when the temperature drops below freezing."

Epstein concludes: "The only material distinction between lawful assistance and murder is plaintiff's consent. Absent such consent, neither would be any more or less a crime because it was either 'passive' or 'active.'"

If the court rejects this argument and refuses to allow tangible assistance, Alcor proposes to instruct Donaldson on how to inject himself with a lethal overdose. Epstein maintains that applying California's law against assisting suicide to such speech would be a violation of the First Amendment. He also argues that the law is unconstitutional on its face, both because it is vague and because suicide itself is not a criminal act.

If Donaldson loses his case and further appeals are unsuccessful, he plans to starve himself to death. At least two Alcor members have already gone this route, including a cancer patient who died after 10 days. It's perfectly legal, and terminal patients who die this way are generally not autopsied. "It's not a very nice thing," Donaldson says. "But it looks like what I'd have to do if I lose the case."

Donaldson recognizes that his suit is destined to be known as a right-to-die case, but he doesn't see it that way. "There are two different views of what's going on," he says. "There's the cryonicist view, and there's the public view. The public view decides that this is suicide, so we're suing for the right to commit suicide. The cryonicist view is that we're suing for the right to cryonic suspension, which is the very opposite of suicide."

Although he supports a broad right to die, Donaldson does not approve of euthanasia—given the alternative of suspension—and he distances himself from organizations such as the Hemlock Society. "My aim is my suspension," he says. "If other people with, I believe, quite fallacious ideas try to use my case for some other purpose, that is not my affair."

Donaldson and other members of the movement are puzzled and frustrated by people who will not or cannot adjust their world views to take account of the opportunities offered by cryonics. As Ettinger puts it with characteristic fervor in the foreword to *The Prospect of Immortality*: "A great many people have to be *coaxed* into admitting that life is better than death, healthy is better than sick, smart is better than stupid, and immortality might be worth the trouble!"

Those who are taking the trouble see life from a different perspective than most of us. "People have asked me how I felt when I was told that I had this tumor that had a high probability of killing me," Donaldson says. "I had already confronted my own death, [so] the first thing I thought was, Well, I guess it's come sooner for me than I expected. The second thing I thought was that arranging for my suspension was the best decision I'd ever made in my life."

Like other cryonicists, Donaldson combines a sometimes unsettling intensity with a surprising sense of humor. During his appearance on *Donahue* last July, he stressed that Alcor's frozen clients are *patients*, not corpses. "The reason they're patients is because we don't think they're dead. And we're right, OK? And all those people who think that they are dead, they're wrong, OK?"

Later in the show, however, Donaldson found a subtler way to express his differences with conventional wisdom. He was pressing a bioethicist to look at cryonic suspension as a risky sort of medical treatment. When the doctor danced around the question, Donaldson interrupted him. "I would like to continue," the bioethicist snapped. "I, too," Donaldson said. "I, too."

PART SIX

CITY LIFE

The Seduction of Planning

By Lynn Scarlett

August/September 1989

n January 1989, the township of Mt. Lebanon, Pennsylvania, issued a comprehensive plan "to lead Mt. Lebanon into the twenty-first century." The report intoned: "Goals not stated cannot be achieved."

Nearly 20 years earlier the same community, under the tutelage of a different set of policy makers, also prepared a comprehensive plan to ensure that the town's housing, transportation, and other needs were met. In the 1970 plan, a proposed mass-transit sky bus system was called the "brightest ray of hope" for the town's transportation needs. By 1988, there was no mention of the sky bus. It had not been built, nor were any plans to build it described. And improving transportation remained among the planners' priorities.

Across a continent, in sprawling Los Angeles, with a population 400 times greater than Mt. Lebanon's, a distinguished committee appointed by Mayor Tom Bradley issued its report, *Los Angeles 2000,* in November 1988. Under preparation for three years, the report resolved that "we can plan wisely and manage the City's growth...or we can allow it to grow by default."

Urban policy makers—in large metropolises and small towns alike—have planning fever. Few communities have escaped the penchant of policy makers to nudge, prod, and force them along the path to someone's idea of utopia. Even statewide urban management plans are now the rage—in Maine, Vermont, Rhode Island, Delaware, Florida, and New Jersey. Details vary, but the thrust is constant: big urban problems require big urban plans.

The idea of urban planning is not new. In the early 1900s, cities began replacing the countryside as the predominant place of employment, and urban populations burgeoned. With growth came problems—crime, pollution, congestion, noise. Today we have vehicle exhaust; in 1900 New York had manure—tons of it. And with these problems has come an understandable urge to mitigate them.

The apparent chaos of cities provided fertile ground for proponents of urban planning. The term itself is seductive, evoking images of order and prospects of perfection. And so, by the '20s, zoning laws—an early planning tool—began to spell out what could be built where. Then came transportation planning and building codes and urban-renewal schemes and redevelopment projects and, most recently, growth-management plans.

Yet urban problems persist. Even the keenest minds with the best intentions can't seem to set the urban landscape aright. How can this be?

With poetic incisiveness, Robert Burn penned in 1785 his often-repeated lines, "The best laid schemes o' mice and men / Gang aft a gley; / An' lea'e us naught but grief and pain, / For promised joy." Planners, or more specifically, public planners, still miss their mark.

This failure is neither surprising nor cause for despair. Much of the chaos that planners fail to mold into order is precisely the dynamism and diversity that drive economic prosperity. "The real problem is not control, but creativity," remarked Jane Jacobs, whose *Death and Life of Great American Cities* upset the discipline of public planning when it appeared in 1961. "Planners' greatest short-coming...is lack of intellectual curiosity about how cities work. They are taught to see the intricacy of cities as mere disorder. Since most of them believe what they have been taught, they do not inquire about the processes that lie behind the intricacy." To the degree that planners fail to quell this perceived disorder, the vitality of cities fortuitously continues.

Although the apparent chaos may be an asset, not a plague, other problems are real. Vehicles clog highways. Pollutants foul the air. Solid wastes accumulate and outpace landfill capacity. Buildings and infrastructure decay. Housing costs soar. Such city woes deserve attention, but plans—even the current breed of "comprehensive," "imaginative," "regional" public plans—are not the answer (and are sometimes even part of the problem).

Consider a recent megaplan devised by Los Angeles-area legislators. This spring the Southern California Air Quality Management District (AQMD), whose jurisdiction includes all of the greater Los Angeles area, held public hearings on a wide-ranging pollution-abatement plan. The plan includes over 140 sets of regula-tions, spanning 18 years, that will touch every aspect of life among South Coast residents and businesses. Leaving virtually no stone unturned, the planners would ban trivial sources of pollution—some backyard barbecues, gasoline-powered lawn mowers, and swimming-pool heaters. And it would take on more-prominent pollution sources—vehicle exhaust, oil refinery emissions, and pollution from hundreds of other industrial and commercial processes.

One by one, industry representatives stood before AQMD officials at the March hearings. The proceedings went something like this. A representative of the water-heater manufacturers would stand up, praise the district for its "pathbreaking plan to deal with pollution," and then add that, unfortunately, the district had its facts all wrong about water heaters. They don't function the way the plan described. Commercial heaters differ dramatically from residential ones, and so on. Next came the swimming-pool representative who also praised the district for its fine work but, alas, lamented that the proposed plan failed utterly to take into account actual swimming-pool heating technology. Then followed the barbecue manufacturers, the furniture makers, the oil companies, the butchers, the bakers, and the candle-stick makers.

No doubt each business was attempting to protect its interests and mitigate any regulatory costs the new plan might impose—a point that student demonstra-tors righteously pointed out with signs denouncing all opponents of the plan as greedy businessmen out to destroy Planet Earth. But the self-interested pleas by representatives of various enterprises also illustrated a fundamental problem of planning—the knowledge problem.

As economist Thomas Sowell observed in *Knowledge and Decisions,* "ideas are everywhere, but knowledge is rare." How, Sowell then asks, "does an ignorant world perform intricate functions requiring enormous knowledge?"

Planning is one popular option. In common political parlance, planning refers to the use of centralized, public decision making to define goals and spell out measures to achieve them. As a decision-making process, it is necessarily formal. It is about rule making and rule enforcement. As a public process, its prescriptions must be specific and leave little discretion to authorities implementing the plan. This inflexibility provides, as Sowell notes, "insurance against the discriminatory use of the vast powers of government. 'Red tape' is an implicit premium paid for this 'insurance.'"

To spell out specific rules, planners need vast amounts of information. To make the AQMD plan work, for example, regulators must accurately predict demographic trends. They must have up-to-the-minute knowledge of the production processes of hundreds of businesses—and, ideally, be able to foresee what new technology might bring. They must be able to ascertain who is not complying with regulations—whether the violators are families enjoying their backyard barbecues or businesses surreptitiously emitting pollutants.

But public authorities, like the rest of us, are not omniscient. Moreover, the planning process is ill-suited to conveying information. In any centralized and relatively inflexible system, feedback about changing circumstances is slow to enter the decision-making loop. And acquiring knowledge about production processes and diverse community needs is expensive and time-consuming. In short, the process is inefficient—a point amply illustrated by the 20th-century performance of massive planning in the Soviet Union.

For seven decades the Soviet Union has tried to plan its economy. Now, Mikhail Gorbachev acknowledges the inefficiencies, persistent shortages, and corruption that once were reported mainly in underground East Bloc jokes. Even on quality-of-life issues, the Soviet experience is unimpressive: life expectancy has declined, mortality rates are up, pollution grays the horizon. So Soviet leaders have ushered in *perestroika*—a liberalization of the economy that includes more decentralized decision making, some private ownership, more freedom. And the West, with some self-complacence, is cheering on these changes.

But what does the Soviet experience tell us? Forget the big debate—communism versus capitalism—and consider only the issue of planning. The Soviet system is a monumental demonstration of its pitfalls. Complex economic systems require the rapid conveyance of vast bits of information about the ever-changing supply of and demand for different resources.

The very complexity so often cited by city authorities to justify master plans in fact warrants just the opposite—decentralized decision making coordinated by the actions of millions of individuals, each privy to information unavailable on a grand scale. Cities are but microcosms of the larger economy. What failed in the Soviet Union for its entire economy is bound to fail also in our cities—and for the same reasons.

Some of the impetus behind planning stems from a very simple fallacy: that only governments plan grandly and only grand plans can bring order. In fact, of course, we all make plans and follow through on them. Many of us even achieve the goals we set out to accomplish. Food gets produced. Buildings get built. Cars get bought. No grand designer spells out a five-year plan for the millions of goods and services we produce and consume. Instead, we rely on that often-neglected process whereby prices reflect the demand for goods in relationship to their supply, informing myriad individual decisions.

Although the overall outcome subscribes to no one individual's particular vision of an ideal community, this is not for lack of planning. And this points up the real function of public plans. They do not establish plans where none exist; they instead replace the plans of individual citizens with those of government officials and the elite that curry their favor.

A telling demonstration of this is found in planners going so far as to instruct builders about the required appearance of their creations. Santa Barbara, California, for example, has decided that only red tile roofs, adobe-colored siding, and earth-colored signage will do for its commercial establishments. Baltimore's planners dictated that its transit facility must have "a cascade of steps," a clock tower, a cafe with umbrella tables, brick walkways, structures of no more than three stories, and so on. Creativity on the part of the developer was, of course, certainly encouraged.

Even as Frank Lloyd Wright was creating his most magnificent buildings, planners had already begun gingerly to impose their visions of grandeur on city development. In New York, one of his buildings had to be constructed behind a wall so that its unconventional concrete-block walls would not mar the view from the street. Today, the structure no doubt couldn't be built at all.

Many planners and citizens deem this issue a spurious one. We cannot concern ourselves with a little loss of freedom of choice when the order and aesthetic appeal of our cities is at stake, they assert. We have to make sacrifices, perhaps even of our freedom, to attain the clean air, pure water, and uncongested roads we all desire.

In fact, however, this loss of freedom will not achieve the intended results. The reasons why are well summarized by Sowell: "The Godlike approach to social policy ignores both the diversity of values and the cost of agreement among human beings." And, he adds, public planning "distorts the communication of knowledge."

Planning involves prescriptions, and prescriptions inevitably raise costs. Developers haggle with city planners to come to some compromise; polluters litigate until they find a technology that will achieve a mandated reduction in emissions; employees demand higher wages in order to keep their employers in compliance with mandated "alternative work schedule" plans. These are all costs of reaching agreements among parties affected by public plans and their accompanying regulations.

Planning also distorts costs by obscuring some costs and increasing others. Banning multifamily dwellings, for example, cuts the supply of housing, and overall housing costs increase. Separating residential from commercial areas drives people into their cars as they commute outside their communities to work. Even as planners may resolve some particular perceived problem, their plans set in motion a series of unintended consequences and unacknowledged costs.

260

If public planning won't work very well, are we destined to breathe foul air and creep along on congested highways? During the AQMD hearings, its proponents repeatedly charged that a vote against the plan was a vote for pollution. The contention is simplistic in its narrow presentation of the options.

The key to successfully resolving urban problems that seem to require master planning is to understand existing decision processes. Some of the "chaos" that planners and established residents seem so eager to suppress is actually the tangible reflection of diverse preferences among different people. And some, as Jacobs observed, flows from the change that inevitably accompanies a dynamic economy. Efforts to eliminate this chaos cannot be accomplished without suppressing freedom and squelching economic prosperity. Such chaos is the sign of an economy that *is* working.

But other urban characteristics, like air pollution and traffic congestion, result from decision-making processes in which important knowledge is not being conveyed. People are, for example, choosing to drive to work at rush hour all alone in their automobiles without recognizing that highway space is limited. Or factories are emitting pollutants into the air as if the atmosphere could, without loss of air quality, absorb the emissions in unlimited quantities. Or low-cost housing is not being built. Here the key issue is how best to convey the missing pieces of information so that people alter their behavior.

All decisions, public and private, are shaped by individual preferences combined with external incentives. To change the outcome of decisions, policy makers can either hope to change people's preferences or alter the incentives they face or ignore both preferences and incentives and legislate behavior. The latter course—the planning approach—erodes freedom and entails high information costs. And changing people's preferences is akin to the ill-fated efforts of various Communist regimes to fashion a "new man." Such efforts have failed even when governments resorted to Draconian "re-education."

It is possible, however, to alter the incentives people face in their daily decisions. At the root of many urban problems, especially air pollution and traffic congestion, is the simple fact that air and roads are "free goods"—treated *as if* they are available in unlimited supply. Commuters pay nothing to use the roadways. Polluters pay nothing to dump byproducts into the atmosphere, and most of us capriciously toss out trash as if landfill were limitless. This means that vital information about the relative scarcity of air and roads and landfill is left out of the decision-making process.

Public planning focuses on the ill effects of this imperfect process and imposes regulations designed to achieve some different outcome. The result: In the case of pollution, an AQMD-style compendium of edicts mandating how Los Angeles residents and businesses are to conduct their affairs and to combat the trash problem, we get mandated recycling programs. But such regulations still convey to commuters and polluters no information about the costs of their behavior.

Or, in the case of housing, planners "downzone" urban areas to reduce crowding and congestion. But by ruling out low-cost, high-density housing, they block the ability of the market to respond to people's needs.

Public planning, espoused in the name of harmony and rationality, actually provokes discord. It interrupts the flow of information from consumer to producer and back. And it does nothing to improve the flow of information about scarcities where the marketplace, with its price-coordinated transmission of knowledge, is not working.

Where price signals are absent, as in the use of air and roads, the most effective approach is to introduce price signals rather than presume to plan away the ill effects of their absence. Create institutions—like air rights or toll roads—that get individuals to take into account the costs of their behavior. Faced with higher costs of driving alone down the freeway at rush hour, for example, some people will switch to public transit. Others will carpool. Still others may move closer to work.

And rather than overcoming the "out of sight, out of mind" mentality toward garbage with mandates and city-financed recycling plans, the more effective solution is to introduce pricing that varies depending on how much garbage people produce. City officials in Seattle did just that. Seattle citizens now have choices. They can buy more recyclable goods and produce less garbage to keep their trash bill low. Or they can maintain their old habits, but pay higher costs for the volumes of waste they generate.

Unlike planned solutions to traffic congestion and landfill scarcity, using price signals lets individuals make their own trade-off, their own choices, about how to respond to changing circumstances. As Sowell neatly summarizes, "more options generally mean better results when the larger number of options includes all the smaller number of options." Planning excludes options. As a result, we are all made worse off.

Flouting the Law, Serving the Poor

By Glenn Garvin

June/July 1985

"How are you doing, Millie?" The man in the yellow Pirates T-shirt, propped indolently against a steel railing in front of the Giant Eagle store, is solicitous. "You gonna be needin' some help today?"

Millie, a wizened and frail little black woman in her 70s, nods. "Please don't let me forget the butter this time," she says to the man as they walk into the store together. Passing them on the way out is a shopping cart piled high with brown grocery bags and shrieking toddlers, guided by a harried young woman in her mid-20s. Her expression brightens as she spots an older man with a blue golf cap.

"Hello, baby," the older man calls. "You ready to go on to the Hill now?" The question is apparently a perfunctory one; even though the woman's attention is distracted by one of the kids, who is assiduously stuffing a plastic Luke Skywalker figure down his throat, the old man begins loading her bags into the back of his big blue Plymouth.

And a few feet away, a complex and emotional negotiation is taking place. "Since *when* has Mower Street been $4.00?" a woman in a blue kerchief demands, shaking a purse in the air. "Since *always*," replies a wiry little man, leaning back out of the path of the purse but setting his jaw nonetheless. "You know it *always* been $4.00 to go over to Homewood."

"I ain't lettin' you rob me like that, no ways," the woman says, stomping off. She stops a few feet away and begins another conversation—more softly—with one of the others who line the sidewalk in front of the Giant Eagle.

The wiry man shrugs his shoulders. There will be somebody else in a few minutes. It is Friday afternoon, grocery-shopping day in downtown Pittsburgh, and the customers are streaming up Highland Avenue to the store. Some of them are on foot, just out of the office. Others are climbing out of the Port Authority buses that stop just a couple dozen feet away. But no matter how they arrive, many of the shoppers will leave in "jitneys."

Virtually everyone in Pittsburgh takes jitneys for granted. But these illicit taxis are actually a remarkable example of entrepreneurs operating successfully in an underground economy, serving Pittsburgh's poor and minorities. The jitneys set their own rates and routes, offer a startling array of services unmatched by any of Pittsburgh's legal transportation companies, and are cheaper than their legal competitors.

Once, jitneys flourished openly (and legally) all over the United States. In the years before World War I, even comparatively small towns like Flint, Michigan, and Ashtabula, Ohio, boasted popular jitney services. Municipal governments, jealous of any competition with their city-franchised streetcar systems, nearly rubbed out jitneys in a frenzy of monopolistic legislation in 1915 and 1916, but some hardy entrepreneurs survived.

You can find their now-illegal descendants still cruising along King Drive in Chicago and hauling commuters up Boulevard East in the Jersey suburbs of New York. They ferry shoppers back and forth to grocery stores in Washington D.C.'s Anacostia neighborhoods, refusing to submit even to the mild regulation of the local Hacker's Commission. A few places, like Atlantic City, even have legal jitneys, but there are illegal jitneys in far more places. There are jitneys in Atlanta, Los Angeles, San Diego, Buffalo, and Philadelphia. Even if they're illegal, there are probably jitneys in your town, too, if you know where to look.

But Pittsburgh is special. Pittsburgh is to jitneys as San Francisco is to cable cars. In Pittsburgh, there are probably twice as many jitneys as there are legal taxicabs. Jitney stands operate openly, sometimes even within shouting distance of cab-company offices. Grocery parking lots are jammed with jitneys. Says an official of one Pittsburgh taxicab company, "The jitneys dominate the market. The jitneys *define* the market. If they decided to cut their prices, we'd have to cut ours."

The local government and the state's Public Utilities Commission (PUC), both of which regulate taxis, don't wink at jitneys so much as they stare. At the Pittsburgh Police Department's Second Precinct headquarters, in the middle of a nest of black honky-tonks and joints known as the Hill, it is not uncommon for officers to summon a jitney to take a drunk home.

A PUC official recently noted that the commission's penalty for illegal jitneys, when it is imposed, is usually a fine of $100 and revocation of the state registration for the vehicle involved. However, he admitted that enforcement in Pittsburgh is "based largely on any complaints we receive," and speculated that the PUC looks at "less than 50" cases per year. Otto Davis, a Carnegie-Mellon University professor who has studied jitneys extensively, thinks the last real effort to crack down on jitneys may have been in the early 1960s, and no one else seems to recall any systematic effort since.

Mass transit is still officially a creature of the government in Pittsburgh, just as it has been almost everywhere else in the country since the advent of the electric streetcar in 1888. Generally, streetcars, buses, and subways either have been operated by cities or have enjoyed monopoly franchises shielding them from the free market. And with a few (but growing number of) exceptions, taxi companies are similar monopolies or are regulated so sharply that they might as well be. The U.S. public-transportation system has been in place so long that hardly anyone questions it anymore.

But Pittsburgh's experience with the jitneys proves that there's another way. "What it proves, I think," says Otto Davis, "is that—at least under some circumstances—a free market in transportation works."

It's a lazy Saturday afternoon in Pittsburgh's Homewood district, a working-class black neighborhood. Morning marketing is over, there are no ball games or concerts today, and Homewood—along with the rest of the city—is quiet. In theory, it should be an easy time to call one of the city's 350 legal taxicabs. But don't bother calling a cab to Homewood, because it probably won't come.

"Yeah, I ain't surprised you couldn't get one," the jitney driver agrees amiably. "They don't like to come over here. Maybe part of it is because folks in this neighborhood ain't got a lot of money. And partly it's the crime. Especially at night, a cab driver don't like to come over here 'cause he's afraid he'll get robbed."

He laughs. "Hell, when I was driving for Yellow Cab I didn't like to come over my ownself at night. Nobody likes to get robbed." He pauses while he turns his big white Dodge. "And maybe," he continues after a moment, "maybe it's 'cause we're black over here. Whatever it is, it don't matter. You got a jitney, didn't you?"

This one came from a jitney stand. There are at least 44 (and probably many more) of these stands scattered through central and north Pittsburgh. Some of them are located in empty filling stations, some in small storefronts, some in garages or even apartments. They usually boast a sign that says "car service" followed by a telephone number. The drivers pay the stand operator $10-20 a week. In return, he prints business cards and places them around the neighborhood—many if not most pay phones in black areas of the city have the cards taped to their front—and he acts as a dispatcher, taking phone calls and directing the drivers to customers who need a ride.

"Mostly we get folks from the neighborhood," says this jitney driver, who says his name is Frank. "I'll take folks anywhere, but mostly they just want to go shopping around here, or maybe go to an office downtown."

Frank does not know he is talking to a reporter—he's just making small talk with a garrulous customer. Although officials have shown little inclination to bother the jitney drivers, they are all very aware that what they are doing is illegal. An open request for information is inevitably met with a blank stare and a mumbled, "I don't know nothin' about no car service"—in some cases, even as customers are getting into the car.

Frank is a typical jitney driver—60 years old, semi-retired, and living on a small pension that he supplements with his jitney earnings. "I used to drive a cab," he says. "But, hell, they wanted $50 a day for me to rent the damn thing from the company. How much money you think I had left over at the end of the day after I paid that $50? The money I make now, it ain't a lot. But it's a damn sight more than I was making from the cab company."

On this Saturday afternoon there are six or seven drivers hanging around in the small brick building that is Frank's jitney station. Their cars are parked on the street outside, everything from big Lincolns to little Datsuns, although the bigger cars seem to predominate. Frank says there are 22 drivers who use the station. "We ain't the biggest, either," he explains. "There's one a few blocks over that has 45 drivers. There's at least 180 jitneys working within a dozen blocks of here—*at least*." He chuckles. "The jitneys are taking over this town."

So it seems. There are four varieties of jitney driver in Pittsburgh. There are the station drivers, like Frank, who are in many ways the most amazing part of the jitney phenomenon. In a business that is supposed to be at least semi-clandestine, the clearly marked jitney stations almost cry out for official retribution. But none seems to be forthcoming.

The other kinds of jitneys are not so screamingly obvious, although any visitor to Pittsburgh can learn to spot them after about an hour in the city. In the downtown area, there are drivers who duplicate Port Authority bus routes; they pull up at certain intersections and honk to call the customers. Generally they charge the same rate as the buses, but they are willing to make short sidetrips from the bus routes to deliver passengers to their doors. These are called "line-haul" jitneys.

Yet other jitney drivers work the airport and the bus station. At the airport, the jitneys seem to coexist peacefully with legal taxicabs and limousines. The cabdrivers will even refer customers to a jitney when some specialized form of service is required—say, a customer who wants to stop at a bank en route to his final destination.

At the bus station, things are somewhat rockier. The taxi drivers are prohibited from entering the station to solicit customers, but the outlaw jitneys scoff at such restrictions. They go into the bus station all the time, getting first crack at fares. There have been some fist fights as a result, and it is darkly whispered among the taxi drivers that a cabbie who was charged with rape a couple of years ago was somehow set up by the jitney drivers.

The final group of jitneys works the supermarkets. These men (in all Pittsburgh jitney lore and legend, there are no reports of any female drivers) not only provide transportation, they offer a sort of Boy-Scout-for-hire service. They help the frail and elderly with shopping, they will walk the cart through the checkout line for a busy customer who has to run across the street, and they load and unload groceries from the car. Like the jitney-stand drivers, they tend to be community types. They call greetings as customers approach the store, exchange gossip and pleasantries, and even act as a neighborhood billboard. At a grocery store on East Liberty Circle, I watched an elderly jitney driver hail a passing woman. "Norma," he called, "your mama's inside the store right now, and she'd like some help with the shopping." Norma smiled, waved, and headed inside. Store managers don't like to acknowledge the jitneys—"I'm not sure what you're talking about"—but they obviously tolerate, if not actually encourage, their presence.

Like Frank, most of the drivers are men between 55 and 75 years old who work four to six days a week. "They sit down there at the supermarkets and the jitney stands, and they talk to each other, shoot the breeze," says Carnegie-Mellon's Davis, who—with Norman Johnson of Florida A&M—conducted a four-year study of jitneys published in the *Journal of Contemporary Studies* last year. "It's both a social thing and an economic thing."

Davis's study showed that 60 percent of the drivers were older and disabled or retired. He also identified two other groups of drivers: middle-aged men who drive part-time to supplement a regular job or during seasonal unemployment, and younger men in their 20s and early 30s who drive jitneys at night while searching for work during the day.

With the exception of the "line-haul" jitneys (the ones that run along bus routes), virtually all the drivers charge by a system of zone fees. Each driver—or group of drivers, in the case of the stations—is free to work out whatever fare schedule he wants, but most jitneys seem to charge roughly the same rates. ("This is a good example of something that most people seem to think requires the government: rate-setting," says Davis. "But these guys set it up themselves, and it seems to work fine.") At jitney stands, all the drivers must abide by the group rate, which is printed and posted, and there seems to be little gouging.

Customer satisfaction seems high. "Yeah, you don't want somebody complaining to the man who runs the station," one jitney driver said. "He'll boot you out. Folks won't come to a jitney stand if they think the drivers are gonna rip them off." When most of the customers are drawn from the neighborhood, the likelihood of complaint is high if a driver makes a misstep.

On the other hand, the jitney driver is truly his own boss and has considerable license to deal with obnoxious customers as he sees fit. I shared a jitney with a woman who was complaining loudly about the car, the upholstery, and the fare, which the driver had told her would be $3.00. She sat in the back, and I was in the front. When we got to my destination, about a block from hers, I started to hand the driver $3.00. He silently signalled me two instead. "I driven her before," he whispered as I got out of the car.

Although the officials who operate the Port Authority buses scream loud, hard, and often about the jitneys in press interviews and public statements, the illegal taxis seem to compete most directly with Pittsburgh's two citywide cab companies. Yet on paper, the law gives the cab companies formidable protection from almost any competition.

Those who dare to enter the taxi market legally are jumping head first into a regulatory thicket. They must apply for a taxi license, called "rates," to the state Public Utilities Commission. According to a commission official, the PUC holds a hearing at which existing companies may challenge the application, then the commission grants rates only if it determines that doing so is "in the public interest." Should the commission grant rates, the lucky applicants must pay one percent of their gross income in taxes to the PUC every year.

There's no official limit on the number of legal cabs, but rates are not handed out frequently. The last serious attempt to get rates from the PUC was in the mid-1970s. The company got rates—but once it began service, it couldn't beat the competition of the jitneys. Indeed, the only legal citywide competition for Yellow is the little People's Cab Company, a 25-car fleet operated by Carnegie-Mellon's Center for Entrepreneurial Development. Although People's does turn a small profit, it is run mostly for experimental purposes.

Can a solitary individual with one car apply for rates? Technically, yes—but the PUC official observed, "I don't recall any case where that's happened. With the need for filing fees, hearings, and attorneys, it's probably not worth it." So for an ordinary entrepreneur who wants to make an honest living by transporting people, the underground economy is the only sensible option available—and a lot of people take that option.

From the customer's standpoint, jitneys stand up well in comparison with Yellow Cab. It operates about 350 vehicles, although drivers say the company's dilapidated cabs break down so frequently that there are rarely more than 200 on the street at any given time.

The jitneys, by almost all accounts, do a better job than the cabs. Jitney drivers are friendlier, more helpful, and more willing to honor a request for unusual service. Jitney drivers will deliver a package, drop off the laundry, pick up a bottle of liquor and bring it by the house, escort a child, and occasionally even carry a customer in return for a promise of payment later in the week. And unquestionably, the jitneys are cheaper. Generally speaking, a $2.60 cab ride will cost $2.00 in a jitney. Moreover, the cab driver will expect a tip, which is unheard of in the jitney trade.

The jitneys have several economic advantages over the taxis, almost all of them related to regulation. The cabbies must buy a chauffeur's license; the jitneys don't do it. The cabbies' revenues are taxed by the PUC; the jitneys' revenues are not. Cabbies are not allowed to assemble groups of passengers headed in the same direction; jitneys do it all the time, especially those that operate out of grocery stores. (This is an advantage especially during rush hour, when heavy traffic keeps a vehicle from making as many trips as it can at other times of the day.)

The cabbies must install meters, which cost $300–500; a jitney's zone-fare card costs a nickel, if that. The cabs, in theory, undergo rigorous safety inspections, which cost time and money; the jitneys don't. (There is good reason to believe, however, that the cab inspections are not all they're cracked up to be. Last year *Pittsburgh Magazine* took a randomly selected Yellow Cab to an inspection station. A mechanic found 18 different violations serious enough to fail the cab and keep it off the road, including cracked brake pads and exhaust leakage into the car. The mechanic tried to talk the cabbie out of driving home. He pleaded, "I wouldn't drive to the pumps in this cab.")

The jitneys do have one major advantage that is arguably unfair—they simply rely on their ordinary auto insurance, since the insurance company has no way of knowing that a driver operates a jitney. The cab companies, on the other hand, pay commercial rates.

"Of course they can operate cheaper than we do," growls an angry Dwight Baumann, president of People's Cab, smacking the table with his fist. "I pay $2,400 a year per car for insurance. They pay $400. We could operate cheaper than we do if you knock that much off our rates."

He continues, "They compete directly with us, and they compete for the riders that all cab drivers want—they compete for the regular, the guy who has to go someplace at the same time every day," he says. "I wish there was something we could do about them."

Al Hayes, the vice president of Yellow Cab, is no more sympathetic to the jitneys. "There's no control on them—no taxes, no anything," he complains. "Anyone who buys a drag-along car is in business with no expenses except for gasoline." Asked how much jitneys are cutting into Yellow Cab's business, he responds, "We're getting about 60 to 70 percent of the business we had 10 years ago. Not all of the decline is because of jitneys, but my best guess is that they're taking about 10 percent of the business we had."

Baumann of People's Cab once tried to do something about the situation. He offered jitney drivers special deals if they'd join his company. His theory was that they would help People's Cab by bringing their current business along, and he could help them by offering radio dispatch service along with group insurance and other conventional business perks.

It didn't work. "They didn't want to pay income tax," he recalls. But, having failed to entice the jitneys into the system, Baumann thinks it's useless to try to crack down on them. "That's been done many times," he says. "It just doesn't get anywhere. If you tried to do the same thing with the rest of the underground economy—if you said, 'Let's regulate the cleaning ladies,' for instance—you'd get the same results."

Yellow Cab's Hayes, in contrast, blames the PUC for the proliferation of jitneys. He says that Yellow hasn't lobbied heavily for a crackdown on jitneys because "we don't have the time nor the money to be the policeman. We feel that's the job of the Utilities Commission, and they could care less."

Just how profitable are the jitneys? Davis, using data assembled by graduate students who actually drove jitneys for a summer, calculated that the average jitney driver makes 3,900 trips a year, bringing in $7,800. After accounting for the costs of gasoline, oil, and other operating expenses, and allowing for depreciation, jitney jobs suddenly don't seem very attractive. The average driver, by those calculations, makes only about $5,000 a year.

But the jitney drivers don't see it that way. "Look, I gotta have a car anyway, right?" said one. "The only thing I'm spending extra to be a jitney is for gasoline." Given that most of the drivers are just trying to supplement an income or to keep their heads above water while looking for other work, jitneys seem like a sensible economic venture. "All you got to have," advised one driver, "is a car and a little bit of knowledge about Pittsburgh."

The inevitable question: If jitneys are such a good deal for drivers and passengers alike, why don't we have more of them? And the answer is, because city governments are greedy. It's certainly not a lack of demand for jitneys, if history is any indication.

The first jitney driver was a Los Angeles man named L.P. Draper. On July 1, 1914, he picked up a passenger in his Model T Ford and drove him a mile or so in return for a nickel. ("Jitney" apparently derives from the French word *jeton*, or token.) Draper seemed to have hit on the proverbial idea whose time had come. In less than a year, there were 62,000 jitneys, operating from San Diego to Portland, Maine. Jitney operators began forming associations, and soon there was even a trade publication, *The Jitney Bus.*

Those early jitneys had but one business strategy, and that was to steal customers who were lined up to ride on electric streetcars. Like the line-haul jitneys in Pittsburgh today who work the Port Authority bus routes, the original jitneys traveled streetcar lines almost exclusively. But customers crowded into them because they were so much faster—they careened about the streets at a reckless 15 miles per hour, twice the speed of the streetcars—and because they could swing off the streetcar route and deliver a passenger to his door. They also lent a touch of excitement to city life; jitneys were constantly smacking into one another as they sped to the curb, trying to pick off customers.

The jitneys specialized in short hauls of a mile or two. and those were precisely the customers the streetcars could not afford to lose. The streetcars were charging everybody a nickel and using the revenues from the short trips to subsidize passengers who went longer distances. (Municipal planners, in those days, thought that was a great idea. They favored "urban decentralization." Municipal planners nowadays refer to that same concept as "urban sprawl." They say mass transit helps to fight it, which just goes to show the miraculous metamorphosis in mass transit over the last 60 years.)

The jitneys were so spectacularly successful in making off with streetcar customers that within five months of L.P. Draper's first foray, the Los Angeles streetcar system was losing so much revenue that it had to lay off 84 employees.

Municipal government fought off a collective wave of nausea at this. They handed out "franchises"—that is, monopolies—to the streetcars in return for road improvements and a cut of the proceeds. And after an unproductive spate of name-calling—the *Electric Railway Journal* sometimes called jitneys "a menace," on other occasions "a malignant growth," and then, when the editor was *really* mad, "this Frankenstein of transportation"—the streetcar companies simply got their pals at City Hall to do some creative legislating. The most common tactic was to impose outlandish fees and bonding requirements on the jitneys.

The cities did not limit themselves to these strategies. They also issued route restrictions and onerous safety requirements. In some cities where anti-jitney laws had to be put to the voters, the streetcar companies were unusually resourceful. In Los Angeles, the streetcar company simply called a holiday on election day and then ordered its employees to shuttle anti-jitney voters to the polls in their autos. Lest there be any doubt about the intent of these new laws and regulations, the *Electric Railway Journal* gleefully discussed new ways "of exterminating the jitney under the guise of regulating it."

The efforts of the city governments and their streetcar quislings were spectacularly successful. In New Orleans, 300 jitneys went out of business in a single day when the city began requiring a $5,000 bond. In Los Angeles, where it all began, the number of jitneys dropped from 1,000 in 1916 to 32 in 1917. By the end of World War I, the jitneys were nearly all gone. Perhaps they derived some posthumous satisfaction from the fact that the streetcar companies could not save themselves through this villainy. The companies began to go bust in the mid-1920s and were soon overrun by bus lines.

Buses, in turn, got into serious financial trouble in the 1950s. They were frequently taken over by the city governments themselves, which soon began to lobby for federal subsidies to keep them afloat. In the 1960s, the federal government began paying for most of the capital improvements to bus systems, and during the next decade, the feds began chipping in toward operating deficits as well. Fares on mass transit—both rail and bus—now cover less than half of the operating costs of such systems.

One problem with fixed-route transportation systems is that none of them—not even the new and fabulously expensive subway systems in Washington and San Francisco—are as convenient, flexible, or adaptable to individual needs as the automobile. Taxicabs carry as many passengers as mass transit does in the United States. But the ubiquitous overregulation of taxis creates problems in that market, as Pittsburgh and other cities have discovered.

Organizations as diverse as the Urban Institute, the American Enterprise Institute, and the U.S. Department of Transportation have all recognized the stupidity—if not necessarily the injustice—of outlawing jitneys. Said a Department of Transportation report in 1972:

*"The present regulatory environment in urban public transportation,
including obsolete franchise limitations and market-entry barriers for
taxicabs and jitneys, restricts the efficient operation of the urban
transportation system. The removal of such regulatory constraints is likely
to lead to more efficient use of the transportation system and increase the
options available to its users."*

Although the DOT report didn't say so, the people who are most vulnerable
to inefficient urban transportation systems are often the poor and minorities. It's
the customers of the Giant Eagle store in Pittsburgh—the ones without cars trying
to make their way home with their groceries on a Friday afternoon—who would
suffer most without an alternative to the official transportation systems tightly
regulated by the state.

Of course, the poor of Pittsburgh are a bit luckier than most. They're
splendidly served by the genial entrepreneur in the yellow Pirates T-shirt and his
colleagues, all of whom ply an honorable trade without letting the law get in the way.

The jitneys do just fine, regardless of what the government thinks or says.
Davis says his conservative estimate of the number of jitneys is 495. The drivers
themselves figure that underestimates the true figure at least by half.

One odd thing Davis reported in his study, which the jitney drivers do not
dispute, is that jitneys in Pittsburgh are a peculiarly black phenomenon. Most of
the passengers are black, and nearly all the drivers are black. Moreover, the jitneys
simply don't operate in all-white neighborhoods.

"We searched like crazy, all up and down the Monangahela Valley," he says,
slowing his car to point out yet another jitney stand in the Hill district, "and we
couldn't find *one*. I'll be damned if I can understand why. It seems like a neat
service. If you're poor and white and living in some white area, you have to arrange
with a friend or a relative to take you to the store. If you live in *this* neighborhood"—he gestures around at the Hill—"you can use a jitney. In a sense, this
neighborhood, even though it is poor and black and no one would ever believe
it—in a sense *this* neighborhood gets better service. Because of the jitneys."

Getting Street-Wise in St. Louis

By Theodore J. Gage

August 1981

om and Susan Jonas stand on their front lawn talking to neighbors. Their two young sons play tag nearby, tumbling gleefully into a wrestling match on the grass. Other children are playing in the middle of a street that seldom sees traffic. It could be a scene from a tree-lined suburban street anywhere in the country.

If Susan Jonas looked away from her children, though, past the wrought iron gates 100 yards away, she would see the autos and 18-wheel rigs roaring past her street, she would see the drunken old man staggering by, clutching a brown paper bag with one hand and stroking his grizzled beard with the other.

On this warm Sunday afternoon in St. Louis, thoughts of the apartment manager who was murdered a few weeks ago in his roach-infested room only a few blocks away do not trouble the Jonases. They do not fear the young toughs who congregate around a boarded up storefront less than two blocks from their quiet neighborhood.

A decade ago, the young toughs and winos were just as close. And most urban planning experts would have predicted that by 1981 the vandals, drunks, and prostitutes would have taken over this quiet street on the west side of St. Louis. In 1970, Westminster Place was a dying street. The peril of urban blight had chased many of its middle-income families—white and black—to the suburbs. Real estate values had plummeted during the 1960s, and even the small enclave of mansions just west and south of this neighborhood was threatened by the creeping urban decay.

But in the early 1970s, people like Fred Hale—a professor at Washington University in St. Louis—got tired of prostitutes strolling past their homes and of watching 6,000 cars a day race down their streets as they bypassed stoplights on nearby boulevards. And people like the Jonases decided that these neighborhoods, with their spacious and lovely three-story brick homes, were worth the effort to save. They moved into an area for which even the experts in urban planning held little hope.

Today, Waterman Place West, the street on which Fred and Lucy Hale live, and Westminster Place, where the Jonases live, are thriving as private streets. Standing up to the urban blight, the crime, and the fear that causes residents to flee, the people in these neighborhoods called on a St. Louis tradition. They found an unconventional solution to a common problem—they bought their neighborhoods.

St. Louis has had private streets since the late 1800s, when the industrialists and businessmen of the booming river city built estates on the outskirts of town and placed barriers around their neighborhoods. Their goal was exclusivity. Later, residents in other neighborhoods would take advantage of the precedent in St. Louis's law books and use private streets to achieve security and stability.

In the 1950s, faced with growing crime rates and declining property values, middle-income residents of some streets petitioned the city to deed the streets to them. This the city did, in return for the residents' assuming responsibility for street, sewer, and streetlight maintenance; garbage pickup; and any security services beyond the normal fire and police protection.

The transfer of ownership is effected via deed restrictions attached to each property on the street. These restrictions require that title to the street be vested in an incorporated street association to which all property owners must belong. They also limit the uses to which the homeowners' property may be put and provide for the association to collect funds from the owners to cover the costs of maintaining the common property.

Most of St. Louis's street associations cover just a block or two. In addition to obtaining legal ownership, residents achieve control over their streets by closing them off to through traffic. With anything from sawhorse and chain to iron fence and gate, a barrier is put at the end of streets, creating cul-de-sacs. The only way to enter these dead-end streets is from other public and private residential streets. The only cars on the streets belong to residents and their visitors.

The result is that on the private streets of St. Louis unfamiliar pedestrians, autos, and even delivery and repair trucks are usually observed by one or more neighbors. It is *their* street, and that ownership gives the neighborhood a high degree of cohesiveness. Unusual noises coming from a neighbor's home, a stranger wandering up and down the street, or even something as harmless as an unfamiliar car parked on the street will draw neighbors out of their homes and elicit phone calls.

"One night about 11 o'clock, I was walking the dog and she got away," related Susan Jonas. "I called out, and the lights in about five houses went on and a couple of people stuck their heads out their doors. It's the kind of thing that makes you feel pretty secure."

During the '60s, the people on many of St. Louis's private streets lapsed into apathy, forgetting the problems that had led them to privatize. They neglected their neighborhood associations, forcing them to make do with a bare minimum of funding and involvement. Consequently, the neighborhoods began declining again, and their middle-income residents turned their sights to suburbia. The familiar problems of changing urban areas were driving residents of both private and public streets from the solid old three-story homes in the heart of the city.

For some people committed to urban living, though, the private street concept again offered a solution in the '70s. Some of them, like Fred Hale, convinced the city to dust off the old laws that made privatizing possible. Others, like the Jonases, bought homes on historically private streets and joined residents working to revitalize their long-dormant neighborhood associations.

Today, not only the Jonases' and Hales' and other private streets but some of the surrounding areas have regained stability. Homes sheltering transients, roomers, and large groups of unrelated people during the '60s are now owned by families with children. Homes that sold for $13,000 in 1969 are valued at $120,000 today and compare favorably to similar homes in St. Louis suburbs in price and quality. Despite the lingering urban problems like crime, vandalism, prostitution, boarded up storefronts, and abandoned apartment buildings that exist only a few blocks to the north on Delmar Boulevard, the area has gained a sense of stability.

Oscar Newman, an architect and urban planner and founder of the Institute for Community Design Analysis, supports the concept of private streets. He has authored books and articles on the subject of possible alternatives to troubled urban living conditions, and he has noted the positive psychological effects of privatizing. "Property is something most people want and identify with," he says. "When you can get people to have pride in their property and a sense of belonging in their community, a number of positive things often happen."

In the mid-70s, Newman did an in-depth study of St. Louis and its private streets. His surveys yielded some intriguing results. For example, on the section of Westminster Place that was private, the crime rate between 1966 and 1973 was far lower than on the adjacent public streets. Relying on the same city police patrolling as the public streets received, Westminster had a crime rate that was 26 percent lower than on Waterman Avenue, one block south of Westminster, and 52 percent lower than on Washington Boulevard, one block north. Although long-time residents said that Washington had historically been a more desirable place to live, between 1960 and 1973 two-thirds of its housing stock, which was similar to that on Westminster, was converted to multiple-occupancy structures, attracting lower-income residents. Not a single home on Westminster had been converted.

More recently than Newman's survey, an informal study by one St. Louis police district showed that during an eight-month period ending April 30, 1981, a particular five-block area of the district consisting of private streets had 34 criminal offenses. The adjoining five-block area, which has no private streets, suffered 120 crimes. The number of reported criminal offenses during the same period in other nearby residential areas without private streets and of equal size and population density ranged from 69 to 137.

The few crimes that occur on the private streets are generally burglaries, home invasions, and thefts of bicycles and lawnmowers from garages. Crimes against persons and "crimes of opportunity"—assault, purse snatching, and thefts from autos, all of which usually occur on the street—have been effectively checked by private street residents.

The private blocks that have hired guards and off-duty policemen to bolster security have fewer crime problems than the blocks that don't. For example, the burglary rate on the 5200 block of Westminster, which employs security guards in the evening, is only a third that of the 5100 block, which employs no private guards but relies solely on city police protection. Still, crime rates are far lower than in adjacent neighborhoods, and the nature of the crimes differs.

But Lt. James Shea of St. Louis's seventh police district, which encompasses much of the private street sector, said he works continually to remind residents that simply constructing gates does not make crime go away. While privatizing streets may cut down crime and allow for tighter control by residents, it is not the entire solution.

"It's true that you have two different worlds a few blocks apart," he explained. "But as long as you have poverty three blocks away from affluence, you'll have crime. It's tempting to hide in your fortress and simply ignore what's going on outside. But the way to continue the stabilizing process and to strengthen the neighborhood is to reach out and help improve the blighted areas."

There is evidence, though, that the mere existence of the private streets is already helping the area. These neighborhoods have provided a nucleus for private enterprise urban renewal efforts.

People from streets like Westminster refer to Delmar, two blocks to the north, as "the DMZ" or "the trenches." Many of the merchants on Delmar have fled their stores, and many of the apartments remain abandoned. But to the south, developers have been restoring apartment buildings and townhouses. Protected by the private streets, which developers agree act as a buffer against the blight to the north, the apartments will be rented to middle-income residents while other buildings will become condominiums.

"At one time, the original private streets and neighborhoods were surrounded by fine apartments," explains Daniel Feinberg, a leading St. Louis real estate agent. "It got to the point where only the private streets were left. The apartments got so bad they had to be vacated. But now developers have the stability of some residential areas to sell and they're back. Besides, most are local developers, and they have a stake in the city's welfare."

The private streets of St. Louis have not been a panacea for all urban problems. Continuing crime in adjacent areas, poor public schools, and the financial burden of maintaining the streets present ongoing difficulties for the residents. But the overall success of this St. Louis Solution has prompted some rethinking of traditional urban renewal efforts and traditional approaches to crime in middle- and low-income neighborhoods. As Oscar Newman writes in his book *Community of Interest*, "These residents have been able to create and maintain for themselves what their city was no longer able to provide: low crime rates, stable property values, and a sense of community."

Privatizing a street is viewed as a drastic move—if ever even considered—by most cities. Even in St. Louis, where the tradition dates back to the last century, local government officials resisted the concept when proposed by residents of the West End in the '70s. But because it seemed to give hope to an almost hopeless setting of spreading urban decay, the city granted the go-ahead for several more formerly public streets to turn private.

Today, the move to privatize streets in St. Louis seems to have come to a halt. Instead, some residents have asked the city to close off their streets to through traffic while allowing them to remain public—a more palatable solution for cities. The increasing high cost of services and street repair has made residents doubt their ability to pay for private garbage pickup, street and sewer maintenance, and guard services.

Washington Boulevard, for example, has been closed off. This street, with private Westminster Place on its south side and Delmar Boulevard on the north, was one of the streets used for comparison in Oscar Newman's studies in the '70s. Washington had a 52 percent higher crime rate and 67 percent versus zero conversions to multiple-occupancy residences.

From the back yards of homes on Washington, residents could see the prostitutes on Delmar. A few of the people still living on Washington remember when police hated to raid the now-vacant apartments on Delmar. Anyone entering the buildings, which stand only 50 yards from some of the homes, had to be fumigated for lice when he left. Drug dealers cruised Delmar and carried their business onto Washington.

Almost two years ago, at the request of a few residents and some young urban pioneers who had recently bought homes on the street, the city agreed to block through traffic on Washington. And it changed the zoning for the area from multiple-2D to single-family housing. Today, the street still has a long way to go. But the progress from when Newman studied it has been astounding.

Developers, encouraged by the stability of the adjacent private Westminster Place and by the presence of other private streets, have bought some of the single- and two-family homes on Washington and have started renovation. Young, lower-middle income couples are purchasing and restoring the old, spacious homes themselves.

There are still a number of abandoned homes, empty lots, and homes housing illegal boarders. But slowly, some of the white and black families living on the street have banded together to form neighborhood associations that they hope will result in citizen crime watches and serve to unite the residents. They have received assurances from the city that it will replace the temporary street barriers with concrete cul-de-sacs and knockdown barriers.

"We are in the trenches," said Eric Smith, president of his block association on Washington. "Over there," he said, pointing to Delmar, "is the front line. We need all the support we can get. But I feel confident we are here to stay."

Eric Smith, a salesman for a steel company, lives in a three-story brick home with his wife, Trudy, and two daughters. The Smiths are renovating the home themselves and use the extra income provided by a student boarder on the third floor to help fund the project. Trudy has less fear of physical violence in her neighborhood than she did two years ago and now lets her daughters play unsupervised in the back yard for short periods—something she would never have done even a year ago.

Street closure is being tried in other communities, too. In Columbus, Ohio, in a neighborhood of low-income federally built row housing, the Metropolitan Housing Authority is constructing concrete cul-de-sacs and putting in fencing at the end of some streets, hoping to reduce much of the traffic, both pedestrian and auto, that makes physical crimes, robbery, and vandalism easy to commit and that facilitates escape. Neighborhood associations have also been started.

"Something like this gives people a stronger sense of their own personal stake in a community," says Steven Bollinger, who headed up the Columbus Housing Authority before taking a job recently as assistant secretary in the federal department of Housing and Urban Development. "By limiting access to the neighborhoods, people who have no business there other than to make trouble have a much harder time. They are highly visible to residents, and the residents often band together and watch out for each other."

In downtown Hartford, Connecticut, in a Department of Justice experiment, the closing off of some streets and narrowing of others has been combined with neighborhood police teams and citizen advisory groups to work with police to improve the physical quality of the neighborhood in a high-density residential area. The Center for Survey Research, associated with the University of Massachusetts, Boston, studied the area from 1973 through 1979 to determine the effect of the program.

To the disappointment of the project directors, police statistics did not show any dramatic drop in crime. Floyd J. Fowler, Jr., director of CSR's study, offers several explanations: Changes in record-keeping procedures may make comparison of police statistics from one year to the next inaccurate. And the percentage of crimes *reported* to police increases, he notes, as people come to believe that they can have an effect on the incidence of crime in their area.

But in any case, says Fowler, the records do show an increase in the rate of arrests for reported crimes. And the project did have an effect on residents' attitudes about the neighborhood. In 1973, only 20 percent of the people living in the area said the neighborhood had improved during the past two years, while 40 percent noted improvement in 1979. And while only 20 percent of the residents in 1973 saw hope for reducing crime and improving the quality of life during the coming five years, 57 percent of the residents in 1979 expected significant neighborhood improvements in the next five years.

"When people feel their neighborhoods are out of control, that's when you get deterioration, crime, and fear," says Fowler. "It is a crucial observation for all future urban planning. It shows that instead of attacking crime and blight by increasing the numbers of patrolling police, you work to stabilize the neighborhoods. By getting things under control, both in terms of the quality of the physical housing and in residents' attitude toward their neighborhood, you can get things under control so people feel secure. That stability is a prerequisite to any efforts to keeping an urban area economically sound."

For maintaining economic stability in neighborhoods comprising owner-occupied residences, Oscar Newman contends that mere closure of streets, even when combined with block associations, is inferior to privatization. Although closure can foster a sense of community and may reduce crime, the residents have no legal mechanism to protect themselves from declining property values, block-busting, zoning changes, or abandonment.

The residents of a private street, however, have a charter stipulating the payment of dues for street services and, in St. Louis's case, for example, generally requiring residents to agree not to use their homes for anything but a residence for their families and not as boarding houses or even to house a single unrelated boarder. If any resident doesn't follow the regulations, the other residents have the power to get a court order for compliance. These private street associations have legal teeth and can place a lien on the property in question.

That legal power is one of the greatest advantages of private street associations. Residents have the ability to force compliance to maintain neighborhood quality. In a few cases during the 1970s, homeowners on private streets in St. Louis asked for and got court-ordered compliance from residents who were not caring for their property or who bought homes with the intention of converting them to boarding houses.

"Closure without privatizing cannot be as effective because there is no legal entity to ensure compliance with things like maintaining a lawn or renting the third floor to boarders," observes Newman. "Block associations get some things done, but they are still not legal entities. And while closing public streets may help, a public street can always be reopened by the city and the old traffic patterns can resume."

Going private, as well as closing off public streets, has not been without its critics. The City of Memphis, when it heeded a residents' petition and decided to close off a street and two alleys to protect residential neighborhoods from an increasing flood of traffic, met resistance from several civic groups that claimed the move was racially motivated.

Auto traffic from a predominantly black area of the city was traveling through a racially mixed but primarily white neighborhood. Residents of those streets asked the city in 1973 to dead-end one of the streets and adjacent alleys. The city council agreed in a 6-to-5 vote, and several civic groups took the case to court.

In 1979, the city went ahead and built the dead ends, and in April of this year the U.S. Supreme Court ruled that the city had the right to close the streets. Justice John Paul Stevens, speaking for the 6-to-3 majority, argued that the action by the city was not racially motivated but was "motivated by its interest in protecting the safety and tranquility of a residential neighborhood."

The stigma of racism attached to street closure and efforts to protect neighborhoods—especially middle-income neighborhoods—has discouraged efforts to close or privatize streets even in St. Louis, says Oscar Newman. Bud Holmes, a Memphis city attorney who worked on the case, said he is sure that "the kind of trouble we had to go to in defending our position has discouraged other communities from even considering such action. But we feel this decision may give cities a green light to preserve middle-class neighborhoods as long as their motivations are legitimate and nondiscriminatory."

It is undeniable that the original private streets in St. Louis were rooted in elitism. The massive gates and palatial mansions built by the wealthy in the 1880s still stand. But the fact that there are several black families on many of the private streets—and the existence of private streets in predominantly black neighborhoods—steals the credibility from an argument that private streets remain a bastion of white affluence against the onslaught of blacks. "It's safe to say that no one on these streets cares what color the person is who moves in, so long as they agree to the principles set down in the street's charter and pay their dues," says Missouri State Sen. Steven Vossmeyer, a private street resident.

Still, it remains an unsettling fact that in the West End of St. Louis the area north of Delmar is predominantly black and poor while the private streets and surrounding residential area south of Delmar are predominantly white and middle-class. Newman insists, however, that, while private streets and similar actions represent efforts to keep middle-income residents in urban environments, it is an economic and not a racial phenomenon.

People must lay aside the stereotyped misconception that trying to save neighborhoods for the middle and working classes automatically means racism, says Newman. "Twenty years ago, I was vulnerable to the argument that by saving middle-income neighborhoods, you were preventing lower-income families from having the chance to buy homes and condominiums," he explains. "I also felt that by saying 'income,' you meant 'race.' But I have watched what has happened. In

St. Louis you have low-income people moving into decent housing stock, and it's three to five years before it deteriorates until it is uninhabitable. Welfare families cannot care for this kind of housing." It is a politically sensitive issue, but one Newman says must be faced.

Concerns about racism are not helped by the fact that in almost all urban situations the school systems are a particularly thorny problem. In St. Louis, most of the residents of private streets send their children to private schools. The St. Louis public school system, typical of many urban systems, is inadequately funded, poorly staffed, and charged with politics. Its students are primarily black—especially in the areas where the private street children would attend. But even the children of black private street residents attend private schools.

"It is an inferior school system, and if you want your child to have an adequate education, you have to make the financial sacrifice required to send kids to private schools," said one mother. Several of the parents, however, are active in local efforts to improve the public school system. "It is my hope that some day the public schools here will be good enough to provide a quality education," said Judy Murphy, a resident of private Kingsbury Place. "But right now, they are not."

These outlooks have prompted additional criticism that residents of the private streets are isolationists and not really involved with the surrounding community. Perhaps the observations have some truth, but without the ability to isolate themselves somewhat from the surrounding urban environment, these residents would probably have moved to the suburbs long ago. As city officials point out, St. Louis would have lost a considerable tax base. And the loss of stability in these neighborhoods might have thwarted all the urban redevelopment now taking place in the surrounding area.

Although acknowledging that it does not offer a short-term answer for the housing problems of the cities' poor, Newman insists that if cities would allow middle-income residents to help themselves, it would be an all-around benefit to the city. The misconception that there is something wrong with housing that is exclusionary because of price must stop, he declares, or there will be a "complete polarization in this country with all the working and middle class in the suburbs and totally dead cities loaded with poor unable to lift themselves up." Private streets and other efforts to keep middle-income people in and near the cities are not racially motivated, he repeats. They are a matter of common sense—a potential private solution to a problem that has resisted the traditional government solutions.

There are indications that the new guard at the U.S. Department of Housing and Urban Development favors such private solutions to urban problems and has plans to encourage and facilitate efforts by citizens and local governments to institute such programs. In mid-May, Newman had a week of meetings with HUD officials. They are consulting with other outside housing experts, too, he says, and, more than any administration in the past 20 years, are open to nontraditional solutions.

"The people at the top feel they are getting a snow job from HUD staffers and city housing authorities," Newman explains. "Even at this point, they sense they are getting the same old solutions, which didn't work, in a different package. They are looking for new ways to do things."

One of the new ways to do things that Newman urged is the St. Louis Solution—private streets. The concept, he told HUD, can be effective in saving the remaining single-family-home neighborhoods in cities and adjoining suburbs, regardless of their racial or ethnic makeup. The hope that young middle-income people are moving back to the cities is just a hope, he pointed out; cities are still rapidly losing their middle-class tax base.

Neighborhoods in Brooklyn and Queens in New York City and other neighborhoods in other cities have considered privatizing for years, he says. "Now they have finally decided, and they come to me and say they're ready. I tell them it is too late. Their neighborhoods have already gone too far down. Too many people have left."

The advantage of a private or in some cases even simply a closed street, he reiterates, is that it encourages residents to stay put and spend money on their homes because they have a sense of stability. "Right now, the individual homeowner in the city is alone. Our government has made each person a pioneer, and people are afraid to put money into their homes because they see the neighborhoods around them crumbling. A private street allows people who were victims of blockbusters and city hall types to have a protection in collective strength. They no longer have to face the problems alone. That is the magic. We need a way to allow governments to give them that collective umbrella—to be the force that encourages these people to unite and find their own solutions. "

In many cases, cities put up arguments against nontraditional solutions. Even in St. Louis, Fred Hale and other residents of the now-private Waterman Place West fought for six years to convince the city that closing the street to through traffic would not throw traffic patterns on the west side of the city into disarray. Privatizing and closing a two-block section of Waterman five years ago meant disrupting a bus route and halting the flow of 6,000 autos a day past the residences on that street. The bus route was moved to a thoroughfare two blocks away, and the cars now use alternative thoroughfares that, city officials admit, have easily accepted the extra traffic.

"I had such a fight to convince the city planners that their fears of total chaos were unfounded," says Fred Hale. "Before the street was closed, this area was a madhouse. Now it's quiet, property values have soared, people are no longer fleeing, and nothing catastrophic has happened to the traffic patterns."

"Cities have a self-protecting bureaucratic mentality that keeps them from supporting nonbureaucratic solutions to their problems," says Steve Savas, HUD's newly appointed assistant secretary for policy development and research. "The notion of private streets and neighborhood associations has a lot of possibilities. It gives residents the chance to do something about improving their neighborhoods.

"I think this kind of idea would definitely be accepted by this administration. The respect we have for the autonomy of state and local governments would prevent us from issuing directives, but we can act as a clearinghouse and research center. We can and I'm sure will encourage these alternatives."

What could local governments do besides deeding property back to residents? They could provide tax incentives. Of the municipal services normally provided in St. Louis, private street residents get only police and fire protection. Yet they pay the same amount of property taxes as other homeowners do. In addition to paying a full city tax, they also pay dues averaging about $350 a year to their private street associations to cover the costs of maintaining their streets, sewers, and so on. This double jeopardy undoubtedly discourages residents on other St. Louis streets from considering the private street alternative. Most other cities don't even have laws that allow privatizing, let alone tax credits for such activity.

Having proponents of private streets and nongovernmental solutions to urban problems in HUD is promising. At this point, encouragement at the federal level seems necessary if local municipalities are to clear the way for nontraditional answers to their problems.

In the institution of these programs, there is a need for government protection of people's rights. In Schaumburg, Illinois, a suburb northwest of Chicago, developers of a subdivision kept the streets private and took advantage of the concept to cut corners in their construction. Now, a decade later, unhappy residents have discovered seeping sewers, cracking foundations, sinking homes, and crumbling streets. During their 10 years of ownership, however, the residents did nothing to maintain their streets and collected no funds to cope with emergencies or needed repairs.

Even in St. Louis, some private street associations have suffered from poor organization and a lack of proper planning. Some of the streets need resurfacing, and residents do not have the funds in their treasuries to make the needed improvements.

Newman has suggested that one of the functions of government might be to provide model fund collection methods to help future private street organizations from getting into financial trouble. In Houston, Texas, the city's Planning Department serves a similar clearinghouse function. Houston has no zoning laws; instead, land use is controlled by the residents themselves, through restrictive covenants attached to property owners' deeds—just as the private street associations of St. Louis protect their neighborhoods.

So while Houston's city government does not do the typical planning, it does, if asked, assist citizens in drawing up covenants that suit the characteristics of their neighborhoods, whether made up of single-family homes, apartments, condominiums, commercial buildings, or a mixture. Instead of pouring more funds into urban renewal programs that are almost universally acknowledged to have been a massive failure, government, both federal and local, could take a similar innovative approach to improving the urban environment.

If the St. Louis Solution to urban decay were encouraged by changes in municipal laws and tax adjustments for the responsibilities that private street residents take over from the city, it is likely that private firms would also step in to fill the need for legal and financial guidance. For example, in response to the growing number of condominium buyers in the last decade, there are now companies that help set up condo associations so that they function smoothly in collecting fees, maintaining common property, and controlling the upkeep of units by individual residents.

Could the private street concept be extended to high-density neighborhoods dominated by multiple-occupancy buildings? Newman, a staunch advocate of privatization in single-family-home areas, is skeptical. When pressed, however, he acknowledges that he's seen it work in University City, a suburb adjacent to the

West End of St. Louis. Yet he believes that in general private streets in such situations would not have the dramatic effects evident in St. Louis because the residents would not be the street owners and so would not regard it as their neighborhood and take care of it accordingly.

It is evident, however, that the owners of apartment buildings would benefit just as much as homeowners from the stability and reduced crime levels that accompany privatization. If that option were made available to them and its potential benefits made clear, it is likely that they would find it in their interest to join in street associations and take measures to reduce crime and maintain the quality of the neighborhood.

Likewise, commercial areas could benefit from the concept. Here, of course, the opposite of closure without privatization—that is, *privatization without closure*—would be appropriate. The benefits to merchants owning their own street would be the ability to control the quality of enterprises on the street (for example, their charter might exclude porn shops or, in a classy commercial strip, fast food restaurants); to require individual owner/members to keep up their property; and probably to jointly purchase private security services, just as some of St. Louis's street associations do.

Extending private streets to more neighborhoods and to untested settings is a radical approach—aimed at a desperate situation. There are so few cases to study that many experts are reluctant to guess how far it might take us toward solving the problem of urban decay. One thing is certain, however: The infusion of billions of dollars in government urban renewal programs has done very little. And the existing evidence on private streets looks promising. For the St. Louis Solution to work on a large scale, though, local municipalities must give residents and merchants tax incentives.

With HUD perhaps ready to steer others in a new direction, the 1980s could be an exciting period for a new kind of urban renewal—one that doesn't depend on government handouts. Instead it can make private citizens and business firms responsible for their own property and welfare. And if some of the nation's leading urban analysts read the signals correctly, the St. Louis Solution stands a chance of working.

Reconstruction

By Virginia I. Postrel

August/September 1992

Police Chief Daryl Gates spent the first evening of the Los Angeles riots at a political fundraiser in Brentwood. People who honestly want to rebuild L.A. might want to spend some time there, too.

To Angelenos, this advice will sound strange. Brentwood is far from South Los Angeles—in miles and in money. On its fringes, you can buy a plain two-bedroom condo for a shade under $300,000. In its heart, home prices stretch into seven figures. The people of Brentwood are wealthy, and they are mostly white.

There are no factories in Brentwood. Shops, yes; restaurants, yes; banks and hairdressers and gas stations, yes. But no factories or movie studios or big law firms. Brentwood looks like a very upscale version of South L.A. before the riots. It has "no jobs."

And the problem with most plans to help the inner cities is that they can't explain why Brentwood isn't poor. From Jack Kemp's enterprise zones, to separatist schemes to "recycle black dollars," to socialist dreams of city-owned rail-car factories, these plans all share a single premise: that the way to make neighborhoods prosper is to put businesses in them.

This vision sounds great. Self-reliance is, after all, a respected virtue in America—and a stark contrast to welfare dependency. Entrepreneurship is inspiring. Ethnic solidarity has provided capital, labor, and upward mobility to countless immigrants. Community self-help has a nice ring.

But with or without investment from the outside, these plans all assume one thing. They assume that South Central will remain a ghetto.

And in a free society, economically thriving ghettos just aren't stable. If new enterprise does spring up in South Central L.A., if neighborhood entrepreneurs start making big bucks and neighborhood workers steady wages, one of two things will happen. Most likely, the newly affluent and the newly middle class will do what their counterparts elsewhere have done. They will get the hell out of South Central. They will use their money to buy safety for their families, and they will commute. Eventually, they will find jobs closer to their new homes. And South Central will remain "the inner city."

But suppose that doesn't happen. Suppose well-to-do residents decide to stay. Suppose they clean up the neighborhood, invest in it, improve it. Suppose by dint of community spirit, political pressure, and hard work, they manage to make South Central once again safe and prosperous. Their investment will pay off. Property values will go up. They will attract more people like themselves. And the neighborhood will gentrify. It will no longer be "the inner city." It will become expensive.

And the people who made it a poor neighborhood, the desirable and the undesirable alike, will have to go elsewhere.

The truth is, poor neighborhoods aren't poor because the neighborhoods don't have jobs. They are poor because the people who live in them don't have jobs. The problem of the inner cities is not a problem of place. It is a problem of people.

On one level, that makes it an easier problem to solve. South Central is a risky place to put a business; even without company-destroying riots, crime defines the inner city. It's hard to overcome the threat of bullets with the promise of tax breaks. It should be simpler to bring the people to the jobs than the jobs to the people. After all, all over the world, poor people travel vast distances in search of work. From Los Angeles alone millions of dollars flow back to Latin America and Asia, retracing the journeys of those who earned them.

But the policy makers concocting ways to "save our cities" ignore this pattern. In Los Angeles, neither Anglo social planners nor black community leaders seem able to imagine how a native-born Angeleno—the child or grandchild of people who crossed the continent to find better work—could take the bus to a job across town. In this city of commuters, no one can imagine a commute from South Central.

This failure of imagination has several sources. One is the habit of mind created by a community dependent on, and insulated by, government checks. On May 1, the Friday of the riots, hundreds of people stood for hours to collect welfare and social-security checks at post offices patrolled by National Guardsmen. In the inner city of Los Angeles, in the inner cities of America, the money comes in; the people don't go out.

Then, there is the current devastation. To be good places to live, neighborhoods do need shops and restaurants and banks and hairdressers and gas stations—the kinds of retail outlets that were sacked by looters and consumed by flames. Insurance companies expect to pay more than $775 million for riot damage, but some business owners say they'll take the money and flee. And with so many businesses gone, it's natural to think about replacing those that won't return.

But such retailers are important not because they provide jobs but because they provide services. They are a convenience to residents, not a path to economic salvation.

What really distinguishes South Central from Brentwood (or from less affluent neighborhoods such as Hollywood) isn't a lack of jobs. It is social isolation, isolation so profound that those who speak for the inner cities assume it will continue forever. In a city that exports imagination to the world, no one can imagine how a young man from South Central might find work on a calmer side of town. No one can imagine hiring him. He cannot imagine it either. He lives in one world. Employers live in another. Jobs must come to South Central because no one can imagine it any other way.

We will not overcome that isolation with a jobs program from Washington. Such programs exist so that local politicians can dole out opportunity locally. Such programs do not widen horizons. They keep things in the district. And while they may provide work experience, they do not teach people how to find real jobs, jobs that involve no political connections.

Indeed, the whole focus on federal programs is destructive. It is unjust to loot the people of Cleveland and Tampa and Santa Fe to rebuild L.A., a city whose reconstruction offers them no conceivable benefit. But it is more than unjust; it is dangerous.

The obvious danger lies in the already apparent backlash—against Los Angeles, against cities, against blacks, against immigrants, even against Rodney King. It is a backlash that for the most part still confines itself to talk-show call-ins and irate letters to the editor. But it will eventually take political form, and it will not resemble anything as benign as a tax revolt.

There are also more subtle perils. Some critics have charged that passing a huge aid package rewards rioting, encourages more of it. This would be true if the aid were going to the rioters, but little of it will reach them directly. Aid does send the wrong message to rioters, but it is not that message.

Rather, aid tells rioters—and the rest of America—that wealth is something to be snatched, to be taken and to be taken lightly. In the unreal world of Washington, billions can be had at the stroke of a pen; adding zeros is a measure of sincerity. Money comes from nowhere and no one. It is nothing personal.

Especially now, we need to send, and to hear, quite the opposite message: that wealth is an embodiment of work, that property is an extension of self, that burning someone's store is a personal attack, an attack no less meaningful than a physical beating. People who believe that property comes free of time and toil— whether they are tax-fed denizens of Congress, the decadent heirs of the rich, or the welfare-supported children of the poor—cannot appreciate what happened in Los Angeles and cannot begin to repair the damage.

For months after Hurricane Hugo struck the South Carolina coast, my family's friend Bob would pack his tools in his car and make weekly trips across the state to the rural enclaves that had been forgotten by the TV cameras, the Red Cross, and the federal government. Along with several friends, he would rebuild and repair the homes of people too poor and often too old to fix things for themselves. He did it, I think, because he felt a connection to these strangers—and because he knew that if he didn't do it, it wouldn't get done.

It was people like Bob who rebuilt South Carolina after Hugo. And it is people like Bob who hit the streets of Los Angeles with brooms and shovels in the weekend following the riots. In a notoriously fragmented city, people from riot-torn neighborhoods worked alongside people from as far away as Riverside County. For a fleeting moment, the people of the inner city were not isolated from the rest of town.

As he shoveled ashes into my garbage bag, a young black man from the Westside commented to me what a revelation the cleanup had been. To see what thriving businesses the area had supported just days before, he said, "blows the lid off" the idea that this neighborhood was some kind of foreign country. How ironic, he thought, that we would never have come there under ordinary circumstances. We were in Pico-Union, not besieged South Central, but he had a point.

Federal aid tells Angelenos that they need no longer concern themselves with reclaiming their city. They've given at the office. Federal aid tells Angelenos that healing their city is none of their business. As Rep. Vic Fazio put it, "The money we provide today will restore the face of Los Angeles but it is now up to Congress and the White House to heal its heart."

By taking the trouble out of things, by giving people reason to think that "if I don't do it, it will get done," federal aid breaks the bonds of community. That, indeed, is part of the point. Aid frees the affluent from worrying about the other side of town. And it permits the inner city to avoid earnest outsiders. Ultimately, it strengthens the walls of the ghetto.

On the left, in fact, it has become quite fashionable to denigrate the cleanup efforts and the spirit behind them, to mock those who suggest that the better angels of our nature have anything to contribute to the future of our city. The ubiquitous Marxist commentator Mike Davis refers to such notions as the "smog bank of sanctimonious rhetoric obscuring our view." (Davis wants $3.7 billion for gangster-administered "social investment.")

Upholding the virtue of community efforts, it seems, detracts from the revolutionary struggle, from the glamour of gang-bangers, from the hate-filled politics of Rep. Maxine Waters. It suggests that private action is important and that we can—and should—live without killing each other. It is too damn judgmental and too damn hopeful.

But the only way to repair Los Angeles, beyond the expensive but superficial job of replacing burned-out buildings, is to break the isolation of the inner city, to bring imagination to South Central. If that happens, jobs will follow—there or elsewhere.

This is a daunting task. It requires, first of all, a concerted effort to make the streets safe—at least as safe as Hollywood, where no car radio is secure but tourists rarely end up dead. As I've suggested elsewhere, citizen patrols could offer a valuable and affordable supplement to community-based policing.

Obviously, public safety would improve the chances of bringing outsiders in. But it would also liberate insiders. When the known world is threatening, the unknown is unthinkable. If you can get shot crossing the street, crossing town becomes too risky to contemplate.

Then, there is transportation. Contrary to popular belief, Los Angeles has lots of public transportation—an extensive bus system. It's just that most people would rather drive. Buses are inconvenient, especially over long distances.

Jitneys, small privately owned cars or vans, would be better. They could offer fewer stops, less waiting, and more flexible routes. They could also provide economic mobility—opportunities for easy-entry entrepreneurship or employment. Entrenched interests, notably the taxi companies and the much-reviled Rapid Transit District, don't like the idea of competition. But surely the lives of inner-city residents count for more than the maintenance of a government bus monopoly. If South Africa can let black entrepreneurs make it big in the jitney business, so can L.A.

In his touchstone book about life in a Chicago housing project, *There Are No Children Here*, Alex Kotlowitz recounts one undilutedly joyous adventure: a family trip to see the store windows of downtown at Christmas time. The children have never been downtown, have never seen skyscrapers, even though they live only miles away. Their mother buys them popcorn, and they have a wonderful time. Pat Conroy tells a similar story in *The Water Is Wide*, only the kids are from a rural island off the coast of South Carolina. Poor people, urban or rural, tend to be provincial. Their worlds are small.

If you live in a small world, it is hard to answer one of the most important questions of all: What do you want to be when you grow up? It's a multiple-choice question, but to see the choices you have to see the world. You have to meet people—in person or in books or on television. You have to find out how to get from here to where you want to be.

Field trips and speakers and programs and books that break the children of America's ghettos out of their isolation are worth more to the future than all the shiny hotels and office buildings Urban Development Action Grants ever built. (And, let's face it, such real-estate subsidies are what "aid to the cities" is all about.) Horizon-expanding encounters aren't expensive, but they require something rare and precious: Somebody has to risk being a stranger in a strange place. Somebody has to cross town.

And that brings us to the heart of the matter. Beyond safety, beyond transportation, beyond field trips, or school choice, or loan pools, or a host of other practical ideas, lies the vague, intangible task of restoring trust, creating empathy, connecting the people of Los Angeles to one another. This is not a collective endeavor. It cannot be accomplished with symbols. The only way for people to learn to see each other as individuals is to see each other as individuals, one by one by one. And that is where the repairs must begin.

PART SEVEN

APOCALYPSE, NO

Economics as if
Some People Mattered

By Petr Beckmann

October 1978

Small is Beautiful is the title of a book by E.F. Schumacher. It is also a slogan describing a state of mind in which people clamor for the rural idyll that (they think) comes with primitive energy sources, small-scale production, and small communities. Yet much—perhaps most—of their clamor is not really for what they consider small and beautiful; it is for the destruction of what they consider big and ugly.

That alone shows that there is more beneath this mentality than the slogan might suggest. Indeed, if its adherents wish to retire into a cottage industry powered by solar collectors and windmills, who's stopping them? There are many lonely places from Maine to Oregon to which the alienated can retreat and live the life they recommend to others. And many have, in fact, done so; but Amory Lovins is not among them, nor was Schumacher (he died in 1977), nor the Creative Initiative Foundation, nor Project Survival, nor Environmental Action, nor any of the other organizations fervently devoted to the small and beautiful.

Corporations, the utilities, the military, big business, profits—and whatever else is supposed to be big and ugly—are not big or ugly enough to stop Lovins from moving into the wilderness. In fact, they are not even big or ugly enough to *make* him move there.

It is, on the contrary, the small-is-beautiful advocates who are trying, and very successfully, to impose their will on the rest of us. And they haven't been imposing it on us by the ballot box: They work through the courts, through the federal bureaucracies and regulatory agencies, through regiments of lawyers and PR men who manipulate behind the scenes; but above all, they spread disinformation through the mass media and the schools and universities. That disinformation plays cleverly on people's desire for a healthy environment and on the fears that these same sources have carefully cultivated.

The way they have been promoting the small and beautiful is neither small nor beautiful. Certainly the money the environmental organizations have been spending to stop economic growth isn't small—it runs into the tens of millions a year, funneled into the environmental coffers in liberal amounts by the liberal foundations. The Creative Initiative Foundation bemoans the greed for worldly possessions out of its $500,000 home in a fashionable San Francisco suburb; a vast literature on the superiority of solar, wind, and tidal power is churned out by innumerable presses, none of which run on solar, wind, or tidal power; the officials of the Natural Resources Defense Council and other conservationists dart about in jumbo jets to lecture their fellow citizens on the virtues of bicycling and other forms of energy conservation.

Clearly, there is more to the small-is-beautiful slogan than its literal meaning. The larger message comes through in two works by outstanding representatives of the movement: Schumacher's *Small is Beautiful—Economics as if People Mattered* and Lovins's "Energy Strategy: The Road Not Taken" in the October 1976 issue of *Foreign Affairs*.

Both of these are well written but would otherwise present little interest since both utterly disregard any factual evidence. What gives them importance is the gushing adulation heaped on them by the TV networks, the press, and the other workshops of the American opinion-molding industry. It has not been fruitless: Congress has been receiving Lovins's testimony amidst much publicity; in November 1977 President Carter not only consulted with Lovins but shortly afterward repeated a string of his concocted figures; and California's governor, Jerry Brown, openly admires and quotes Schumacher.

The two publications have much in common in several respects, but perhaps the most striking feature is that they are both credos of unquestioning faith, palmed off to the reader as objective analysis. Lovins's piece is, in this respect, the more dishonest of the two, for while Schumacher's book contains little more than shallow technophobia ("What do I miss, as a human being, if I have never heard of the Second Law of Thermodynamics? Nothing. And what do I miss by not knowing Shakespeare? I simply miss my life."), Lovins's piece is adorned with a string of fabricated figures and doctored data.

The tone of Schumacher's book is set in the preface by Theodore Rozsak, who deplores "the phony plebiscite of the marketplace" and condemns economics as a science that "must hope and pray...that people will never be their better selves, but always greedy social idiots." (Note the "science that must hope and pray"—a contradiction in terms that says more about Roszak than about economics.)

Schumacher himself continues in the same spirit: "The market is the institutionalization of individualism and nonresponsibility. Neither the buyer nor the seller is responsible for anything but himself....To be relieved of all responsibility except to oneself means of course an enormous simplification of business. We can recognize that it is practical and need not be surprised that it is highly popular among businessmen."

Throughout his book, Schumacher gives copious evidence of being utterly unfamiliar with issues of safety in power generation, public health, and technology in general, which is somewhat surprising for one who worked for the British Coal Board until 1971; and his economics shows the same erudition. Schumacher was an avowed socialist, but his argument against the free market is particularly inept and some 200 years out of date.

The free market does not, of course, eradicate human greed, but it directs it into channels that give the consumer the maximum benefit, for it is he who benefits from the competition of "profit-greedy" businessmen. The idea that the free market is highly popular among businessmen is one that is widespread, but not among sound economists. It was not very popular in 1776, when Adam Smith's *Wealth of*

Nations was published, and it has not become terribly popular with all of them since—which is not surprising, for the free market benefits the consumer but disciplines the businessman.

If the free market is so popular with business, what are all those business lobbies doing in Washington? The shipping lobby wants special favors for U.S. ships; the airlines yell rape and robbery when deregulation from the governmental CAB cartel threatens; the farmers' lobby clamors for more subsidies. What all these lobbies are after is not a freer market but a bigger nipple on the federal sow.

And responsibility? It is the welfare bureaucracy that robs homo sapiens of responsibility: If someone dies after eating detergent, who is responsible? In currently fashionable wisdom, the manufacturer who failed to provide a warning label "not for internal consumption"; the FDA, OSHA, EPA, and dozens of other regulatory agencies; government and society at large, which failed to train, coerce, and watch over its helpless, moronic subjects—everybody and nobody. In contrast, the free market indeed breeds individual responsibility.

As a statement, "small is beautiful" is senseless. The small-is-beautiful people will quickly confirm this. They prefer the big bus of collective transit to the small automobile; they love solar power even if it involves collectors on hundreds of square miles; and they hate the nuclear plants that can produce the same power on tiny sites.

Much as they would love to have size and everything else decreed by those who know what is good for us, size is something that evolves to its own optimum, at least in the fields where the Schumachers and Lovinses have not been able to interfere. In nature, for example, species evolve to the "right" size. Warm-blooded animals living in the cold must be a minimum size. There are polar bears, but no polar mice; penguins, but no polar sparrows.

Buildings cannot grow beyond a certain size—skyscrapers significantly taller than the Sears Tower or the World Trade Center would waste too much space on elevator shafts for all those people in the upper stories, and the building would become uneconomical, even though technically it would be feasible to make it taller.

Quite often it happens that a technology develops toward increasing sizes of the product because twice the size will cost less than twice as much; this is called economy of scale. Typically, an oil tanker brings in revenue proportional to the volume of oil carried; but its investment costs are (roughly) proportional to the amount of material used, and its operating costs are partly determined by the fuel needed to propel it. If the linear dimensions of the tanker are doubled, its cargo space increases eightfold, but its surface area only fourfold, and the required propulsion power only threefold (all in very rudimentary theory; the actual figures are slightly different, but the principle and savings remain). Oil tankers, therefore, become more economical with increasing size, which is why they have recently grown to as much as 500,000 tons displacement.

In other cases, of course, economy works in exactly the opposite direction. Typically, semiconductor technology and integrated circuits have *reduced* the size of electronic equipment to an astounding degree. Electronic watches, for example, now worn on wrists and available for under $20, are not fundamentally new. Electronic, quartz-controlled watches have been around since the 1920s, though only central radio stations and astronomic institutions were able to afford them. When made with vacuum tubes, they cost many thousands of dollars, produced great amounts of waste heat, and usually needed a whole (air-conditioned) room to house them. So the modern digital watch might be a case where small is beautiful (but Schumacher and Lovins, presumably, would prefer sundials or hourglasses).

But they are wrong in the case that interests them most—that of energy sources, particularly electric-power plants. Largely through economies of size—larger central power plants—the price of electricity declined from a high of 13.3 cents per kilowatt-hour in 1922 to a low of 3.4 cents in 1974 (both in constant 1967 dollars). Main reason: *Large systems waste less energy*. And unlike skyscrapers, electric-power plants do not yet seem close to a limit. In fact, looking centuries ahead, some analysts have suggested that our present "energy cells," in which electricity is transmitted over a few hundred miles, will be replaced by far larger "cells" in which hydrogen will be piped over thousands of miles with far smaller losses. The hydrogen, of course, must be produced by investing energy to extract it from water—on a scale for which nuclear energy is the only currently viable candidate.

But whatever the future may hold, the past development of energy sources has shown a consistent trend to more efficient and bigger power plants. The alternative Lovins proposes is energy waste on a gigantic scale: diesel engines in your back yard, fluidized-bed coal furnaces in your basement (they haven't been developed yet—better men than Lovins are still working on them). And why not do it the efficient, clean, and safe way—with centrally generated nuclear power? Because, says Lovins, in a metaphor that has since been adopted by every sensitive and aware cocktail hostess, that would be like using a chainsaw to cut butter, for the electricity is made in reactors at temperatures of millions of degrees. This type of agglomeration of words into a meaningless string can be traced back to Barry Commoner, a Marxist biologist who believes thermodynamics can be abused for political ends. But the Commoner-Lovins wisdom is both false and irrelevant. It is false, because the temperature in a reactor, at its hottest point at the axis of a fuel rod, is about 4000F (600F at the surface of the pellets); and it is irrelevant, because for what is the energy of the uranium conserved if it is left in the ground?

A discussion of the economic and technological blunders in Schumacher's *Small is Beautiful* could fill a whole book; in Lovins's case, it *has* filled a whole book, mainly devoted to his outsized technical errors (*Soft vs. Hard Energy Paths*). There are less obvious, but equally distasteful, aspects of the small-is-beautiful mentality. One of these is its deeply antidemocratic, authoritarian undertone.

The energy sources recommended by Schumacher, Lovins, and the other small-and-beautiful people have been tried before—on the feudal manor. Not only are they technologically similar or even identical, but their "softness" consists partly in their small capacity: no more (and, practically, very much less) than needed by a single home.

What exactly constitutes "soft" energy is mushy and ill-defined in the small-and-beautiful literature; *soft* seems to mean *primitive*, *pitiful*, and often *unavailable*. But to Lovins, who rejects solar energy converted in large, centralized (and more efficient) plants, it seems to be determined by the feudal feature of everybody producing his own goods for consumption.

Large-scale division of labor is something that has come about only with large-scale industrialization. It has not always been true that some organizations make only shoes, while others make only cloth, and that the man who makes only shirts is rewarded with a salary, some of which he exchanges for shoes, shirts, both, or neither, at his choice. Only a few hundred years ago there was no (significant) division of labor; every family made its own shoes, wove its own cloth, and sewed its own shirts. Families also provided their own energy. Most of it came from muscle power—animal muscles or their own. What little other energy they harnessed came from the type of sources Schumacher and Lovins advocate—solar, wind, water. The sun, in those days, gave approximately one kilowatt per square meter at the best of times, just as it does today; and whether amorphous semiconductors will eventually become available to replace medieval forms of harnessing solar energy will make precious little difference to the general idea.

But the absence of the division of labor is not, by itself, what made the feudal system. The vast majority of people were serfs, bound to the land with which they were bought and sold, working for the owner of that land, the seignior or lord of the manor, and completely at his mercy within the harsh code of the medieval Church. Economically, the manors were virtually self-sufficient and in peacetime only loosely tied to the "central" authorities—king, emperor, bishop, pope—who were too far away to make much difference to the local authoritarian system.

Now to go back to feudal energy sources and feudal methods of production *could* merely be inept; it does not necessarily follow that it would have to be authoritarian, too. Perhaps not, although probably it would.

In any case, the small-and-beautiful people leave us with little doubt as to their attitude toward authority: They worship it. The Creative Initiative Foundation's *Primer for Living* is full of it. Schumacher's admiration for Marx, Mao Tse-tung, and what amounts to feudal technology will make the wary reader think, "Next thing he will do is bemoan people's mobility compared to the good old times when they were bound to the land." Next thing he does is bemoan people's mobility compared to the good old times when they were bound to the land. "A highly developed transportation and communication system...makes people *footloose*," he writes (his italics). "Everything in this world has to have structure, otherwise it is chaos....Before the advent of mass transport, the structure was simply there, because people were relatively immobile....Before this technological intervention,...people and things were not footloose; transport was expensive enough so that movements, both of people and of goods, were never more than marginal....The basic requirements of life had of course to be indigenously produced."

That is the type of system, along with feudal energy sources and feudal technology, whose praises are sung by Schumacher; and lest there be any misunderstanding, the point is driven home repeatedly. The automobile and jet plane have, to millions in the West, fulfilled man's ancient dream of mobility, and physical mobility has resulted in social upward mobility as well. But to Schumacher, this spells the "footloose society," and he laments the passing of the times when "the movement of populations, except in periods of disaster, was confined to persons who had a very special reason to move, such as the Irish saints or the scholars of the University of Paris." These idyllic times have not, of course, passed away everywhere. In some countries, movement of populations is still confined to persons who have very special reasons—in the USSR and mainland China, for example.

Schumacher, it should be said, does not *consciously* advocate feudalism. But his vision of cottage industries in small communities with primitive technology, and his call for discipline and authority, are so suggestive of feudalism that just about the only thing missing is the *primae noctis* (the right of the lord of the manor to bed any serf girl on the night before her wedding).

Lovins's ideas are no less feudal than Schumacher's. "In an electrical world," says he, "your lifeline does not come from an understandable neighborhood technology run by people you know are at your own social level, but rather from an alien, remote and perhaps uncontrollable technology run by a faraway, bureaucratized, technical elite who have probably never heard of you."

True enough for electricity. But how about your shoes (or anything else but homemade doughnuts)? They don't come from an understandable neighborhood technology, either, and certainly the people who made them "have probably never heard of you." The implication of this disturbing state of affairs is clear: We must go back to the times when every family made its own shoes. At least, that is what Lovins concludes in the case of electricity.

But it is not merely feudal economics that Lovins finds attractive; he also emerges as a firm believer in authority and the proper place for the common rabble. The "soft," that is feudal, path is incompatible with the "hard" path of efficient and central energy conversion, he asserts. Is it because there is only enough capital for one but not for both of these paths? If so, there is a simple and time-honored way to find out how capital is best allotted: from the investors who allot that capital. The reason they know so much more about it than Lovins is twofold: One, they study the question with all the zeal that comes with putting one's own money on the line; and two, there are so many of them that the great majority is never permanently wrong—snake-oil stocks do not soar for long. But for the small-and-beautiful, economic decisions are not to be made by those who risk and therefore understand; the economy must be legislated, decreed, regulated, and regimented.

Considerations of capital, however, do not seem to be the only reason why Lovins has ruled the two paths incompatible. The capital investments possible with conservation, says he, are far less than those needed to increase "most" kinds of energy supply, and "a largely or wholly solar energy economy can be constructed in the U.S. with soft technologies that are now economic or nearly economic." And elsewhere: "An affluent industrial economy could advantageously operate with no central power stations at all." Not to mention that "in the soft path, conversion and distribution losses have been all but eliminated" (with this claim, Lovins not only revolutionizes economics but revokes a basic law of physics) and that domestic fluidized-bed coal furnaces (not yet invented) have combustion efficiencies of over 80 percent.

That is a lot of good news all at once. The puzzle is that the "greedy" princes of capitalism are not yet trampling each other to death in the mad rush to exploit these fabulous technological innovations. Obviously, they are too stupid to know what is good for them. But Lovins's home team, the Friends of the Earth, together with a dozen other well-heeled organizations, will coerce them for their own good. Not, of course, via the ballot box—a diabolical institution that should never have been given to the rabble—but by the courts, the regulatory agencies, the federal bureaucracy, by guerrilla tactics that price "hard" technologies out of the market, and by whatever other forms of coercion, intimidation, and misinformation are available to them.

Some of the present "soft" technology already carries the seeds of coercion. Gigantic windmills that produce pitifully small amounts of power but cost millions of dollars are paid for not by the consumer's free choice but by the taxpayer, whose money is being squandered by reckless politicians. The "100 billion dollar bailouts" and "oligopolies" with which Lovins charges the energy industry are entirely mythical, but billions of dollars of taxpayers' money are to be handed out by the government in the form of tax credits, rebates, subsidies, and incentives to a solar industry that might not make it on its merits. Indeed, the many sensible, if limited, applications that solar energy does have will not emerge as the best that were filtered out by a free market; they will be hidden, and perhaps smothered, by the lemons and rackets kept alive with the subsidies from the governmental sun worshipers.

But the small-and-beautiful crowd's love for coercion and contempt for the ballot box is best illustrated by the case of nuclear power. In the 1976 elections, in seven states representing 20 percent of the U.S. electorate, the small-and-beautiful placed on the ballot what was in effect a ban on nuclear power. These states were picked by the nuclear opponents as the most likely to approve such a ban. Instead, they defeated it by an average margin of two-to-one!

The tactic that was then adopted, and proved more successful, was to price nuclear power out of the market by abuse of the legal system and forcing artificial delays. But such obstructionism, supported by a broad assault of horror fiction in the mass media, was still not enough. In the summer of 1977, the small-and-beautiful met in Salzburg, Austria (the conference was attended by both Schumacher and Lovins), and decided to "raise the social and political costs of nuclear power" by acts of lawlessness, such as occupying construction sites of nuclear power plants. In Europe, these tactics provoked large-scale violence, with at least one dead and hundreds injured. In the United States, the small-and-beautiful openly admire such violence and have tried hard to instigate it in New Hampshire, California, Oregon, and other places.

The way of the small-and-beautiful does not lead through the ballot box; it is the way of the rope puller and manipulator, and it is not averse to the way of the storm trooper.

Another ill-defined concept pervading Schumacher's and Lovins's writings is that of vulnerability, a disadvantage attributed to "hard" but not to "soft" energy sources. Vulnerable to what? To war, to routine outages, to sabotage, to industrial strife, to fuel shortages? It never quite comes through the mush. But though Lovins uses the term *vulnerability* flexibly to boost the varied aspects of his far-out theories as needed, the main use seems to be reserved for propaganda against nuclear power, the use of which would allegedly lead to a police state. Constant repetition will not make this inept argument any better: Thirty years of shipping large quantities of nuclear bombs, not harmless fuel assemblies, have not turned this country into a police state; ensuring the security of hydroelectric dams, which are more difficult to guard, more easily sabotaged, and far more lethal than a nuclear plant in the disaster they could cause, has not done so either. The idea that nuclear *power* could lead to proliferation of nuclear *bombs* is just false.

In general, nuclear power is safer, cleaner, and environmentally more benign than any other source of electricity. The fact that the advocates of the small-and-beautiful, and typically Schumacher and Lovins, consistently ignore the comparison with other power sources should tell us clearly that they have very little interest in safety or a clean environment.

The idea that a small, community-wide electrical system would be less "vulnerable" than the interstate power grids is laughable. The very idea of a grid is the pooling of resources, so that a local net in trouble can receive aid not only from its own but also from other utility systems, often in other states. The Lovinsian mini-system of windmills and chicken manure could probably never be tested in sabotage, war, or industrial strife: It would scarcely make it through the first snow storm.

And yet the U.S. energy system is indeed horribly vulnerable in a way that the Lovinsian fantasies not only ignore but help to exacerbate.

In 1976 the United States imported oil and petroleum products at the rate of 7.12 million barrels a day, 40.6 percent of its total demand. New oil and gas is being kept underground by price controls; both digging and burning of coal is hamstrung by environmentalist obstructions; nuclear power, which with breeder technology could provide this country with its electricity for 1,000 years, is being hounded and harassed by an unholy alliance of the mass media with the environmentalist zealots in the Carter administration.

Now take a look at the world map of major oil fields, 60 percent of which lie in the crescent-shaped area inside the USSR or dominated by it. The USSR is now the world's biggest oil producer (bigger than Saudi Arabia), and its production is rising; that of the United States is declining. The USSR is moving into a position of control of the world's oil spigots and of sea lanes from them, and that control means economic, military, and possibly political control of the nations that must import their oil from that crescent-shaped area of the world—the United States among them.

Only the utterly naive would fail to recognize the signs that the USSR is, in fact, actively pursuing such a goal: the feverish build-up of the Soviet navy; the all-out effort to dominate the Middle East; the effort to control the oil shipping lanes to Europe and the United States, including the political campaigns against Israel and South Africa; the effort to dominate the African horn; the conquest of Angola—these are some of the signs of a consistent Soviet foreign policy.

But for those who are blind to these signs, there is also documentary evidence that the Soviets are pursuing a deliberate policy of making the West more pliable by disrupting its energy supplies. Andrei Sakharov, the courageous dissident scientist who, as father of the Soviet hydrogen bomb, was high up in the Soviet establishment in 1955, has given this testimony:

"I often remember how in 1955 a high official of the Soviet Council of Ministers spoke to a group of scientists and told them that now (Shepilov, a member of the Presidium of the Central Committee of the Communist Party, had just returned from Egypt) the principles of a new Soviet foreign policy in the Middle East were being worked out. He said that the long-term aim of this policy was using Arab nationalism to create difficulties in the oil supply of European countries and thus to make them more pliable."

That was in 1955. Twenty-three years later, it is clear the Soviet policy has been spectacularly successful. And we may safely assume that it is no longer limited to making the West more pliable by disrupting its energy supplies but that it is aimed at controlling the West by being able to interdict them.

The prospect of the United States losing control over its economic—and therefore ultimately political—destiny is the most ominous and acute threat of the U.S. energy crisis. And what is the answer of the small-and-beautiful people—in particular, Amory Lovins—to this paramount threat? The deindustrialization and ruralization of the United States.

It does not follow, of course, that the small-and-beautiful advocate deindustrialization *in order* to help the Soviets. Far more likely than helping the Soviets, they are trying to help themselves.

It is conceivable that Lovins and the other spokesmen of pseudo-environmentalism kid themselves that they are motivated by the desire to live in harmony with nature and to do mankind a good turn. This may be highly interesting to the psychologist, but is utterly irrelevant to the issues. If Lovins were a genuine safety advocate, he would support the type of energy that is safer than any other, which is nuclear (see my *Health Hazards of Not Going Nuclear!*) He would not advocate diluting the dangers of energy by millions of windmills, hundreds of millions of solar collectors, and energy storage in every home, which *per energy produced* would lead to carnage unheard of with any large-scale source of electricity.

If he were a genuine environmentalist or conservationist, he would know that breeding nuclear fuel can provide the world's electricity for the next millennium, the volume disrupted by mining being 5,000 times smaller than that for coal yielding the same energy. And if he were genuinely interested in preventing proliferation, he would not conceal the fact that making bombs via the nuclear *power* fuel cycle is the most time-consuming, expensive, dangerous, and inept way of the *eight* available methods.

But it does not matter all that much what motivates Lovins personally. There are people who think the earth is flat and people who think they can communicate with the dead; a man who doctors his data to show that an industrial giant can run on windmills and chicken manure is not all that interesting.

The real point about the Lovins phenomenon is that he is received by a president of the United States who parrots his fantastic figures, that the mass media adulate his piffle, that many professionals (and their spouses) in academia and business are in ecstasy over it, and that the politicians who have discerned the vote-garnering powers of this naive dream are drooling in transported rapture.

But who is it that *doesn't* swoon? The common man, for he would be the big loser.

The blue-collar worker, for one, knows the worth of a home energy system that substitutes an investment of thousands of dollars for the purchase of electricity at a nickel a kilowatt-hour. Neither he nor the labor unions are willing to go back to brute muscle power after central power plants have been abolished, large-scale industry crippled, and jobs eliminated by the millions.

The American farmer, with the world's highest per-acre yields, knows the worth of energy; it goes, not just into his tractor fuel, but above all into his fertilizers. He sells food not only to Sweden and Switzerland (whose small energy consumption is quite falsely held up by Lovins) but also to countries where most of the inhabitants go hungry—because they still have a Lovinsian economy.

And the poor? Lovins goes through the obligatory ritual of saying that they suffer most from energy shortages, whereupon he proceeds with details of the energy sources that only the affluent can afford. His concern for the poor is heartbreaking; but how many chapters do his Friends of the Earth have in Harlem or in Watts? Evidently the poor do not yearn for Lovins to be so good to them.

Lovins's soft-headed energy paths are, in fact, popular only among a very small section of the American people. The members of this tone-setting elite, no matter how much they may kid themselves about environment and ecology, resent the common man, for he is crowding "their" highways, beaches, national parks, and airlines; but even more bitterly, they resent technology—"vulgar," "gone berserk," and "equivalent to war"—for it has enabled the common man to crowd them and needs a population of engineers, technicians, and workers who understand it, when the world should really be dependent only on the sensitive who ponder the mysteries of the transcendental. They resent the free enterprise system because it lets people buy and do what they want to, when they really should buy and do what they *ought* to. And what they ought to do should be planned by the tone setters who know what is good for the people. They know technology is bad, for it has wounded them with the ultimate insult: They don't understand it anymore.

The influential social position of this elite, then, is threatened by the mass prosperity that is bred by technology and free enterprise. What better way to keep the riff-raff in its place than to kill both by abolishing all but feudal energy sources? The gospel taught by the small-and-beautiful, the ecologists, the population controllers, the antinukes, the no-growth crusaders, the regulators, and the other regressionists comes in many versions; but its fundamental commandment is, *There are too many of you others.*

Schumacher subtitled his book *Economics as if People Mattered*, but what the small-is-beautiful mentality amounts to is economics as if only *some* people mattered; and what it advocates can only be achieved by coercion. Small for you is beautiful for Lovins.

Love Canal: The Truth Seeps Out

By Eric Zuesse

February 1981

Y ou're about to be untricked. If you believe that the guilty party in the Love Canal tragedy is the Hooker Chemicals & Plastics Corporation, which the Justice Department is suing, rather than the Niagara Falls Board of Education, which bought the dump from Hooker in 1953; or if you believe that Michael Brown's famous book that has become the popular authority on the whole mess, *Laying Waste: The Poisoning of America by Toxic Chemicals*, sets out the truth, the whole truth, and nothing but the truth about Love Canal, then you've been snookered. In fact, as I'm going to show, hardly ever has there been a more blatant example of Big Brother successfully hiding the skeletons in his closet or of a gullible investigative reporter and compliant major media going along with the cover-up so that a bunch of bureaucrats can pass the buck to some bewildered private interest. The irony is that the target of this particular smear, Hooker Chemicals, may very well have botched others of its many chemical dumps, but not Love Canal, the very site that has brought the company so much adverse publicity and a flood of government and private lawsuits.

I first suspected that something might be wrong with the press reports about Love Canal—I had not yet read Michael Brown's book—when I noticed that only passing mention was being made of the fact that the Niagara Falls Board of Education has owned the site since 1953. Twenty-plus years after Hooker deeded the property to the board, the canal is seeping huge quantities of poisonous chemicals. These toxic substances have been down there a long time, I thought. Why are they percolating up only after such a long sleep? Could something have disturbed the chemicals buried there? Or was the oozing inevitable? Had Hooker unloaded the property on the school board back in the '50s, hoping to avert the very claims for damages now being pressed against it?

My curiosity sparked, I obtained a copy of the Love Canal deed. It opens: "This Indenture [is] made the 28th day of April, Nineteen Hundred and Fifty Three, between Hooker Electrochemical Company...and the Board of Education of the School District of the City of Niagara Falls, New York," which would, "in consideration of One Dollar" paid to Hooker, receive title to the described property. The kicker is the deed's closing paragraph:

> "Prior to the delivery of this instrument of conveyance, the grantee herein has been advised by the grantor that the premises above described have been filled, in whole or in part, to the present grade level thereof with waste products resulting from the manufacturing of chemicals by the grantor at its plant in the City of Niagara Falls, New York, and the

grantee assumes all risk and liability incident to the use thereof. It is therefore understood and agreed that, as a part of the consideration for this conveyance and as a condition thereof, no claim, suit, action or demand of any nature whatsoever shall ever be made by the grantee, its successors or assigns, against the grantor, its successors or assigns, for injury to a person or persons, including death resulting therefrom, or loss of or damage to property caused by, in connection with or by reason of the presence of said industrial wastes. It is further agreed as a condition hereof that each subsequent conveyance of the aforesaid lands shall be made subject to the foregoing provisions and conditions."

So Hooker had shifted to the board "all risk and liability incident to the use" of the property. In addition, the deed specified that the future owner(s) of the property could not make any claims against Hooker for injury or death or property damage arising even from "the *presence* of said industrial wastes." It's not surprising that Hooker would have wanted this shift of liability incorporated into the deed. After all, it had made clear that these "waste products resulting from the manufacturing of chemicals" could cause not only property damage but "injury" and "death." That's pretty dangerous stuff.

Looked at one way, these provisions would seem to indicate that Hooker had been quite anxious to unburden itself of responsibility for this property. On the other hand, since the first condition, assumption of liability for use, only makes explicit what normally accompanies any property exchange, and since the second would protect Hooker only from claims made by the board and subsequent owners, and not from claims by third parties, it would seem that these provisions are more in the nature of a warning. By incorporating them into the deed, Hooker had provided clear notice, recorded for all time, that its use of this property had been such that any future owner would have to take care to use it in a safe manner so as to avoid causing harm.

Certainly the last sentence in the indenture must be interpreted in this way. Not only the school board but "its successors and assigns"—any future holder of the property obtaining rights to the canal after or from the board—had already been drawn into the shift of liability. So why add the closing sentence, about "each subsequent conveyance of the property"? The concern seems to have been with preventing catastrophe to innocent third parties by making sure that, down through all future generations, whoever obtained this property would be warned that it contains dangerous chemicals and reminded of the corresponding obligation to use it in a manner reflecting this hazard. So the inclusion of that last sentence in the deed doesn't fit in very well with the ruthless and negligent attitude I'd been led by most press accounts to believe that Hooker has been displaying in the Love Canal matter.

Ruthless and negligent? As I was subsequently to learn, Hooker had evidently been so concerned that the board know what it was getting in taking over the canal that the company had not left to chance whether school board officials would physically inspect the property prior to acquiring it. Instead, Hooker had escorted them to the canal site and in their presence made eight test borings—into the protective clay cover that the company had laid over the canal, and into the surrounding area. At two spots, directly over Hooker's wastes, chemicals were encountered four feet below the surface. At the other spots, to the sides of the canal proper, no chemicals showed up.

So whether or not the School Board was of a mind to inspect the canal, Hooker had gone out of its way to make sure that they *did* inspect it and that they did see that *chemicals* lay buried in that canal. Yet the subsequent behavior of the school board would lead the casual observer to conclude that its members never knew the facts about the property they were acquiring.

I decided to try to talk with some of the people who sat on the board during the key years of 1952 through 1957 and so had firsthand knowledge of the events. In the latter year, the board was debating whether to sell portions of the Love Canal to real estate developers; Hooker officials came to the board meetings to urge that these sales not be consummated. For this and other reasons, 1957 served as a turning point in the history of the Love Canal—the beginning of its precipitous slide into becoming a hell pit.

I introduced myself to the first former member of the school board I'd managed to track down and get on the phone, Peter Longhine, by saying that I was a reporter who wished to speak with someone with firsthand knowledge of the board's transactions with Hooker. That's all—I made no mention of courts, legal liability for Love Canal, or anything even remotely threatening. But Longhine would say only: "I don't want to get involved in giving any court testimony. It's better to let sleeping dogs lie. But I can tell you one thing—the Board of Education didn't do anything wrong. Anyway, we don't have any legal responsibility for it." This seemed to me an odd reaction, considering that I had just introduced myself and had not suggested even remotely that the Board of Education was in any way culpable, much less legally liable.

I got another former school board member on the phone, Robert Brezing. This time, I wasn't even able to finish my introduction. He abruptly hung up the phone, and I found myself trying to protest to a dial tone. Now I knew that something was fishy. I packed my bags, camera, and cassette recorder and left for Niagara Falls.

The first thing that struck this newcomer about the town of Niagara Falls was how very normal the place is. Because of its famous namesake falls, I had expected the town itself to have a character different from your typical American small city, but that's just what the place turned out to be. The people, I found, are pleasantly friendly and open, and if there is a wrong side of the tracks anywhere to the right or left of Main Street, it's hard to find.

Visually, it would perhaps be more accurate to describe Niagara Falls not as a small city so much as an endlessly sprawling suburb of 75,000 people without a core city. There are only two commercial streets, Main and Pine, both of which intrude upon otherwise uninterrupted expanses of suburban-style houses, which extend row upon row on each side of the two chief thoroughfares. In any event, whether it's seen as a town or merely as a suburb without a city, Niagara Falls struck me as a singularly odd kind of place to serve as a bellwether for the souring of America's dream of an insect-free plasticized world—"better living through chemistry," to quote the commercial from DuPont. There's an irony to this place: On the one side of town is the eternal majesty of nature grandly displayed in the water tumbling over the Niagara escarpment; across the city stands a stark symbol of the incompetence and perhaps greed of man—the acrid fumes and boarded-up houses along the periphery of the now-infamous chemical ditch.

But as it turns out, that festering blister of the industrial age known as Love Canal isn't quite as incongruous a fixture in Niagara Falls as it might seem at first blush. You don't have to be around this place long before you'll hear about how the local economy was built even more upon the chemical industry than upon tourism. Back in the 1950s, the locals will tell you, the putrid air from the industrial stacks made the eyes and lungs continually smart. The smog was so bad that the city was recognizable from an approaching plane by the dark grayish-brown cloud of pollution that blanketed the earth below.

Of course, this was in an era when *conservation* meant leaving the wild bears alone, *nutrition* meant "fruit, cereal, milk, bread, and butter," and *pollution* was a term that only communists, oddballs, or crazy people ever used. Niagara Falls considered itself fortunate back then to be one of the capitals of the world's chemical industry. The townspeople felt proud to be in the vanguard of the coming technological society. When the Atomic Energy Commission handed out awards to Niagara Falls chemical plants for work on radioactive substances, it made page-one headlines in the local newspapers. Chemical row along Buffalo Avenue, which skirts the southernmost edge of town bordering the Niagara River, was not only the Falls area's chief source of employment but also a source of considerable civic pride.

Now, however, the long-anticipated chemical future has at last come to the world, and a lot of people in Niagara Falls are finding that they don't like it. The theory used to be that industrial wastes need only be shoved under the rug and they would be gone. Out of sight was out of mind. But as events at Love Canal and elsewhere were ultimately to make clear, today's faraway rural chemical dump is tomorrow's suburb, where you may someday live and where your children may end up going to school.

Of course, many people don't care about tomorrow and never did. According to the popular wisdom, this kind of dangerous shortsightedness is an attribute of private businesses more than of governmental bodies, and this perception has colored the way the Love Canal story has been reported. But my own investigation shows that this popular interpretation of the Love Canal tragedy is 180 degrees off.

Back at the turn of the century, an ambitious entrepreneur by the name of William Love envisioned building a huge hydroelectric project in the Niagara Falls area. Thomas Edison had just harnessed the force of electricity; but because the state-of-the-art allowed only for transmission by direct current, which was uneconomic over long distances, industries had to be located near the source of electrical generation. Love planned his hydroelectric canal project as a means of supplying this electrical power to nearby industry and even dreamed that his "Love's Canal" would become the basis for a booming model city. But the economic recession of 1894 and Nikola Tesla's pioneering system of alternating current, which facilitated transmission of electricity over long distances, combined to bankrupt Love's Canal after only short segments of it had been dug. The 3,200-foot-long section that Hooker started filling with waste chemicals in 1942 has now come to be known internationally as *the* Love Canal.

Hooker says that it chose the site because the soil characteristic of the area—impermeable clay—and the sparse population surrounding the canal at the time made the pit outstandingly suitable for disposing of dangerous chemical wastes. The customary practices then were to pile up such wastes in unlined surface impoundments, insecure lagoons, or pits, usually on the premises of the chemical factory, or else to burn the wastes or dump them into rivers or lakes. Except for disposal into water supplies, these practices were all legal until 1980, when the Environmental Protection Agency began issuing regulations implementing the Resource Conservation and Recovery Act of 1976.

The EPA estimates that 90 percent of chemical wastes are currently being disposed of in ways that do not meet its proposed standards (controlled incineration, treatment to render the waste nonhazardous, secure landfills, or recovery). An attorney I spoke with from the New York State Department of Environmental Conservation told me that "at least 50 percent of chemical waste dumping [in that state] is contracted out to organized crime." If true, however, such was not to be the case with Love Canal.

Hooker in 1941 began studies of the suitability of using the canal as a chemical dump. The findings were affirmative, and by April of the next year the company completed the legal transactions to commence dumping what ultimately amounted to approximately 21,800 tons of the company's waste before the canal property (which included a strip of land on either side of the canal) was donated by Hooker to the Niagara Falls Board of Education in 1953, under pressure from the board that if Hooker didn't willingly deed the land the property would be seized under eminent domain for the building of a school.

It's also worth noting here that other wastes besides these 21,800 tons from Hooker have apparently been dumped into the canal. According to New York state officials, federal agencies, especially the Army, disposed of toxic chemical wastes there during and after World War II. The city of Niagara Falls also regularly unloaded its municipal refuse into this Hooker-owned pit.

There were two reasons why the school board wanted to acquire Hooker's Love Canal property. One was that the postwar baby boom had produced a need for construction of more schools, and virtually every available open lot of suitable size was being eyed voraciously by the Board of Education's Buildings and Grounds Committee for possible construction of new schools. The other was that since the area was not built up (one of Hooker's reported criteria for the site's suitability), land prices around this dumpsite were low, and the board was strapped for cash. On October 16, 1952, the very same day that Hooker sent a letter to the Board of Education agreeing to donate the canal property for the token price of $1.00, the board itself recorded, in its minutes for that evening's meeting, that "a communication was received from the Niagara Falls Teachers Association stating that teachers are becoming more and more uneasy because of their uncertain financial prospects."

Looking over the school board minutes from the early '50s, one notes two concerns that dominated and practically obliterated all others: construction of new buildings and overcoming the monetary shortage. There is no indication that any long-term consequences were being thought of; the attitude seems to have been that the future could take care of itself. For example, the 99th Street School, which was built beside Love Canal, was being planned by the school board at the same time as another, the 66th Street School, and the *Niagara Gazette* reported on September 13, 1978, that high radiation had been found at that other location. It turns out that this school also may have been built upon a former dumpsite. The Board of Education's deed to the site (donated by the federal government) refers to the presence of radioactive substances.

The negotiations that culminated in Hooker's transfer of the Love Canal property to the Board of Education took place over a period of several years. The contemporary documentary record is very sparse, consisting of three perfunctory letters and the deed itself. Virtually all of the negotiations were oral rather than written.

One thing, however, is clear: According to the school board's own records, the board was already well along in its planning of the 99th Street School more than two years before Hooker deeded the canal to the board. And the board meant business. It was gearing up for a string of condemnation proceedings for the canal site and all properties abutting it. First, there's a map, dated March 1951 and labeled "School Site Study Plan A" (Plan B was for the 66th Street School). This map not only shows the projected school being built right over the very center of the canal itself but also shows the assessed condemnation values for the canal property and each of the properties bordering it.

Then there are two letters from the school board's attorney, Ralph Boniello— one dated September 4, 1952, informing the board's business manager, Frank Lang, that procedures were under way to purchase four lots abutting the canal; the other dated September 19, 1952, addressed to Carmen J. Caggiano and sent by registered mail, return receipt requested, informing Caggiano that since he had refused the board's "price offered of $10 per front foot" for the strip of 10 lots he owned along the east side of the canal, "The purpose of this letter is to apprise you of the institution of an action in condemnation to acquire the above-described property for educational purposes."

According to reporter Michael Brown, in his book and other writings, the school board's attorney at the time denies that the threat of property condemnation was ever held out against Hooker for the Love Canal site. Brown neither questions nor documents this. Yet when Hooker, in 1957, addressed to the president of the Board of Education a letter that was read out loud and passed around at the board's meeting on November 21 of that year, and when that letter recalled that in 1952 board officials had threatened "that condemnation proceedings might be resorted to," there wasn't a peep of protest from any board member or official present—not from Wesley Kester, head of the board's Buildings and Grounds Committee in 1957, who had served in the same capacity in 1952 and so must have been very prominently involved in the negotiations with Hooker at the time; not from Arthur Silberberg, another member of the same committee who had also served in the same capacity throughout that period with the board; not from Frank Lang, a board member who had served as manager of business affairs throughout the period and was always involved in such matters as property condemnations; not from William Small, who was superintendent of schools throughout the period and who had personally accompanied Hooker's executive vice president, Bjarne Klaussen, to Love Canal in March 1952 when the test holes were bored into the clay cover over the canal and into the surrounding area to check for chemical leakage; not from the board's attorney, William Salacuse, who had been its president back in 1952 and who had also been present at that test at the canal site; not from anyone at all, though the printed minutes of that evening's board meeting make conspicuous mention of this letter from Hooker.

One might wonder why Hooker deeded the property to the school board for $1.00 rather than let it be condemned and seized under eminent domain. After all, condemnation would clearly have freed the company from future liability for the chemical dump, saving Hooker the trouble of spelling out such matters in the deed.

Hooker claims that it had wanted any future property holder there to know of the dangerous chemicals and that it had therefore agreed to donate the property, subject to the board's recognition that, to quote Hooker's letter of October 16, 1952, to the board, "in view of the nature of the property and the purposes for which it has been used, it will be necessary for us to have special provisions incorporated into the deed with respect to the use of the property and other pertinent matters." Had the land been condemned and seized, says Hooker, the company would have been unable to air its concerns to all future owners of the property. It is difficult to see any other reason for what it did.

The school board, however, ultimately refused to accept the special provisions proposed by Hooker concerning the use of the property. Hooker wanted to require that the donated premises "be used for park purposes only, in conjunction with a school building to be constructed upon premises in proximity to" them. And it wanted the board to agree that, should the property ever cease serving as a park, title to it would revert to Hooker. Instead of these restrictions, which the board rejected, the company had to settle for the liability provisions and warnings in the last paragraph of the deed hammered out in meetings between Hooker and board representatives.

On April 28, 1953, Hooker's secretary and general counsel, Ansley Wilcox—the same man who later, as the company's vice president and general counsel, was to be the author of the letter read out at the meeting of the Board of Education on November 21, 1957—submitted to the board the final draft of the deed. Nine days later, the board's attorney, Boniello, wrote to the board that, because of the provisions contained in the deed's closing paragraph, "In the event that the Board shall accept this deed, it is my opinion that there is placed upon the Board the risk and possible liability to persons and/or property injured or damaged as a result thereof arising out of the presence and existence of the waste products and chemicals upon the said lands referred to in the said deed." In short, the board's own attorney at the time was emphasizing to his client that if it were to accept the Canal it would be getting as part of the package liability for personal and property damage, which ultimately happened to homeowners in the area surrounding the Love Canal.

Nonetheless, on May 7, 1953, the board voted unanimously to accept the deed. Similarly, the board had voted unanimously to accept the deed to the site of the 66th Street School; that deed's reference to radioactivity at the site served as no deterrent either. Both sites, incidentally, had already, on December 30, 1952, been approved by the Niagara Falls Planning Board.

In August 1953, before construction work had begun on the school, the board voted (unanimously) to remove 4,000 cubic yards of "fill from the Love Canal to complete the top grading" at another school, on 93rd Street, whose construction was already well under way. This school, like the one on 99th Street nearby, is now closed down because of public concerns about the school children's exposure to chemical waste residues.

On January 21, 1954, the board approved the removal of 3,000 more cubic yards of fill from the Love Canal. On the same date, the architect for the 99th Street School wrote to board member Wesley Kester, chairman of the Buildings and Grounds Committee, saying that "the General Contractor...hit a soft spot in the ground. This turned out to be a filled drain trench which gave off a strong chemical odor. Upon further investigation the excavator made contact with a pit filled with chemicals and immediately stopped work in this area. The General Contractor contacted one of his employees who formerly worked on this property for one of the former owners. From this man we learned that...these pits were filled with chemical waste, some of which was in 55 gallon drums." Suggesting that these chemicals "might be a detriment to the concrete foundations," the architect advised soil tests with a view toward possible "revisions of building location," and the building was shifted 30 feet eastward.

When the *Buffalo Courier-Express*, in the wake of the recent recognition of chemical seepage in the Love Canal area, interviewed the architect about this in 1980, he "said the records indicated only 'poor soil conditions' as the reason for the move." The newspaper's reporters didn't say that this was a gross understatement, apparently because they had never gone to the Board of Education to see the letter from which I've just quoted, which shows that the records indicate a lot more than just "poor soil conditions."

A set of architect's plans dated August 18, 1955, reveals that another 10,000 cubic yards of soil were to be removed from the top of the canal in order to grade the surrounding area. Part of the area from which this soil was to be scooped out had been filled with Hooker's wastes. The grading was executed as shown in these plans. Later in the year, the Buildings and Grounds Committee donated some of the property immediately surrounding the school to the city so that streets and sidewalks could be paved. (The school building had been completed and its doors opened to 500 students in February 1955.)

On June 25, 1956, the architect wrote to the contractor for the school's playground, changing the location of the kindergarten play area "so as not to interfere with the apparent chemical deposit" and informing him that "this revision has been approved by Dr. Small, Superintendent of Schools." In an October report on this contractor's work, the architect reiterated that "these changes were discussed with school authorities" and had been made "because a chemical dump occurred at the originally located play area." The architect further pointed out that "these chemical pits are continuously settling."

The whole character of this correspondence between the architect and the board and contractors is in the manner of a somnambulist executing his accustomed routines, as in a deep, quiet fog that is never interrupted by the sound of the 55-gallon drums clanking around in the pits. One would be led to believe that they had signed the Love Canal deed with their eyes closed and their ears shut. The superintendent of schools approved relocation of the play areas so as to avoid "chemical deposits" and "chemical pits" and never once took it upon himself to advise the architect that more was at stake here than "detriment to the concrete foundations" due to "chemical pits...continuously settling." It is evident that the architect had never seen the deed. He and the contractor had to *discover* that this place had once been a chemical dump. The superintendent *knew* that it had been; he had been present at the drilling of test holes at the site; he had read the deed but evidently never imparted any wisdom therefrom to the architect or the contractor. He didn't tell them, for example, about the danger of injury or death.

The Board was finally jarred awake in November 1957. The precipitating event was a proposal from two developers who owned land on another site that the board was hungrily eyeing. The developers had suggested a trade whereby they would have gotten chunks of the Love Canal property in return for their properties plus some cash. The deal would have netted the board $11,000, and Wesley Kester and the rest of the Buildings and Grounds Committee were strongly in favor of it. But Hooker got wind of the proposal and was just as strongly opposed.

Hooker sent its attorney, Arthur Chambers, to attend the meeting of the board on November 7. As reported in the *Niagara Gazette* the next day, Chambers admonished the Board of Education that it had "a certain moral responsibility in the disposition of the land." After reminding the board that chemicals were buried under the surface, he explained that this "made the land unsuitable for construction in which basements, water lines, sewers and such underground facilities would be necessary." He referred to "negotiations at the time the land was deeded to the board," in which Hooker had urged that it be used only for surface constructions or parks. According to the board minutes from that evening, Chambers conceded "that his company could not prevent the Board from selling the land or from doing anything they wanted to with it," but he made clear Hooker's "intent that this property be used for a school and for parking. He further stated that they feel the property should not be divided for the purpose of building homes and hoped that no one will be injured."

The head of the Buildings and Grounds Committee, Wesley Kester, was furious. According to the article in the *Niagara Gazette*, he spluttered, "The land is a liability to us. There's something fishy someplace. Now they tell us it shouldn't be used." The battle lines were now clearly drawn.

Hooker was determined to prevent, if it could, the selling of this land to subdividers. The showdown came at the board meeting of November 21. Arthur Chambers again made his appearance, this time reinforced with a lengthy letter from the company's vice president, Ansley Wilcox, in which the board was reminded in no uncertain terms of the details of the mostly verbal negotiations and unwritten promises that had preceded the transfer of this property to the board more than four years earlier. In addition, Hooker's position on the proposed sale was again stated. According to the board minutes, "They feel very strongly that subsoil conditions make any excavation undesirable and possibly hazardous." As the *Niagara Gazette* quoted him the next day, Chambers told the board, "There are dangerous chemicals buried there in drums, in loose form, in solids and liquids." The *Buffalo Courier-Express*, too, referred to Chambers's speech about this "chemical-laden ground."

But perhaps the deciding factor in the board's ultimate vote wasn't the address by Arthur Chambers so much as the letter from Ansley Wilcox. Now even Wesley Kester's memory was refreshed. One no longer heard from him, "Now they tell us...," since, as Wilcox pointed out, they'd told it all before.

As I stated earlier, Wilcox's letter was being heard this evening by an audience that included, besides Kester himself, other key people on the board who had been involved in the negotiations with Hooker during 1952 and 1953. It contains the most thorough recounting of these negotiations on record anywhere, and the officials present protested not a single item in Hooker's recounting—not that Hooker had been approached by Small and other representatives of the board in the interest of acquiring the property; nor that Hooker had "explained in detail to Dr. Small the use which we were making of the property"; nor that Hooker had expressed its reluctance "to sell the same, feeling that it should not be used for the erection of any structures"; nor that the school board was nevertheless "so desirous of acquiring the same" that its representatives had brought up the option of condemnation proceedings; nor that Hooker had then agreed to donate the property subject to certain restrictions upon its use; nor that Hooker had proposed and the board had refused to agree that the Love Canal property be used "for park purposes only" and that the school building be constructed only on premises "in proximity to" the same; nor that any of these events had transpired in the way described, which indeed made Hooker look like the opposite of the negligent and shortsighted company it is now widely thought to have been. In fact, as evidenced by Wilcox's letter, Hooker was adamant in its long-range view, noting "that even though great care might be taken" in development of the property, "as time passes the possible hazards might be overlooked [and] injury to either persons or property might result."

The board's vote that evening was practically unprecedented. They split 4 to 4, with one member abstaining, and thus failed to pass Wesley Kester's resolution to sell the land. For once, the board did not vote unanimously; they had been shaken awake from their slumber.

As it turns out, these tumultuous board meetings of November 1957 were just so much "sound and fury signifying nothing" anyway. Apparently unbeknownst to Hooker, on the very same two November days when the company's representatives were urging the board that the subsurface chemicals made the land unsuitable for underground construction, city workmen were busy at the canal constructing a sewer that punctured both of its walls and the clay cover. From September through December 1957, work was in progress on this sanitary sewer between 97th and 99th streets beneath Wheatfield Avenue, a soon-to-be-paved street that lay right across the middle of the canal property.

This sewer pipe was laid 10 feet below the surface on a gravel bed and covered with gravel, providing a highly permeable violation of both canal walls. Any loose and liquid chemicals buried in this part of the canal could now escape, flowing along the gravel sewer bed not only under Wheatfield but also under 97th and 99th streets, and so throughout the neighborhood. To top this all off, a manhole was dug from the top of the canal down through the fill to this sewer system 10 feet below the surface.

Whether or not any of Hooker's chemicals were in fact buried in this part of the canal is not clear from public records. Hooker says that its practice was to fill various parts of the canal, creating an earthen dam with clay, pumping out the standing water, dumping waste to within four feet of the surface, then covering the section with clay. From Board of Education maps indicating the approximate location of Hooker and city wastes in the canal, and another map showing the location of streets and the 99th Street School, it can be estimated that Wheatfield Avenue crossed over the canal at a spot just south of a Hooker dumping area. It is doubtful, however, that these maps are precise enough to make a positive determination. One of them carries a notation showing that the Hooker dumping spot in question—the same one that, by the same approximations, would have been invaded at its northern end during construction of the school building—was used by Hooker to dispose of "fly ash, trash, and HGI spent cake," the latter, according to a Hooker spokesman, being an abbreviation for lindane (a chlorinated hydrocarbon pesticide more toxic than DDT).

Whether or not this sewer was laid through Hooker chemicals, however, one thing is clear from the record: Hooker was opposed to *any* construction through *any* part of the canal, precisely because of such risks. And work on this sewer system was being done by the city of Niagara Falls at the same time as the warnings that such construction was "dangerous," "injurious," and not "safe" were appearing in the local newspapers. But nobody made the connection; it is as though the printed word had not existed. The sleepwalkers kept bumping around in the night. Hooker was protesting into an abyss; no one was there who would hear and who would make connections between the real world and the printed warnings. Yet now Hooker is being excoriated.

This marked the first time in history that the canal walls had been penetrated. Maps in the city engineer's office show that there were no sewers into the canal before this one. But another was soon to be built. This was a storm sewer under Read Avenue. It was put in between May and September 1960 and penetrated only the west canal wall, running from a catch basin sunk into the canal out to 97th Street. Again, the sewer bed was gravel.

The drawings of these sewers are available for public inspection at the office of the city engineer in the town hall. One member of the public who, it seems, never cared to look at them—nor at the voluminous printed records and correspondence regarding Love Canal that are also available at the Board of Education—is Michael Brown, the author of the Pulitzer-prize-nominated book on the subject of waste dumping.

In addition to these publicly recorded breaches of the canal walls, there were two other, though lesser, man-made incursions upon the surface of the canal: one a French drain that the school board had placed around the school, the other an illegal catch basin put in by a 97th Street homeowner. Both of these were noted by Stephen Lester, who, under the auspices of the New York State Department of Transportation, served as a consultant to Love Canal area residents during remedial work on the canal. Of course, like the sewers put in by the city, Hooker had nothing to do with these constructions.

Following Hooker's successful defeat of the Buildings and Grounds Committee's proposal to sell Love Canal property to developers in 1957, the board sought every means possible to transfer liability for the property to somebody else. They wanted to dump the canal like a hot potato. First, they tried to palm it off onto the local Junior Chamber of Commerce for a playground area. But the Jaycees wouldn't move ahead without liability insurance, which, it seems, no firm was willing to supply. So that deal fell through. Then, on June 2, 1960, the Board "dedicated to the City" the section of canal property that lay north of the school. Hooker's restrictive provisions were included in the deed.

All that remained to unload now was the southern section. This was put up for public auction in December 1961. On the bidding sheet was duly imprinted the last paragraph of the deed from Hooker, with all those ghoulish warnings, and with one revealing addition: the indemnification clause to protect Hooker was now expanded to include the Board of Education, so that the board would pass liability along with the property. The difference this time was that the new owner would be receiving the property in dangerous condition and, in spite of the warnings in the deed, without any mention of all of Hooker's admonitions concerning suitable use of the property.

When the sole bid was opened, the board found that they had been offered $1,200, which they voted unanimously to accept. The fellow who bought the land—a former firefighter, now a motel keeper, by the name of Ralph Capone—ended up paying $5,400 in local paving assessments and $1,500 in property taxes, even though the city, every time he tried to get a building permit to develop 50 or so houses, confronted him with regulations that, as he later put it, "would have cost me millions." Then in 1972 the city ordered him to do $100,000 worth of work on his plot "to correct...strong chemical odors permeating from ground surface" and to alleviate "potentially hazardous conditions" there. Finally, after spending a total of $13,000 on the property, he gave up in 1974 and sold this bundle of headaches to a friend for $100.

Capone says that when he bought the property for $1,200 he had considered himself lucky. The release clause on the bidding sheet and in the deed had struck him as having been just so much lawyerese, hardly meriting a second wink. As he recently put it in an interview with the *Niagara Gazette*'s Paul Westmoore, "Back then I never would have believed a public body would have sold land it felt was dangerous." In fact, however, the board had known quite well what it was selling; and the minutes of the board, under the date of January 4, 1962, show the following reaction to Capone's bid: "Three members of the committee visited this plot of land on 99th Street and checked from one corner to the other. We all agreed that, if we could sell the property, it was the thing to do."

It is on the question of apportioning blame for Love Canal that the media have fallen down the most. Practically every level of government has been involved over the years in violating either the canal's walls or the protective clay cover that Hooker says it had laid four feet thick on top of its wastes. Even the New York State Department of Transportation, which now shares major responsibility for remedial work on the canal with New York's Department of Health and the federal Environmental Protection Agency, ripped into the canal in 1968, at the southern end where Hooker had done most of its dumping. In the construction of an expressway and the moving of Frontier Boulevard northward, chemicals were contacted, and Hooker was requested to, and did, cart away 40 truckloads of chemical wastes. Just as Hooker had worried in 1957, as time passed the possible hazards of construction on the property had been put totally out of mind.

Quite in line with media reports, then, which have picked up on very little of this governmental involvement in the Love Canal disaster, is the lawsuit filed in December 1979 by the Justice Department on behalf of the EPA, seeking to collect from Hooker $124.5 million for cleaning up the Love Canal area. Evidently, with the public so misled, the government's lawyers thought they could get away with laying all the blame at the doorstep of the only nongovernmental body involved, Hooker Chemicals and Plastics Corporation and its parent, the Occidental Petroleum Corporation.

Although the suit also names the Niagara Falls Board of Education, the city, the County Health Department, New York state, and UDC-Love Canal (a state agency set up to purchase the homes of families evacuated from the surrounding area), not one of these governmental bodies—and here again the media have missed a step—is implicated in the responsibility for the problems at Love Canal. "The City is named herein as a defendant only to insure that the remedial measures requested by the plaintiff [EPA] can be fully implemented by the City's action with regard to its own property." And so on and so on. For each of the governmental units named in the suit, there is a reassuring paragraph noting that it is so named only to enlist cooperation in remedial work.

The government's case against Hooker contains a great many charges and allegations that I have seen disproven in the documentary records at the Board of Education and the office of the city engineer. Hooker hasn't supplied me with its own supplementary documentation, but that wouldn't be necessary except on one point that has served as a focus for many of the EPA-Justice charges: the adequacy of the clay cover Hooker laid over its dumpings.

Residents of the Love Canal area have contended that at least some of Hooker's wastes were covered only with fly ash. These are recollections of what happened 30 years ago. There *is* evidence that there was plenty of fly ash in the area. Not only did Hooker itself use part of the canal to dump fly ash, which accumulated in the bottom of its furnaces, but school board records show that Hooker, and probably the city also, were asked to supply fly ash to fill in the portions of the canal that were still an open trench when the board took over the property. There is no evidence, however, that Hooker used fly ash to cover its chemical dumpings.

Hooker claims—and notes on the maps at the Board of Education dating from the early '50s tend strongly to support this—that the company laid four feet of clay

313

over its fill. Furthermore, a private engineering firm, Conestoga-Rovers Associates of Waterloo, Canada, hired by the city in 1979 to evaluate the Love Canal dumpsite, has concluded that Hooker's practices there cannot be faulted, even by the standards of the Resource Conservation and Recovery Act (RCRA) being implemented in 1980—the only existing federal law concerning the hows and wheres of industrial dumping. (Of course, even without a statute on the books, Hooker would be liable, subject to the relevant statute of limitations, for damage to third parties due to negligence, were its practices in fact negligent. But it would be hard for such a claim to get very far if Hooker's practices decades ago met and exceeded regulations, generally regarded as stringent, effected only in 1980.)

Although the Conestoga-Rovers report had not yet been delivered to the city at press time, Frank Rovers has stated to Senate staff members considering toxic-waste cleanup legislation that, as summarized by the Washington representative of the American Institute of Chemical Engineers, on whose RCRA Task Force Rovers was serving, "The design of the Love Canal site was well within the standards of RCRA. What went wrong with Love Canal can be attributed in large part to lack of monitoring, invasion of the site itself, and lack of remedial work." And the invading construction, which raised the need for remedial work, can only be laid at the feet of the school board, the city, and the state Department of Transportation. (The other main factor that precipitated the crisis was that in 1976 Niagara Falls experienced record rains that poured down into the by-then opened canal, forcing large quantities of the chemicals up and out; in October of that year, there surfaced the first reports of nearby basements being invaded by chemicals attributed to Love Canal.)

The EPA's own chief of hazardous waste implementation, Mr. William Sanjour, was quoted in *The New York Times* on June 30, 1980: "Hooker would have had no trouble complying with these (RCRA) regulations. They may have had a little extra paperwork, but they wouldn't have had to change the way they disposed of the wastes." Ironically, Sanjour's admission here was a bold and direct contradiction of a key charge leveled by the EPA itself in its suit against Hooker, filed in federal court six months earlier.

Reading this EPA-Justice Department lawsuit, one senses how desperate its drafters must have been to implicate Hooker on whatever grounds could be dredged up. In paragraph 23 it's charged that "two storm sewer systems...were built in 1952 before Hooker sold the Canal property to the Board." It is not claimed that the two sewers in question penetrated the canal walls; the fact is that these systems—Colvin–100th Street and Frontier–100th Street—didn't even come close. Interestingly, the suit does not mention the real villain-sewers, constructed in '57 and '60, which would, of course, have implicated party or parties other than Hooker.

In paragraph 35 we find that "vegetation in the vicinity of the Love Canal is suffering from stress." The Love Canal homeowners might wilt upon hearing that one, as though their own travails were not enough to bring Hooker down if Hooker is guilty.

Paragraph 108 informs us that "Hooker never applied to the Secretary of the Army for and does not have a permit authorizing the deposit of wastes into navigable waters at the Canal." This is one of the few allegations in the suit that

Hooker doesn't contest as false. Did you know that there are "navigable waters at the Canal"? Can you imagine sailing a ship upon this chemical dump? Well, of course, nobody's ever done it, nor even tried it. In fact, the canal never was navigable, even before it became a dump in the early '40s; it wasn't even being dug for that purpose when its construction was abandoned in 1910. "Navigable water," indeed.

But in the court of public opinion, Hooker is already adjudged guilty. Playing into the hands of the feds on this has been that intrepid "investigative reporter" Michael Brown, whose book, *Laying Waste*, has been praised to heaven, despite the fact that its tale of Love Canal is unrecognizable to anyone who has examined the actual documents. Jessica Mitford said, "This extraordinary and terrifying book is one of the best examples of tenacious, dedicated journalism I've ever read." Sen. Daniel P. Moynihan pronounced the book "strong, clear, credible, and humane." Ralph Nader said, "*Laying Waste* takes the reader on a macabre journey from the notorious Hooker Chemical Company waste dump at Niagara Falls to..." and called the volume "an advance briefing" on America's future of "cancerous, toxic cesspools left by callous corporations." Sen. Bill Bradley applauded it as "a clear call for the massive effort necessary to clean up the horrors." Paul Ehrlich praised it as "a vitally important book." Jane Fonda said, "I hope every American is awakened by this book." So let's dip a bit into *Laying Waste*.

On page 8 Brown says, "At that time [1953], the company issued no detailed warnings about the chemicals; a brief paragraph in the quit-claim document disclaimed company liability for any injuries or deaths that might occur at the site." He doesn't quote from the deed and mentions it again only once, curtly.

Would you know from his description of the "brief paragraph" (which I quoted in full earlier) that this is the longest paragraph in the entire deed, running 17 full lines of type, or that it speaks of these chemicals as being capable of *causing* injury and death? Furthermore, there's an innuendo here that is simply not true: that there is no evidence that Hooker had verbally warned the board repeatedly and in strong terms about the chemicals. Ansley Wilcox's letter, which Brown never even mentions in his book, is strong documentation to refute this innuendo.

On page 9 Brown says: "When I read [the Love Canal] deed I was left with the impression that the wastes would be a hazard only if physically touched or swallowed. Otherwise, they did not seem to be an overwhelming concern." That's his other reference to the deed, and it's equally misleading. Brown's introduction of "touching" and "swallowing" into the deed's restrictions are his own concoctions. Neither they nor any equivalents are in the deed, and even Brown's inference of them is drawn entirely from thin air. And although "injury" and "death"—which are in the deed—may "not seem to be an overwhelming concern" to Michael Brown, they did to relevant parties at the time, contrary to what Brown claims.

Also on page 9 Brown writes: "Ralph Boniello, the board's attorney, said he had never received any phone calls or letters specifically describing the exact nature of the refuse and its potential effects, nor was there, as the company was later to claim, any threat of property condemnation by the board in order to secure the land."

Boniello, however, had not *needed* any phone calls or letters. The very passage in the deed that Michael Brown saw as not "an overwhelming concern,"

Boniello warned his client at the time to take seriously. Boniello would later describe it as "like waving a red flag in front of a bull." The school board members "were forewarned. But all that they felt was that they were getting a big piece of land for free." If Brown had read the newspaper for which he himself was a reporter, the *Niagara Gazette*, he would have known that this was Boniello's opinion, because that's where it was quoted, on August 9, 1978, more than a year before Brown's book went to press. In this interview with Paul Westmoore, Boniello further stated: "I suggested they get a chemical engineer to inspect it [Love Canal]. They never did, to my knowledge."

On the property condemnation issue, my phone conversation with Boniello on the evening of October 16, 1980:

"Q: Is it possible that Hooker could have been verbally threatened with land condemnation at Love Canal by the board's representatives, such as Wesley Kester, head of the Buildings and Grounds Committee, while you might not have been informed of this?

"A: Oh yes. My function was only come in afterwards and close a deal, not to negotiate or make deals. The board decided what they wanted done and told me to draw up the papers. I was brought in after the fact. So all I can say is that I was never instructed to initiate condemnation proceedings on the Love Canal property. Whether condemnation was actually threatened verbally by the board is a question I am not competent to answer, since I wasn't in a position to know."

On page 10: "In 1958, the company was made aware that three children had been burned by exposed residues on the surface of the canal, much of which, according to the residents, had been covered over with nothing more than fly ash and loose dirt. Because it wished to avoid legal repercussions, the company chose not to issue a public warning of the dangers only it could have known were there." This strings three distortions together into one big lie.

First, Brown fails to mention anywhere in his book that not only Hooker but the city had been dumping into the canal; that this municipal waste may well have been covered over with fly ash and dirt; and that, in any case, the Board of Education had used fly ash at this site, as the record shows it had at other school sites, to grade the property. Therefore, Brown's slur of Hooker—the implication that fly ash and dirt is what Hooker had "really" laid over its wastes and that this gives the lie to the company's claim of having laid a clay cover over its dumpings—is at best a fudging of the available documentation and at worst a vicious distortion.

Second, Brown offers no evidence of Hooker's alleged wish "to avoid legal repercussions." The Board of Education, of course, in accepting the deed, had explicitly assumed liability for any injury attendant to its use of the property, which use, as we now know, had unearthed those chemicals. For its part, Hooker was apparently confident that its own practices at the canal had all been entirely legal, not just matching but surpassing the safeguards then in normal usage (which were zilch, even according to the EPA itself).

Third, as to the charge that Hooker "chose not to issue a public warning of the dangers only it could have known were there," this is false in both clauses. Brown never mentions in his book the very public warnings that Hooker had made in November 1957, which were published in the local newspapers at the time (including the *Niagara Gazette*, for which Brown later reported, but which, again, it appears he never consulted). These warnings preceded by less than a year this 1958 incident. So not only Hooker but the Love Canal area residents and the city government could have known of the dangers there.

Yet while Hooker was issuing these warnings the city was ripping through the canal to build a sewer. That the children's exposure to chemicals took place only months later lends plausibility to the hypothesis that this construction disturbed buried chemicals, just as Hooker had feared. Brown also fails to mention anywhere in his book the earlier warnings that Hooker had communicated to the board, also brought to public light in 1957; and he furthermore leaves entirely out of the picture the correspondence between the board and the school's architect, which shows how intimately the board was involved with these "chemical pits."

When Hooker, in a letter to the editor in the July 1980 *Atlantic*, pointed out in response to Brown's article on Love Canal in an earlier issue that the chemical dump under Hooker's management in the '40s and '50s had been found by a chemical engineer to be "well within the standards of RCRA"—the strict law of 1980—Brown's evasive printed reply, which ignored these very findings, was that it would not comply with RCRA because "those standards, among other things, propose that landfills not be located near so populated an area, and mandate that a landfill not be in a position to poison a water source. The Love Canal has leaked into the Niagara River, and probably is still doing so." Brown's reply neatly avoided mentioning the lack of evidence for any such leakage while Hooker had managed the canal and the abundant evidence of the dump's mismanagement by the school board and the city for decades afterward—the "invasion of the site itself" noted by the engineer hired by the city.

And for Michael Brown to claim that the Love Canal dump in 1953 had failed to meet RCRA standards because the surrounding neighborhood was subsequently to become populous simply makes one's mind reel. Even Brown himself, in his book, acknowledges that in 1953 the surrounding area had been sparsely populated. Well, Brown's book won three Pulitzer nominations, so who cares about such insignificant matters as accuracy and truth!

When I spoke with the president of the Love Canal Homeowners Association, Lois Gibbs, on October 17, 1980, I learned that Michael Brown has been one of her chief sources of information about Love Canal. This surprised me, because I expected that the information flow would have been in the reverse direction, since Brown relied so much on residents' testimony. But as it turned out, Gibbs knew practically nothing about the canal itself, although she has said a great deal about the dump.

This is a matter of some consequence, because Lois Gibbs has appeared prominently on network TV news programs and as a guest on national TV talk shows and has been much quoted in the newspapers and over the wire services. She has certainly been one of the chief sources for Mr. and Mrs. America's idea about what went wrong at Love Canal. Apparently, however, no interviewer or reporter has ever checked her facts; nor has she, so far as I am aware, ever been asked probing questions to determine the documentation for her positions.

As with Michael Brown, the basic thrust of her position is that, as she put it in response to my question, "Who was primarily responsible [for Love Canal]?": "I believe fullheartedly that Hooker is primarily." On Hooker's role at the canal, she said: "They left open avenues of swale, pipelines, and so forth. They didn't deposit the waste in 55-gallon drums, as they say they have. They also knew children were being burnt on the canal proper and never made that public knowledge. And when they told the Board of Education there were wastes buried there, they never truly explained what the wastes were and what the ramifications of the wastes moving around in the ground and surfacing in the school could cause."

Gibbs, I soon learned, is fond of snowing the listener with technical terminology that she herself, as it turns out, doesn't understand. So for the perplexed reader who, like myself, has never encountered the term *swale*—which she later defined for me as "underground stream beds"—I subsequently found that it refers to a line of surface-water runoff. Every plot of land necessarily has swales. As for her intended charge of underground streams at Love Canal, there is not a shred of evidence for the allegation. And what we know and don't know about "pipelines" will be made clear below.

As to her charge that Hooker "didn't deposit the waste in 55-gallon drums as they say they have, " Hooker's actual statement, as reported in the *Niagara Gazette* on November 22, 1957, was: "There are dangerous chemicals buried there in drums, in loose form, in solids and liquids." The rest of her statement is pure Michael Brown and has been dealt with earlier.

I asked her: "Are you aware that the Board of Education back in 1951 had drawn up a map of the Love Canal area and that it showed the assessed condemnation value of each property?" Her reply: "No." The head of the homeowners had never even gone to the Board of Education to check its records so as to make an informed judgment about the roots of their tragedy.

When I asked her about the sewer under Wheatfield Avenue, whose installation in 1957 may well have precipitated the ultimate catastrophe, she denied my assertion that it was "surrounded with gravel." She claimed that this underground excavation was instead "backfilled with clay." The city engineer could straighten her out on that one.

In response to my question whether she'd ever heard of the American Institute of Chemical Engineer's Task Force on RCRA and the findings of one of its members about why the Love Canal had seeped, she said, "No." But, she continued: "Let's pretend that the Canal hadn't been disturbed. It still would have leaked.

"Q: How so?

"A: Because there were farmers' field tiles that were connected to the canal, and these were clay pipes 6 inches to 8 inches in diameter.

"Q: When were these tiles put in?

"A: Probably before the canal was used as a dump. Furthermore, there are open avenues of swale, which are underground stream beds, that were backfilled with rubbish—not a solid fill.

"Q: Is this in Stephen Lester's report [which she had mentioned earlier]?

"A: I think so. If not, it's in Beverly Paigen's."

Beverly Paigen is not an engineer but a biologist, so of course her study had nothing to do with the structure of the canal. Instead, it was an epidemiological study of the incidence of health problems among Love Canal area residents. (This report created a sensation—and panic—when it was released in February 1979 with the conclusion that area residents showed high rates of pregnancy disorders, birth defects, and other illnesses. Subsequently, a five-member panel of scientists reviewed this study and concluded that it is "literally impossible to interpret" and "cannot be taken seriously as a piece of sound epidemiological evidence.")

Stephen Lester is not an engineer either. He is a toxicologist and environmental researcher hired by the New York Department of Transportation in 1979 to assist the Love Canal area residents during remedial work being done by the department. In the course of observing that work, says Lester, he did see clay pipes running from the canal, which, he speculates, were probably used to draw water from the canal to irrigate the orchards that surrounded the area before it was built up.

Did they exist along the entire length of the canal? Had Hooker removed any such pipes or backfilled them with clay in the sections used by the company for dumping chemicals? Lester's report has no answers to such questions; nor does the city engineer's office, which contains no records of the existence or location of such pipes; nor do the people working at Hooker 30 years later. But it strains credulity to believe that Hooker would have chosen this site, prepared a section at a time for dumping, and covered its wastes with clay—rather than just dumping anywhere into the canal's waters—and not have seen and attended to any such clay pipes. Of course, of what the Army did when it dumped toxic wastes there, we know nothing. And what would have happened had the canal not been disturbed after Hooker owned it, we shall never know.

Love Canal may or may not have polluted its neighborhood beyond repair. But the question now is, has it polluted the media beyond repair? Except for *The Wall Street Journal*'s publication of the minutes of the two November 1957 school board meetings under the headline "What Hooker Told Whom, When About Love Canal," and the *Journal*'s two editorials on the facts therein, none of the national media has delved into the history of the Love Canal mess. This story has been butchered in the press. The executioners have been a motley band, led by the U.S. Justice Department, the EPA, the New York state departments of you-name-it, Michael Brown, and Lois Gibbs. Why has their joint exercise in public deception been so overwhelmingly successful? More to the point, why hasn't Hooker's counterfight so far been more effective?

It makes me blush to say it, but in an op-ed article of mine in *The New York Times* in late 1979, the editor there cut out a slashing comment I had made in a preliminary draft, calling Hooker's actions at Love Canal "criminal." I've learned since then to be more circumspect about the truthfulness of what I read (and write!) in the papers. There genuinely are big corporate criminals, and the public's outrage at this, and at their frequent success, is good and healthy—but only if one can still keep one's eyeglasses clean when approaching the facts of each particular case. But that's hard to do.

It hasn't helped that Hooker and its parent, Occidental Petroleum Corporation, have met the public-relations challenge of Love Canal with a practically unbroken string of catastrophically bad decisions. At first, when the story was strictly a local one, before Love Canal had hit the national press in the summer of 1978, Hooker's response was to stonewall. The company refused to provide even basic information requested by both the homeowners and the local news reporters. After Love Canal exploded across the nation's front pages during the first half of 1979, cracks started appearing in Hooker's stonewall, but this change got under way too slowly and too late.

In the summer of 1980 the company published a booklet, *Love Canal: The Facts*, which for the first time presented Hooker's detailed public defense against the accusations that were now being hurled at the firm from every corner. Most of the damage to the company had already been done, however. Michael Brown and Lois Gibbs had made their starring appearances on the network TV talk shows, and the ghastly pictures of Love Canal's chemical oozings had finished their sensational runs on the nightly news shows—with prominent mention of the fact that the canal had once been a Hooker dump.

Even now, the response of Hooker and Occidental remains strictly defensive. Having permitted the Love Canal spark to ignite a conflagration that (according to present Wall Street estimates) has burned off a half billion dollars' worth of Occidental Petroleum stock value, the best that Hooker and its parent firm can come up with is still a meek squeak: "We didn't do it." Hooker has not sued Michael Brown and his book publisher, Random House, for libel; to the public, this means that Hooker must be guilty.

When I asked Hooker's PR department why the company isn't challenging in a court of law the allegations by Brown and others, I was told, in effect, that that was a matter for the legal department—and that none of Hooker's lawyers was talking to any reporters. Then, on November 3, I phoned Occidental Petroleum, which referred me to Philip Wallach Associates, the parent corporation's public relations counsel. Wallach told me that it was he who had advised Occidental not to file a libel suit against Michael Brown and Random House, because "to do so would only have given the book free publicity." When I asked Wallach, "But isn't it sometimes the case that the best defense is a good offense?" he agreed with me that this was so. And when I further inquired why he was more concerned about preventing some negative publicity for Brown's book than he was about giving his own bloodied corporate client some desperately needed positive exposure—and especially increased credibility—he told me, "Well, you have a point there. I suppose maybe I should reconsider." That's where the matter now stands. To think that $500 million of a corporation's stock value can hang on decisions made in such a manner!

Can more Love Canals happen? There's no reason why not. Niagara Falls is not the only town that's been gung ho on technology without concern for consequences. This kind of attitude may still prevail there; it certainly can be found elsewhere, and Love Canal may well turn out to have been just the opening battle in a long hot war between the present and the future.

Despite the popular myth that Love Canal is the result of a single corporation's greed and heartlessness, the actual explanation is far more complex. It's clear to anyone who digs into this matter that Hooker may well have been the only party to the affair to behave responsibly. Hooker chose an exceptionally fine chemical dumpsite; it ceded the dump to the school board under circumstances in which the threat of condemnation was real and the reality of condemnation was already under way for adjoining properties; it warned the school board that the chemicals could kill and insisted that the board pass this warning on to any subsequent owner of the property; it urged the board not to construct the school or any other buildings directly over the canal; it protested the prospect of any subsurface construction on the canal.

These warnings were repeatedly ignored, however, by the governmental bodies involved in desecrating this chemical tomb: the school board itself, the City Planning Board, the city engineer, and the state Department of Transportation. In addition, other governmental agencies have been busy spreading misinformation about the canal: the Niagara County Health Department, the state Department of Health, the U.S. Environmental Protection Agency, and the U.S. Department of Justice.

Despite all these nefarious governmental involvements, nothing has happened up to the present time to reduce the likelihood of similar governmental crimes being committed in the future. Even if the new federal legislation on waste dumps, RCRA, proves effective against corporate violators, it could never be effective against governmental bodies. Just on the outside chance that an RCRA suit might someday be filed against a town, school board, or other public agency, what would be the probability that any governmental criminals would be penalized? No matter how guilty they might be, it is the taxpayers who would end up paying the tab on any resulting fines, and it is unlikely that any government bureaucrat would be imprisoned, even if his crimes included the deaths of innocent victims.

When the Justice Department and the EPA joined the fray in December 1979 with their suit against Hooker, they were tacitly acting to protect the interests of all the governmental agencies that throughout the years seem clearly to have produced the Love Canal mess. The federal authorities could instead have chosen to file charges against those governmental bodies, but this would have made some important New York state politicians unhappy during an election year—and New York was a crucial state for Jimmy Carter. With the press and the homeowners screaming, the federal government apparently felt compelled to "do something" about the matter, and Hooker turned out to be the most suitable punching bag under the circumstances.

The federal attorneys must certainly have seen much of the evidence that I've presented here and so must have known how shoddy their case against Hooker really was, yet they slogged through their legal mire and came up with the obligatory political document. If instead they'd sued the governmental agencies, that would have made considerable news but even more considerable political enemies. It would also have deflated the Michael Brown bubble, but why do that when it could be exploited, since Brown had conveniently placed blame upon the same scapegoat that the politicians now found so suitable?

Perhaps because of the visibility of what went wrong at Love Canal, even if there has been little attempt to understand *how* it went wrong, there is an increased public awareness that in environmental matters the future *doesn't* take care of itself. But that would not alone prevent future Love Canals. It would not get at any of the fundamental structural problems that aided and abetted the environmental disaster.

At the very least, governmental criminals should not be protected from paying the price for their actions. And when businesses share in the blame, they too should be hotly pursued for every ounce of damage to persons and property. If nothing else, that's the protection that should be afforded citizens by a proper system of property rights, whereby you may do what you will with your property and what is in it and on it, so long as it does not infringe on my rights to my life, my liberty, and my property.

Certainly the worst thing we could do would be to hand to the corporate world some of the same kind of protection from responsibility that we've allowed government officials. Yet, ironically, one of the hottest new items from Congress—the recently passed "Superfund" legislation for cleaning up toxic chemicals in the environment—will serve, in part, to lessen the risks of mismanagement on the part of individual firms involved in disposing of toxic chemical wastes.

Any environmentalist who believes that this set-up is a super idea should pay heed to our experience with legislatively limited liability in another industry where the risks of injury are high: nuclear power. Back in the 1950s, when "the peaceful atom" was but a fervent dream on the part of the Atomic Energy Commission, Congress stepped in as the promulgator of devil-may-care. Faced with a drawing-board industry unable to obtain insurance (for reasons that themselves have much to do with government—see "Who Caused Three Mile Island?", August 1980), Congress passed the Price-Anderson Indemnity Act in 1957, dictating that, in the event of a major nuclear accident, the first $500 million in claims would be footed by U.S. taxpayers, the next $60 million by the firm (through its insurance), and anything over and above that—practically everything in a serious accident—would simply go uncompensated.

The nuclear-power industry was born as a direct result of this legislation. While it may well have come into existence anyway—eventually, and when reactor designers and so on had satisfied insurers' safety experts that nuclear-power generation was insurable—the indisputable effect of this legislation has been to reduce the incentives for individual firms or the industry as a whole to make sure that they are employing and coming up with the best, safest procedures possible.

How could we even think of imposing a similar system upon the public as a way of "controlling" the chemical industry? Said Sen. Jennings Randolph in urging the Senate's passage of its Superfund bill: "We cannot afford another Love Canal." But the senator entirely misses the point. Any society that socializes risks while it privatizes rewards is earning every Love Canal it gets.

Debunking Doomsday

By Phil Gramm

August 1978

The doomsday philosophy has more credibility today than it's ever had in the history of mankind. Why that's so is difficult to determine, but no doubt the computer has given new credibility to a type of prediction that is thousands of years old. It's important to realize that all doomsday philosophies have a central scientific core in that they are based on data—or at least purported data—about the world. So we find doomsday philosophies accompanying the rudimentary beginnings of science in the time of the ancient Greeks.

The Greeks viewed the world as possessing a fixed stockpile of resources, and they viewed man's role within this conception as one of adaptation. When man was successful at adapting, he had prosperity and plenty, and when he was unsuccessful he faced hardship and starvation. And using this conception of the fixed stockpile of resources, man has throughout history predicted doom for mankind.

The ancient Athenians, for example, were very concerned about what would happen to the resource base in ancient Greece if the other city-states approached the level of living that had been achieved in Athens. Our best economic and anthropological estimates are that, when this concern was a hotly debated topic in Athens, per-capita income was $8.00 or $10 per annum. Yet the Athenians were probably right in their concern that, given the resource base defined by their technology, it might have been difficult, if not impossible, for the other city-states during that period to achieve Athens' level of living.

Using this basic concept of a fixed stockpile of resources as a fundamental assumption about the world, we've seen numerous predictions of doom. Economics has been in the forefront of these predictions—ranging from the new forecasts of ecological collapse to the old Malthusian predictions that we would see exponential growth in population, arithmetic growth in the means of production, and thus ultimate starvation. Of course, Malthus never foresaw the great technological innovations in agriculture and therefore never envisioned the possibility that someday a foolish government might pay people not to grow food.

All the predictions of doom floating around have basically three things in common. One, they assume a fixed stockpile of resources. Two, they assume that technology is either fixed or bounded. Three, all of these predictions that have had a timetable which has elapsed have proven to be wrong. And they've failed to materialize for a fundamental reason: The basic premise is false. Resources are not fixed.

What practical man has known and proven for thousands of years, modern science in this century has finally realized. *Resources are not fixed.* They are a function of science and technology. Man creates resources like he creates everything else—by rearranging what he finds in nature. As science and technology progress, new resources are born and old resources die. We need only remember that for the man who ran naked in the forest, the only mineral resource was a stone. Of course, by learning to sharpen that stone he increased his resource state a millionfold. And we, by using resources—mineral resources in particular, which to the man running in the forest were valueless—have been able to walk on the moon. Whether or not that was a productive exercise, it was a tremendous technological achievement.

What this indicates is that there are only two constraints on the resources available to us. One is the limit to our imaginations, but we really shouldn't be particularly concerned about this constraint, because very little that has ever bound society has been caused by its pressures. There is every reason, however, to be very concerned about the second constraint—the limits on our freedom of action.

If one looks at historical experiences, nations and civilizations do not die by exhausting their resource base. Nations and civilizations die by consuming their institutions, by destroying the process that has historically provided the incentive for civilizations to arise and flourish and for people to solve problems. So it seems difficult to believe that the fundamental problem in the American economy today is an energy depletion problem. It seems more likely that the energy problem, "the energy crisis," is simply a manifestation of another problem, a very real problem, in society.

In fact, there is no evidence whatsoever to substantiate on a historical basis the contention that we woke up in October of 1973 and found the world had run out of petroleum products. There is no radical change to be seen in the factors that economists have to rely on to judge the economic scarcity of a resource. History has seen its "resource crises," and by studying them economists have discovered a traditional price pattern for a resource that is becoming exhausted in an economic sense. First, there is a prolonged period of increase in the price of that resource relative to the general increase in prices. Such a process continues until the same creative genius that is at first diverted to trying to augment the supply of the diminishing resource finally is transferred to producing an alternative to that resource and ultimately destroys its market.

The history of the whale-oil crisis is a perfect example of the exhaustion of a natural resource in an economic sense— exhaustion to a point. There were clear indications by 1800 that whales were being killed more rapidly than they were replenishing themselves, and by 1820 it started to show up in price. Then, over a 40-year period, there was a sustained, consistent increase in the price of whale oil. The price increased 400 percent in constant purchasing-power dollars. And it elicited the standard consumer response and called forth the standard producer response—tremendous technological innovation in the whaling industry. Production in the industry increased 1,000 percent in these 40 years, despite clear evidence that fewer whales were available in 1860 than in 1820. The rise in relative price year after year triggered a transformation of investments in the whaling industry and, ultimately, in the energy industry, so that we see man moving from the Arctic Ocean to Pennsylvania, looking for a new energy resource.

Now, if one looks at the price pattern of energy in the American postwar period, it does not fit the historical pattern of resource exhaustion. If we take the prices of energy resources consumed by the American public—gasoline, heating oil consumed directly, and natural gas—and we weight each of these prices by the amount spent by the public on them, we can create an energy price index much as the Bureau of Labor Statistics calculates a consumer price index. If we then take this energy price index and deflate it by the wholesale price index, we get real energy prices, adjusted for the increase in the general price level. So we can look at what happened from 1950 until the Arab embargo.

On a five-year basis, this is the pattern. From 1950 to 1955 real energy prices fell 3.1 percent. From 1955 to 1960, real prices fell 3.9 percent. In the next period they were down 6.5 percent, and in the next, 8.1 percent. And from 1970 to October 1973 real energy prices fell by 9.4 percent on a five-year basis. This is not the price pattern of a resource becoming depleted in an economic sense. Quite the contrary. It's the price pattern of a resource becoming more abundant. What happened with the Arab embargo was the imposition of political constraints that reacted with a deep-seated problem that had been building in American energy production for two decades and, in the process, triggered a worldwide energy problem. But this is a far cry from the traditional price pattern of the economic depletion of a resource.

There is no doubt that the petroleum era will come to an end—but not because we've run out of petroleum. The era will come to an end because as we begin to press up against economic constraints we will, if individual initiative is maintained, experience the kind of stimuli that can function through the system to engender the creation of a new energy resource, or a myriad new energy resources. So we must totally reject the notion espoused by President Carter and the president of Exxon and the great bulk of the petroleum industry that the age of cheap energy is over. There is absolutely no historical evidence to suggest that. In fact, the evidence is that, in the whole energy consumption history of mankind, there has not been a new energy resource that in terms of a fundamental measure of constant value did not ultimately turn out to be cheaper than the previous energy resource. New energy resources come on line only when they're cheaper than old energy resources in terms of new technological development—at least in a society that allows any semblance of a market system to function.

Our "energy problem" is not that we are running out of petroleum—or "cheap energy." The real problem is that we have not let the market system work. We have stifled the production of energy in the United States. There has been a great deal of discussion about the impact of Federal Power Commission price controls on natural gas; how this has stifled the development of a cheap and clean burning domestic fuel; how by maintaining an artificially low interstate price, the consumer in the Midwest and Northeast has gotten away with paying lower prices than the Texas consumer. The last is political rhetoric and nonsense. They *should* be so lucky to pay $2.25 per thousand cubic feet for the natural gas.

The really significant result of the artificially low prices for natural gas is that they have been forced to buy substitutes that have cost them as much as $6.25 per thousand cubic feet. In the recent past the pipelines going into the Northeast have been 15-percent empty, which is by no means a measure of the real shortage of natural gas in the Northeast. In buying synthetic gas, in buying liquefied Algerian gas, and in buying heating oil, consumers there have spent more money to make up for that 15-percent shortage than they spent to buy the 85 percent of natural gas that was delivered. In reality, FPC regulation of natural gas prices, like every price ceiling ever imposed in the whole history of mankind, drives up prices to the American consumer, stifles technological development, and benefits in overall economic terms only those who produce fuels more expensive than natural gas.

Similar considerations apply to the petroleum industry, to environmental restrictions that have held up drilling in the continental shelf, to the Alaska pipeline, to the lag in licensing of nuclear reactors. All point to the conclusion that the real constraint that we face—and probably the most serious constraint that faces the American people today—is a constraint on our initiative and a constraint on our freedom of action. We *could* face a real energy crisis. Our children might live in a world that is "incapable" of meeting its energy demands. That will not occur, however, because people are too stupid to do something about it. It will not occur because our schools stop turning out people who can drill oil and gas wells, who can convert coal, who can find and produce and market resources that we've never dreamed of. It will only happen if we foolishly destroy the incentive system that rewards the hard-working and the inventive. That system, of course, is the free-enterprise system—the only legitimate consumer movement in the whole history of civilization.

The real issue is not how much oil and gas exists in the continental shelf of the United States, or what volume of natural gas can be found in tight gas formations all over the country. There are those who are competent to make those assessments, although they're still not very good at it. It's important to remember that scientists have a terrible record of predicting the future. In the 1870s, after crude petroleum had broken the whale-oil market, the U.S. Revenue Commission sought to get Congress to invest in the development of new technology to gasify coal for use in the 1880s and 1890s, when our petroleum deposits were expected to be exhausted. In December of 1900 the U.S. Geological Survey, which basically was in cahoots with Standard Oil, went to Beaumont, Texas, did a study of Spindle Top, and concluded in a report that would be published after January 10 that, despite some favorable findings in Corsicana, Texas, oil would never be produced west of the Mississippi. On January 10, of course, a well came in on that hill outside Beaumont that, while it flowed, produced more oil than all the other wells in all the rest of the world combined. If you want to know about the future, you need to talk to science-fiction writers, not scientists. Science-fiction writers generally share a belief, borne out by history, in human inventiveness, in humans' capacity to solve problems.

And when we ponder how that creativity is to be directed toward our present problem, it is important to look at the system that has worked in the past. There's a cliche among collectivists to the effect that, "Sure, the market system will work in doing things that are not very important. But in crucial areas, upon which our very existence depends, we can't rely on the market." That's a falsehood. We might rely on collectivism to produce goods that we don't really need and goods that we have a lot of substitutes for; but those things that we must have—that we cannot live without, at least in the manner in which we choose to live—those things have got to be reserved for private production, not government production. The sooner we let the same system that put bread on our table for lunch put gasoline back in our cars and cooling and heating back in our homes, the sooner we're going to get on with solving the "energy problem."

Apocalypse Whenever

By Andrew Ferguson

April 1990

Michael Clark is the executive director of Friends of the Earth, and he's a little anxious about this whole Earth Day thing. He's in a hurry. What's the rush? "We are driven by the fact that we don't have much time left to act, maybe 10 years," he told *The New York Times* late last year.

And you thought you had problems. The guy from the *Times* didn't say to Mike, "Yeah? Ten years? Then what happens?" because he didn't have to. The reporter, being an environmental reporter, already knows from talking to environmental activists (it's his job) what happens then: What happens then is it, the apocalypse, Armageddon, curtains, the end.

Environmentalists long ago learned what every auto mechanic and Bible-belt rabble-rouser and real estate panic artist has always known: Bad news is profitable news. As a sales device, the apocalypse—unlike, say, oil deposits in the North Sea—is an endlessly renewable resource. It never goes away. The sound of the ticking clock fetches us all. News of looming doom works today, it will work tomorrow and tomorrow and tomorrow—just as it worked yesterday and the day before.

It certainly worked 20 years ago, around the time the first Earth Day was getting cranked up. Eco-pests never descended to strapping on sandwich boards and walking the length of Hollywood Boulevard and back again calling sinners to repent (their Earth Shoes would have made the trek impossibly painful); they didn't need to.

They had the press. The first Earth Day thus gained rivers of ink and miles of footage on the evening news and managed to induce a kind of coast-to-coast, day-long hysteria in which millions of normally sane Americans did things they would never have dreamed of doing for a fraternity hazing.

Time magazine described some of the proceedings in an article titled "Memento Mori" (literally, I think, "Memo for Morons"): "At the University of Wisconsin, 58 separate programs were staged, including a dawn 'earth service' of Sanskrit incantations. Car wreckings—followed by interment of the beasts—were a common protest. Some students at Florida Technological University held a trial to condemn a Chevrolet...." In Cleveland, *Time* recounted cryptically, "a student held aloft a plastic bag full of garbage and intoned: 'This is my bag.'" (I don't understand it either.) There was much more: cooking cowpies, hugging pigs, listening to speeches by John Lindsay.

Why did Americans do such things? Because some of it was fun, of course, but more importantly because the end was near. Considering the reams of apocalyptic treatises then blanketing America, it's a wonder we didn't all start waving

327

bags of garbage. To every side the chorus was singing the same tune that Michael Clark is crooning today. Norman Cousins, the editor, announced that "the human race is operating under the starkest of deadlines." *Life* magazine told us that by 1980 city dwellers would need gas masks. And NBC's Edwin Newman, his sunken eyes darkening with portent, warned his viewers that by 1980 the mighty rivers of this great nation "would have reached the boiling point."

Scary, yes. But a skeptic could ask, with some justification: What does Norman Cousins, widely recognized even then as an all-purpose crank, know? Or the editors of *Life*, for that matter? And Edwin Newman—wasn't grammar his thing?

The tribe of apocalyptics understood that it helps if your witch doctor is indeed a *doctor*, and to silence the skeptics the movement enlisted one Paul Ehrlich as chief whooper-upper. He was catholic in his alarmism, but it was the subject of "overpopulation" that really set his bells to ringing. He became the Quasimodo of the cause.

Now, Dr. Ehrlich was an entomologist by training, and some immediately recognized that after many years of rigorous study he had lost the capacity to distinguish between an army of hideous little arthropods swarming over his desk in a Stanford laboratory and an upwardly mobile population of homo sapiens building tract houses in Palo Alto. Each for him was equally unpleasant; each brought chaos. But, hinged or unhinged, he *was* a doctor, and that seemed good enough for everybody. It was enough, in any event, for *Playboy* and *Look* and *Reader's Digest* and *McCall's* and the dozens of other slick magazines that got him to dispense his wisdom in their pages. And it was enough for Johnny Carson, who throughout the '70s made the bug man a regular guest on his show.

For Ehrlich had the tone just right. "We face a very real crisis this instant," he told *Reader's Digest* readers in 1968. *This instant*: petulant, barely choking down the sob, vaguely threatening to hold...my breath...until...you *pay attention to me*. But the tone, however undignified, was necessary; this was, let's not forget, apocalypse. Even if the world's food supply tripled by the year 2000, he continued in his *Digest* article, "it is already too late to prevent a drastic rise in the death rate through starvation." And how late is it, as Johnny's audience might have called out? "The time of famines will be upon us full-scale in 1975." But then a cruel shrug: "What's done is done."

Nevertheless, the inevitable end has a sunny side. It's already too late, but we still get to take *drastic action*. A Federal Department of Population and Environment, a head tax for families with children, mandatory birth-control education in the schools, lots of abortions, an end to "death control" (an apocalyptic term meaning "medical research"), and finally, soon or late, "compulsory birth regulation." Come again? "We might, for instance, institute a system whereby a temporary sterilant would be added to a staple food or to the water supply." Earth Day was a mother lode for fans of drastic action. And to think that right-wingers were worried about fluoride!

Had enough? Dr. Ehrlich lets no one off that easy. He leaves *Digest* readers with a dirge of questions to ponder. "We must look to the survivors," he writes, "if any."

"Will they have to wear smog masks as a matter of routine? [Yes! Haven't you been reading *Life*?] Will they enjoy mock steaks made from processed grass or seaweed? Will they accept regimentation and governmental control at a level previously unheard of? Above all, will they be able to retain their sanity in a world gone mad?"

The answer to the last question, quite obviously, is no. Dr. Ehrlich wouldn't let them. Before and during Earth Day and for years thereafter, he was inescapable, even if you were one of those rare Americans who never watched *The Tonight Show* or who never read *Look* or who never bought *Playboy* just for the articles. He called the American people a "cancer on the planet," and the cancer cooed. It embraced him, it cuddled with him, it set him upon its knee and bounced him up and down. "I'm booked a year ahead on personal appearances," he said in 1970, "and get around two dozen requests a day." His manifesto, *The Population Bomb*, sold a cool million, and he logged 80,000 miles a year. His vasectomy was covered in *Life*.

Apocalyptics is fun, as I say, and soon everybody was joining in. Eschatologists crowded the magazines, the op-ed pages, the airwaves. I have noted Norman and Ed, but space prevents me from servicing them all. Gaylord Nelson, then a senator from Wisconsin, deserves special mention, if only because he (along with several dozen competitors) claimed credit for devising Earth Day. He used that paternity to elbow his way into the pages of *Look* and grab a national audience.

There he relieved himself of several predictions, all ecstatically dreadful. The breathing masks, of course, will be de rigeur by the 1980s, but only when we're outdoors. He cites the secretary of the Smithsonian, S. Dillon Ripley, to the effect that by 1995, "between 75 and 80 percent of all the species of living animals will be extinct." Not that we'll have time to miss the furry koala or the cretinous buffalo or the gentle giraffe, for a mere five years later, the natural environment will no longer be able to sustain any life at all.

Nelson's prescriptions are much what you would expect of a senator from the state that gave us Robert LaFollette. Each urgently needed policy marches out with capital letters unfurled: a National Land Use Policy, a National Policy on Air and Water Quality, a National Policy on Resource Management, a National Policy on Oceans, a National Policy on Population. Having limned this impressive program, he makes the complaint that "thousands of government-agency offices are protected from public scrutiny by layer on layer of bureaucracy"—nothing, surely, that a National Policy on Bureaucratic Layers can't fix. And then, stirringly, he closes: "We need action. The cost of not acting will be far greater than anything we have yet imagined."

At this point the question naturally arises: How do we imagine a cost greater than the extinction of all life on earth by the year 2000? There's no evidence that anyone ever asked it of the Hon. Gaylord. Taken item for item, many of the eco-predictions were mutually exclusive by their very nature, and the key to understanding Earth Day then and now is to know that nature had absolutely nothing to do with it. And accuracy, thank God, had nothing to do with it either. We Americans never did, so far as I recall, get water rationing and a ban on flush toilets by 1974, though several eco-experts divined that these would be crucial; nor did we get food rationing by 1980; nor a 500-percent increase in dysentery by the mid-70s. (Imagine an outbreak of dysentery with no flush toilets!)

There was one other thing the apocalyptics were wrong about—Earth Day itself. A presidential candidate, Ehrlich predicted in 1970, would spring from the Day's fertile loins, and the doctor's own organization, Zero Population Growth, would form the nucleus of a new political party. Earth Day, he wrote, "is going to have a tremendous impact....The movement is going to generate a lot of civil disobedience, similar to what we saw in the early days of civil rights....Among other things, people are just going to stop paying their bills." Gladwin Hill, the national environmental reporter for *The New York Times*, said the occasion marked the beginning of "what may become the greatest movement ever to sweep the country." And the editors of *The Progressive* were also, as is their wont, wrong: Earth Day would "become the birthday of a new and more hopeful movement affecting all our lives in all ways."

Instead, as we now know, Earth Day 1970 went the way of all media events. It faded into the pages of *Look* and *Time* and *Newsweek*, yellowing in bound volumes, gathering dust in library stacks. It was a close call, however. And in the heaving bosom of every environmentalist there is a fountain of hope that never runs dry. Hence Earth Day 1990. The executive director of an organization boosting the great event, Christina Dresser, recently had this to say: "The point is not an event, but launching a decade of environmental activism." Don't worry. She'll be dead wrong.

The Green Road to Serfdom

By Virginia I. Postrel

April 1990

I f there is one popular cause in the 1990s, it is the environment. Motherhood and apple pie, baseball and the flag— all may be subjects of controversy. But the environment is beyond debate. As *Time* magazine puts it, "our stand on the planet is that we support its survival." Could any cause be more humane, or less questionable?

"Protecting something as wide as this planet is still an abstraction for many," said California Gov. Jerry Brown in 1979. "Yet I see the day in our lifetime that reverence for the natural systems—the oceans, the rain forests, the soil, the grasslands, and all other living things—will be so strong that no narrow ideology based upon politics or economics will overcome it." As we enter the '90s, Brown's prophecy seems to be coming true.

But beneath the rhetoric of survival, behind the Sierra Club calendars, beyond the movie-star appeals, lies a full-fledged ideology—an ideology every bit as powerful as Marxism and every bit as dangerous to individual freedom and human happiness. Like Marxism, it appeals to seemingly noble instincts: the longing for beauty, for harmony, for peace. It is the green road to serfdom.

If we are not to turn down its path, we must first recognize it for what it is. Just as socialism seduced many people by masquerading as an elaborate form of charity, so this green-ideology-without-a-name disguises itself as simple concern for a cleaner world. But there is a difference between the ordinary desire for clean air or pretty places to hike and the extraordinary passion to remake the world.

The green idea is dangerous precisely because it appeals so strongly to deep longings shared by many people. It evokes a world of natural beauty and human scale, in which people will fully understand the tools they use and will provide for themselves without depending on experts or specialists. It speaks of slowing life down and of viewing life whole. It taps the power of wilderness and the poetry of the pastoral. It offers a sense of place, of rootedness. It invokes "ancient wisdom" and "grassroots democracy." It promises "quality of life." It has much to say about ends, little about means. It speaks poetically about much, plainly about little.

Ideologies are messy. They tend to associate disparate ideas in unexpected ways. Rarely do their advocates agree precisely on what they are advocating. Viewed up close and personal, no two socialists or conservatives or classical liberals believe exactly the same thing.

The greens are no different. They have their internal quarrels and their ideological factions. The German Green Party alone can be split either of two ways: between the "realos" and the "fundis" or between the "Red-Greens" and the

331

"Green-Greens." The former division captures attitudes about how much to compromise for short-term political gain; the latter, the influence of Marxism.

Similar divisions exist in the United States. Grass-roots-oriented "eco-activists" maintain the vision while Washington-based "envirocrats" write and enforce the laws. Mystical "deep ecology" promoters square off against neo-Marxist "social ecology" advocates. In the middle, making up the rank and file, are people who want both stronger regulation out of Washington and more recycling at the household level, who like what deep ecology says about spirituality and saving nature for its own sake but think social ecology is right to emphasize practical politics, who admire the uncompromising stand of direct action groups like Earth First! but find spiking trees to prevent logging a bit extreme—who, in short, pick and choose among green ideas and organizations the ones that suit their own temperaments.

As quarrelsome as its adherents may be, however, every ideology has a primary value or set of values at its core—liberty, equality, order, virtue, salvation. For greens, the core value is stasis, "sustainability" in the approved jargon. The ideal is of an earth that doesn't change, that shows little or no effect of human activity. History is not an arrow, but a circle. On the evil of growth, both Murray Bookchin, the Marcusean doyen of social ecology, and Arne Naess, the intuitive apostle of deep ecology, agree. "Limits to growth" is as much a description of how things *should* be as it is of how they *are*. There is a sacred quality to the earth. Nature is best left undisturbed. The greatest sin is to make the desert bloom.

Green politics, write British greens Jonathon Porritt and David Winner, "demands a wholly new ethic in which violent, plundering humankind abandons its destructive ways, recognizes its dependence on Planet Earth and starts living on a more equal footing with the rest of nature....Reformist environmentalism, as practised by single issue pressure groups and advocated by environmentalists in the main political parties, is nowhere near enough. The danger lies not only in the odd maverick polluting factory, industry, or technology, but in the fundamental nature of our economic systems. It is industrialism itself—a 'super-ideology' embraced by socialist countries as well as by the capitalist West—which threatens us."

Green ideology is certainly shared by people who call themselves Greens, troop off to conferences in Oregon wearing Gaia T-shirts and Birkenstock sandals, and engage in debates over whether it is proper to transport food across bioregional boundaries to feed starving people. These Greens are undoubtedly green. But so, eventually, are the hundreds of thousands of people who read publications like the *Utne Reader* and the *L.A. Weekly* and absorb, bit by bit, green ideas. So, in a sense, are the 80 percent of respondents who told *New York Times* pollsters that the environment should be protected "whatever the cost."

Despite some activists' desire for a pristine party that will advocate a bright green ideology, most greens realize that success will come in other ways. Their values will become part of the general *zeitgeist* and work their way into news stories and movies and the Democratic and Republican party platforms. The radicals will keep pushing, advocating ever more "principled" ideas, shifting the background of the main debate further and further away from balancing costs and benefits to preserving nature for its own sake.

Green ideologues often disavow mainstream environmentalists—at least those willing to make their peace with markets, private property, or industry in an effort to reduce pollution or conserve natural resources. But rare is the mainstream representative who will repudiate the "purists" who inhabit the fringes.

"I think groups like Greenpeace and Earth First! make a significant contribution to the educational process," former Sen. Gaylord Nelson, now with the Wilderness Society, told writer Brandon Mitchener in a laudatory article on direct action groups in *E* magazine. Said National Audubon Society Vice President Robert SanGeorge: "Hopefully with the different strategies of the different environmental organizations, something better will happen for the world."

David Brower, the "Archdruid" of the U.S. environmental movement, understands well the dynamics of ideological crusades—how increasingly radical factions push the "mainstream" to greater and greater extremes. "I founded Friends of the Earth to make the Sierra Club look reasonable," he told *E*. "Then I founded the Earth Island Institute to make Friends of the Earth look reasonable. Earth First! now makes us look reasonable. We're still waiting for someone to come along and make Earth First! look reasonable."

Already, the most influential environmentalists in Washington include Jeremy Rifkin, an unabashed advocate of extreme green ideology, and Lester Brown, an ardent fellow traveler. One need not accept the Earth First! slogan, "Back to the Pleistocene!" to abet the ideology behind it. "In one way or another," wrote the green prophet E.F. Schumacher, "everybody will have to take sides in this great conflict."

In a sense, green ideology is a *cri di coeur*: "Stop the world, I want to get off!" Technology is too complicated, work too demanding, communication too instantaneous, information too abundant, the pace of life too fast. Stasis looks attractive, not only for nature but also for human beings.

"The pressure and strain of living," wrote Schumacher in *Small Is Beautiful*, "is very much less in, say, Burma than it is in the United States, in spite of the fact that the amount of labour-saving machinery used in the former country is only a minute fraction of the amount used in the latter."

Rifkin describes the green coalition as "time rebels," who "argue that the long-term psychic and environmental damage has outstripped whatever temporary gains might have been made by the obsession with speed at all costs. They argue that the pace of production and consumption should not exceed nature's ability to recycle wastes and renew basic resources. They argue that the tempo of social and economic life should be compatible with nature's time frame."

To slow economy and society to the approved *adagio*, the greens have some fairly straightforward prescriptions: Restrict trade to the local area. Eliminate markets where possible. End specialization. Anchor individuals in their "bioregions," local areas defined by their environmental characteristics. Shrink the population. Make life simple again, small, self-contained.

It is a vision that can be made remarkably appealing, for it plays on our desire for self-sufficiency, our longing for community, and our nostalgia for the agrarian past. We will go back to the land, back to the rhythms of seedtime and harvest, back to making our own clothes, our own furniture, our own tools. Back to barn raisings and quilting bees. Back to a life we can understand without a string of Ph.D.s.

"In living in the world by his own will and skill, the stupidest peasant or tribesman is more competent than the most intelligent workers or technicians or intellectuals in a society of specialists," writes Wendell Berry, an agrarian admired by both greens and cultural conservatives. Berry is a fine writer; he chooses words carefully; he means what he says. We will go back to being peasants.

Greens share with communitarian conservatives like Berry a suspicion of modernity, of individualism, of rootless cosmopolitans and the cities they inhabit. But where the conservatives exalt authority and tradition, the greens reject the traditions to which they themselves are heirs. Conservatives uphold the Western, the Christian—the medieval manor, perhaps, or the yeoman farmer.

Greens look to the East, past the skyscrapers of Hong Kong, beyond the Ginza, to the Ming China that destroyed its ships lest they sail beyond the horizon. Granted, no medieval Chinese would recognize the blend of nature-worship, feminism, Zen, Taoism, Marxism, and egalitarianism that makes up green thought. But many greens would embrace the vision described by the *Tao Te Ching* and quoted in the 1985 book *Deep Ecology*:

> *Let people recover*
> *The simple life:*
> *Reckoning by knotted cords,*
> *Delighting in a basic meal,*
> *Pleased with humble attire,*
> *Happy in their homes,*
> *Taking pleasure in their*
> *Rustic ways....*
> *Folks grown gray with age*
> *May pass away never having*
> *Strayed beyond the village.*

On the virtue of such a life—indeed, on its necessity—there is little disagreement between the mystics and the Marxists or the "principled" and the pragmatic. The only question is how to get there.

Greens often hint that energy shortages or the greenhouse effect will force the transformation they seek. *Ought* quickly becomes *is*. *Should* becomes *will*. Things will change because they must. The greens may not buy Marx's historical dialectic, but they share his determinism.

Writes Porritt, who heads Britain's branch of Friends of the Earth: "From all the knowledge we now have about environmental issues, the inevitable conclusion is that our way of life cannot be sustained without grave damage to the Earth and our own health. We've done enormous damage by sustaining our way of life thus far, and by seeking to sustain it into the next century, we willfully and criminally endanger future generations who will share our planet. Simply put, our modern society is unsustainable. Unsustainable means that *we cannot go on living as we do now*" (emphasis in the original).

Porritt, however, is no naif. Like many greens, he believes people's attitudes must change and speaks easily of "the spiritual dimension of the ecology movement." But he knows it is not enough. "My strong feeling is that we need to step in tune with the Earth but we also need to engage in the political processes in order to protect it," he writes. "However uncomfortable it makes people, that means political confrontation."

Greens, especially those of the non-Marxist, earth-goddess-worshipping variety, are indeed rhetorically uncomfortable with political confrontation. They like consensus and preach nonviolence. They exalt decentralism (though they stop short of decentralizing all the way down to the individual). But with their radical wing crying, "No compromise in defense of Mother Earth!," the greens are as driven to political confrontation as the pro-life movement was to blocking abortion clinics.

And greens show plenty of zest for political power—at the local, state, national, and international levels. Opposing environmentally destructive central planning, they may sound downright Hayekian, but offered a chance to enforce *their* will by treaty or ordinance, they dump consensus like so much toxic waste. As a German Green told columnist Alston Chase, "Grass-roots democracy sounded wonderful before we were elected to Parliament. But now we are in power, centralized solutions seem far more effective."

For the most part, green political power still manifests itself in relatively mild-mannered ways: telling a farmer he can't sell his land to a developer, rezoning the site of someone's dream home as "open space," banning the sale of car air conditioners (as Vermont has), ordering some people to work nine-day, 80-hour weeks (as the Los Angeles Air Quality Management District has). We haven't yet gotten to emptying the cities, Khmer Rouge-style.

But consider the green-influenced response to the AQMD's intrusive, and most likely ineffective, plan to control air pollution in Los Angeles by—among other edicts—dictating working hours, banning deodorants, and regulating numerous industries out of business or out of town. That the plan was decreed from above and written by a handful of unelected "experts" didn't matter. That it lumped insignificant sources of pollution in with important ones didn't matter. That it failed to weigh costs against benefits or even to demonstrate that it would, in fact, significantly reduce air pollution didn't matter. All that mattered was that it was extreme and that it was comprehensive. It was "serious." Lester Brown, the much-quoted head of the Worldwatch Institute, lavishes the same sort of praise on China's draconian one-child policy. How "serious" greens get will depend primarily on how much power they can grab.

Most greens can still consider themselves nonviolent for one reason: Their victims don't fight back. So far no one has taken up arms to defend his logging equipment against Earth First! sabotage or his factory against EPA closure. But some greens, at least, see the inherent contradiction in their views.

Writes longtime activist Stephanie Mills, contemplating a battle over whether to allow a golf course to be built: "The ecofascist in me finds it hard to trust even the outcome of a democratic process, let alone a paradigm shift, because the demos is, through no fault of its own, largely ignorant of biology. I fear that our culture is so confused and our information systems so polluted with irrealities that people will vote, time and time again, to let the golf course be built."

Mills equates land ownership with slavery, herself with the abolitionists. But, unlike a human being, land cannot own itself. Freed slaves can decide what to do with their lives. They can speak for themselves in court. But some human being has to speak for the land, has to decide what will become of it. Mills and her fellow greens volunteer to be those spokespersons. In effect, *they* will own the land.

But without paying for it. After all, writes Mills, "there's far more land to preserve than there is government or philanthropic ability to compensate the owners. So it is a win-lose situation as long as the dominant paradigm, which maintains that land can be owned, holds sway." Suddenly, we are back to liquidating the kulaks.

Mills is a remarkably frank writer, and her book *Whatever Happened to Ecology?*, recently published by Sierra Club Books, provides some of the most interesting peeks at the green world to come that can be had by the general public. Mills garnered national attention in 1969, when she delivered a college commencement address entitled "The Future Is a Cruel Hoax" and declared she'd never have children. The book traces the evolution of the environmental movement and of her ideas since then. Today, she and her husband live on a farm in northern Michigan, where they pursue their bioregionalist ideal of "reinhabiting" the land by restoring some of its wildness and blocking future development. A journalist, not a theorist, Mills speaks not only for herself but for the intellectual movement of which she is a part. Her words are chilling:

"We young moderns resort to elaborate means of getting physical experience. Yogic practice, fanatical running, bicycling, competitive sports, bodybuilding. All of these recreations are voluntary and may not cultivate the endurance necessary for the kind of labor required to dismantle industrial society and restore the Earth's productivity." *Are voluntary...the endurance necessary...the labor required...dismantle industrial society.* The prose is pleasant, the notions it contains disturbing. Are we to conscript a slave army to restore the earth? Shall green-clad drill instructors run us through endurance-building workouts? To what is Mills alluding? She never explains.

She continues: "One summer afternoon a few days after a freak windstorm, I made a foray out to buy some toilet paper. (Every time I have to replenish the supply of this presumed necessity, I wonder what we're going to substitute for it when the trucks stop running.)" *When the trucks stop running.* There is a history of the future buried in those words, fodder for several science-fiction novels—but, again, no explanation of when and why the trucks will stop. Or who will stop them.

People don't want to be peasants: The cities of the Third World teem with the evidence. And certainly, the typical subscriber to the *Utne Reader* (a sort of green *Reader's Digest* with a circulation of nearly 100,000 after only five years of publication) doesn't envision a future of subsistence farming—much less the hunter-gatherer existence preferred by deep ecologists. More to the reader's taste is, no doubt, the cheery vision offered by Executive Editor Jay Walljasper.

It's 2009. Nuclear weapons have been dismantled. Green publications have huge circulations. Minneapolis has 11 newspapers and its own currency ("redeemable in trout, walleye, or wild rice"). Sidewalk cafes sell croissants and yogurt. A local ordinance decrees a 24-hour work week. Cars are nearly nonexistent (a delegation from the "People's Independent Republic of Estonia" is in town to help design better ski trails for commuters). Citizens vote electronically. The shopping mall has become a nature preserve.

Walljasper is clearly having fun—after all, he puts Aretha Franklin's face on the $10 bill—and he doesn't consider any of the tough questions. Like how all those magazines and newspapers exist without printing plants or paper mills. How the Estonians got to town without airplanes or the fuel to run them. (Jeremy Rifkin specifically names the Boeing 747 as the kind of product that can't be produced in the small-is-beautiful factories of the coming "entropic age.") How the chips to run the electronic voting got etched without chemicals. Where the chips were made. How a 24-hour work week produced the sustained concentration needed to write software or the level of affluence that allows for restaurant croissants.

And, above all, Walljasper doesn't explain why after millennia of behaving otherwise, humans simply gave up wanting *stuff*. If the Walljasper of 2009 still overloads on reading material, why should we assume that people whose fancy runs toward fast food and polyester (or fast cars and silk) would be struck with a sudden attack of bioregionally approved tastes? How *exactly* did that shopping mall disappear?

"The root of the solution has to be so radical that it can scarcely be spoken of," says movie director and British green John Boorman (*Hope and Glory*, *The Emerald Forest*). "We all have to be prepared to change the way we live and function and relate to the planet. In short, we need a transformation of the human spirit. If the human heart can be changed, then everything can be changed."

We have heard this somewhere before. People are forever seeking to change the human heart. They usually begin with persuasion, and persuasion sometimes works. We did, some of us, stop killing each other in the name of God.

But the greens want people to give up the idea that life can be better. They say "better" need not refer to material abundance, that we should just be content with less. Stasis, they say, can satisfy our "vital needs." They may indeed convince some people to pursue a life of voluntary simplicity, and that is fine and good and just the kind of thing a free society ought to allow. Stephanie Mills is welcome to her farm.

But I do not want to give up 747s (Rifkin), or cars (Kirkpatrick Sale), or glasses (Joan McIntyre), or private washing machines (Bookchin), or tailored clothing (Schumacher), or long work weeks spent at a computer I could never build. I do not want to return to the world in which Chaucer's clerk dreamed of owning 20 books. (Neither, I daresay, would these prolifically writing greens).

The "debased human protoplasm" that Mills holds in contempt for their delight in "clothes, food, sporting goods, electronics, building supplies, pets, baked goods, deli food, toys, tools, hardware, geegaws, jimjams, and knick-knacks" will not go down nonviolently. Many ordinary human beings would like a cleaner world. They are prepared to make sacrifices—*trade-offs* is a better word—to get one. But ordinary human beings will not adopt the Buddha's life without desire, much as E.F. Schumacher might have ordained it. And many ordinary human beings will not give up the right to own land without a fight, complete with guns.

Green ideology springs from the rift C.P. Snow described as "the two cultures," the split between scientific and literary intellectuals. We have yet to come to terms with that split—itself a product of understandable, and largely necessary, specialization. It has produced an ideological crisis.

Ideologies are, by definition, created in the world of ideas, by intellectuals. They are created with words. When science and technology became too complex for those who wield words to easily understand, some of the writers rebelled. Rather than bone up on science or accept tools they didn't comprehend, they demanded that the world get simpler. They got their science from popularizers and built an antiscience worldview on it.

From the life sciences, they learned that chemicals cause cancers—without understanding that our methods of measuring both chemical concentrations and minute dangers have grown ever more sensitive. From popularizers who said that physics no longer differs from Eastern mysticism, they learned that reality is radically subjective, reinforcing the intuitive approach of deep ecology. From ecologists who posited that the earth acts as a single system to maintain conditions conducive to life, they learned that the earth is alive. Mistaking metaphor for reality, they took James Lovelock's Gaia hypothesis and turned earth into a goddess. From the Second Law of Thermodynamics, Rifkin justifies an entire system of political economy based on the ideal of never expending energy. From quantum physics, Fritjof Capra derives justification for a new world order.

Writing in *The Tao of Physics*, he declares: "I believe that the world-view implied by modern physics is inconsistent with our present society, which does not reflect the harmonious interrelatedness we observe in nature. To achieve such a state of dynamic balance, a radically different social and economic structure will be needed: a cultural revolution in the true sense of the word." How we get from quarks and quanta to a new social order is best left to a less popular Capra work, *Green Politics*, about the rise of the German Green Party.

Pseudoscience has always appealed to half-educated intellectuals—Marxism lured many a disciple with its talk of "scientific materialism." The greens claim to have equally scientific proof that industrial civilization is "unsustainable," that we must give it up or die. Some of their ideas do indeed draw on the work of serious scientists. But green ideologues would be genuinely unhappy if the greenhouse effect turned out to be insignificant, even less happy if technological advances refuted their apocalyptic claims. Their greatest nightmare is the discovery of cheap, safe, clean energy. It would be "like giving a machine gun to an idiot child," population-control advocate Paul Ehrlich said when the excitement over cold fusion suggested that prospect. "It's the worst thing that could happen to our planet," Rifkin told the *Los Angeles Times*.

Greens wrap themselves in science, but many dislike the spirit of inquiry that drives the scientific process. They want the world to be simple and simply understood—or so subjective it *cannot* be understood. Deep ecologist Arne Naess says, "People can then oppose nuclear power without having to read thick books and without knowing the myriad facts that are used in newspapers and periodicals." Schumacher pooh-poohed science as mere "know-how," inferior to humanistic pursuits. His answer to Snow, who wanted educated people to know both Shakespeare and science, was to declare: "What do I miss, as a human being, if I have never heard of the Second Law of Thermodynamics? The answer is: Nothing."

Some greens may be comfortable with scientific inquiry (at least if it doesn't disturb nature) and prefer facts to mystical insight, but all oppose both the technological optimism that often drives science and the economy that sustains it. They speak much of ecology and note, correctly, that we have learned that the natural world is made up of complicated connections we can only begin to understand. But they demand that the human world, in which similar connections create markets and cities and communications networks, be smashed into its component parts.

Schumacher attacked markets because they "take the sacredness out of life, because there can be nothing sacred in something that has a price." He refused to recognize that prices express the value real human beings put on things, that they allow us to "be in touch with more than a very limited number of persons at any one time"—something he said can't be done.

He criticized modern transportation and communications for making people "footloose," for letting them easily move to suit themselves and especially for letting them create crowded cities. He preferred the world when people were "relatively immobile," when "the movement of populations, except in periods of disaster, was confined to persons who had a very special reason to move, such as the Irish saints or the scholars of the University of Paris." When, in short, only the intellectual elite could change its geographical station in life.

In 1959, Snow, a socialist, saw where the two cultures would lead. And he passionately defended the industrialism the greens aim to dismantle: "Industrialisation is the only hope of the poor. I use the word 'hope' in the crude and prosaic sense. I have not much use for the moral sensibility of anyone who is too refined to use it so. It is all very well for us, sitting pretty, to think that material standards of living don't matter all that much. It is all very well for one, as a personal choice, to reject industrialisation—do a modern Walden, if you like, and if you go without much food, see most of your children die in infancy, despise the comforts of literacy, accept twenty years off your own life, then I respect you for the strength of your aesthetic revulsion. But I don't respect you in the slightest if, even passively, you try to impose the same choice on others who are not free to choose. In fact, we know what their choice would be. For, with singular unanimity, in any country where they have had the chance, the poor have walked off the land into the factories as fast as the factories could take them."

At its extreme, green ideology expresses itself in utter contempt for humanity. Reviewing Bill McKibben's *The End of Nature* in the *Los Angeles Times*, National Park Service research biologist David M. Graber concluded with this stunning passage: "Human happiness, and certainly human fecundity, are not as important as a wild and healthy planet. I know social scientists who remind me that people are part of nature, but it isn't true. Somewhere along the line—at about a billion years ago, maybe half that—we quit the contract and became a cancer. We have become a plague upon ourselves and upon the Earth. It is cosmically unlikely that the developed world will choose to end its orgy of fossil-energy consumption, and the Third World its suicidal consumption of landscape. Until such time as Homo sapiens should decide to rejoin nature, some of us can only hope for the right virus to come along."

It is hard to take such notions seriously without sounding like a bit of a kook yourself. But there they are—calmly expressed in the pages of a major, mainstream, Establishment newspaper by an employee of the federal government. When it is acceptable to say such things in polite intellectual company, when feel-good environmentalists tolerate the totalitarians in their midst, when sophisticates greet the likes of Graber with indulgent nods and smiles rather than arguments and outrage, we are one step farther down another bloody road to someone's imagined Eden. All the greens need is an opportunity and a Lenin.

PART EIGHT

DEATH OF AN EMPIRE

USSR: The Crumbling of an Empire

By Robert W. Poole, Jr.

April 1981

A s I write, Soviet troops are poised on the border of Poland, and the world once more is holding its collective breath. Will it be another Hungary, another Czechoslovakia, another Afghanistan? Whatever the Kremlin leaders decide, they have trapped themselves in a no-win situation.

If they fail to invade, they will have given their consent to the de facto overthrow of Marxist-Leninism in a vital component of their empire. Besides its symbolic value as a confession of ideological bankruptcy, such a move would entail direct, practical risks. Not only would it encourage the workers of Hungary, Czechoslovakia, Lithuania, the Ukraine, et al. to go and do likewise, it would also destroy a vital link in the Warsaw Pact's logistics system. (The USSR's 19 divisions in East Germany are crucially dependent on supply lines through Poland.)

If the Soviets do invade, however, they will pay a heavy price. Once more they will have had to resort to naked force to maintain their hold on the inhabitants of a workers' paradise. The threat of protracted resistance is very real—not just from Polish workers but from the Polish army as well. By invading, the Kremlin will cut off any possibility of Western banks rolling over the $12 billion in loans to Poland coming due this year. They will also demolish the lingering prospects of SALT talks, their $12-billion gas pipeline from Siberia to West Germany, and further Western grain bailouts.

In his stunningly prophetic book *Will the Soviet Union Survive Until 1984?*, Andrei Amalrik 12 years ago predicted a U.S.-China *rapprochement*, revolt by Eastern European satellites, and internal decay in the Soviet Union, fueled by nationalistic rivalries and the failures of central planning. What keeps the lid on, he wrote, is the gradual improvement in Soviet living standards. Nevertheless, he warned, "a sharp slowdown, a halt or even a reversal in the improvement in the standard of living would arouse such explosions of anger, mixed with violence, as were never before thought possible."

Such a reversal is now occurring (and not just in Poland). As the chilling article "Russian Disorders" by George Feifer (*Harper's*, February) makes eloquently clear, the Soviet economy is falling to pieces. "The centralized planning Russians used to regard as the solution to major economic problems is now considered a condemnation to economic absurdity." Huge shortages and surpluses, food and toilet-paper rationing, soaring prices, bloated bureaucracies, diversion of *18 percent* of GNP to the military—these are a few of the obvious symptoms.

More ominous is the demoralization brought on by people's disillusionment with a system that has promised them material and spiritual progress—but has given them fraud, manipulation, and deceit as a way of life, simply to get enough to eat in an economy that cannot deliver the goods.

Twelve years ago this malaise and cynicism were the concerns of Amalrik's intellectual strata. Today, as Feifer demonstrates, they are the concerns of the demoralized working class. Alcoholism has become the national pastime—one-third of all consumer spending in food stores is for alcohol. And the result has begun showing up in statistics: Alone among modern nations, life expectancy in the Soviet Union is declining, infant mortality is increasing. The country is slowly committing suicide.

What should be clear from all this is that the increasingly popular view of the Soviet Union as an all-powerful behemoth is simply not true. "In the last analysis the main source of Soviet strength is Western incomprehension of the great and growing internal tensions which threaten the fabric of the Soviet system," says Leszek Kolakowski, the ex-communist philosopher who was expelled from Poland in 1968. "If the Soviet leaders suspected for one moment that the Western world knew what *they* know about their system, their worries about the staying power of the Soviet Empire would increase immeasurably" (*Encounter*, January).

What does all this imply for U.S. foreign policy? To begin with, while there is no question that U.S. defenses must in some respects be strengthened, there is hardly call for the near-panic expressed in some quarters on the right. The Soviets are *not* 10 feet tall.

The salient fact is that the Soviet empire is increasingly vulnerable to disintegration. The aim of U.S. policy should be to hasten the process, if possible—without triggering either a nuclear war or a situation in which the Kremlin can fall back on whipping up patriotism to preserve its control. The latter prospect should make for caution about directly threatening moves—covert arms shipments to potential rebels, for instance. But encouraging the liberalization of policies in China (while avoiding military aid) would serve very well to keep the pressure on the Soviets.

And there is wide scope for other sorts of pressure. On the one hand, since it is economic issues that have made real to Soviet workers the manifest failures of socialism, there's a good case for not bailing out the commisars. At the same time, increasing the amount of information available about life in the West would increase the likelihood of Soviet citizens demanding reforms.

More fundamentally, the *moral* case for capitalism needs to be articulated in the West and communicated to the East. No one can read Feifer's brilliant piece without seeing that socialism's moral bankruptcy has become obvious even to the Soviet workers. "More and more now regard [socialism] as poison to social relationships as well as individual consciences. 'Everyone knows that to get ahead in the country, it is almost required that you be a liar or a cheater—often a swine,'" one of Feifer's Russian friends told him. Yet again and again he found that "with their old ideals and hopes shattered, most people have none to replace them."

Here is the opportunity of our lifetime. "One cause around which we might be able to build something like an ideology is liberty," a cautious Kolakowski tells his interviewer. Indeed. Some of us are already trying.

How to Dismantle the Soviet Empire

By Jack Wheeler

November 1983

My crampons dug into the ice as Nick belayed me up the summit ridge of Mount Elbrus. If I slipped, and Nick failed to arrest me, I would fall into a cluster of large rocks bulging out of the glacier a thousand feet below. As I carefully made my way up to him, over 18,000 feet in the sky, it never occurred to me that my life was connected to and dependent upon a Russian. The man above me, whom I was counting on to save my life if need be, was Nikolai Chernyi—a Soviet Communist, whose government is the sworn enemy of my country and has countless megatons of nuclear bombs aimed at my home. But in that moment, he was simply Nick, a fellow mountaineer whom I trusted on the mountain without reservation, as he did me.

When we reached the summit and stood on the very pinnacle of Europe (Elbrus, which lies in the Caucasus Mountains between the Black Sea and the Caspian Sea, is the highest peak in Europe), we did so as fellow human beings experiencing a bond of spiritual exultation that only a shared victory in the sky can bring. The thought that we were, or should be, enemies would have been absurd.

Some days later, I found myself in a disco bar late at night on the 22nd story of a new Moscow hotel. It was filled wall-to-wall with Muscovite teeny-boppers boozing and boogying to the throbbing beat of Western rock 'n' roll.

I was dancing and talking with a young girl named Tanya, who bubbled over with youthful energy, gaiety, and innocence. As I talked with her and her friends—they all spoke some English—I was once again struck by the fact that despite their almost total isolation from the outside world and the government's continuous barrage of hate-filled propaganda against America, most Soviet citizens not only do not hate Americans but are fascinated to meet one.

"You are really from America?" they asked excitedly.

"I sure am," I happily replied.

"Are you a socialist or a capitalist?" Tanya wanted to know.

A grin spread across my face as I looked right at her to announce proudly: "I am a capitalist!"

"*You Are? Really?*" was the wide-eyed, shocked, incredulous response. I had actually admitted it in public.

"And what, Tanya, do you think you and your friends are by being here?"

They all looked at me with puzzlement. "What do you mean?" she asked intently.

"Tanya, I know this is all new to you, just since the last Olympics, but here you are drinking English gin and bopping around to Pink Floyd and Blondie. How decadent and bourgeois can you get? Where do you think all this *came* from?"

The multicolored disco lights started to flash, and the music began to blast through the room again, so we all got up to boogie some more. As I watched the young gyrating bodies around me, I knew there was little difference between these kids and those in the West. It was impossible, a bad joke, to look on them as enemies.

At various times in its history, America has been at war with the English, the Spanish, the Germans, the Italians, the Mexicans, and the Japanese. All are today our friends. There is nothing in the nature of things that makes it impossible for such a turnaround to occur someday with the Russians, as well.

There is only one basic requirement for this to happen. If the Soviets want peaceful coexistence, detente, disarmament, it is really very easy—all they have to do is stop trying to rule the world.

With his clenched fist raised in fury toward America, Nikita Khrushchev thundered the famous threat, "We will bury you!" And from Lenin to Andropov the Soviet Union has unwaveringly proclaimed its aim of overthrowing political democracy wherever it may be. Khrushchev's words were those of Lenin and Stalin, and today their threat remains a firm goal of every member of the Soviet Central Committee, for whom Tanya's father works. Like it or not, against its will, America is engaged in a life-or-death struggle with the Soviet Union. The vast majority of the *people* of the Soviet Union may not be deadly enemies of our country, but the *government* of the Soviet Union is.

If a peaceable citizen is attacked by a thug in an alley, he is morally entitled to take whatever measures are necessary, including injuring or even killing the thug, to protect himself and his property. The right to self-defense in the face of aggression is an evident moral given for human beings individually—and collectively, as entire nations.

How to best defend ourselves against the Soviets' grand design is a question that has puzzled American administrations and citizens for decades. Answers to this question have by and large failed to observe a basic strategy of defense against any enemy: discover his weakness.

Since the founding of the Grand Duchy of Muscovy in 1462, the Russian state has on the average increased its territory by the size of Denmark every single year, or by the size of the entire country of Italy every seven years. Today, the Soviet Union contains over 100 separate ethnic groups and cultures. Since 1917 it has swallowed several entire nations, bit off large chunks of others, and violently subjugated into colonies 8 of the 13 countries on its border, as well as numerous others around the world.

Within the past decade, the Kremlin has added more than a dozen other nations to its sphere of influence. What was once French Indochina should now be considered Soviet Indochina—Laos, Kampuchea (Cambodia), and Vietnam. The USSR and its clients are now in control in Angola, Mozambique, Ethiopia, South Yemen, Benin, the Congo Republic, Grenada, and Nicaragua. The latest addition is Suriname. The genocide and chemical warfare being conducted in Afghanistan is only a dramatic variant of the ubiquitous hunger, bloodshed, and brutal dictatorship that always accompany Soviet colonization.

In the turmoil of the Bolshevik counterrevolution (which fascistically over-threw the real revolution of Kerensky, who had replaced the Czar's autocracy with a parliamentary democracy), enormous portions of the Russian empire declared themselves independent of Great Russian rule. In 1920, Finland, Latvia, Estonia, Lithuania, Belorussia, the Ukraine, Georgia, and Azerbaijan were all independent sovereign nations. All were subsequently conquered by Soviet military force, their borders subsumed within the borders of the USSR. Only Finland managed finally to escape.

When Hitler's troops marched victoriously into Kiev, the capital of the Ukraine, in September 1941, the Ukrainian people welcomed them as liberators, deluging them with flowers. Millions of people in the Soviet Union joined the Nazis to fight against Stalin. It was only after Hitler began butchering and enslaving them as much as did Stalin that the latter was able to appeal to patriotism and launch a counteroffensive.

The history of Russia and the Soviet Union is filled with the Great Russians' subjugation of other peoples and cultures— the Little Russians, or Ukrainians; the White Russians, or Belorussians; the Georgians, Balts, Moravians, Poles, Ruthenians, Slovaks, Bessarabians, Crimea Tatars, Volga Germans, Tadzhiks, Turkmen, Armenians, Mongols, Azerbaijani, Uzbeks, Kazakhs, Kirghiz, and Afghans. The Kremlin has been occupied since 1917 by men obsessed with missionary Marxism and imbued with the ancient Great Russian desire for empire.

Because of this virulent synergy of missionary Marxism providing a religion-like justification for Great Russian imperialism, the principal purpose of the Soviet economy is the manufacture of weapons. It is correctly noted that while the United States has a military-industrial complex, the Soviet Union is one. Engaging in the most massive military build-up in history, the Soviets have achieved strategic superiority over the United States. The Soviet Navy is now acknowledged to be our equal in many areas, and a vast outpouring of tanks and conventional arms from Soviet munitions factories continues unabated.

Wherever in the world—particularly now in our very backyard in Central America—there is a chance to destabilize America and the West using terrorists, guerrilla war, subversion, propaganda, or whatever, the Soviets are there with guns and money. Moreover, the United States faces nuclear extinction at the hands of a state that has issued apocalyptic threats.

It is thus with good reason that the Reagan administration wishes the United States to take action. Its solution, however, is that the government vastly increase U.S. military spending. This is quite curious, because "conservatives" constantly condemn "liberals" for always wanting to solve social problems by the government throwing billions of tax dollars at them.

What neither the conservatives nor the liberals see is that the Soviet Union is in reality utterly weak and vulnerable. It is this failure that, ironically, assures the Soviets a continued existence. Once the world recognizes the powerlessness of the Soviet Union—that the emperor has no clothes—the Soviets are through, the game is up.

Everyone knows of the outer colonies of the Soviet empire—the "satellites" of eastern Europe, Outer Mongolia, Cuba, etc. But it is less well recognized that the Soviet Union is itself a collection of *inner colonies*—the Ukraine; the Baltic countries of Latvia, Lithuania, and Estonia; the Transcaucasian countries of Georgia, Azerbaijan, and Armenia; and the IslamicTurkic countries of central Asia. Soviet imperialism is practiced first and foremost on its own people within its own borders. And, like Humpty Dumpty in the children's rhyme, if the Soviet Union is ever broken up in any way, it can never be put back together again.

One of the most potent forces for political change in this century, especially since World War II, has been anti-imperialist nationalism. Accordingly, we should not seek to promote individual freedom in the Soviet Union so much as tribal freedom, that is, anti-Soviet, anti-Great Russian ethnic nationalism.

The best defense is a good offense. America and the West are under attack by the most dangerous imperialist power in history. It is about time Americans started doing to the Soviets precisely what they have been trying to do to us, employing a strategy of quid pro quo in subversion and propaganda. For the Kremlin is far more vulnerable to its own medicine than we are.

And the way to do it for real entails, interestingly enough, no massive arms race or increases in the defense budget. It means spending money with a great deal more effectiveness, such as on developing and supporting a number of national liberation movements within the Soviet Union itself.

The goal of such a strategy would be either to establish a genuine peace with the Soviet Union such as America enjoys with former enemies like Japan, West Germany, Spain, and England, or to render the Soviet Union incapable of being any sort of real threat to the United States, up to and including by dissolution of the USSR as a political entity.

The Kremlin must be driven to the conclusion that it cannot conduct a war with the West—nuclear or conventional—without a civil war breaking out among the USSR's inner colonies. The risk of war must be made so great for Moscow that this equation becomes inescapable: war with the West = dismemberment of the Soviet Union.

To achieve this, the U.S. government must define a foreign policy whose goal is to secure from Moscow the realization that there is no exit from this equation: that the USSR's only alternative to political extinction as a nation-state is to abandon its strategy of global domination and its support of terrorist and subversive groups around the world, concentrating instead on developing the Soviet economy.

Such an alternative entails major, radical disarmament. The message to Moscow must be clear: *disarmament or dismemberment.*

When we look at a Mercator projection world map on which the globe's curved lines have been straightened out on a flat surface, the USSR appears as a vast, seamless, monochrome blob, dwarfing the rest of Europe and Asia. But this is an illusion. Africa, for example, which looks smaller than the USSR, is much bigger: The entire Soviet Union plus the entire continental United States could be fit into Africa with room to spare.

Moreover, private mapmakers should be encouraged and government cartographers should be mandated to depict the Soviet inner colonies in separate colors with each designated "Soviet occupied." It is vital that the world change its perspective on the Soviet Union: It is not a monolithic, impregnable giant but a glued-together, imperialist empire that must some day come apart at its many seams.

The greatest potential weapon we have at our disposal against the Soviets is not the MIRVed ICBM, the Trident nuclear submarine, or even the incredible cruise missile. It is the CIA and a multitude of private, voluntary organizations. The most cost-effective move we could make in defense spending would be to shift the focus of CIA operations, giving this agency the directive to make trouble for the Soviet Union. At the same time, the government should make it clear that the neutrality laws will not be interpreted in such a way as to prevent private organizations from playing an active role in such activities.

A program to undermine the Soviet empire should not waste time on grandstand plays like assassinations and coups d'état. It should instead concentrate on taking tiny bites, causing small, irritating problems all over the place—worker unrest, ethnic unrest, complaints and moanings in three dozen places. In other words, make the Kremlin suffer, as the Mongols say, the death of a thousand cuts. Here are a few examples of what could be done.

ISLAMIC REVIVAL. There are over 47 million Moslems in the Soviet Union. While the elite of the Moslem clergy have been accorded power and privileges, the Moslem laity and the rank-and-file clergy have little freedom to practice their religion. In czarist Russia there were over 26,000 mosques; today there are only 200 in the entire USSR. With the resurgence of fire-breathing Islam throughout the Middle East, it should not be difficult to stimulate an Islamic revival among Soviet Moslems.

Such a revival would encourage the already-proliferating secret Moslem brotherhoods that have led recent large-scale anti-Soviet riots in Tashkent, Dushanbe, and Chimkent. It would spark a resurgence of the famed "Basmachi" guerrilla movement among the Kazakhs and Kirghiz in the '20s and '30s. It would help bring to Soviet Moslems the true story of Soviet genocide being perpetrated upon their fellow Moslems in Afghanistan. And it would spark demands for greater religious freedom, the construction of more mosques, and most especially the freedom to make a *hadj*, a pilgrimage to Mecca. (To make a *hadj* is one of the five "commandments" of Islam, but only the political hacks among the Moslem clergy in the USSR are allowed out of the country. A hue and cry should be raised throughout all of Soviet Central Asia demanding equal rights for Soviet Moslems.)

ETHNIC SAMIZDAT. A network of underground ethnic newsletters could be developed by teaching ethnic groups throughout the Soviet Union how to make pan-hectograph printing presses.

SABOTAGE AND HARASSMENT. Militant resistance groups could be organized in the European inner colonies—Latvia, Lithuania, Estonia, Belorussia, and the Ukraine. These would be similar to the French Resistance during World War II but updated for the '80s, trained to commit sophisticated acts of political sabotage against government and military facilities, records, and equipment. The publicly announced goal of these inner-colony national liberation movements would be outright national sovereignty and political independence à la Finland.

The Soviet Union, for example, is dependent for its functioning on computers, just as the West is. But Soviet computers are primitive compared to ours and are thus more vulnerable to sabotage.

America is home to many talented computer experts who are from Soviet-bloc countries and could be recruited to disrupt the functioning of Soviet computers. They could indulge, say, in "the entropy defense," adding extraneous, made-up data to important records. Adding millions of fake names to the government's lists of dissidents, workers under suspicion, and so on, would make such lists useless.

Scrambling citizens' identification numbers on computer files would generate awe-inspiring chaos in virtually every government agency. Computer "virus" programs could be introduced into a system; these eat and destroy other files in the entire system.

Military phone networks in the USSR are connected to the military computer systems and to the public phone system as well. An ingenious computer manipulator could figure out how to gain access via public phones to the military's own computers. Of course, the cooperation of inside informants and accomplices is necessary, but given this, the possibilities for the most delightfully catastrophic computer sabotage are endless.

Handbooks on harassment techniques should be prepared and distributed, describing how to squirt epoxy glue into door locks, make antigovernment stickers with adhesives that etch the message into glass and can't be removed, get government officials to think their phones are tapped by other officials, and make homemade napalm from soap suds, egg whites, and gasoline. All such techniques of sabotage and harassment should be directed to impairing the government's ability to intimidate and control, while avoiding endangering the lives of private citizens.

UNREST. Agents provocateurs could be used within all the inner colonies to foment worker, student, and ethnic unrest: complaints, demands, small strikes and demonstrations, in dozens of factories and universities. Workers would be encouraged to demand independent unions; students, less ideology and an end to compulsory courses on Marxism; ethnic groups, more autonomy and a return to their own cultural and legal traditions; and people everywhere, an end to the hated "internal passport," so they could travel throughout the country as they please.

This all must begin very slowly, sporadically, building up over time. Outbursts in one area that may die down as soon as the government cracks down will break out all over again in another, then another, then another, so that reports such as this one from the *Los Angeles Times* in October 1981 begin to appear commonplace:

> *"Dissident sources in Moscow reported the arrest of the leading*
> *nationalist figure in Soviet Georgia, Zviad Gamsakhurdia, after a human*
> *rights demonstration two weeks ago. Gamsakhurdia, 41, spent two years*
> *in prison in the 1970s on anti-Soviet slander charges. The latest*
> *demonstration reportedly took place Oct. 12 in a suburb of Tbilisi, the*
> *Georgian capital. A dissident source said about 200 people gathered to*

protest Soviet controls over the Georgian national language and literature."

UNDERGROUND ECONOMY. The black market, the "second economy" in the Soviet Union, is already so large that the value of exchanges there may very well equal or exceed the official gross national product. Every ruble siphoned off from the state is one ruble less that can be spent on armaments and one ruble more that contributes to the collapse of governmental control over the economy and people's private lives.

A program could be developed to finance and assist promising black marketeers and entrepreneurs in setting up clandestine consumer-goods factories and in moonlighting private services—on state time and using state materials, of course. Underground distilleries for *samogon* (moonshine) offer great possibilities. Sovietologist Murray Feshbach of Georgetown University reported in 1982 that urban Soviet families devote nearly the same proportion of their weekly budgets to alcohol as American families do to food.

BROADCASTING INFORMATION. Since its inception, the Soviet government has maintained an information barrier around its citizenry, a monopoly on all forms of media reaching the average Soviet citizen. The only systematic and effective breach of this barrier is international radio: the Voice of America (VOA), Radio Free Europe-Radio Liberty, the British Broadcasting Corporation (BBC), Deutsche Welle, and RIAS (U.S.-funded, from West to East Berlin).

This breach can and should be widened by the improvement of programs currently directed toward the major non-Russian ethnic minorities, which are broadcast in their own native languages. They should operate with the explicit purpose of encouraging liberation-secessionist activities and various other modes of rebellion against the rule of Moscow.

While the recent proposal for a "Radio Free Cuba"—Radio Martí, named after a Cuban patriot—is a welcome step in the right direction, this is an attack on the periphery. There should be a "Radio Free X" station not only for all of the outer Soviet colonies but for the inner colonies as well—a Radio Free Ukraine, Radio Free Georgia, Radio Free Estonia, Latvia, Lithuania, Belorussia, Azerbaijan, Kazakhstan, Uzbekistan.

Each should broadcast programs providing information about the lives and traditions of its people, helping to preserve its cultural heritage and national identity; historical episodes of its resistance to Great Russian domination; news reports embarrassing to the Soviet government such as crime and corruption statistics, details on the latest crop failure, and juicy gossip about the Kremlin elite; and bulletins on the latest activities of emerging national liberation movements within the inner colonies.

Moreover, the VOA—or, better yet, a group of private individuals—could build an additional station with a transmitting power on the order of, say, a million watts, direct it toward all of western Russia, and operate it just like a big-city, DJ-hip, 24-hours-a-day, eat-to-the-beat rock 'n' roll radio station in the United

States. It could be laced with news breaks, tips for teens, gossip on rock stars and groups (particularly emerging Russian ones like Time Machine, the latest heart throb of Moscow teeny-boppers), hip commercials for various popular contraband items available in the black market, and songs played by special request.

Tanya and millions of her fellow Soviet teenagers are ready to be corrupted by good old decadent bourgeois rock 'n' roll. It becomes increasingly unappealing to listen to Yuri declaiming how you should slave and sacrifice your one life for the good of the masses when you can instead listen to the Stray Cats. And you're unlikely to develop a murderous hatred for America when you're dancing to its music and it makes you feel so good.

As effective and influential as radio can be as a device to disseminate information and foment unrest, there is another available medium that is even more powerful—television. The technology exists to broadcast TV programs via satellite directly into private homes throughout the Soviet Union and Eastern Europe. To see actual events that the Soviet government desperately suppresses or distorts on its "news" would strengthen the profound cynicism and rage that so many average Soviet citizens already feel toward their government media. (There are bitter jokes that everyone in the USSR knows. Q: Why do Soviet televisions come with windshield wipers? A: To wipe the spit off.)

The two alternatives for direct broadcasting involve either a very-high-powered geosynchronous satellite, capable of beaming a continuous signal receivable by normal home-TV antennas, or multiple low-orbit satellites of lesser power, each providing about 10 minutes' worth of signal. The former would be about 10 times more costly; its signal, however, would be uninterrupted and harder to jam.

SUBVERSIVE WORDS. When it comes to the print media, there is no breach whatsoever in the information barrier that the Soviet government has thrown up around its citizenry. In the Soviet Union, you can read only what the government lets you, and it's all their side of the story.

That is why copies of *Playboy* magazine can go for 100 rubles (about $30) or more in Moscow. When we gave the latest *Playboy* and *Penthouse* that we sneaked past customs to our guides on Elbrus, they smiled so much that they might have had lockjaw.

Certain Christian groups in the United States have become skilled at smuggling Bibles into the Soviet Union. Equally subversive would be a program to smuggle in thousands of copies of *Playboy*, as well—for the average Russian to see the hundreds of pages of ads celebrating the vast cornucopia of goods available to the magazine's American readers would be demoralizing enough, not to mention the departures from socialist realism for which the magazine is well noted.

Also, if the anti-Communist, Bible-smuggling Christians were really smart, they would cooperate with Moslems to smuggle Korans into Soviet Central Asia.

In addition, people interested in getting more information to Soviet citizens could work to distribute throughout the Soviet empire vast numbers of Lippman-emulsion microdots (a quart jar would contain over 100 million) encoded with the texts of various books, current magazines, and newspapers. Microdots are pinhead-sized pieces of photographic film on which a large quantity of information (for example, the Bible on one microdot) can be put; Lippmann-emulsions, discovered in the 19th century, are particularly easy to make. These microdots can be read with a simply-made glass-bead microscope.

GUERRILLA ARMS. The pen is mightier than the sword, but the sword still has its place. For example, the Afghan rebels (more accurately, the patriots) should be supplied with Redeyes—handheld, shoulder-launched, heat-seeking missiles—to neutralize Soviet helicopter gunships. And in retaliation for the Soviets' widespread use of chemical warfare in Afghanistan, show the patriots how to make an "Afghan cocktail."

The Afghans could also be encouraged and enabled to expand their activities across the border, attacking military targets in the three Soviet Moslem republics adjoining Afghanistan—Turkmenistan, Uzbekistan, and Tadzhikistan. This would deny the Kremlin a sanctuary from which to launch its campaign of Afghan genocide.

Beyond any doubt, the Kremlin easily has the might to squash any single small disruption or movement, just as a person can squash a bee whose single sting is only a minor annoyance. But several dozen stings by a swarm of bees is another matter. By giving the Soviet government so many problems of so many different varieties in so many different places throughout its empire, the USSR's might would be rendered impotent.

All of these offensive strategies are the sticks, designed to take advantage of the Achilles heel of the Soviet Union, to take it out of the game. But where there is a stick, there should also be a carrot, an enticement to play the game on our side. Diplomatic strategy should provide the carrot.

The Russian people and their leaders are not some crazed, bloodthirsty horde like the Mongols under Genghis Khan. Russians have made great contributions to Western civilization. Cultural greats, for example, include such Russians as Tchaikovsky, Rimski-Korsakov, Dostoyevsky, and Tolstoy.

The Russians have clearly demonstrated their capacity to behave barbarically, as have the Germans. Nonetheless, today there is an affinity between Germany and the other cultures of the West, certainly including America—and reasonably so. Russia and the Russian people also can become an ally of America's, and not as in World War II, when there was a marriage of cynical convenience to fight a common enemy, but on the basis of cultural affinity, trust, and friendship.

There do not have to be adversaries in the world, as the Marxist, fixed-pie view of reality suggests. The nations of the world can grow and prosper together.

So why does the Soviet Union look upon the United States as an adversary? It certainly isn't because we are capitalists rather than socialists or communists. After all, the Soviet Union's greatest adversary is China, yet China's government spouts nearly the same Marxist-Leninist line as the Kremlin does.

Let's face it: America really isn't a belligerent, warlike country. There is more compassion, honest concern, and actual cash on the barrelhead given away by Americans for the well-being of mankind than by any other nation on earth. America simply isn't an imperialist power. It gave back Cuba and the Philippines and Okinawa and isn't trying savagely to colonize all over the world.

America's diplomatic attitude and operating principle toward the Soviets should be: Don't attack us, and we won't attack you—morally, ideologically, subversively, economically, or militarily. Stop acting like an imperialist power, stop trying to foment disruptions and rebellions, *stop trying to make trouble*. Get the Cubans and East Germans out of Angola and Ethiopia and South Yemen and Nicaragua, and get yourselves out of Afghanistan. Cease the constant outpouring of lies and childish propaganda about us. If you do, we'll leave you alone. If you don't, we'll dismantle you as a political entity.

The only way to negotiate with the Soviets is through strength; the only viable diplomacy is to make them an offer they can't refuse. As the son of Don Corleone reported in the movie *The Godfather*: "My father placed a gun at the man's head and told him that either his signature or his brains would be on the contract." Likewise, it must be made breathtakingly clear to the old men in the Kremlin that either their signature or their brains will be on a verifiable disarmament treaty.

It is true that the Kremlin is between the proverbial rock and a hard place: Either it continues its massive military build-up and constant expansionist foreign policy, or the entire system of oppression and control starts to disintegrate. So it seems that if the Soviet Union disarms, the Soviet Union dissolves. But there is an out—the path chosen by China.

For the choice is not limited to being our friend or our enemy. What is necessary is for the Soviet Union to understand that its very survival requires its becoming, at the very least, *nonbelligerent* toward America and the West, as China has done.

China poses little threat to us. Its government is not aggressively imperialist and isn't voraciously colonizing all over the world. With the insanity of the Cultural Revolution behind them, the Chinese are concentrating instead on developing their own economy—without going on a credit binge and with a panoply of semicapitalist, private-incentive measures.

The Soviet Union should be in the same boat. At the very least, the Soviets must concentrate on keeping theirs afloat and must refrain from trying to sink ours. If they do not, the task of our diplomacy should be to explain to them that we can no longer refrain from simply pulling their plug.

We live in a risky world, perhaps the riskiest ever. All military graveyards are full of dead heroes. This is no time or place for rash moves, for a political charge of the light brigade leading us all into a nuclear Balaklava.

Yet America is in a fight for its life. Either we give up, lie down, and culturally die, or we figure a way to win, a way to take the bastards out.

Of course "the Commies" have enough nuclear weapons to blow us all off the map many times over. But we do not need to immobilize ourselves with panic over the prospect of *nuclear* war any more than, say, *germ* war. All-out biological germ warfare, for which the Kremlin is actually better prepared than we, would wreak just as much of a holocaust. It is fully as frightening as a nuclear war, and yet we single out the latter in which to wallow in fear-stricken anguish.

The Soviets do have immense military power, unimaginably horrible power. But they also have a problem. They can't use it. For them to use the bomb would be an act of suicide—not because of the physical destruction that would be wrought by a retaliatory attack, but because of the political devastation that would result.

The Soviet Union is really Humpty-Dumpty. The "union" is not voluntary: The strong centrifugal forces within its borders are kept in check only by constant oppressive force. Today, with major demographic shifts, economic decline, disillusionment with Marxism, and the Polish situation, these centrifugal forces are coming into sharper and sharper focus—making the present a most propitious time for programs and policies that heighten the USSR's mortal ethnic problem.

A major purpose of such programs is to ensure that no matter what futile and hypocritical appeals to a nonexistent patriotism the Great Russians make to the other nations and cultures under their sway, no matter what precautions the Soviets take for a nuclear attack upon them, the vast destruction of such an attack would chaotically disrupt and break lines of communication and control between the Kremlin and a great many places throughout its empire. And once that empire is literally broken up into isolated, separate pieces, it can never be put back together again.

Once the Kremlin loses control—even if only for a matter of days—of several portions of what previously was the USSR and its outer colonies, it will be unable to regain that control. The centrifugal forces will be unleashed; the inner colonies as well as the outer will say, "Do svidanya, Yuri!" The Soviet Union will simply vanish as an intact political entity; and whatever political structures will arise in its place, there will be many of them, and they won't be taking orders from the Kremlin.

This is why, for example, the Warsaw Pact, and the possibility of its being a coordinated offensive threat to Western Europe, is such a fraud. NATO needs to develop its capacity for *subversion*, not its capacity to repel hypothetical attack by Eastern Europeans eager to conquer or die for the glory of Great Russia.

None of this means that anyone should consider for a pico-second calling the Soviets' bluff or a preemptive first strike against them. It means, rather, that the U.S. government should be doing hardball negotiating with the Kremlin.

We *can* decisively put the Kremlin on the defensive in such negotiations. The particular techniques I've suggested for a subversive strategy of promoting ethnic nationalism within the Soviet Union are illustrative examples only. The employment or rejection of any one of them is not in itself important. What is vitally important is that the United States and the rest of the West go on a quid pro quo offensive against the Soviet Union and begin at last to exploit resolutely and confidently the USSR's mortal weaknesses.

There is enormous risk to us and the world no matter what we do. The Soviet Union is a society in a serious state of decay. There may well be more risk, however, in a policy of apprehensive, apologetic timidity than in trying to hasten and control to our benefit the Red empire's dissolution.

The course suggested here—to go for the USSR's jugular, to take advantage of the Soviet Union's Humpty-Dumpty vulnerability—is no more inherently risky than any other. It will require liberal doses of courage, caution, patience, skill, cool nerves, conviction, and self-confidence. But these are requirements for success and survival, both for individuals and entire cultures in the first place.

America need have no fear of the Soviet Union. The state whose leaders have promised to bury us can be made to suffer the death of a thousand cuts—unless it chooses peace.

Welcome to the
Domino that Didn't Fall

By Maurice M. Tanner

July 1986

I don't like it any more than you do, but there is nothing we can do about it. The Vietnamese can take this country any time they want to. If they march across the border, they'll be in Bangkok in two weeks. But they won't have to do that— they'll do it the easy way. They'll step up the insurgency and wait until the country falls like a ripe mango.

I t was 1977 and a colleague and I were arguing over the future of Thailand, a country where we had both spent a fair portion of our Foreign Service careers. We both spoke the language, and we both had reputations as bright, albeit somewhat eccentric, Thai country experts. We were in total disagreement.

"You're selling the country short," I argued back. "There is no way that 45 million Thai are going to let themselves be put in the same bag with the tragedies that have happened next door."

"You're being naive," he told me. "Look what the insurgents have going for them. They have hundreds of miles of shared border with Laos and Cambodia. They have a dedicated cadre that's been in place for 15 years and a new group of intellectuals and student leaders that the '76 coup drove into the jungles. Worse yet, they will have all those M-16s we left behind in Vietnam. It will be the best-armed insurgency in the world."

He wasn't the only one making predictions of doom back then. Just about all of the international experts on insurgency were convinced that things looked grim for Thailand. The Communist Party of Thailand had everything that Mao said it would need for victory. Besides the arms and the cross-border sanctuaries, there were masses of rural poor with good reason to distrust and hate government officials. The insurgents faced a national army that was more a political party than a fighting force. The Thai government seemed to be in a state of constant chaos, bouncing back and forth between attempts at elected parliamentary government and sudden coups followed by military dictators.

Even so, I was convinced that the other experts were wrong, for they were ignoring the impact that a free-enterprise system was making on the country, especially the rural populations that were supposed to be the primary recruiting ground for the insurgency.

Back in those days, about the only people I could find who agreed with my assessments were a few Thai officials and businessmen. One of those was Khom-son, a jeweler in Bangkok.

"Too many people believe what they read in the paper," he told me one evening over a Peking duck. "Thailand's the place to invest your money these days."

"Then why are so many people moving their capital out?" I asked.

"I've got some friends that are getting their money out of the country," he answered as he carefully used his chopsticks to wrap a bit of duck skin in the rice-flour tortilla. "They're crazy. You don't make interest off a Swiss bank account."

"You mean, you think that this country is going to survive?"

"Absolutely," he told me. "Ninety percent of the people in this country don't want anything to do with communism. Sure, a lot of them are scared because of what happened in Vietnam, but that doesn't mean they will roll over and play dead."

"I hope you aren't counting on the Americans moving in and saving you," I said. "We tried that in Vietnam and it didn't work."

"We won't need you," he answered. "We can do it ourselves."

My chubby friend with years of good living wasn't volunteering to go out in the jungle to fight for his country. He was convinced he wouldn't have to do that. He knew something about his countrymen that the outside experts were ignoring.

The jeweler who bet on his own country is a rich man today. A lot of other Thai citizens who took similar risks and invested their money in local enterprises aren't doing that badly either. Despite all the apparent advantages, the Communist Party of Thailand lost. By 1983, the Thai government was legitimately proclaiming victory over the Communist insurrection. Today, everyone agrees that the insurgency is over, that Thailand will survive.

The Communists lost because massive quantities of weapons, cross-border sanctuaries, and a dedicated cadre are not enough if ordinary citizens refuse to participate. Power may come out of the barrel of a gun, but it requires people willing to hold and aim guns to exercise power. In Thailand, the Communists never succeeded in recruiting the masses of the rural population to the side of the revolution. They had the guns—they didn't have the people to pull the triggers.

Now that it is all over, the experts are arguing about why it didn't happen the way they predicted. Some credit enlightened Thai government policies, including extensive investment in economic development and an open-arms treatment of insurgents who surrendered. Others credit the China-Soviet competition, which forced China to drop its support for the insurgents in return for good relations with the Thai government. Some even claim that the U.S. intervention in Vietnam saved Thailand, by giving the Thai the breathing space they needed to solve critical national problems while massive U.S. spending in the country during the Vietnam War years added an economic boost.

They all miss the point. Thailand was never in the danger the counterinsurgency experts claim it was in.

In making their predictions of imminent disaster, the Cassandras ignored the 90 percent of the Thai population who never saw a Communist, never took a pot shot at a government official, and continued through it all to live lives dedicated, not to some political ideology, but to making themselves and their families as comfortable as possible.

I first became aware of this other part of Thailand shortly after my arrival in Bangkok in 1967. Of a class of young State Department officers just out of language training, I was the only one who was not assigned to one of the counterinsurgency jobs in our expanding diplomatic effort to ensure that Thailand didn't follow the Vietnamese example.

Disappointed by having to worry about the size of rice crops, the impact of American military spending on the local inflation rate, and the problems of Bangkok Port congestion instead of being out on the front lines of the free world like my colleagues, I worked out my frustration by taking weekend trips into the rural provinces around Bangkok. A day's travel could include a train trip behind a wood-burning steam locomotive, a run down a river in a double-decked boat, even a long-tailed speedboat dash through a canal. I talked to dozens of passengers as we bounced down rutted roads or glided along the smooth, muddy-brown waterways.

I didn't find people seething with hate and discontent over the unfairness of life, people looking for an excuse to start killing somebody. I found people who were worried about rice prices and curious about a foreigner who spoke their language. I found people who weren't content with today but who had plans to make it better; people who loved to play but worked hard when they had to.

In every village and town I visited I found small markets stocked with a surprising selection of basic consumer items and a lot of things I would have thought would be luxuries for the farm population—radios, sports equipment, toys, and watches. I had discovered a rural society that looked poor at first glance but turned out to be a demonstration of how a free-enterprise system can meet the demands of rising expectations.

By the end of my first four years in Thailand, I had visited every one of the 72 provinces. Along the way my travels introduced me to farmers, local officials, and small-town businessmen.

Somchit the medicine man was typical of many of the small businessmen I met back in those days. He lived in one of the larger rural towns of Lopburi Province, where he owned a factory located behind his house in a building that looked like it should be roosting chickens rather than a pharmaceutical operation.

Inside the old wooden building, we found a half-dozen workers mixing various white chemical powders together in washtubs. The different chemicals were being shoveled out of 50-pound bags. The chemical factory labels on the bags revealed that Somchit's special medicine was an aspirin-based headache powder. His workers were packaging individual dosages in tiny paper envelopes that carried his own special brand.

It was labor-intensive, but even with the low wages he paid his workers, Somchit couldn't compete with the provincial city pharmacies and their displays of machine-packaged pills.

So Somchit had to go out looking for customers in places that didn't have corner drugstores. He made his money by personally peddling those single-dose envelopes in villages and small towns throughout the Northeast, the very heartland of the supposed insurgency explosion. With a small magic show and a couple of large, defanged king cobras, Somchit drew crowds to listen to his sales pitch.

"What about the Communist insurgents?" I asked him. "Isn't it dangerous to go into these kinds of areas?"

"As long as I mind my own business, they don't bother with me," he shrugged. "I guess they have headaches too."

There was an army of those small merchants traveling throughout the rural areas of Thailand, selling anything that would make a profit. They offered aspirin, vitamins, toothpaste, soaps, cough remedies, and Ovaltine—anything a villager might want and a few more things the villager didn't even know about until the merchant showed up with a sales pitch.

These itinerant merchants didn't just sell things that had the approval of government planners and social engineers. The businessmen were out there for their own profit, and they sold what people wanted. If rural dwellers wanted nylon panties for their wives and cheap whiskey for themselves, that's what they got, if they had the money to pay for it.

These merchants were feeding the very thing the government was supposed to be worried about, the tide of rising expectations. With an evening's entertainment and a sales pitch, they were creating more unhappiness and unfulfilled wants than a month's worth of propaganda on the Communist radio station broadcasting out of China.

Yet the unhappy Thai farmer who wanted some of the goodies that the merchants were offering didn't go into the jungle and join the Communists. Instead, the potential customer worked to make a bit more money so he could buy the next thing on his growing list of wants.

Because there were things the rural dwellers wanted to buy, there was an incentive to make their own labor more efficient, whether by increasing yields, adding new crops, or reducing the amount of labor used on the farm, thus freeing family members to find jobs in towns and cities.

Farmers trying to increase profits so they would have cash for consumer goods discovered that pesticides, fertilizers, and herbicides were cost-effective. Their teachers were not the bureaucrats but merchants—often people at an income level not much above the farmer—who went into the villages to sell the chemicals. Those small merchants also lent the money to the farmers to buy what they were selling, taking a short-term mortgage with the crop as collateral.

They didn't do that for altruistic reasons. They charged discount or interest rates that the social engineers called usurious. But they were there with money in their hand, sometimes in areas where the government didn't go because of insurgent activity.

I wasn't the only American official who recognized that free enterprise was running rampant in the countryside. In 1972 the U.S. Agency for International Development (AID) sent one of its young interns to Roiet Province in the Northeast. His assignment was to look into the possibilities of AID funding a project to develop the rural marketing infrastructure.

"What I found," he recently told me as we reminisced about the old days, "was a well-developed marketing system already in place. The Sino-Thai merchants were traveling all over the province, buying the crops the farmer had to sell and offering farm supplies and consumer products the farmer wanted to buy.

"I wrote a report concluding that a marketing system project wasn't needed, that an effective system already existed. My supervisors told me it was a good report, except for the conclusions. They wanted me to keep the data but to change the results so the report would justify the creation of a project proposal."

Fortunately, the man refused to change the conclusions. The idea of a project was buried in the massive bureaucratic paper pile we produced as part of our development aid to Thailand.

As farmers looked for ways to increase profits, cheap farm machinery began to replace animal and human power. Again, it was the merchant and entrepreneur who had what the farmer wanted.

In the late '60s, the United Nations development agency in Southeast Asia at the time, ECAFE, announced a contest to design a machine that would replace the water buffalo.

"We want a machine that a family can use just like they use the water buffalo," the contest's creator explained to me while we chatted over scotch and sodas at one of the endless parade of diplomatic cocktail parties. "It will have to be able to run in flooded rice paddies so it can be used to pull a plow. But it will also move along a highway carrying goods to market."

The international bureaucrats eventually judged the winner a contraption based on an unsuccessful military rice-paddy vehicle. It was a square, open personnel carrier that ran on six balloon tires, three on each side. It may have been fun to ride in, but it was useless as a plow and far too expensive for the average family to buy for a drive along the highway.

While ECAFE was using blind men to redesign the elephant, some business-men introduced the "iron buffalo," a cheap, low-horsepower gasoline engine mounted on a hand-guided plow with steel paddle wheels. The engine can easily be removed and mounted on a water pump or a simple tractor that can pull a wagon loaded with family or produce along the highway.

In June 1978, I drove through the province of Sukhothai along with a Thai advisor on my staff. The province contains some of the richest rice land in the country and it was planting time.

"Have you noticed?" my Thai friend asked after we had been driving for a couple of hours. "We must have passed at least a hundred farmers plowing their fields and we haven't seen a single water buffalo pulling a plow."

In just five years, the entire province had moved to the iron buffalo.

The introduction of new crops was as important to increasing farm income as new machinery and chemicals. In the early '60s, Thai farmers grew rice and not much else. Between 1965 and 1968, corn production jumped from nothing to become a major export crop. Farmers started growing jute, cotton, tapioca, and sugar. Many of these new crops could be grown in the dry season when the rice paddies had always lain fallow.

The spread of these new crops was not the result of any massive government extension program. It was directly tied to the world market and to the small merchants who went into rural areas to buy the crops when the farmers grew them.

When extension work was done, it was often done by the private sector. The international tobacco industry showed the way. The world market demanded a new source of Turkish-style tobacco, a labor-intensive crop. To meet that demand, tobacco companies like Adams International put in place privately financed extension programs that soon taught thousands of farmers in the Northeast how to grow high-quality Turkish tobacco.

With the bottom dropping out of the world rice market these days, the search for new crops continues. Only last year, I went with some representatives of the Simplot Company, a U.S. potato processor, to visit potato farmers in northern Thailand. Simplot was interested in introducing the russet potato to meet the demands of the new fast-food industry that has now reached Bangkok. McDonald's wants to serve the Thai customer the same kind of french fry he ate while studying or touring in the United States. That translates into more income opportunities for Thai potato farmers.

One of the American commercial agronomists traveling with us was surprised to find himself discussing a brand-new and more expensive variety of herbicide with a little farmer dressed exactly like the peasants in the pictures of a travel brochure. The farmer not only knew what the herbicide was, he had already purchased a small amount from a local supplier and tried it to see if it was cost-effective. It wasn't a government extension agent who told him about the new chemical—he had read the advertising at his local farm-supply store.

Not every rural dweller can make extra money by planting new crops or increasing yields. Many of those who wanted new things had no choice but to leave the farm and go looking for work. Sometimes that meant a job found a long way from home. Take the case of Huan Pakpok. Huan, like thousands of other Thai men, went all the way to Saudi Arabia to find a job.

"It was the most miserable two years I ever spent," he recently told me. "The Saudis don't let anyone have fun. No whiskey, no women—it was nothing but work, eat, sleep, and back to work."

He may have been miserable, but every month he sent back $350, and his wife put most of it in the bank. He's been back in Thailand for a year now. He runs his own small carpentry business. He and his wife still live in the house where he grew up, a wooden shack that sits on high stilts. But they have fans, a kitchen blender, a radio, a refrigerator, and a brand-new color TV. Huan is also the one who can afford store-bought whiskey when someone throws a party in the village.

Huan and the other Saudi contract workers also helped solve a national problem: the foreign exchange disaster caused by the sudden jump in oil prices in the '70s. It was the private-enterprise solution. Thailand traded labor for oil.

Not everybody benefited, not everybody succeeded. But those most likely to succeed in a freewheeling private-enterprise system were the people who would have made the best insurgents, the ones with daring, initiative, and a willingness to try something new.

The free-enterprise system came naturally to Thailand. For hundreds of years the Thai kings encouraged trade and provided protection to merchants moving through Thai territory. As Thailand was never colonized, it never suffered the interruption of free trade and commerce that was imposed by European governments in the other countries of Asia.

Following the end of the monarchy in 1932, Thai civilian leaders, many of whom had been thoroughly exposed through education to European statism, attempted to impose a more centrally controlled order on the Thai economy. Fortunately, such efforts failed to have much impact, in part due to the greed of the economically unsophisticated military officers who held controlling political power and who quickly discovered the personal benefits to be reaped by looking the other way when statist laws interfered with a businessman's profits.

None of this is to say that the government had nothing to do with meeting the rising expectations of the rural population. Things like irrigation and rural electrification projects benefited rural populations and encouraged the growth of private enterprise.

The single most important government contribution was the massive road-building program implemented over a 20-year period. Initially, road building was financed as a security measure. The government had to get troops and tanks into the areas where the insurgents were recruiting villagers. The army used the roads occasionally. But an army of merchants used the roads continually, usually before construction was even completed. During the worst of the insurgency, the merchants would go places the army didn't dare go.

The highway from Phitsanuloke to Lomsak was one such road. It cuts through a valley that separates two mountain areas in northern Thailand, where in 1972 and '73 some of the most vicious fighting in the war against the insurgents took place.

It was 1977 before the U.S. Embassy finally decided the road was safe enough for Americans to travel, provided we did so in unmarked civilian vehicles. By this time, I was assigned as the consul in northern Thailand. On my first trip through the valley between the two mountains, still held by the insurgents, it was easy to see what had happened.

The road had opened up a new area for land settlement. Landless farmers quickly moved in to squat and plant crops. The merchants followed them, both the ones who came to buy and sell for the day and those who set up small stores, restaurants, gas stations, and even movie houses.

According to Maoist revolutionary doctrine, all of those people, most of whom had gone broke someplace else before moving into the area, should have been prime candidates for recruitment into the insurgency. Instead, they were more interested in growing and selling cabbages to the long line of merchant trucks traveling up and down the highway. Each new arrival in the area helped to build a corridor of farm villages and small-merchant towns that cut apart the insurgent armies on each side of the valley more than any number of military battalions ever could have done.

Using the free-enterprise model, from 1960 to 1984 Thailand experienced sustained growth averaging 7 percent in real terms. It wasn't an evenly distributed growth, and the cities prospered far more than the rural countryside. The rich got richer, and the gap between the rich and the poor grew broader. But not all the poor got poorer. They did discover wants they never had before. They weren't able and still aren't able to fulfill all those wants. They never will be. But the average family can count on acquiring something new every year.

First it might be the medicines. Next, cloth and clothes made in a factory instead of by hand. Then come bicycles, transistor radios, wristwatches, and, for the most successful, motorcycles, TV sets, and even an occasional pickup truck. A free-trade policy ensures that almost anything they might want is available.

A short history of private enterprise in rural Thailand could be written just focusing on the exploding sale of corrugated tin roofing. In the 1950s, almost all rural farmers lived under thatched roofs. As merchants began selling sheets of corrugated tin, the tin roof became the status symbol in farm villages all over the country.

By the late '70s, thatched roofs were rare in many parts of the country. At a wedding party in Chiang Mai one evening, I sat at a table with a couple of businessmen who had made small fortunes from tin roofing. I jokingly asked them what they were selling now that everyone had a tin roof.

"Linoleum," one of them quickly answered. "That's where the money is these days. Every woman in the North wants a pretty floor covering." The other fellow joined in, and I sat there fascinated as they argued over the merits of different types of floor coverings and whether or not Japanese, Korean, or the locally produced product brought the most profit to the businessman.

Now, several years later, plastic or asphalt-based floor coverings are almost as common as the tin roof. Who knows what the Thai farm housewife will decide she wants next? The person who discovers that valuable piece of information will not be a government planner.

Development on the free-enterprise model is not without its problems. Most Thai farmers, like farmers everywhere, still live on the brink of disaster, facing ruin from weather, unstable world-market prices, and just bad judgment.

The less successful farmers are losing their land to more productive neighbors and are forced to seek work in the cities. Bangkok slums are filled with those who came to the city hoping for jobs they sometimes can't find.

The social ills of a free economy have taken their toll on families and individuals. Slum children spend their days selling flowers to Bangkok motorists instead of taking advantage of free education. The daughters of rural families often sell themselves, or are sometimes sold, into prostitution.

Yet even here the free-enterprise system can offer solutions, if people are only willing to try. Take the Paknet family as an example. It may not be a typical rural Thai family, but it's the family I know the best, since the youngest daughter paid me the great good favor of becoming my wife.

Plod and Samniang Paknet were successful rice farmers in rural Ayuthaya Province until Plod died of tuberculosis back in 1954. His widow and a couple of the children tried to work the farm for a few more years but ended up selling out. Today, none of the children work on farms or are married to farmers. They all had to seek jobs as servants in the homes of the rich in Bangkok or as workers in nearby textile mills or furniture factories.

Some might describe the story as another rural tragedy, the kind of thing that breeds insurgency. It's not. All the children have families of their own and high hopes for their own children. They are too busy climbing into Thailand's new urban middle class to worry about what might have been. They are doing it without benefit of welfare payments, unemployment compensation, farm subsidies, government-financed loan programs, or any financial support from the one daughter who married into money.

Samniang still lives in the old family house, which she managed to keep when she lost the farm. Her son, who works in a small factory a few kilometers from the village, and his wife live with her. An American social worker would describe their house as an example of abject poverty. They sit on the floor to eat and the meals are cooked over open charcoal fires. Samniang doesn't think she's poor. In the last 10 years, she's acquired electricity, fans, a TV set, a refrigerator, and spray cans of Off mosquito repellent.

I have met people like the Paknet family in every province of the country. They know that living free is neither safe nor easy, but that's the only way they want it. When people like the Paknets fail in rural Thailand, they place the blame on themselves or forces outside the control of human beings. They don't blame the government for having failed to provide for them. Of course, there are some who do. Every society has its malcontents, and the foreign journalist out to prove a point can always round up a few people eager to complain about the inequalities of life, which must all be the fault of whoever currently holds power in Bangkok.

Somehow critics of free enterprise in the Third World never seem to find people like Khun Thongbai to interview. Thongbai's family never had any property, at least as far back as anybody in the village could remember. The village still talks about how poor he was as a kid. He went to school in rags and bare feet. Somewhere along the way, Thongbai scraped together enough baht coins to buy a few eggs from another villager. He walked into the nearest town and sold them for a small profit. That worked so well that he kept doing it. Eventually he earned enough to feed himself a bit better than he was used to, though he kept living poor.

He lived so poor that no one imagined that he was saving a bit of money each week—until the day he put in the high bid on a piece of property another villager was selling. Thongbai doesn't buy the eggs he sells these days. On that piece of land, he has 5,000 chickens in modern coops that lay eggs for him. His two trucks haul the eggs to market.

But there were insurgents. The Communists had to have something to entice young men and women into the jungle to fight. They couldn't have all been common criminals and psychopaths. Something must have been wrong to keep the size of the insurgency growing through the '60s and most of the '70s.

The first point that many of the foreign experts tended to ignore was that the insurgency was only developing in the more-remote areas of the country, places where lack of communication and poor crop land made it very difficult for the free-enterprise system to operate—not impossible, just difficult. Frustrations in these depressed areas did lead to higher levels of dissatisfaction. Sometimes, people got so angry and frustrated that they wanted to kill somebody.

While the developing insurgent situation obviously required a military response, few assessments were ever made of whether or not the same kind of discontent that was feeding the insurgency in the remote areas of the Northeast also existed in the more heavily populated areas. It was accepted almost without challenge that Thai people everywhere were fed up and that the insurgency would spread under its own force unless the government took drastic action.

There were a few American voices that questioned the general assumptions. One of my colleagues in the embassy's political section in 1968 did an assessment that concluded that the Thai rural population was not seething with open discontent. His report claimed that the free-enterprise system that had long been in place was meeting the rising expectations of the populace. People were opting to work harder rather than drop out. They were trying to find new jobs, plant new crops, and try new kinds of economic activity rather than pick up their guns and go into the jungle.

The report made it all the way to Washington and drew considerable comment and quite a bit of challenge for a few weeks. Then the experts went back to counting the few hundred villages that had fallen under Communist control and forgetting about the 10,000 villages where the game of free enterprise still played.

At least a few Thai businessmen and government officials understood that the average village peasant wanted nothing more than to be left alone to make his own decisions. They realized that free farmers considered the political agitators as much a threat to their personal peace as did the government officials sitting in Bangkok.

On a cold (for Thailand) January evening in 1977, a colleague, the British consul in Chiang Mai, and I were invited to a small party thrown by a local businessman at his vacation cottage high up the mountain overlooking the largest city in the North. The other guests included the deputy governor, the provincial police chief, and several other businessmen.

Late in the evening, after we had stuffed ourselves with minced pork and chili and bet on the outcome of a fight between two horned beetles locked in combat on the field of a sugar-cane stick, the talk turned serious. The officials and the businessmen were worried about reports that some of the students who had fled into the jungle after the October 1976 coup were working in the villages around Chiang Mai, trying to recruit local youth into the insurgency.

The Thai men all agreed that the village leaders didn't want the students around, but they didn't have adequate equipment to defend the villages. The solution was obvious and the bargain was struck. The businessmen agreed that each would donate a substantial amount of money to purchase weapons, and the government officials agreed to make sure the weapons got distributed to the villages that the student activists were threatening.

My British colleague, who also spoke Thai, and I sat there with stunned expressions on our faces. Our insurgency experts in our embassies in Bangkok were screaming concern about the weapons that were supposedly flowing across the border out of Vietnam, yet these local community leaders were going to pass even more weapons around the rural villages! Those Thai businessmen understood something that we Americans seemed to have forgotten. Free people can be trusted with weapons, because 99 percent of them will use those weapons to ensure their own freedom, not to threaten the freedom and property of others.

In explaining why some young people joined the insurgency, one factor in recruitment that was often ignored was the role of boredom. Rural Thailand had always been subject to massive underemployment. This meant that people had lots of time on their hands, and life in a remote village can be pretty dull if you're young and adventurous but see nothing ahead but long days and quiet evenings.

Some jumped at the chance of adventure the insurgent recruiters were offering. Many of those who went singing into the jungle eventually discovered that they had made a bad deal. Life in a jungle camp proved to be more than just dangerous; most of the time it was even more boring than life in the village had been. At least in the villages, one didn't have to put up with the constant propaganda harangue and the strict rules of personal behavior that the insurgent leaders imposed on their troops.

Right at the time that the pessimist was predicting a Communist victory, the Communist Party of Thailand was suffering massive defections. Whole units were following their leaders over to the government side. The Communist Party of Thailand not only failed to recruit the peasant army they had counted on, but the party eventually lost those they did recruit.

Long before the final victory, an astute observer could see it starting to happen. As early as 1973 we were seeing a rash of defections from the insurgent camps in southern Thailand.

"What am I supposed to do?" one intelligence officer complained to me one day in Songkhla as he pointed to a pile of defector interrogation reports on his desk. "The boss wants me to go through these reports and come up with an erudite political explanation for the defections, something we can use in designing a psy-war campaign to encourage more of them. They'll think I've gone 'round the bend if I tell them the truth. It's lack of nooky."

"You mean they're defecting because they want to get laid?" I asked in disbelief.

"That, and everything else you can get in a city but not in a jungle camp run by Maoist puritans," he answered.

The Communist Party of Thailand offered the young men and women who were bored with the monotony of village life the challenge of the jungle, the chance to get even with the oppressor government, training in how to shoot a gun and ambush a military convoy, and the promise of a brave new world.

The free-enterprise system offered them movies, cheap bus fare to the big city, pop music, blue jeans, running shoes, Ovaltine, Fab, contraceptives, and Vicks Vaporub. In massive numbers, the disgruntled opted for the temptations of the modern world.

In 1983, I accompanied some Thai government workers on a walk into a Hmong hill-tribe village in Nan province. The people living in that village had fought for 10 years with the Communist Party insurgency. They had only just surrendered to the government side when we made our visit.

We spent the night with one of the villagers, his two wives, and his children. For 10 years, his crops had fed Communist insurgent soldiers. Two of his daughters had been trained in China as jungle combat nurses. As we sat passing around a small bottle of whiskey, one of the Thai officials asked our host why he decided to defect.

"It wasn't any fun being an insurgent," he told us. "Somebody was always ordering us around. Now we do what we want to do. We can sell things we grow. We can take the money and go to town. We can buy anything we want."

The next morning we walked out with him to his fields. It was the off-season, so the rice had been harvested and the money crops planted. He was growing ginger, cotton, and kidney beans. His wives and his daughters were collecting sweet seeds that grew wild in the jungle and brought a good price in the nearest town.

Our host was ambitious, not content. "We have to sell our crops to the man that drives the truck up here," he complained. "We know what he gets in Nan City, but we don't have any way to get them down to market ourselves. We have to sell at his price."

One of the Thai officials in our party suggested that he and his neighbors in the village pool their resources, set up a cooperative, and buy their own truck. Our host listened politely, then shook his head. He had been part of a grand cooperative for 10 years, sharing equally what he produced with all in the group. He didn't want any more of it.

"I've got it figured," he explained. "In three years I can save enough to make a down payment on a used pickup. Then, I'll make the money." He was probably a damned good insurgent; he was a lousy Communist.

The Thai example has important ramifications for other parts of the world where the United States places its prestige on the line. Too often the American public judges the prospects of an allied country not by what is happening with the 90 percent of the population that is busy looking out for themselves and their families but by the small, vocal group of malcontents who demand an instant remake of society and government solutions to all social and cultural ills.

Too often our press and political leaders judge the worthiness of another government for our support solely on the basis of how closely their electoral system matches our own. Too often, once governments are elected, the leaders decide that the only way they can compete with the Marxist challenge is by adopting Marxist principles. And all too often, they are encouraged to do so by the development "experts" we send out to advise them.

Such countries then embark on programs of unsound and uneconomical land reform, currency and exchange controls, public housing, artificially depressed basic commodity prices, and farm subsidies, all accompanied by major tax increases and massive international borrowing to pay for the programs. They justify such state-controlled programs by claiming that if wealth is not redistributed by the elected government, then the poor will fill the ranks of the insurgents. Too often, they only succeed in preventing the private sector from engaging in the activity that is necessary to meet the demands of the ordinary citizen, who wants to get some of the benefits of the modern world.

It's time we learned one of the most important lessons of the Vietnam era, the one taught by Thailand. The free-enterprise system does work. It offers the only way in which a society can meet the demands of rising expectations without the tragedy of violent revolution.

1988, Year of Hope

By Marty Zupan

January 1989

Whit hen the balance sheet for 1988 is added up, it must surely be deemed a year of surprising gains in the struggle for freedom. Burma, which had suffered for 26 years under one-party socialist rule, offered the most drama. At first it seemed we were witnessing a replay of Filipino people power. Massive street revolts forced the resignation of iron-fisted Ne Win and then of his successor, the former head of state security. But, just when it appeared that the opposition had routed a despotic government, the Burmese military unexpectedly resurrected the iron fist.

But as hopes were being dashed in Burma, the universal yearning for human freedom bubbled up elsewhere. In Poland a series of strikes provoked by a new generation of Solidarity leaders forced the hand of the Polish government. The government called a special session of the legislature—heretofore a familiar response only in Western democracies—to deal with the crisis.

In Czechoslovakia, 10,000 protesters turned out for a march commemorating the reformist Prague Spring 20 years earlier. It was the first mass protest since 1969.

In Hungary, miners engaged in the first officially acknowledged strike in more than 30 years, demanding pay increases to reduce the squeeze of new taxes. A reform-minded government quickly conceded a point, slashing new income taxes on bonuses.

In the Baltic countries of Estonia, Latvia, and Lithuania, forcibly incorporated into the Soviet Union in 1940, the natives are growing restless. This year, "popular fronts" were formed in all three, and they now rival the local Communist Party in membership. These fronts have held several-day congresses to hammer out platforms demanding measures of autonomy ranging from economic self-determination, the right to veto mandates from Moscow, and an end to atheistic education in the schools (Latvia), to constitutional guarantees of private property and an end to compulsory military service (Estonia). The Estonian front even announced plans to run its own candidates in 1989 elections (not even Solidarity has attempted such a challenge to Communist Party rule).

Halfway around the world, the citizens of Chile peaceably voted against eight more years of Gen. Augusto Pinochet, the dictator whose junta seized power in 1972. In troubled Haiti, an internal revolt of 30 young military officers and noncoms brought to power Lt. Gen. Prosper Avril, who moved quickly to clean up pervasive graft in the military, end its bloody oppression, and effect a transition to democracy.

Why this seemingly contagious ferment for freedom? Some of the possible reasons augur well for millions of oppressed people around the globe.

Consider first how the information revolution is hopelessly complicating the life of the dictator. Except in places such as Albania and Ethiopia, where rigidly imposed isolation or grinding poverty prevent the speedy and thorough spread of information, it has become next to impossible for governments to keep people from knowing what is happening both outside and inside their own country.

Can anyone doubt that protesting students and workers in Burma drew inspiration from the dramatic events in the Philippines two years earlier? Estonian economists now propose that their country operate as a special economic zone within the USSR, with its own currency and rights to foreign trade; their model is Communist China's lately devised special economic zones.

Within countries, the technology of the information revolution is likewise debilitating the best efforts of dictators who may still be able to shut down the press (Burma) or control the supply of newsprint (Nicaragua). The personal computer is still relatively expensive—and controllable. But the lowly radio and tape recorder, ever cheaper and smaller, are widely available.

From China come reports that a student speech pleading for democratic freedoms will be taped, copied, and distributed through the underground. In Latvia, people kept up with the two-day meeting of the Popular Front on radios held to their ears, just like baseball fanatics in America following their favorite team. A Roman Catholic Mass at the conclusion of Lithuania's Popular Front meeting was broadcast live on radio and television—a first in a Communist country. And this summer a young East German woman may have been directly saved by a video camera. In broad daylight and in full view of Western tourists, she jumped into the river Spree to swim from East to West Berlin. A guard in a pursuing patrol boat had his gun aimed; but a British visitor on the West German side had his video camera aimed as well, and the East German police backed off.

Second, and relatedly, even dictators are not all immune to opinion, that of their own people and that of the world. It is strange but possibly true that Chile's Pinochet, having restored a measure of economic prosperity, would like to be remembered as a ruler who had the guts also to restore democracy. Certainly Haiti's new military head of government seems so motivated: "My vision," he told American journalists, " is to enter history as one who has saved the country from anarchy and dictatorship and who has asked for the establishment of an irreversible democracy."

The Economist suggests that even one of the most unbudgeable tyrants, Romania's Nicolae Ceausescu, could be pressured out of his ruthless scheme to uproot half the villagers of Romania and resettle them in "agro-industrial centers." "Ceausescu longs for flattery in the big wide world. Insult this vanity—by vocal condemnation and ridicule at...international gatherings—and western countries might just prevent a lot of senseless destruction in Romania."

Finally, it does not seem too soon to speculate that Mikhail Gorbachev's push for economic reform in the Soviet Union, whatever its own ultimate outcome, may be rippling in unintended yet beneficial ways throughout the world. Hungary is openly critical of its comrades' latest scheme in Romania, home to nearly 2 million people of Hungarian descent. But Gorbachev, what with holding down the home front, has declined to intervene. Likewise the stirrings of independence in the Baltic states are benignly tolerated, in evident hopes that Gorbachev will win much-needed popular support. And now, political turmoil in Yugoslavia—nonaligned but ever-mindful of the might of the Soviet Union—is leading some observers to speculate that it may become the first Communist nation to abandon the creed.

Of course, it would be foolish to predict that 1988 marks a turning point in history, a moment from which future observers will date a measurable flowering of freedom. We cannot predict. We can only hope.

Fin de Siècle

By Virginia I. Postrel

November 1991

*The lamps are going out all over Europe. We shall not see them
lit again in our lifetime.*

Sir Thomas Grey, 1914

The people who walked in darkness have seen a great light. The shadow that descended in August 1914 has lifted. In Moscow, when it counted, the worst lacked all conviction and the best were filled with passionate intensity. Yeats's blood-dimmed tide at last recedes. The 20th century is over.

Centuries, like decades, exist not in the neat and tidy pages of the calendar but in the expanses of the imagination. They are defined not by what is forgotten—"What were the peasants doing?" our teaching assistant used to ask of the age of Machiavelli and Luther, Galileo and Shakespeare—but by what is remembered. The details fade, like faces recalled in a dream. What remains is but a caricature, a sketch suggesting truth by dominant features, characteristic gestures.

Of the 20th century, especially in Europe, we shall remember that it was nasty, brutal, and mercifully short—77 years that murdered millions. It was the century in which all but the naive and the wicked lost faith in progress, when every idea became its extreme. Nationalism begat racism; racism begat genocide. Equality liquidated the kulaks and marched the cities of Cambodia into the killing fields. We bided time until someone would push the button. If we can destroy the world, we thought, we will.

In the 20th century, liberty seemed an endangered species, a little bird whose every nest fell prey to marauding beasts. The destroyers claimed history as their ally, a force as impersonal and inevitable as a tidal wave or earthquake. The long twilight struggle had the fatalism of Norse legend. As the free world grew smaller, pessimism seemed only logical.

Europe got its tragic sense of life from World War I, America from Vietnam. But the results were the same. We cowered before history. The president of the United States was afraid to invite Alexandr Solzhenitsyn to dinner. It wouldn't have been prudent.

The left declared us "better Red than dead," positing those as the only alternatives. We were, they said, on the "wrong side of history," in Africa and Asia and, by implication, in Europe and America as well. In response, the right told us that democracies perish and totalitarianism endures. Freedom was worth fighting for, they said, but we shouldn't expect to win.

371

Fatalism cannot, however, long sustain freedom. For that, one must have confidence, defiance, cheek. And somehow, somewhere, sometime between the invasion of Afghanistan and the fall of the Wall, the people of the West recovered their courage—and their convictions. We began to believe, once again, that we were *right*, that the liberal society was not decadent but good and true, that capitalism was liberation, that freedom was more than nothing left to lose.

In part, it was bravado born of desperation. But there was substance as well. Franco set Spain free, and Juan Carlos stood up to fascists who would have reenslaved her. Portugal stopped a communist coup. Hong Kong and Taiwan, South Korea and Singapore, put their communist neighbors to shame. Japan, not China, became the next superpower.

Latin America followed Franco. The College of Cardinals elected a Polish pope. Solidarity survived. Margaret Thatcher and Ronald Reagan proclaimed the Anglo-American gospel of liberalism and sometimes even acted on it.

When Reagan called the Soviet Union an evil empire, the left deemed him a dangerous madman. When he said communism was doomed, the right thought him a fool. A man out of his time, he did not partake of pessimism. He infuriated those who admired him most.

"His trust in the future, his sunny belief that change, big change, was possible—the very things that occasionally infuriated the young of his administration—turn out to have been appropriate to the times," writes Peggy Noonan in *What I Saw at the Revolution*. "Sometimes the shrewdest thing is not to be too skeptical, not to be too 'wise.'"

In the heart of darkness, a new Soviet man was born. Vladimir Bukovsky wrote of the old version in his 1977 memoir, *To Build a Castle: My Life as a Dissenter*: "I despised Soviet man—not the one depicted on the posters or in Soviet literature, but the one who existed in reality, who had neither honor nor pride, nor a sense of personal responsibility, who was capable of tackling a bear alone with a pitchfork but who shrank away and broke into a cold sweat at the sight of a policeman, who would betray and sell his own father to avoid the boss thumping his fist on the desk at him. The tragedy was that he existed inside every one of us, and until we could overcome this Soviet man within, nothing in our life would change." Dissidents like Bukovsky and Solzhenitsyn, Sharansky and Sakharov overcame the Soviet man inside because they could not do otherwise. They could not live by the lie. Others followed—less brave, less bold, less public, but nonetheless important. Soviet man became weaker, and the Soviet Union changed.

The old Soviet man undoubtedly still exists. After all, only a tiny percentage of Moscow's millions turned out to protect the "White House" from the expected onslaught of tanks. But thousands did. And, as Tatyana Tostaya notes in *The New Republic*, each did so not as a mob but as an individual: "Every one of the men and women who assembled outside the Russian Parliament building left his or her home alone, and headed in the rainy night toward the danger without any certainty that they were joining anything larger or safer than themselves."

372

Some still claim that history is the product of impersonal forces. But in August 1991 it was made by great men and women—many of them nameless. There was greatness on the streets of Moscow and in the halls of the Russian parliament. It resounded in Yeltsin's address from atop the tank and in Gorbachev's "The hell with you" response to the coup plotters. History spoke in the voices, and the deeds, of individuals.

The lamps are going on all over Europe, all over the world. We walk again in the light. The 20th century is over.

About the Authors

(We have made every effort to procure current information on the authors listed here. Where we have no current information, we have included the author's affiliation at the time *Reason* published the article written by that author.)

PETR BECKMANN is professor emeritus of electrical engineering at the University of Colorado and editor and publisher of the monthly newsletter *Access to Energy*.

JAN BELLAMY worked for a law firm.

TOM BETHELL, a contributing editor of *Reason,* is Washington Correspondent for *The American Spectator*.

ROGER BISSELL, a professional musician and self-taught philosopher, was chairman of the Nashville Tax Alternatives Committee. He is currently president of the Southern California chapter of the Association for Psychological Type and a musician at Disneyland.

DAVID BRUDNOY is New England's leading nighttime radio talk show host (WBZ-AM) and a commentator with the region's leading TV station (WCVB-TV).

PATRICK COX is a freelance writer.

EDITH EFRON is a contributing editor of *Reason.* She is the author of, most recently, *The Apocalyptics*.

ANDREW FERGUSON was an editorial writer for Scripps Howard News Service. He is currently a senior writer at *Washingtonian* magazine.

SARAH E. FOSTER is a freelance writer. She now writes frequently for the Institute for Contemporary Studies in San Francisco.

MILTON FRIEDMAN, a senior research fellow at the Hoover Institution, was awarded the 1976 Nobel prize in economics. He is the author of *Capitalism and Freedom* and co-author, with Rose Friedman, of *Free to Choose*.

THEODORE J. GAGE was a freelance journalist in Evanston, Illinois.

GLENN GARVIN was a staff writer for *The Washington Times.* He is the author of *Everybody Had His Own Gringo: The CIA and the Contras*.

GEORGE GILDER is the author of *Wealth and Poverty* and *The Spirit of Enterprise*.

PAUL GORDON was an assistant editor of *Reason*.

WILLIAM GORENC, JR. is an attorney with a Cleveland law firm.

PHIL GRAMM taught economics at Texas A&M University. He is now a Republican U.S. Senator from Texas.

THOMAS W. HAZLETT, a contributing editor and monthly columnist for *Reason,* teaches economics and public policy at the University of California, Davis.

BILL KAUFMANN was assistant editor of *Reason.* He is now a contributing editor to *Liberty* magazine and the author of a novel, *Every Man a King.*

MANUEL S. KLAUSNER was an editor of *Reason.* He is now a trustee of the Reason Foundation and an attorney with Kindel & Anderson in Los Angeles.

JOEL KOTKIN was the West Coast editor of *Inc.* magazine and co-author of *The Third Century: America's Resurgence in the Asian Era.* He is a senior fellow at the Center for the New West in Denver and for the Progressive Policy Institute. He is the author, most recently, of *Tribes: How Race, Religion, and Identity Determine Success in the New Global Economy.*

DAVID MATHISEN was a science journalist, environmental engineer, and novelist in Minneapolis.

MICHAEL MCMENAMIN, a contributing editor of *Reason,* is an attorney with a Cleveland law firm.

CHARLES MURRAY is the author of *Losing Ground* and *In Pursuit.*

CHARLES OLIVER is assistant editor of *Reason.*

ROBERT W. POOLE, JR. was editor of *Reason.* He is now publisher of *Reason* and president of the Reason Foundation.

VIRGINIA I. POSTREL is editor of *Reason.*

THOMAS SZASZ, a contributing editor of *Reason,* is professor of psychiatry emeritus a the SUNY Health Science Center in Syracuse and author, most recently, of *Our Right to Drugs: The Case for a Free Market.*

LYNN SCARLETT was book review editor of *Reason.* She is now vice president for research for the Reason Foundation.

JACOB SULLUM is associate editor of *Reason.*

MAURICE M. TANNER was in the U.S. diplomatic corps in Bangkok.

JACK WHEELER traveled around the world reporting on anti-Soviet guerrilla insurgency movements. He is now president of the Freedom Research Foundation and of Jack Wheeler Expeditions, both based in Washington D.C.

KARL ZINSMEISTER, a contributing editor of *Reason,* was an adjunct research associate at the American Enterprise Institute. He is now a writer in Ithaca, New York.

ERIC ZUESSE was a freelance writer and director of Consumers' Alliance, a New York-based consumer advocacy group.

MARTY ZUPAN was editor-in-chief of *Reason*. She is now a vice president at the Institute for Humane Studies at George Mason University.